Critical Thinking Skills

Developing Effective Analysis and Argument

Critical Thinking Skills

Developing Effective Analysis and Argument

Second edition

Stella Cottrell

palgrave
macmillan

First edition published 2005
Second edition published 2011

First published 2005 by
PALGRAVE MACMILLAN

Palgrave Macmillan in the UK is an imprint of Macmillan Publishers Limited,
registered in England, company number 785998, of Houndmills, Basingstoke,
Hampshire RG21 6XS.

Palgrave Macmillan in the US is a division of St Martin's Press LLC,
175 Fifth Avenue, New York, NY 10010.

Palgrave Macmillan is the global academic imprint of the above companies
and has companies and representatives throughout the world.

Palgrave® and Macmillan® are registered trademarks in the United States, the
United Kingdom, Europe and other countries.

ISBN-13: 978–0–230–28529–3   paperback

This book is printed on paper suitable for recycling and made from fully
managed and sustained forest sources. Logging, pulping and manufacturing
processes are expected to conform to the environmental regulations of the
country of origin.

A catalogue record for this book is available from the British Library.

A catalog record for this book is available from the Library of Congress.

Printed in China

Self-evaluation sheets, planners and activity sheets may be photocopied
by individual students for their personal use only.

Contents

Introduction   viii
Glossary   xii
Acknowledgements   xiv

1   What is critical thinking?   1

Introduction   1
What is critical thinking?   2
Reasoning   3
Why develop critical thinking skills?   4
Underlying skills and attitudes   5
Self-awareness for accurate judgement   6
Personal strategies for critical thinking   7
Critical thinking in academic contexts   8
Barriers to critical thinking   10
Critical thinking: Knowledge, skills and
   attitudes   13
Priorities: Developing critical thinking abilities   14
Summary   16

**2   How well do you think? Develop
   your thinking skills**   17

Introduction   17
Assess your thinking skills   18
Scoring sheet   22
Focusing attention   23
Focusing attention: Identifying difference   24
Focusing attention: Recognising sequence   25
Categorising   27
Activity: Categorising text   28
Close reading   29
Information about the sources   31
Answers to activities in Chapter 2   32

**3   What's their point? Identifying
   arguments**   37

Introduction   37
The author's position   38
Activity: Capturing the author's position   39
Argument: Persuasion through reasons   40
Identifying the argument   41
Activity: Identifying simple arguments   44
Activity: Reasons and conclusions   45
Hunting out the conclusion   46
Summary of features   47
Summary   48
Information about the sources   48
Answers to activities in Chapter 3   49

**4   Is it an argument? Argument and
   non-argument**   51

Introduction   51
Argument and disagreement   52
Activity: Argument and disagreement   53
Non-arguments: Description   54
Non-arguments: Explanations and summaries   55
Activity: What type of message?   56
Distinguishing argument from other material   58
Activity: Selecting out the argument   59
Summary   61
Information about the sources   61
Answers to activities in Chapter 4   62

**5   How well do they say it? Clarity,
   consistency and structure**   63

Introduction   63
How clear is the author's position?   64
Internal consistency   65
Activity: Internal consistency   66
Logical consistency   67

Activity: Logical consistency	68
Independent reasons and joint reasons	69
Activity: Independent reasons and joint reasons	70
Intermediate conclusions	71
Intermediate conclusions used as reasons	72
Activity: Intermediate conclusions	73
Summative and logical conclusions	74
Activity: Summative and logical conclusions	75
Logical order	76
Activity: Logical order	77
Summary	78
Information about the sources	78
Answers to activities in Chapter 5	79

6 Reading between the lines: Recognising underlying assumptions and implicit arguments | **85**

Introduction	85
Assumptions	86
Activity: Identify the underlying assumptions	87
Identifying hidden assumptions	88
Implicit assumptions used as reasons	89
Activity: Implicit assumptions used as reasons	90
False premises	91
Activity: False premises	92
Implicit arguments	93
Activities: Implicit arguments	94
Denoted and connoted meanings	95
Activities: Associations and stereotypes	97
Activity: Denoted and connoted meanings	98
Summary	99
Information about the sources	99
Answers to activities in Chapter 6	100

7 Does it add up? Identifying flaws in the argument | **105**

Introduction	105
Assuming a causal link	106
Correlations and false correlations	107
Activity: Identify the nature of the link	108
Not meeting the necessary conditions	109
Not meeting sufficient conditions	110
Activity: Necessary and sufficient conditions	111
False analogies	112
Activity: False analogies	113
Deflection, complicity and exclusion	114
Other types of flawed argument	115

Unwarranted leaps and castle of cards	116
Emotive language; Attacking the person	117
More flaws	118
Misrepresentation and trivialisation	119
Tautology; Two wrongs don't make a right	120
Summary	121
Information on the sources	121
Answers to activities in Chapter 7	122

8 Where's the proof? Finding and evaluating sources of evidence | **125**

Introduction	125
Primary and secondary source materials	126
Searching for evidence	127
Literature searches	128
Reputable sources	129
Authenticity and validity	130
Currency and reliability	131
Selecting the best evidence	132
Relevant and irrelevant evidence	133
Activity: Relevant and irrelevant evidence	134
Representative samples	135
Activity: Representative samples	136
Certainty and probability	137
Sample sizes and statistical significance	138
Over-generalisation	139
Controlling for variables	140
Facts and opinions	141
Eye-witness testimony	142
Triangulation	143
Evaluating a body of evidence	144
Summary	145
Information on the sources	145
Answers to activities in Chapter 8	146

9 Critical reading and note-making: Critical selection, interpretation and noting of source material | **147**

Introduction	147
Preparing for critical reading	148
Identifying the theoretical perspective	149
The relation of theory to argument	150
Categorising and selecting	151
Accurate interpretation when reading	152
Making notes to support critical reading	153
Reading and noting for a purpose	154
Concise critical notes: Analysing argument	155
Concise critical notes: Books	156
Concise critical notes: Articles and papers	157

Critical selection when note-making 158
Activity: Critical selection 159
Commentary on critical selection activity 161
Note your source of information 162
Summary 164
Information on the sources 164
Answers to activities in Chapter 9 165

10 Critical, analytical writing: Critical thinking when writing 167

Introduction 167
Characteristics of critical, analytical writing 168
Setting the scene for the reader 170
Activity: Setting the scene for the reader 171
Writing up the literature search 172
Words used to introduce the line of reasoning 173
Signposting alternative points of view 175
Words used to signpost conclusions 177
Words and phrases used to structure the line of reasoning 178
Drawing tentative conclusions 179
Activity: Writing conclusions 180
Critical analysis for essays: essay titles 181
Academic keywords used in titles 182
Critical analysis for essays: reading 183
Critical analytical essays: introductions 184
Structured argument: the body of the essay 185
Essays: Bringing the argument together 186
Citing and referencing your sources 187
What do I include in a reference? 188
Summary 189
Information on the sources 189
Answers to activities in Chapter 10 190

11 Where's the analysis? Evaluating critical writing 191

Introduction 191
Checklist for evaluating Essay 1 192
Evaluate Essay 1 193
Evaluation of Essay 1 195
Commentary for Essay 1 196
Checklist for evaluating Essay 2 198
Evaluate Essay 2 199
Evaluation of Essay 2 201
Commentary on Essay 2 202
Evaluating your writing for critical thinking 204
Summary 206

12 Critical reflection 207

Introduction 207
What is critical reflection? 208
Why engage in critical reflection? 210
Decide your approach and purpose 211
Approach: outcome, focus, model, method 212
Approach: method and audience 213
Approach: relating experience and theory 214
Decide your approach: summary 215
Resource: Outline approach to reflection 216
Reflection phases 1 and 2 218
Examples of phase 1 reflection 219
Examples of phase 2 reflection 220
Models of reflection 221
Deciding on your model for reflection 222
The Core Model for critical reflection 223
Applying reflection to professional practice 225
Reflection and professional judgement 226
Good and bad critical reflection 227
Presenting your reflection to others 229
Summary 230
Information about the sources 230

Texts for Activities in Chapters 8, 9 and 11 231

Texts for activities in Chapters 8, 9 and 11 233

Practice activities on longer texts 239

Practice 1: Features of an argument 240
Answer to Practice 1: Features of an argument 244
Practice 2: Finding flaws in the argument 247
Answers to Practice 2: Finding flaws in the argument 251
Practice 3: Features of an argument 255
Answers to Practice 3: Features of an argument 261
Practice 4: Finding flaws in the argument 266
Answers to Practice 4: Finding flaws in the argument 271

Appendix: Selected search engines and databases for on-line literature searches 277

Bibliography 278
Index 280

Introduction

Nobody is an absolute beginner when it comes to critical thinking. Our most everyday activities require us to make use of some of the basic skills involved in critical thinking, such as:

- working out whether we believe what we see or hear;
- taking steps to find out whether something is likely to be true;
- arguing our own case if someone doesn't believe us.

However, just because we can think critically this doesn't mean we always do, or that we do it well. This is to be expected, as we don't need to employ the same level of critical thinking for everything we do.

For everyday activities, we take a certain amount on trust, and this saves us from having to recheck every detail. We have to decide on how much information is really required and what level of doubt is acceptable for each new circumstance. The levels and types of knowledge we need vary depending on the task, such as whether we are simply switching on a light, inventing a new form of electrical circuit or treating someone for electrocution. Similarly, critical thinking involves:

- identifying correctly when we need to gain more information;
- selecting effectively the right type and level of information for the purpose.

Success in most professions requires good critical thinking skills. Academic study also requires increasingly sophisticated levels of critical analysis at every level of study. Whether for work or for study, you may be expected to apply critical thinking to:

- what you hear, see, and do;
- the material you read;
- how you interpret new situations and events;
- what you write, say or present to other people;
- your own learning and professional practice.

Aims of this book

This book aims to help readers develop an understanding of what is meant by critical thinking and to develop their own reasoning skills. These skills are essential to those progressing to higher levels of academic study, whether at advanced or degree level. However, the underlying concepts are useful to anyone who wishes to:

- understand the concepts used in critical thinking;
- develop clearer thinking;
- interpret and produce argument more effectively;
- be more observant of what they see and hear.

This book focuses mainly on aspects of critical thinking that can be applied to work and study, and which help individuals to think about how they think. It is not intended to be an advanced study of abstract reasoning or logic. For these, the reader is referred to works such as A. Garnham and J. Oakhill (1994), *Thinking and Reasoning*, and A. Fisher (1988), *The Logic of Real Arguments*. Rather, its purpose is to focus on the basics of clear thinking.

For those new to critical thinking

The book will assist you in practical ways such as helping you to:

- recognise and understand the technical terms in critical thinking so you know what other people are referring to when they mention these, and so you can apply them yourself as relevant;
- build confidence in your own ability to apply critical thinking techniques;
- examine closely the opinions, views and arguments presented by other people;

- challenge other people's views from an informed perspective when this is appropriate.

For students

Students will find the book particularly useful in developing the ability to:

- recognise the arguments of specialist authors;
- locate arguments in key texts with greater speed;
- engage with the arguments used by both experts and their peers;
- produce better critical analytical writing of their own for marked assignments;
- recognise the difference between critical analysis and other kinds of writing, such as description.

Activities in the book

Critical thinking is an activity. It isn't sufficient to read about it: it has to be practised. The book offers activities to apply the concepts it introduces and to practise new skills. It may be that, after completing one or two of the activities that accompany a new concept, you find that aspect very easy. If so, move on to the next aspect. However, many people find some or all aspects of critical thinking to be difficult at first. If this is true of you, be reassured that this way of thinking becomes easier with practice.

The answers pages do not simply provide a correct answer: they also explain the reasons behind the answers so as to develop further the concept that has been practised. Reading through these should help you to clarify your understanding about that aspect of critical thinking.

A wide range of topics is used as examples and as practice material. You do not need any background knowledge of the subjects covered in these. It is possible to do all the activities no matter what your subject discipline or area of interest. The activities require you only to apply critical thinking to the material provided.

Passages used in the book

All of the passages in the book have been specially designed to illustrate the key points of each chapter and to provide appropriate practice material. They draw on a range of different academic disciplines but are written in such a way that you do not need to be an expert in the subject to understand the material.

None of the passages in this book is reproduced from any other text. However, some draw on the writing of others for background information. Where this is the case, details of the original source are given at the end of the chapter to enable you to follow up subjects that interest you.

Purpose of short and longer passages

For the main body of the book, especially the early chapters, the passages are short in order to introduce new learning points and to give you the opportunity for quick practice in applying these. Usually, at least three examples of each learning point are provided, as that is regarded as the minimum number of practice tries required in order to anchor new learning into memory.

In articles, books and other source material, the learning points will not always be as apparent as in the short passages provided here in the early chapters. It is important to develop the ability to apply critical awareness when reading longer texts. For these, you will need to balance different perspectives and weigh up material from a range of sources, synthesising the material to form your own judgements.

Longer practice passages are provided in Chapters 4 and 11 and in the practice section towards the end of the book. These enable you to work on several aspects of critical thinking simultaneously.

Terminology: author and audience

The different aspects of critical thinking covered in this book can be applied to material in varied media, whether written, audio or televisual. However, in order to simplify the text, the terms 'author' and 'audience' are used throughout, irrespective of the type of media.

Author

This refers to the person who creates the message, whether this is written, spoken or delivered through another medium. It doesn't necessarily mean the 'author' of a book.

Audience

This refers to whoever receives the message, whether through conversation, books, television,

DVD or other medium. The audience, in this respect, may be a viewer, a reader, a listener, or an observer.

Glossary

A glossary of technical terms used in critical thinking is provided on page xii.

Contents of the chapters

The book is organised to help you build your skills in critical thinking, starting from a basic understanding of what critical thinking is, through to applying techniques and strategies when reading and producing your own critical writing.

Chapter 1 introduces critical thinking, looking at the range of underlying skills and attitudes associated with critical thinking, and why it is beneficial to develop critical thinking skills. It emphasises the importance of self-awareness as an aspect of making accurate judgements and bringing suitable objectivity to critical reasoning. Many people find critical thinking to be a challenging activity when they first begin. The chapter looks at the barriers that might prevent you from developing critical thinking skills and ways of overcoming these. You are invited to evaluate your current skills in order to focus on those aspects of the book that are the most useful for you.

Chapter 2 looks at aspects of thinking skills such as focusing your attention, identifying similarities and differences, sequencing, categorising, and close reading. These are skills that underlie more advanced critical thinking as well as personal management skills, so improving these can benefit many aspects of academic work and personal and working life. The chapter provides an opportunity for you to evaluate these skills and then to practise those aspects which need further development.

The third chapter, 'What's their point?', introduces argument as a central aspect of critical reading. It identifies the main features and components of arguments within critical thinking, and provides practice in identifying these different elements. This is useful in helping you to find the most important aspects of your specialist texts, and to do so more quickly.

Chapter 4 builds on the previous chapter, looking at the differences between critical arguments and other types of writing that may appear to be

arguments, such as disagreements. It also looks at how, when reading, to distinguish critical argument from summaries, explanations and descriptions. As arguments can become lost within other details, this chapter gives practice in identifying more easily the material relevant to the main argument. Such skills are also useful for improving reading speed and accuracy and in helping you to identify whether your own writing has a sufficiently critical focus.

Chapter 5 focuses on the quality of reasoning. It gives you practice in evaluating how well authors present their arguments in terms of structure, logical order, internal consistency, the way in which reasons are used to support each other, and the use of interim conclusions. Understanding the structure of an argument is beneficial both in making reading faster and more effective, and in structuring your own arguments.

Chapters 6 and 7 develop skills in analysing the details of an argument. These skills help you to read texts and interpret arguments at a deeper rather than a superficial level. This is especially important for evaluating academic arguments or, for example, checking that you understand the implications of contracts in the workplace or the nuances of political arguments used at election time. As you develop these skills, you will be better able to engage in debating the issues raised by experts or by specialist authors, checking whether they are consistent in what they are saying and whether their arguments contain flaws that are not immediately obvious.

Chapter 6 focuses on 'reading between the lines', identifying aspects of the author's position and argument that are not directly stated. These include underlying assumptions and 'implicit arguments'. The chapter also looks at what is meant by the 'premises' on which arguments are predicated and at identifying 'false premises'. Finally, it examines what is meant by denoted and connoted meanings, and the importance of identifying hidden connotations within an argument.

Chapter 7 provides a different perspective on evaluating an argument, this time focusing on flaws within the reasoning. It looks at confusions that are made between cause and effect, and introduces the concept of 'meeting necessary and sufficient conditions'. It also introduces the most common types of flawed argument, such as false analogies, unfair use of emotive language, tautology, and misrepresentation.

Chapter 8 focuses on finding and evaluating sources of evidence to support an argument. It examines the difference between primary and secondary sources, looks at how to conduct a literature search, and provides criteria for evaluating and selecting different kinds of evidence. Concepts such as authenticity, validity, currency and reliability are introduced. It also looks at a range of methods used to ensure the evidence is robust, such as checking for representative sample sizes and levels of probability, and triangulating evidence.

Chapter 9 looks at specific ways of applying critical thinking to reading and note-making, such as orientating to the task of critical reading, making accurate interpretations, and categorising and selecting material in order to make the process of reading and note-making more effective. It examines the relationship of theory to argument, and looks at ways of categorising theories in order to ease comparison between different arguments. The chapter also emphasises the importance of noting the sources of evidence, as an essential aspect of critical note-making.

The next two chapters focus on the application of critical thinking to the act of writing. Chapter 10 looks at characteristics of critical writing, and especially the importance of maintaining a focus on your own potential readers and setting the scene for them. It gives details about how to use language to structure and signpost arguments so that the reader is clear which stage of the argument is being presented and the direction of your argument. Critical writing uses tentative language to express conclusions and this is also examined. The chapter looks specifically at how students can apply what they have learnt about critical thinking to each stage of writing their own essays.

Chapter 11 provides an opportunity to evaluate two critical essays. The emphasis in this chapter is not on identifying and evaluating arguments, but rather on evaluating longer texts as pieces of critical writing. The two essays differ in how effective they are at applying the conventions required for critical, analytical writing. Checklists and commentaries are provided to help you approach the task and to evaluate your responses. A further checklist is provided as an optional tool for you to use, or adapt,

to evaluate your own critical writing. Additional practice activities are provided at the end of the book (pages 239–76).

Chapter 12 looks at critical thinking from a different perspective. Critical reflection is used, increasingly, within professional practice and for student assignments. The chapter provides practical means of addressing this challenging form of critical activity, taking you through the steps of planning your reflection, relating personal experience to theory and practice in a critical way, and presenting these skilfully for assessment.

Reflection 📖 The implications

As with all academic work and professional good practice, you will benefit from reflecting upon the points raised in each chapter and, in particular, your own current ways of approaching these. Some chapters provide prompts to assist such reflection.

You are likely to gain more from using the book if, as you work through a section, you pause to consider from time to time how that aspect of critical awareness would benefit your own study, writing, or professional work.

It is well worth taking such time to pause and consider the implications of the key points in order to help you see the significance and relevance of the materials and critical strategies to your own work or study.

Glossary

When we discuss arguments, a number of specific terms are sometimes employed. Some that are useful to know in the initial stages of learning about critical thinking are listed below.

Argument   Using reasons to support a point of view, so that known or unknown audiences may be persuaded to agree. An argument may include disagreement, but is more than simply disagreement if it is based on reasons.

Argument – the overall argument   The overall argument presents the author's position. It is composed of contributing arguments, or reasons. The term 'line of reasoning' is used to refer to a set of reasons, or contributing arguments, structured to support the overall argument.

Arguments – contributing arguments   Individual reasons are referred to as arguments or 'contributing arguments'.

Assertions   Statements which are made without any supporting evidence or justification.

Conclusion   Reasoning should lead towards an end point, which is the conclusion. The conclusion should normally relate closely to the author's main position. In critical thinking, a conclusion is usually a deduction drawn from the reasons, or evidence. The final section of an essay is also referred to as the conclusion. This is examined in detail on page 185.

Conclusion – intermediate conclusions   The author may draw interim conclusions during the course of an argument, before arriving at final conclusions. Each interim conclusion is based on only some of the evidence or a particular set of reasons. These intermediate conclusions may be used to provide evidence, or to serve as reasons, in the next stage of the argument.

Consistency – internal consistency   An argument is *internally consistent* when all parts of the line of reasoning contribute to the conclusion. Nothing then contradicts or undermines the main message. An argument may be internally consistent but still be inconsistent in other respects, such as not being consistent with the evidence or with the opinions of experts in the field.

Consistency – logical consistency   An argument is logically consistent when the reasons are provided in a logical manner – that is, in the best order, with each linked to previous or following arguments so as to build up a case. A logically consistent argument will be internally consistent. In a logically consistent argument, the reasons support the conclusion.

Discursive   Discursive writing develops and elaborates an argument, moving successively from one point to the next in a given direction, towards conclusions. It does this in a thoughtful way that engages critically with the evidence base and the theories and arguments of others, drawing out implications and significance.

Line of reasoning   The line of reasoning is established through the order in which reasons and evidence are presented. This order should make it clear to the reader how the argument is to be interpreted and what the structure of the argument is. The line of reasoning should lead forwards with a clear direction, with one piece of reasoning leading in an obvious way to the next, rather than hopping from one point to another in a random way, or leading the audience round in circles.

Logical order   Good arguments present reasons and evidence in a structured way, so that information builds on what has already been said. See 'line of reasoning' above.

Position   A point of view, supported by reasoning.

Predicate   The foundation of the argument; the aims of the argument; an underlying point of view; the assumption that underlies the argument. For example: *the argument was predicated on a Marxist interpretation of wealth; the programme was predicated on the assumption that the prisoner was innocent.*

Premises   Propositions believed to be true and used as the bases for the argument; the basic building blocks for the argument – that is, the reasons for believing that the conclusion is true. Premises that are not well-founded are referred to as *false premises*.

Propositions   Statements believed to be true and presented as arguments or reasons for consideration by the audience. A proposition may turn out to be true or false.

Reasons   The contributing arguments put forward to support the overall argument or line of reasoning.

Reasons – independent reasons   The author may use several reasons to support the conclusion, each of which may be valid in its own right but may have nothing to do with the other reasons given.

Reasons – joint reasons   The reasons provided to support an argument when they are connected in some way and mutually reinforce each other.

Salience   'Salient' simply means 'relevant to the argument'.

Substantive point   The central point that is being made, or the core of the argument. This expression is used to focus attention on the main point, especially if an argument has been diverted towards more minor issues and when the key message is becoming obscured.

Tautology   Unnecessary repetition, when the author makes the same point but in different words. For example, in poor arguments, a tautology may be used to make it appear as if there are two reasons to support a conclusion, when the first reason has merely been reproduced in a different way.

Example of key terms used together

- *Proposition 1*: One of the expedition team is suspected of having pneumonia.
- *Proposition 2*: A serious storm has been predicted in the area.
- *Proposition 3*: The mountainside can be dangerous during some storms.
- *Proposition 4*: Some members of the team are not familiar with the area or with mountaineering.
- *Conclusion*: It isn't a good moment to launch an expedition into the mountains.

Premises

It is not a good time for the expedition to go into the mountains as a storm is expected and some of the team may not have the health or experience to cope with this.

False premises

The argument against launching the expedition sounds convincing. However, it could be based on false premises: a storm may not be due, the dangers might be exaggerated, or the team may be more experienced than described, or the team member may have only a minor cold. In that case, the argument against launching the expedition would be based on false premises.

Predicate

The argument against the expedition is predicated on an assumption that the safety of the team should take priority over the requirements of the expedition.

Salience

The question of safety is salient to the debate about whether to launch the expedition. Other things may not be salient to that argument. For example, the facts that a team member was good at sports at school 20 years ago, or had hiccups yesterday, are probably not salient to the discussion.

Acknowledgements

I offer many thanks to all those who have contributed to bringing this book into being. First of all, I thank all those students who used study skills sessions with me to develop strategies for improving their own critical thinking skills. For many, this involved taking courageous steps in asking for help. I hope that their efforts and bravery may now also help others, especially those who find the mysterious words 'more critical analysis needed' on feedback to their work. Secondly, I thank the lecturers who took the trouble to point out to students that they needed to improve their critical and analytical abilities and sent them in the direction of help. Thirdly, I thank the readers of the early draft of the book, who made excellent suggestions for its improvements: any remaining errors and weaknesses are my own. I owe a great deal to the research into various disciplines undertaken by others. Where I have drawn on this as background reading, this is acknowledged at the end of the chapter or in the bibliography. I owe, too, an enormous debt to the many readers and reviewers who have provided feedback on the first edition and their various recommendations for enhancing the text.

I am grateful to the students who have given permission for their work to be used, especially Charlotte French and Sophie Kahn for their extracts from their reflective journals, summary and project rationale. I also thank Jacqui Ambler for her work on student projects and the reflections she brought to my attention.

I am grateful, as ever, to the many staff at Palgrave Macmillan who work so hard behind the scenes to pull together all the different aspects of the book, and to Suzannah Burywood in particular, for making everything run so smoothly. I am grateful, too, to Valery Rose and Jocelyn Stockley for editing the script and preparing it for the printers, and for the enormous care they take with the small details. Above all, I thank my partner 'for everything', but especially for all the good things to eat as I laboured and for endless patience.

S.C.

Chapter 1

What is critical thinking?

Introduction

This chapter provides a general orientation to critical thinking. It examines what is meant by 'critical thinking', the skills associated with it, and the barriers that can hinder effective development of critical approaches. Many people can find it difficult to order their thoughts in a logical, consistent, and reasoned way. This book starts from the premise that skills in reasoning can be developed through a better understanding of what critical thinking entails, and by practice.

Critical thinking is a cognitive activity, associated with using the mind. Learning to think in critically analytical and evaluative ways means using mental processes such as attention, categorisation, selection, and judgement. However, many people who have the potential to develop more effective critical thinking can be prevented from doing so for a variety of reasons apart from a lack of ability. In particular, personal and emotional, or 'affective', reasons can create barriers.

You are invited to consider, in this chapter, how far such barriers could be affecting your own thinking abilities and how you will manage these.

What is critical thinking?

Critical thinking as a process

Critical thinking is a complex process of deliberation which involves a wide range of skills and attitudes. It includes:

- *identifying other people's positions*, arguments and conclusions;
- *evaluating the evidence* for alternative points of view;
- *weighing up opposing arguments* and evidence fairly;
- *being able to read between the lines*, seeing behind surfaces, and identifying false or unfair assumptions;
- *recognising techniques* used to make certain positions more appealing than others, such as false logic and persuasive devices;
- *reflecting on issues* in a structured way, bringing logic and insight to bear;
- *drawing conclusions* about whether arguments are valid and justifiable, based on good evidence and sensible assumptions;
- *synthesising information*: drawing together your judgements of the evidence, synthesising these to form your own new position;
- *presenting a point of view* in a structured, clear, well-reasoned way that convinces others.

Scepticism and trust

Ennis (1987) identified a range of dispositions and abilities associated with critical thinking. These focused on:

- the ability to reflect sceptically;
- the ability to think in a reasoned way.

Scepticism in critical thinking means bringing an element of polite doubt. In this context, scepticism doesn't mean you must go through life never believing anything you hear and see. That would not be helpful. It does mean holding open the possibility that what you know at a given time may be only part of the picture.

Critical thinking gives you the tools to use scepticism and doubt constructively so that you can analyse what is before you. It helps you to make better and more informed decisions about whether something is likely to be true, effective or productive. Ultimately, in order to function in the world, we have to accept the probability that at least some things are as they seem. This requires trust. If we can analyse clearly the basis of what we take as true, we are more able to discern when it is reasonable to be trusting and where it is useful to be sceptical.

Method rather than personality trait

Some people seem to be more naturally sceptical whilst others find it easier to be trusting. These differences may be because of past experiences or personality traits. However, critical thinking is not about natural traits or personality; it is about a certain set of methods aimed at exploring evidence in a particular way. Sceptical people can require structured approaches that help them to trust in the probability of an outcome, just as those who are more trusting require methods to help them use doubt constructively.

Critical thinking and argument

The focus of critical thinking is often referred to as the 'argument'. Chapter 3 identifies the features of an argument in critical thinking. The argument can be thought of as the message that is being conveyed, whether through speech, writing, performance, or other media. Critical thinking helps you to identify the obvious and the hidden messages more accurately, and to understand the process by which an argument is constructed.

Reasoning

Knowing our own reasons

Critical thinking is associated with *reasoning* or with our capacity for *rational* thought. The word 'rational' means 'using reasons' to solve problems. Reasoning starts with ourselves. It includes:

- having reasons for what we believe and do, and being aware of what these are;
- critically evaluating our own beliefs and actions;
- being able to present to others the reasons for our beliefs and actions.

This may sound easy, as we all assume we know what we believe and why. However, sometimes, when we are challenged on why we believe that something is true, it becomes obvious to us that we haven't really thought through whether what we have seen or heard is the whole story or is just one point of view. There are also likely to be occasions when we find we are not sure what we consider to be the right course of action or a correct interpretation.

It is important to examine the basis of our own beliefs and reasoning, as these will be the main vantage points from which we begin any critical analysis.

Critical analysis of other people's reasoning

Critical reasoning usually involves considering other people's reasoning. This requires the skill of grasping an overall argument, but also skills in analysing and evaluating it in detail.

Critical analysis of other people's reasons can involve:

- identifying their reasons and conclusions;
- analysing how they select, combine and order reasons to construct a line of reasoning;
- evaluating whether their reasons support the conclusions they draw;
- evaluating whether their reasons are well-founded, based on good evidence;
- identifying flaws in their reasoning.

Constructing and presenting reasons

Reasoning involves analysing evidence and drawing conclusions from it. The evidence may then be presented to support the conclusion. For example, we may consider that it is a cold day. Someone who disagrees may ask why we believe this. We may use evidence such as a thermometer reading and observation of weather conditions. Our reasons may be that the temperature is low and there is ice on the ground.

We use basic examples of reasoning such as this every day. For professional and academic work, we are usually required to present such reasoning using formal structures such as essays, or reports with recommendations. This requires additional skills such as knowing how to:

- select and structure reasons to support a conclusion;
- present an argument in a consistent way;
- use logical order;
- use language effectively to present the line of reasoning.

Why develop critical thinking skills?

Benefits of critical thinking skills

Good critical thinking skills bring numerous benefits such as:

- improved attention and observation;
- more focused reading;
- improved ability to identify the key points in a text or other message rather than becoming distracted by less important material;
- improved ability to respond to the appropriate points in a message;
- knowledge of how to get your own point across more easily;
- skills of analysis that you can choose to apply in a variety of situations.

Benefits in professional and everyday life

Skills in critical thinking bring precision to the way you think and work. You will find that practice in critical thinking helps you to be more accurate and specific in noting what is relevant and what is not. The skills listed above are useful to problem-solving and to project management, bringing greater precision and accuracy to different parts of a task.

Although critical thinking can seem like a slow process because it is precise, once you have acquired good skills, they save you time because you learn to identify the most relevant information more quickly and accurately.

Ancillary skills

Critical thinking involves the development of a range of ancillary skills such as:

- observation
- reasoning
- decision-making
- analysis
- judgement
- persuasion

Realistic self-appraisal

It is likely that you already possess some or all of these skills in order to cope with everyday life, work or previous study. However, the more advanced the level of study or the professional area, the more refined these skills need to be. The better these skills are, the more able you are to take on complex problems and projects with confidence of a successful outcome.

It is likely that many people over-estimate the quality of the critical thinking they bring to activities such as reading, watching television, using the internet, or to work and study. It is not unusual to assume our point of view is well-founded, that we know best, and that we are logical and reasonable. Other people observing us may not share this view. A lack of self-awareness and weak reasoning skills can result in unsatisfactory appraisals at work or poor marks for academic work. Certainly, comments from lecturers indicate that many students are prevented from gaining better marks because their work lacks evidence of rigorous critical thinking.

Underlying skills and attitudes

Critical thinking rarely takes place in a vacuum. Higher-level critical thinking skills usually require some or all of the skills and attitudes listed below.

Underlying thinking skills

Critical thinking assumes abilities in a range of skills such as categorising, selection and differentiation, comparing and contrasting. These skills are examined in Chapter 2.

Knowledge and research

Good critical thinkers can often detect a poor argument without a good knowledge of the subject. However, critical thinking usually benefits from background research. Finding out more about a subject helps you to make a more informed judgement about whether relevant facts, alternative explanations and options have been covered sufficiently.

Emotional self-management

Critical thinking sounds like a dispassionate process but it can engage emotions and even passionate responses. This should not surprise us when we consider that reasoning requires us to decide between opposing points of view. In particular, we may not like evidence that contradicts our own opinions or beliefs. If the evidence points in a direction that is unexpected and challenging, that can rouse unexpected feelings of anger, frustration or anxiety.

The academic world traditionally likes to consider itself as logical and immune to emotions, so if feelings do emerge, this can be especially difficult. Being able to manage your emotions under such circumstances is a useful skill. If you can remain calm, and present your reasons logically, you will be better able to argue your point of view in a convincing way.

Perseverance, accuracy and precision

Critical thinking involves accuracy and precision and this can require dedication to finding the right answer. It includes:

- *Attention to detail*: taking the time to note small clues that throw greater light on the overall issue.
- *Identifying trends and patterns*: this may be through careful mapping of information, analysis of data, or identifying repetition and similarity.
- *Repetition*: going back over the same ground several times to check that nothing has been missed.
- *Taking different perspectives*: looking at the same information from several points of view.
- *Objectivity*: putting your own likes, beliefs and interests to one side with the aim of gaining the most accurate outcome or a deeper understanding.
- *Considering implications and distant consequences*: what appears to be a good idea in the short term, for example, might have long-term effects that are less desirable.

Reflection 📖 Emotional self-management

For me, the emotions that are most difficult to manage when others disagree with me are:

I deal with these by:

Self-awareness for accurate judgement

Good critical thinking involves making accurate judgements. We noted above that our thinking might not be accurate if we are not fully aware of the influences that affect it. These can include such things as our own assumptions, preconceptions, bias, dislikes, beliefs, things we take for granted as normal and acceptable, and all those things about our selves and our world that we have never questioned.

People who are outstanding at critical thinking tend to be particularly self-aware. They reflect upon and evaluate their personal motivations, interests, prejudices, expertise and gaps in their knowledge. They question their own point of view and check the evidence used to support it.

Becoming more self-aware takes courage. It can be unsettling to find out things about ourselves we didn't know, as most of us like to think we know ourselves very well. It is also challenging to question our belief systems. We think of these as part of our identity and it can be unsettling if we feel our identity is called into question.

Furthermore, the result of your critical thinking might place you in a minority amongst your friends, family or colleagues. Nobody else might interpret the evidence in the same way as you. It takes courage to argue an alternative point of view, especially when it is possible that you might be wrong.

Reflection 📖 Influences on my thinking

For me, the influences on my own thinking that I need to be most aware of so they don't prejudice my thinking are:

I will deal with these by:

Reflection 📖 Challenging opinions

For me, the things I find most difficult about challenging the opinions of other people are:

I deal with these by:

Personal strategies for critical thinking

Below, three lecturers describe how they view critical thinking.

Example 1

- I may make a quick first reading to get the overall picture and check my initial response. I see whether it rings true or contradicts what I believe to be true.
- I compare what I read with what I already know about the topic and with my experience.
- I summarise as I go along, and hold the overall argument in my head to make sense of what comes next.
- I look for the author's position or point of view, asking 'What are they trying to "sell me"?'
- As I read, I check each section and ask myself if I know what it means. If not, I check again – sometimes it is clearer when I read the second time. If it is still unclear, I remind myself to come back to it later as the rest of the passage may make it clearer.
- I then read more carefully, seeing what reasons the writers present and checking whether I am persuaded by these.
- If I am persuaded, I consider why. Is it because they make use of experts in the field? Is there research evidence that looks thorough and convincing?
- If I am not persuaded, then why not? I check if this is a 'gut level' thing or whether I have good reasons for not being convinced. If I have relied on a gut response, I check for hard evidence such as whether I have read other material that contradicts it.
- I then create my own position, and check that my own point of view is convincing. Could I support it if I was challenged?

Here the lecturer is describing an overall strategy for reading and analysing the text in a critically analytical way. The final point refers to 'creating' a personal position by synthesising the available material – and then submitting this to critical analysis too.

The example below indicates that, as well as the words on the page or material being critiqued, there are wider contextual and other considerations to be taken into account.

Example 2

I put my energy into looking for the heart of the issue: what is really being said, and why? The answers may not be on the page; they may be in the wider history of a debate, a cultural clash, or conflicting bids for project money. It is surprising how often the wider context, popular debates, even a desire to be seen to be saying what is currently in fashion, have a bearing on what a given passage is really saying.

The third lecturer wouldn't disagree with what has gone before, but adds another dimension. Analysis encourages a focus on the detail, and on considering many different angles. This can generate a large body of evidence or long list of points for consideration. An important aspect of your critical analysis is to sift through this wealth of information, and make good judgements about what is the most significant.

Example 3

The trick is being able to see the wood for the trees; identifying what is relevant amongst a mass of less relevant information. It isn't enough just to understand; you have to be constantly evaluating whether something is accurate, whether it gets to the heart of the issue, whether it is the most important aspect on which to focus, whether it is the best example to use – and whether what you are saying about it is a fair representation of it.

All three examples illustrate different aspects of the critical thinking process:

- an analytical strategy for the material;
- understanding of the wider context;
- an evaluative and selective approach;
- being self-critical about your own understanding, interpretation and evaluation.

Critical thinking in academic contexts

Development of understanding

Students are expected to develop critical thinking skills so that they can dig deeper below the surface of the subject they are studying and engage in critical dialogue with its main theories and arguments. This is usually through engaging in critical debate in seminars, presentations or writing produced for assessment or publication.

One of the best ways of arriving at a point where we really understand something is by doing, or replicating, the underlying research for ourselves. However, as undergraduates, and indeed in everyday life, there simply isn't the time to research everything we encounter. The depth of understanding that comes through direct experience, practice and experimentation has to be replaced, at times, by critical analysis of the work of other people.

Students need to develop the ability to evaluate critically the work of others. Whilst some find this easy, others tend to accept or apply the results of other people's research too readily, without analysing it sufficiently to check that the evidence and the reasoning really support the main points being made. Bodner (1988), for example, describes chemistry students as being unable to 'apply their knowledge outside the narrow domain in which it was learnt. They "know" without understanding.' Bodner suggests that, instead of focusing primarily on standard chemical calculations in books, students should be looking for answers to questions such as 'How do we know . . . ?' and 'Why do we believe . . . ?'

Bodner's description is likely to be just as true of students in other subjects. It is not unusual for students, and for people generally, to rely unquestioningly on research that is based on a small sample of the population, or that is based on faulty reasoning, or that is now out of date. Evidence from small or isolated projects is often treated as if it were irrefutable proof of a general principle, and is sometimes quoted year after year as if it were an absolute truth. Chapter 8 looks further at critically examining and evaluating evidence.

Reflection 'Knowing without understanding'?

Do you recognise anything of yourself in Bodner's description of students? What effect would the approach he suggests have on your learning and understanding?

Both positives and negatives

In academic contexts, 'criticism' refers to an analysis of positive features as well as negative ones. It is important to identify strengths and satisfactory aspects rather than just weaknesses, to evaluate what works as well as what does not. Good critical analysis accounts for *why* something is good or poor, why it works or fails. It is not enough merely to list good and bad points.

Comprehensive: nothing is excluded

At most English-speaking universities, students are expected to take a critical approach to what they hear, see and read, even when considering the theories of respected academics. Normally, any theory, perspective, data, area of research or approach to a discipline could be subjected to critical analysis. Some colleges, such as religious foundations, may consider certain subjects to be out of bounds, but this is not typical.

The idea or the action, not the person

A distinction is usually drawn between the idea, work, text, theory or behaviour, on the one hand and, on the other, the person associated with these. This is also true when making critical analyses of other students' work, if this is a requirement of your course. Even so, it is worth remembering that people identify closely with their work and may take criticism of it personally. Tact and a constructive approach are needed. Giving difficult messages in a way other people can accept is an important aspect of critical evaluation.

Your work's rubbish, of course but as a human being, you'll do, I suppose!

Irma wasn't famed for her tact

Non-dualistic

In our day-to-day lives, we can slip into thinking everything is right or wrong, black or white. In the academic world, answers may occur at a point on a continuum of possibilities. One of the purposes of higher-level thinking is to address questions which are more complicated and sophisticated, and which

do not lend themselves to straightforward responses. You may have noticed yourself that the more you know about a subject, the more difficult it becomes to give simple answers.

Dealing with ambiguity and doubt

With the internet at our fingertips, we are more used to obtaining answers within minutes of formulating a question. However, in the academic world, questions are raised in new areas and answers may not be found for years, or even lifetimes. This can feel uncomfortable if you are used to ready answers.

This does not mean, though, that vague answers are acceptable. If you look at articles in academic journals, you will see that they are very closely argued, often focusing on a minute aspect of the subject in great detail and with precision. Students, too, are expected to develop skills in using evidence, even if drawn from other people's research, to support a detailed line of reasoning.

It is worth remembering that in academic work, including professional research for business and industry, researchers often need to pursue lines of enquiry knowing that:

- no clear answers may emerge;
- it may take decades to gain an answer;
- they may contribute only a very small part to a much larger picture.

Critical thinking as a student means:

- finding out where the best evidence lies for the subject you are discussing;
- evaluating the strength of the evidence to support different arguments;
- coming to an interim conclusion about where the available evidence appears to lead;
- constructing a line of reasoning to guide your audience through the evidence and lead them towards your conclusion;
- selecting the best examples;
- and providing evidence to illustrate your argument.

Barriers to critical thinking (1)

Critical thinking does not come easily to everyone. Barriers vary from person to person, but can usually be overcome. This section looks at some key barriers to critical thinking and encourages you to consider whether these might be having an impact on you.

Misunderstanding of what is meant by criticism

Some people assume that 'criticism' means making negative comments. As a result, they refer only to negative aspects when making an analysis. This is a misunderstanding of the term. As we saw above, critical evaluation means identifying positive as well as negative aspects, what works as well as what does not.

Others feel that it is not good to engage in criticism because it is an intrinsically negative activity. Some worry that they will be regarded as an unpleasant sort of person if they are good at criticism. As a result, they avoid making any comments they feel are negative and make only positive comments. They may not provide feedback on what can be improved. This is often an unhelpful approach, as constructive criticism can clarify a situation and help people to excel.

Over-estimating our own reasoning abilities

Most of us like to think of ourselves as rational beings. We tend to believe our own belief systems are the best (otherwise we wouldn't hold those beliefs) and that we have good reasons for what we do and think.

Although this is true of most of us for some of the time, it isn't an accurate picture of how humans behave. Most of the time our thinking runs on automatic. This makes us more efficient in our everyday lives: we don't have to doubt the safety of a tooth-brush every time we brush our teeth.

However, it is easy to fall into poor thinking habits. People who get their own way, or simply get by, with poor reasoning, may believe their reasoning must be good as nobody has said it isn't. Those who are good at winning arguments can mistake this for good reasoning ability. Winning an argument does not necessarily mean that you have the best case. It may simply mean that your opponents didn't recognise a poor argument, or chose to yield the point for their own reasons, such as to avoid conflict. Imprecise, inaccurate and illogical thinking does not help to develop the mental abilities required for higher-level academic and professional work.

Barriers to critical thinking (2)

Lack of methods, strategies or practice

Although willing to be more critical, some people don't know which steps to take next in order to improve their critical thinking skills. Others are unaware that strategies used for study at school and in everyday situations are not sufficiently rigorous for higher-level academic thinking and professional work. With practice, most people can develop their skills in critical thinking.

Reluctance to critique experts

There can be a natural anxiety about critically analysing texts or other works by people that you respect. It can seem strange for students who know little about their subject, to be asked to critique works by those who are clearly more experienced. Some students can find it alien, rude or nonsensical to offer criticism of practitioners they know to be more expert than themselves.

If this is true of you, it may help to bear in mind that this is part of the way teaching works in most English-speaking universities. Critical analysis is a typical and expected activity. Researchers and lecturers expect students to question and challenge even published material. It can take time to adapt to this way of thinking.

If you are confident about critical thinking, bear in mind that there are others who find this difficult. In many parts of the world, students are expected to demonstrate respect for known experts by behaviours such as learning text off by heart, repeating the exact words used by an expert, copying images precisely, or imitating movements as closely as possible. Students of martial arts such as tai chi or karate may be familiar with this approach to teaching and learning.

Affective reasons

We saw above that emotional self-management can play an important part in critical thinking. To be able to critique means being able to acknowledge that there is more than one way of looking at an issue. In academic contexts, the implications of a theory can challenge deeply held beliefs and long-held assumptions. This can be difficult to accept, irrespective of how intelligent a student might be.

This is especially so if 'common-sense' or 'normality' appears to be challenged by other intelligent people or by academic research. It can be hard to hear deeply held religious, political and ideological beliefs challenged in any way at all. Other sensitive issues include views on bringing up children, criminal justice, genetic modification, and sexuality.

When we are distressed by what we are learning, the emotional response may help to focus our thinking but very often it can inhibit our capacity to think clearly. Emotional content can add power to an argument, but it can also undermine an argument, especially if emotions seem to take the place of the reasoning and evidence that could convince others. Critical thinking does not mean that you must abandon beliefs that are important to you. It may mean giving more consideration to the evidence that supports the arguments based on those beliefs, so that you do justice to your point of view.

Barriers to critical thinking (3)

Mistaking information for understanding

Learning is a process that develops understanding and insight. Many lecturers set activities to develop expertise in methods used within the discipline. However, students can misunderstand the purpose of such teaching methods, preferring facts and answers rather than learning the skills that help them to make well-founded judgements for themselves.

Cowell, Keeley, Shemberg and Zinnbauer (1995) write about 'students' natural resistance to learning to think critically', which can mean acquiring new learning behaviours. Cowell et al. outline the problem through the following dialogue:

> Student: *'I want you (the expert) to give me answers to the questions; I want to know the right answer.'*
> Teachers: *'I want you to become critical thinkers, which means I want you to challenge experts' answers and pursue your own answers through active questioning. This means lots of hard work.'*

If you feel that critical thinking is hard work at times, then you are right. There are lecturers who would agree with you. However, if it wasn't difficult, you would not be developing your thinking skills into new areas. In effect, you are developing your 'mental muscle' when you improve your critical thinking skills.

Insufficient focus and attention to detail

Critical thinking involves precision and accuracy and this, in turn, requires good attention to detail. Poor criticism can result from making judgements based on too general an overview of the subject matter. Critical thinking activities require focus on the exact task in hand, rather than becoming distracted by other interesting tangents.

When critically evaluating arguments, it is important to remember that you can find an argument to be good or effective even if you don't agree with it.

Which barriers have an effect upon you?

On the table below, tick all those barriers that you consider might be affecting your critical thinking abilities.

Barrier	Has an effect?
Misunderstanding what is meant by criticism	
Lack of methods and strategies	
Lack of practice	
Reluctance to criticise those with more expertise	
Affective reasons	
Mistaking information for understanding	
Insufficient focus and attention to detail	

Reflection Managing barriers

Consider what you could do to manage these barriers in the next few months.

Critical thinking: Knowledge, skills and attitudes

Self-evaluation

For each of the following statements, rate your responses as outlined below.
Note that 'strongly disagree' carries no score.

4 = 'strongly agree'   3 = 'agree'   2 = 'sort of agree'   1 = 'disagree'   0 = 'strongly disagree'

		Rating 4–0
1	I feel comfortable pointing out potential weaknesses in the work of experts	
2	I can remain focused on the exact requirements of an activity	
3	I know the different meanings of the word 'argument' in critical thinking	
4	I can analyse the structure of an argument	
5	I can offer criticism without feeling this makes me a bad person	
6	I know what is meant by a line of reasoning	
7	I am aware of how my current beliefs might prejudice fair consideration of an issue	
8	I am patient in identifying the line of reasoning in an argument	
9	I am good at recognising the signals used to indicate stages in an argument	
10	I find it easy to separate key points from other material	
11	I am very patient in going over the facts in order to reach an accurate view	
12	I am good at identifying unfair techniques used to persuade readers	
13	I am good at reading between the lines	
14	I find it easy to evaluate the evidence to support a point of view	
15	I usually pay attention to small details	
16	I find it easy to weigh up different points of view fairly	
17	If I am not sure about something, I will research to find out more	
18	I can present my own arguments clearly	
19	I understand how to structure an argument	
20	I can tell descriptive writing from analytical writing	
21	I can spot inconsistencies in an argument easily	
22	I am good at identifying patterns	
23	I am aware of how my own up-bringing might prejudice fair consideration of an issue	
24	I know how to evaluate source materials	
25	I understand why ambiguous language is often used in research papers	
	Score out of 100	

Interpreting your score

Going through the questionnaire may have raised some questions about what you know or don't know about critical thinking. The lower the score, the more likely you are to need to develop your critical thinking skills. A score over 75 suggests you are very confident about your critical thinking ability. It is worth checking this against objective feedback such as from your tutors or colleagues. If your score is less than 100, there is still room for improvement! If your score is under 45 and remains so after completing the book, you may find it helpful to speak to an academic counsellor, your tutor or a supervisor to root out the difficulty.

Priorities: Developing critical thinking abilities

- In column A, identify which aspects of critical thinking you want to know more about. Give a rating between 5 and 0, giving 5 for 'very important' and 0 for 'not important at all'.
- In column B, consider how essential it is that you develop this aspect soon. Give a rating between 5 and 0, where 5 is 'very essential' and 0 is 'not essential at all'.
- Add scores in columns A and B to gain an idea of where your priorities are likely to lie.
- Column D directs you where to look for more information on that point.

	Aspects I want to develop further I want to:	A Want to know more? Rate from 0 to 5 5 = 'very important'	B How essential to develop it now? Rate from 0 to 5 5 = 'very essential'	C Priority score Add scores for columns A and B.	D See Chapter
1	understand the benefits of critical thinking				1
2	remain focused on the exact requirements of an activity				2
3	pay better attention to small details				2
4	know what is meant by a line of reasoning				3
5	identify the component parts of an argument for critical thinking				3
6	recognise the words used to signal stages in an argument				3 and 10
7	distinguish argument from disagreement				4
8	distinguish argument from summaries, descriptions and explanations				4
9	pick out the key points from background information				4
10	be able to analyse the structure of an argument				5, 10
11	evaluate whether arguments are internally consistent				5
12	understand what is meant by an intermediate conclusion				5
13	be able to structure an argument				5, 10 and 11
14	be better at reading between the lines				6
15	recognise underlying assumptions				6
16	recognise when an argument is based on false premises				6

	Aspects I want to develop further I want to:	A Want to know more? Rate from 0 to 5 5 = 'very important'	B How essential to develop it now? Rate from 0 to 5 5 = 'very essential'	C Priority score Add scores for columns A and B.	D See Chapter
17	recognise implicit arguments				6
18	understand what is meant by denoted and connoted meanings				6
19	be aware of how cause, effect, correlation and coincidence can be confused				7
20	be able to check for 'necessary and sufficient conditions'				7
21	identify unfair techniques used to persuade readers				6, 7
22	recognise tautology				7
23	recognise flawed reasoning				6 and 7
24	be able to evaluate source materials				1 and 8
25	understand what is meant by authenticity, validity, and reliability				8
26	evaluate when samples are representative				8
27	understand what is meant by 'triangulation'				8
28	check for levels of probability				8
29	apply critical thinking when making notes				9, 10
30	use language more effectively to structure argument				3, 10 and 11
31	present my own arguments clearly in writing/for essays				10, 11
32	be able to undertake good critical reflection for assignments or my job				12

Priorities for action

- Look back over the priorities table above. Identify the three aspects to which you gave the highest scores. If more than three have the highest score, select three to start with.
- Write the three priorities here as actions starting with 'I will . . .', using words that are meaningful to you – e.g. 'I will find out what tautology means.'

1	I will	
2	I will	
3	I will	

Summary

Critical thinking is a process that relies upon, and develops, a wide range of skills and personal qualities. Like other forms of activity, it improves with practice and with a proper sense of what is required. For some people, this may mean changing behaviours, such as paying attention to detail or taking a more sceptical approach to what they see, hear and read. Some need to focus on developing critical thinking techniques, and this is the main purpose of the book.

For others, weaknesses in critical thinking abilities may stem from attitudes to criticism, and anxiety about potential consequences. Barriers associated with attitudinal and affective responses to critical approaches were considered in this chapter. Sometimes, it is sufficient to become more aware of these barriers, and to recognise the blocks to effective thinking, for the anxiety to subside. If you find that these difficulties persist, it is worth speaking to a student counsellor about your concerns. They will be familiar with such responses and may be able to help you to find a solution that fits your personal circumstances.

Developing good critical thinking skills can take patience and application. On the other hand, the rewards lie in improved abilities in making judgements, seeing more easily through flawed reasoning, making choices from a more informed position and improving your ability to influence others.

Having undertaken an initial personal evaluation of your critical thinking skills, you may now wish to follow up the priorities you identified. This is a particularly useful approach if you have already worked on your critical thinking skills. If you are new to critical thinking, you may find it useful to progress directly to Chapter 2 in order to test, and practise, your underlying thinking skills. Alternatively, proceed now to Chapter 3 and work through the chapters in turn.

Chapter 2

How well do you think?
Develop your thinking skills

Learning outcomes

This chapter offers you opportunities to:

- identify foundation thinking skills which contribute to critical thinking
- assess your recognition of patterns and your attention to detail
- practise focusing attention

Introduction

We use basic thinking skills in everyday life, usually with little difficulty. However, many people find it difficult to apply these same skills automatically to new contexts, such as more abstract problem-solving and academic study. This is partly because, although people use these skills in contexts familiar to them, they are not always sufficiently aware of the underlying strategies that they are using so as to be able to adapt them to new circumstances. The more used we are to applying skills easily in one context, the more difficult it can be to identify the underlying skills.

Critical thinking skills are based on underlying sets of thinking skills such as:

- focusing attention so as to recognise the significance of fine details;
- using attention to fine detail in order to recognise patterns, such as similarities and differences, absence and presence, order and sequence;
- using recognition of pattern in order to compare and contrast items and to predict possible outcomes;
- sorting and labelling items into groups, so that they form categories;

- using an understanding of categories to identify the characteristics of new phenomena and make judgements about them.

These skills are not only useful for critical thinking in academic and professional life, but are tested as part of the procedures for selecting job applicants for interviews.

The next pages provide several short self-assessment activities for you to assess how good you are already at these skills. In particular, these give you practice in attending to fine detail, and the level of mental discipline that critical analysis involves. Student critical writing is often weakened by a lack of sustained and close attention to detail in one or more stages of the critical process. Improving your ability to pay attention to detail, selectively and at speed, is likely to have benefits for your study and assignments.

If you find the assessment easy, then progress to a chapter that is more useful for you. Otherwise, use the rest of this chapter to practise these skills further.

Assess your thinking skills (1)

Comparison

The following activity enables you to check how good you are at identifying similarity and difference. For each set of boxes below, identify which one is the odd one out. An example is given first.

Example

1	2	3	4	5	6
← ← ← ←	→ → → →	← ← ← ←	← ← ← ←	← ← ← ←	← ← ← ←

Here, box 2 is the odd one out as the arrows point in a different direction from those in the other boxes. Now try the following.

A

1	2	3	4	5	6

B

1	2	3	4	5	6

C

1	2	3	4	5	6

D

1	2	3	4	5	6

Sequence

This activity assesses your ability to recognise how a sequence is structured. Each set of boxes forms a sequence. Below each sequence is a set of options. Choose one option to replace the question mark and complete the sequence.

Example sequence

◆	✳	◆	✳	◆	?

Options for the example sequence

1	2	3	4	5	6
▱	☾	◆	💬	✳	✉

The answer is 5, as the sequence in the example is one of alternating diamonds and stars. Now complete the following sequences.

Sequence A

✸	✸	✸	✸	✸	?

Options for sequence A

1	2	3	4	5	6

Sequence B

1	2	3	4	5	6

Options for sequence B

1	2	3	4	5	6

Answers: see p. 32. ▶

Assess your thinking skills (2)

Sequence C

Options for sequence C

1	2	3	4	5	6

Sequence D

Options for sequence D

1	2	3	4	5	6

Categorising

This activity enables you to check your ability to categorise information. For each box, organise the set of items into two groups. Each group should be distinct with its own particular characteristic. Identify the characteristic of each group. There may not be the same number of items in each group.

A	mouse		typing		drive
	printer		talking		monitor
	screen		scrolling		eating

B	pyramid	vast	oasis	gigantic
	palm-tree		desert	massive
	enormous	Nile		immense

C	topaz	agate	silver	ruby
	gold	opal		platinum

D	Empty	Gate	Shoal	Divan	burst
	chops	Kenya	hertz	micro	Pound

Following directions

Answer the following questions as directed.

A Use the multiple choice responses below to answer the question: How many legs has a cow?

1 A cow has three legs.

2 A cow has two legs and two tails.

3 A cow has four legs and a tail.

4 A cow has four legs.

B Use the multiple choice responses below to answer the question: Of which atoms is water comprised:

1 Water is comprised of oxygen and hydrogen.

2 Water can exist as a solid, fluid or gas.

3 Water is comprised of oxygen and hydrogen and is rarely, if ever, found on any planet except earth.

4 Water forms ice when it is frozen and is then considered to be a solid.

Assess your thinking skills (3)

Close reading

This activity enables you to check your close reading skills. Each passage below is followed by a series of questions about the text. For each question, circle:

A If the statement follows logically from the information given in the passage.

B If the statement is untrue or it does not follow logically from the information given in the passage.

C If the passage does not give enough information for you to say whether it is true or follows logically from the information that is given. Consider what other information you would need.

Passage 2.1

The Arctic

The Arctic region at the top of the northern hemisphere forms a broad cold band that encompasses both Greenland and Siberia. Conditions in the Arctic are harsh. Vegetation is sparce and temperatures are low for most of the year. Inhabitants of the region enjoy three months of continual daylight in the summer. However, in winter the sun never appears. For three months of the year there is perpetual night, the only natural light coming from the moon, the stars and the northern lights.

1   The main argument is that summers in the Arctic are very short.

       A   **B**   **C**

2   The vegetation of the Arctic is not good to eat.

       A   **B**   **C**

3   The sun never appears.

       A   **B**   **C**

4   There is daylight for some or all of the day during nine months of the year.

       A   **B**   **C**

5   There is no electricity in the Arctic.

       A   **B**   **C**

Passage 2.2

George Washington Carver

George Washington Carver Jr. (1865–1943) was an agricultural scientist of repute. His research contributed to the development of over 300 products from peanuts alone. Amongst over 100 industrial applications he helped to develop from agricultural products such as soybeans, were rubber substitutes, paints and textile dyes. His work was celebrated by President Franklin D. Roosevelt with a national monument in 1943. Carver became a symbol to many different groups. As the first Black student to attend his college, he was proof of what a former slave could achieve through education. Given Carver's claim that God was his inspiration, religious groups embraced his discoveries as a sign of God's blessing for materialism. Southern businessmen saw in him a living example of New South Philosophy and materialism. Through him, the South was transformed from being a one-crop cotton-based producer to a multi-crop economy with industrial outlets. As with many great men, the stories surrounding Carver's life have taken on mythic aspects, which are now hard to disentangle from the truth.

6   Franklin D. Roosevelt succeeded George Washington Carver as President of the USA.

       A   **B**   **C**

7   Roosevelt constructed a monument to Carver after his death in 1943.

       A   **B**   **C**

8   Carver was not really a great man as his story is based on myths.

          A   **B**   **C**

9   Religious groups thought God favoured materialism.

          A   **B**   **C**

10   Before Carver, no Black students had attended college in the USA.

          A   **B**   **C**

11   Before Carver, the Southern USA was a multi-crop economy with industrial outlets.

          A   **B**   **C**

12   Carver helped to invent over 100 industrial applications from soybeans.

          A   **B**   **C**

Recognising similarities

Which of the following two passages, option 1 or option 2, is closest in meaning to Passage 2.1, *The Arctic*, above (p. 20).

Option 1

As you move further north, the environment deteriorates to one of icy climatic conditions for much of the year, with few plants, and months without any daylight at all.

Option 2

The Arctic region in the northern hemisphere is best avoided as conditions are so harsh, and yet the inhabitants enjoy living there. They like the continual daylight in the summer and the natural light of the moon and the stars.

Which of the following three passages, option 3, 4 or 5, is closest in meaning to Passage 2.2, *George Washington Carver*, above (p. 20).

Option 3

Carver claimed that he owed his success to God's inspiration. This shows that if you put your faith in God, he will help you to be successful as an inventor and as a materialist.

Option 4

Carver was an important symbol for Black groups in the South. He was born a slave and was the first Black student to go to his college. Southern businessmen and religious groups would not have expected that education would have such an effect upon people they had regarded as slaves. Carver's celebration by a President of the United States was given in recognition that the economy of the Southern states no longer relied on cotton.

Option 5

The economy of the South was diversified by Carver's discoveries in agricultural science, resulting in Carver becoming something of a symbol and mythic figure for Southern groups.

Answers: see p. 33. ▶

Use the scoring sheet on the next page to add up your score and evaluate your performance.

Scoring sheet

Work out your score

Check the answers on pp. 32–3. Use the scoring sheet below to add up your score.

Item	Possible score	Your score
Comparison	4	
A	1	
B	1	
C	1	
D	1	
Sequence	9	
A	2	
B	2	
C	2	
D	3	
Categorising	14	
A	3	
B	4	
C	4	
D	3	
Following directions	4	
A	2	
B	2	
Close reading	15	
1	1	
2	1	
3	1	
4	1	
5	1	
6	1	
7	2	
8	1	
9	1	
10	2	
11	1	
12	2	
Recognising similarities	4	
Arctic	2	
Carver	2	
Total	50	
Double your total to find your percentage score	100	

Evaluate your score

This is only a rough test for you to see for yourself how easily you performed some of the underlying skills associated with critical thinking. People who find critical thinking hard often have a difficulty in one or more of these skills. However, this is not always the case. There can be many reasons why people do well at one task and not another, so do not be discouraged if you found this difficult or gained a low score.

86–100   Excellent! This score suggests that you already have very good overall basic thinking skills to apply to critical thinking skills.

60–85   Good! If this is distributed evenly across all the items in the assessment, then you are likely to have a good basis for developing critical thinking skills. Note whether there were any areas where your score was lower than others, or which you found more difficult. You might benefit from more practice in those areas before proceeding or if you find critical thinking difficult.

30–60   Well done! You have obviously already gained a basis for developing your basic and critical thinking skills. Some people find critical thinking easier when it applies to real situations rather than in small activities, and that might be true of you. However, you are likely to benefit from practising these skills further, both through the activities in the rest of this chapter and taking more time on tasks which require close attention to detail.

Less than 30   Well done for sticking with the task. It may be that today wasn't your day for this kind of activity. Have a go with the activities in this chapter and see if you develop some strategies for improving these skills. If not, and if you find critical thinking to be difficult, it is worth speaking to a tutor or lecturer to discuss the assessment.

Focusing attention

Attentional processes

Attention isn't the same as concentration. Concentration is associated with maintaining a focus on a task, even when it is difficult to do this. Attentional processes may include such concentration, but do not necessarily do so. Attentional processes that are important to critical thinking include:

- knowing where to look, where to focus the attention;
- being aware of when we are unable to maintain attention, and when to rest, so that we are able to maintain a sharp focus;
- becoming used to conventions, whether for reading, writing, tests or exams, so that we can use these to help us use attention efficiently;
- being aware of the conventions or rules for jokes, puzzles, television programmes, videos, different types of text or spoken information, so that we can use that knowledge to direct our attention efficiently;
- being aware of where there may be tricks, false impressions or illusions;
- remembering previous experience so that we can use it to direct attention.

Automatic thinking and frames of reference

We can train our attention so that we are better able to notice relevant information. Much of the time, our mind operates 'on automatic pilot'. This makes it efficient for a range of activities other than critical thinking. Our brain tends to be effective at finding ways of saving us mental energy. Where it can, it takes short cuts and uses what it already knows to make sense of anything new it encounters. It tends to do this on an approximate basis, so it isn't always accurate.

Our mind uses its previous experiences to provide frameworks, known as 'frames of reference', to help categorise incoming information. When the brain thinks it knows what it is looking at, it will naturally stop trying to categorise the experience. That is how optical illusions or magical tricks work: our brain thinks it knows what it is seeing even though it is being tricked, so it stops looking for further explanations.

Our frames of reference can be more or less sophisticated. At a basic level, we sort situations into safe/not safe, as this helps our survival. We can usually pick out our name from background noise, even when we are not paying attention, as that also helps our survival. We sort other information according to our vocabulary, knowledge and experiences. The more experience we have of consciously thinking through how our experiences are interconnected, and labelling those experiences, the more likely it is that we can organise our thoughts and direct our attention in particular ways when we want to.

Activity: Find the 't'

Read the following text. Read it a second time, and identify how many times the letter 't' occurs.

Terrifying torrents and long dark tunnels are used to create the excitement of the thrilling train ride at the park.

The answer is on p. 34.

The activities in the self-assessment on pages 18–21 focus on some attentional processes that underlie critical thinking. To complete these activities, we need to pay attention to detail so as to notice patterns within the 'bigger picture'. If we can recognise patterns, we can compare items, drawing out similarities and differences. If we can recognise sequence, we are in a better position to identify trends, predict the next step and distinguish between cause and effect. The following pages give more practice in developing attentional skills.

Focusing attention: Identifying difference

This activity gives you further practice in comparing different patterns in order to identify which item does not belong to the set. For each set of boxes, identify which box is the odd one out.

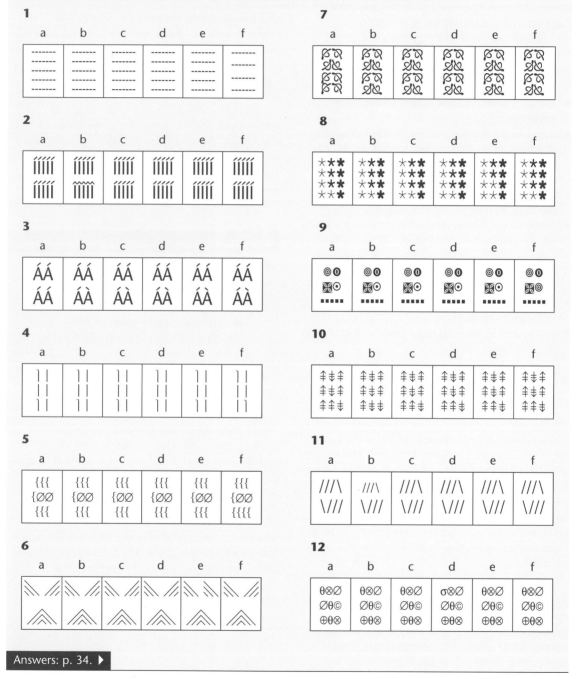

Answers: p. 34. ▶

Focusing attention: Recognising sequence (1)

The following activity gives you further practice in recognising sequence. As in the previous assessment exercise, work out what the sequence is. Select an answer from the choice below, to replace the question mark and complete the sequence in each case. Answers on pages 34–5.

1

a	b	c	d	e	f
#	# #	# # #	## # #	## ## #	?

Options for sequence 1

1a	1b	1c	1d	1e	1f
# # #	## ## ##	#	# #	## ## #	## #

2

a	b	c	d	e	f
ωξ	ωξ	ωξ	ωξ	ωξ	?

Options for sequence 2

2a	2b	2c	2d	2e	2f
ωξ	ωξ ω	ωξ ωξ	ω	ωξ	ω ξ

3

a	b	c	d	e	f
ΧχΧ χΧχ ΧχΧ	χΧχ ΧχΧ χΧχ	ΧχΧ χΧχ ΧχΧ	χΧχ ΧχΧ χΧχ	ΧχΧ χΧχ ΧχΧ	?

Options for sequence 3

3a	3b	3c	3d	3e	3f
ΧχΧ χΧχ	χΧχ ΧχΧ χΧχ	χΧχ ΧχΧ χΧχ	χΧχ ΧχΧ χΧχ	ΧχΧ χΧχ ΧχΧ	ΧχΧ χΧχ ΧχΧ

4

a	b	c	d	e	f
⊃	⊃ ⊄	⊃ ⊄ ⊄	⊃⊃ ⊄⊄	⊃⊃ ⊄⊄ ⊄	?

Options for sequence 4

4a	4b	4c	4d	4e	4f
⊃⊃ ⊄ ⊄	⊃⊃ ⊄⊄ ⊄	⊃ ⊄	⊃⊃ ⊄⊄ ⊄⊄	⊃⊃ ⊄ ⊄	⊃ ⊄ ⊄

5

a	b	c	d	e	f
←Ψ →↓ ⇦↓	Ψ↓ ←↓ →⇦	↓↓ Ψ⇦ ←→	↓⇦ ↓→ Ψ←	⇦→ ↓← ↓Ψ	?

Options for sequence 5

5a	5b	5c	5d	5e	5f
←← Ψ⇦ ↓↓	Ψ Ψ →⇦ ↓↓	Ψ← ⇦↓ ↓↓	⇦Ψ →↓ ↓↓	→← ⇦Ψ ↓↓	←← ⇦↓ Ψ↓

6

a	b	c	d	e	f
◻◯ ◻◯	◻◯ ◻◯	◼◯ ◻◯	◼◯ ◻◯	◼● ✳◯	?

Options for sequence 6

6a	6b	6c	6d	6e	6f
◼◯ ◻◯	◼● ✳◯	◼◯ ◻◻	◼◯ ◼◯	◼● ✳●	◻◯ ◻◯

Focusing attention: Recognising sequence (2)

7

	a	b	c	d	e	f
	✛✗	✛✗	⊙◗	⊙◗	⊙◈	
	✛✗	⊙◗	⊙◗	⊙◈	⊙◈	?
	⊙◗	⊙◗	⊙◗	⊙◈	✛✗	

Options for sequence 7

	7a	7b	7c	7d	7e	7f
	⊙◈	⊙◈	✛✗	⊙◗	✛✗	⊙◈
	⊙◗	✛✗	✛✗	✛✗	⊙◗	✛✗
	⊙◈	⊙◈	⊙◗	✛✗	⊙◈	✛✗

8

Options for sequence 8

9

Options for sequence 9

10

Options for sequence 10

11

Options for sequence 11

12

Options for sequence 12

Answers: p. 34. ▶

Categorising

Categorising skills are important to critical thinking as they enable you to sort information into appropriate groups and recognise which information has relevant connections to other kinds of information. In critical analysis, this helps you to compare the right things, so that you compare 'like with like'. This is necessary for constructing sophisticated arguments, such as in debate or for essays and reports.

Comparisons

Drawing comparisons is essentially about finding similarities and identifying differences. The same two items may be considered to be similar or different depending on the context and the criteria used for comparison, as the following set of questions demonstrates.

Q1	What do these eight items have in common?

| zebra | cat | puppy | goldfish |
| whale | kitten | seal | elephant |

Q2	What do these items have in common which makes them different from the other items in the list in Q1?

| cat | goldfish | kitten | puppy |

Q3	What do these items have in common which makes them different from other items in the list?

| kitten | puppy |

The items in Q1 are all animals. Q2 has focused in on animals that are common domestic pets and Q3, on *young* domestic pets. In each case, the selection focuses in more detail on a narrower range of shared characteristics.

Salient characteristics

'Salient' simply means 'relevant to the argument'. In the above examples, your existing knowledge of animals and pets probably made it easy to recognise the characteristics that the items in each group shared. When you recognise the characteristics

that a set of items holds in common then, in effect, you are sorting these into groups, or categorising. A category is simply a group of items with shared characteristics. Any kind of category is possible: tall pointed objects; green vegetables; current prime ministers.

Activity: Categorising

Identify the following categories (in other words, what does each group have in common?)

(a) pond   lake   sea   pool
(b) Indian   Irish   Iranian   Bolivian
(c) lair   den   pen   burrow   hutch
(d) biology   chemistry   physics   geology
(e) creates   stellar   engines   soothes
(f) decide   deliver   denounce   devour
(g) never   seven   cleverest   severe
(h) memory   language   problem-solving
(i) appendicitis   tonsillitis   colonitis
(j) rotor   minim   deed   peep   tenet
(k) cheluviation   illuviation   leaching   salination
(l) 21   35   56   84   91
(m) oligarchy   exarchy   plutarchy,   democracy
(n) cete   herd   colony   flock   drove

Answers: p. 35. ▶

Categorising involves not merely identifying shared salient characteristics, but also having the right background knowledge and vocabulary to label the group once identified. You may have found this an issue when trying to describe some of the groups above. Good background knowledge and vocabulary do make it easier to find, sort and use information at speed, making critical thinking more efficient.

The above items were easier to categorise because you already knew that they formed a category. This meant you only had to find the salient characteristics of ready-formed groups. Pattern-finding skills also make it easier to identify similarities when a group is not already pre-formed.

Activity: Categorising text

For each of the following sets of three texts, identify which two carry the most similar message.

Passage 2.3

Matter

(a) Different ages have classified matter in different ways. Aristotle's view was that all material substances consisted of air, earth, fire and water. This view held sway for a long time. Today, we describe liquids, solids and gases in terms of their chemical properties.

(b) Systems for classifying matter have varied over time. Although we now analyse matter in terms of chemical properties, Aristotle's division into earth, fire, air and water was used for a long time.

(c) Different ages have classified matter in different ways. Aristotle's view that all material substances consist of air, earth, fire and water was clearly erroneous and was replaced by the correct version we hold today. We describe liquids, solids and gases in terms of their chemical properties.

Passage 2.4

Anointing oil

(a) When Elizabeth II was crowned queen of England, she was anointed with a mixture of essential oils. A mixture of oils including cinnamon, rose, jasmine and civet was invented in the days of Egforth of Mercia, who was the first English king to be anointed in the manner of the Old Testament. This has been used ever since and is prepared by the royal physicians before a coronation.

(b) The anointing of kings and queens has always been an aromatic affair. Coronation oil is prepared by royal physicians, and contains a mix of essential oils. For that of Elizabeth II, these included cinnamon, rose, jasmine, civet, musk and neroli. Such a mix of oils has been used for hundreds of years, perhaps even all the way back to 785, when Egforth of Mercia was the first English king to be anointed in the manner of the Old Testament.

(c) Essential oils have always played an important part in coronation rituals. When Elizabeth II was crowned queen of England, a mixture that included cinnamon, jasmine, benzoin and neroli was prepared by the Surgeon-Apothecary. It is possible that such ingredients were used even as long ago as 785, when Egforth of Mercia was crowned.

Passage 2.5

The right hemisphere

(a) The right hemisphere of the brain controls our capacity to identify what is real. When either hemisphere is damaged, it is difficult for people to perform tasks such as differentiating their mother from a cupboard. When the right hemisphere is damaged, some individuals lose their power of imagination. They also may not be able to envisage what problems they have. This is not the case with left hemisphere damage.

(b) The right hemisphere of the brain controls the ability to recognise what is real in the outer world, such as differentiating your mother from your cupboard. When the right hemisphere is damaged, some individuals find it impossible to recognise or imagine the problem they have. This is not the case with left hemisphere damage.

(c) Our capacity to recognise what is real is controlled by the right hemisphere of the brain. If this is damaged, the individual may find it impossible to imagine what problems are created by the damage. Individuals with syndromes of the left hemisphere are able to grasp what problems are created by the syndrome.

Answers: see p. 35. ▶

Close reading (1)

Critical thinking frequently requires you to read in very precise ways, paying attention to fine detail in order to make an accurate interpretation. This may require you to read more slowly, although, with practice, your critical reading skills can also become faster. This chapter provides practice in reading precisely.

In the activity below, you are required to answer a series of multiple-choice questions about a passage. There is a set of questions for each passage. Go through the passages in turn. You may find it helpful to check the answers for one passage before going on to another.

If you do not get all the answers correct, give some thought to where you were going wrong before moving on to the next passage.

Activity

For each statement, circle:

A If this is consistent with what is said in the passage or follows logically from the information given.

B If this is not consistent with what is said in the passage or does not follow logically from the information given.

C If the passage does not give enough information for you to conclude whether a statement is true or follows logically from the information given. Consider what other information you would need.

Passage 2.6

Traditional legends

Traditional legends from the Americas are drawn from very diverse people and regions. They cover what would have been the particular experiences of many groups: coping with natural disasters, migrations, encounters with animals, journeys and events, distilled into myths in which many peoples can see their own story. The legends illustrate cosmic themes, such as the directions of North, South, East and West. Legends are not just quaint stories. They continue a tradition of beliefs and religion that link people culturally and ethically.

1 Legends serve social and cultural purposes.

     A   B   C

2 The themes found in legends are common to many different peoples.

     A   B   C

3 All legends address cosmic themes such as the directions of North, South, East and West.

     A   B   C

4 The passage implies that if you understand these myths, you will have a better sense of direction.

     A   B   C

5 Although different people produced the legends, the legends are all the same.

     A   B   C

6 The passage suggests that people share common experiences and can see their stories reflected in the legends produced by others.

     A   B   C

Answers: see pp. 35–6. ▶

Close reading (2)

Passage 2.7

Transformation

Disease and developmental disorders can bring about unexpected benefits. Whilst the conditions may bring unhappiness and pain, they can also bring us face to face with what we want the most out of life; many people have seen illness as a transformative event. Whilst certain opportunities close down, others can open up unexpectedly. Where certain neural pathways of the brain are blocked, for example, others may be forced into action, bringing about new ways of doing things, and sometimes even new ways of being.

7   People on benefits are more likely to get diseases.

      A   **B**   **C**

8   Disease and developmental disorders are essential to neural development.

      A   **B**   **C**

9   Most people find illness to be a transformative event.

      A   **B**   **C**

10 If a person loses the capacity to perform an activity because of a disease, it is possible that they can learn an alternative method.

      A   **B**   **C**

Passage 2.8

Clinical trials

Before a new pharmaceutical drug reaches the market, it must undergo clinical trials. The raw data from clinical trials of drugs are rarely published and what is published may be very misleading. The results of clinical trials that indicate that a drug is beneficial are likely to be published whereas tests that suggest the same drug is not effective are not published, and the public do not get to hear about them. The result is that even academic articles written about new drugs, and which are normally based on the same data, can be very inaccurate. Not only that, but even our understanding of what an illness is can become distorted. For example, it was widely believed that depression was caused by people having a serotonin deficiency. Clinical trials suggested taking drugs that raised serotonin levels would result in greatly reducing the risk of suicide. This is contested in *The New Brain Sciences* (Rose, 2004), which argues that such drugs, far from reducing the effect of suicide, may even increase its risk, and that there is very little evidence that depressive illness has anything to do with serotonin levels.

11 The reasons given to explain depressive illness are flawed.

      A   **B**   **C**

12 Raw data from clinical trials are less likely to be published than the results of trials that indicate that a drug is beneficial.

      A   **B**   **C**

13 Clinical trials are not undertaken frequently enough to establish whether the effects of drugs change as a person grows older.

      A   **B**   **C**

14 Academic articles are normally more accurate than the results of trials produced by drug companies.

      A   **B**   **C**

15 Decreased serotonin levels lead to an increased risk of suicide.

      A   **B**   **C**

Answers: see pp. 35–6. ▶

Close reading (3)

Passage 2.9

If a person carrying a cane collapses, they are likely to receive help very quickly. This suggests that people are altruistic, but not everyone receives such help. A third more people are likely to offer help to a person who appears to be lame than to those who are bleeding or have a facial disfigurement. If a person appears seriously wounded, helpers are more likely to offer indirect assistance by seeking more expert help. People are more likely to help if the cost of helping is low or if intervention is perceived as likely to be effective. Almost all potential helpers take flight if the victim appears drunk. However, in the USA, black people were more likely to help a black drunk and white people to help a white drunk (Piliavin et al., 1981). In other circumstances, there were no obvious racial differences in willingness to assist a victim.

16   If a drunk person is bleeding, they are less likely to receive help than if they are not.

      A   **B**   **C**

17   White people are generally more likely to help other white victims than black victims, except when they are drunk.

      A   **B**   **C**

18   People with facial disfigurements are less likely to receive help than people who are lame.

      A   **B**   **C**

19   People are more likely to help if they feel they can be of use.

      A   **B**   **C**

20   It is likely that people think either that the cost of helping a person with a cane is low or that help in such cases is likely to be effective.

      A   **B**   **C**

Check your method

If you do not get all the answers correct, give some thought to where you were going wrong before moving on to the next passage. If it is not obvious why you got an answer wrong:

- Read the passage several times, focusing on the lines related to the question you got wrong.
- Focus on the exact wording. Check whether you misread anything.
- Check whether you jumped to conclusions for which there isn't evidence in the passage.
- Check whether you read more into the passage than is actually written on the page or more than can logically be deduced from the information given.
- Did you bring other information to the passage which is not actually written down? The instructions are to use only information which is in the passage – not your general knowledge.

Answers: see pp. 35–6. ▶

Information about the sources

Carwell, H. (1977) *Blacks in Science: Astrophysicist to Zoologist* (Hicksville, NY: Exposition Press).

McMurray, L. (1981) *George Washington Carver* (New York: Oxford University Press).

Piliavin, J. A., Dovidio, J. F., Gaertner, S. L. and Clark, R. D. (1981) *Emergency Intervention* (New York: Academic Press).

Rose, S. (2004) *The New Brain Sciences: Perils and Prospects* (Milton Keynes: The Open University).

Sachs, O. (1985) 'Right hemisphere syndromes', *The Man Who Mistook His Wife for a Hat* (London: Picador).

Worwood, V. A. (1999) *The Fragrant Heavens: The Spiritual Dimension of Fragrance and Aromatherapy* (London: Bantam Books).

Answers to activities in Chapter 2

Assess your thinking skills: answers

Use the scoring sheet on p. 22 to record your answers.

Comparison (p. 18)

A   The odd box is 5. In all the other boxes, the line of circles in the second row is larger than in the other rows. Score 1 for a correct answer.

B   The odd box is 1. In all the other boxes, the set of scissors in the bottom right-hand corner has white blades whereas the set in box 1 has black blades. Score 1 for a correct answer.

C   The odd box is 4. The left-hand image in the bottom row is presented back to front in this box. Score 1 for a correct answer.

D   The odd box is 6. The middle item in this box is different. Score 1 for a correct answer.

Sequence (pp. 18–19)

A   selection 1. Score 1 for a correct answer.
    The first three boxes repeat a pattern, with the tail to the right. The next set repeat the pattern with the tail to the left.
    Score 1 for identifying the reason correctly.

B   selection 4. Score 1 for a correct answer.
    Every second box has the same pattern.
    Score 1 for identifying the reason correctly.

C   selection 5. Score 1 for a correct answer.
    In each successive box, the top row from the previous box becomes the bottom row.
    Score 1 for identifying the reason correctly.

D   selection 2. Score 1 for a correct answer.
    Stars increase by one for the first three boxes then start again from one. Stars also move from top to bottom in alternate boxes. Boxes 4 and 5 start to repeat the same sets of lines (∫ and ≤) as earlier boxes, but these alternate between being at the top or the bottom of the box.
    Score 2 for identifying the reason correctly.

Categorising (p. 19)

A   (i)   parts of a computer: mouse, drive, printer, monitor, screen

    (ii) verbs (or words ending in –ing): typing, talking, scrolling, eating
          Score 1 for categorising items correctly.
          Score 1 for identifying why group (i) belong together.
          Score 1 for identifying why group (ii) belong together.

B   (i)   items associated with Egypt: pyramid, oasis, palm-tree, desert, Nile

    (ii) words that indicate that something is large: immense, vast, massive, enormous, gigantic
          Score 1 for categorising items correctly.
          Score 1 for identifying why group (i) belong together.
          Score 2 for identifying why group (ii) belong together.

C   (i)   precious stones: agate, topaz, ruby, opal

    (ii) precious metals: gold, silver, platinum
          Score 1 for categorising items correctly.
          Score 1 for identifying why group (i) belong together.
          Score 2 for identifying why group (ii) belong together.

D   (i)   words beginning with a capital letter: Empty, Gate, Shoal, Divan, Kenya, Pound

    (ii) words that begin in the lower case (i.e. without a capital letter): chops, hertz, micro, burst
          Score 1 for categorising items correctly.
          Score 1 for identifying why group (i) belong together.
          Score 1 for identifying why group (ii) belong together.

Answers to activities in Chapter 2 (continued)

Following directions (p. 19)

The aim of this activity was to enable you to check how closely you followed directions, especially when not forewarned. Academic work and exams usually require you to answer the question exactly as it is worded.

A   Answer 4 is correct: a cow has four legs. If you answered C, check the exact wording of the question again: it only asks how many legs a cow has. Score 2 for a correct answer.

B   Answer 1 is correct: water is comprised of oxygen and hydrogen. This is all that the question asks. Although the other responses may be true, they do not answer the exact question posed. Score 2 for a correct answer.

Close reading (pp. 20–1)

The Arctic

Score 1 for each correct answer.

1   **B**   The passage does state that summers are short but the main argument is that conditions in the Arctic are harsh.

2   **C**   This may be true or false: the passage does not say.

3   **B**   Untrue. The passage says the sun doesn't appear for three months – but it can during the rest of the year.

4   **A**   True – this follows logically. The passage states that there is no daylight for 3 months.

5   **C**   The passage does not give enough information about non-natural forms of energy.

George Washington Carver

6   **B**   Untrue. This is not stated in the passage and does not follow logically from what is stated. Score 1 point.

7   **C**   The passage does not give exact dates so the monument could have been built while Carver was still alive. Score 2 points.

8   **B**   Untrue. The passage states that there are mythic aspects to Carver's life, and implies that this is because he was a great man. It does not state that Carvers' life, in its entirety, was a myth. Score 1 point.

9   **A**   True. The passage states that religious groups believed this because Carver declared that God was the inspiration for his discoveries. Score 1 point.

10   **C**   We would need more information. The passage refers only to Carver's own college, not to all the other colleges in the USA. Score 2 points.

11   **B**   Untrue. The passage states the opposite, that this was the case as a result of Carver's inventions. Score 1 point.

12   **C**   The passage states that Carver helped to develop over 100 industrial applications from agricultural products *such as* soybeans: we don't know how many of these were from soybeans themselves and how many from other agricultural products. Score 2 points.

Recognising similarities (pp. 21–2)

For each passage, score 1 for identifying the correct option, and score 1 for finding the reason.

Option 1 is the nearest in meaning to passage 2.1 (*The Arctic*). Option 2 states that inhabitants like living there, which we do not know from the passage.

Option 5 is the nearest in meaning to the *George Washington Carver* passage, and is a summary of its key points. Options 3 and 4 focus on only some aspects of the passage, and make assumptions that are not in the passage. Option 3 expresses religious views that are not stated in the passage. Option 4 is inaccurate in stating why the monument was set up: the exact reasons are not given in the passage.

Answers to activities in Chapter 2 (continued)

Focusing attention

Find the 't' (p. 23)

There are 14 't's. These are highlighted below.

> Terrifying torrents and long dark tunnels are used to create the excitement of the thrilling train ride at the park.

If you counted less than 14 the first time round, this is not unusual. It is likely that your brain used its 'auto-pilot' to read the short words such as 'to' and 'the' automatically as a whole unit, rather than as a sequence of letters, even when you were trying to focus on the individual letters. If this happened to you, it may indicate that your brain works efficiently for most reading purposes.

Identifying difference (p. 24)

1 = f	5 = f	9 = f
2 = b	6 = e	10 = b
3 = a	7 = a	11 = b
4 = f	8 = e	12 = d

Recognising sequence (pp. 25–6)

1   = 1b   An additional symbol is added in each successive box.

2   = 2e   Boxes a and b are repeated in each successive pair of boxes.

3   = 3c   Boxes a and b are repeated in each successive pair of boxes.

4   = 4d   Each box adds one item, first to the left-hand column, then to the right-hand column.

5   = 5e   Each symbol travels anti-clockwise around the box, moving one place in each successive box.

6   = 6b   Each new box is repeated once.

7   = 7f   The bottom row doubles in the next box along and also moves up one place.

8   = 8a
✳▨✳ moves up one place each row.
O moves along the row from left to right and descends a row each box.
↺✳¤ at top of box for two boxes then at bottom for two, then top for two.
❧ repeats for two boxes then shifts one place.

9   = 9d   The symbol ◎ moves from left to right along each row in turn. All the other symbols do the same. Once a symbol arrives at the bottom right-hand corner, it starts again in the top left-hand box.

10   = 10f   The top row alternates in each successive box. The last three boxes of the middle row form a mirror image to the first three boxes of that row. The third row adds one dot in each successive box, for a sequence of three, then starts again.

11   = 11e
■·■ moves down a row in each successive box for four boxes (and then starts again from the top).
The diamond pattern ·◆· moves down a row in each successive box for three boxes (and then starts again from the top). It also alternates to a larger diamond coming first, ◆·◆t, in alternate boxes.
The □O◎ pattern moves down a row in each successive box for four boxes (and then starts again from the top). Within the pattern, the square moves one place to the right in each successive box.
☽ moves down a row in each successive box for four boxes (and then starts again from the top). It also doubles on alternate boxes.

12   = 12b
The row of 5 squares, ▪▪▪▪▪, moves clockwise around the edge of the box from one box to the next.

Answers to activities in Chapter 2 (continued)

◆◆◆ alternates between the top and second lines, and changes to ◆◆ on the top line.
•• alternates between the third and second lines, and changes to ••• on the second line.
✳O alternates between the fourth and third lines, and changes to O✳ in alternate boxes.

Categorising

Categories (p. 27)

(a) Bodies of water
(b) Nationalities
(c) Animal habitats
(d) Science subjects
(e) Seven-letter words
(f) Verbs with the suffix (i.e. starting with) 'de-'
(g) Words containing 'eve'
(h) Cognitive (thinking) skills
(i) Inflammatory conditions of bodily organs
(j) Palindromes: words that read the same backwards and forwards
(k) Terms that refer to the development of a soil profile
(l) Multiples of 7
(m) Forms of government
(n) Collective nouns for types of animal

Categorising text (p. 28)

Passage 2.3   Matter

Passages (a) and (b) are the most similar as they merely describe the two sets of classification. Passage (c) makes value judgements about the systems.

Passage 2.4   Anointing oil

Passages (b) and (c) are the most similar. Passage (a) makes a claim that the mixture of oils was invented in Egforth's reign whereas the other two passages express this only as a possibility.

Passage 2.5   The right hemisphere

Passages (b) and (c) are the most similar. Passage (a) attributes difficulty in differentiating reality to both hemispheres whereas (b) and (c) attribute this only to the right hemisphere. Passage (a) also claims that right-hemisphere damage leads to loss of imagination in general, which the other two do not.

Close reading (pp. 29–31)

Passage 2.6   Traditional Legends

1   A   This follows logically from the final line of the passage.

2   A   This follows from what is said in the second sentence.

3   C   There is not enough evidence in the passage to know this, as the passage refers only to myths of the Americas.

4   B   No, the passage does not say anything about a sense of direction.

5   B   This does not follow from the passage.

6   A   This is consistent with what is written in the passage.

Passage 2.7   Transformation

7   B   The passage does not say anything about people on benefits.

8   B   The passage does not state this and it does not follow logically from information in the passage.

9   C   The passage does not state this and we would need more data to know if most people did find illness to be transformative.

10   A   This is consistent: it paraphrases what the passage states.

Answers to activities in Chapter 2 (continued)

Passage 2.8 Clinical trials

11 **A** The statement is consistent with the passage, which argues that depression is wrongly attributed to levels of serotonin.

12 **A** This is consistent with the passage, as it states that raw data are rarely published whereas the results of beneficial tests are more likely to be published.

13 **C** The passage does not provide information about ageing effects.

14 **B** This is not consistent with the passage. The passage suggests that academic articles are normally just as inaccurate, as they are based on the same data.

15 **B** This is not consistent with the information given in the passage, which argues that there is insufficient evidence about the links between serotonin levels and depression.

Passage 2.9

16 **C** No data are provided on this in the passage.

17 **B** This contradicts the message of the passage, which is that in most circumstances there are no obvious racial differences in patterns of assistance.

18 **A** This is consistent with the third sentence, which states that a third more people are likely to help someone who is lame.

19 **A** This is consistent with the sentence in the middle of the passage that says people are more likely to help if they think they will be effective.

20 **A** This is consistent with the first sentence, about the speed with which people help those with canes compared with others, and the sentence in the middle of the passage about when people are more likely to offer help.

Chapter 3

What's their point?
Identifying arguments

Learning outcomes

This chapter offers you opportunities to:

- identify the key components of an argument
- develop strategies for identifying reasons, conclusions and arguments within a message
- practise identifying simple arguments

Introduction

Critical thinking focuses on 'argument'. This chapter looks at what is meant by 'argument' within the context of critical thinking, and how to recognise its key features. If you are able to detect the main argument, you are better able to direct your attention to the salient, or most appropriate, material. This, in turn, enables you to direct your reading to the most relevant material, and to save time by reading more efficiently.

There are many short passages used in this chapter to help you practise critical thinking skills. It is worth noting that the activities may ask you to make judgements about the arguments, but none ask whether you agree with them. You may not agree with the reasons or conclusions given. However, critical thinking requires an evaluation of

arguments in terms of the merit of their formal features, such as the quality of the reasoning, and not whether these support our own opinions. Good critical thinking includes recognising good arguments even when we disagree with them, and poor arguments even when these support our own point of view.

Doug never recognised a good argument.

The author's position

When we read, watch television or listen to people talking, we are presented with other people's arguments. Underlying those arguments are points of view or 'positions' that they aim to convey to us, their audience.

We should increase prison sentences for crime (1)

Increasing prison sentences isn't helpful (2)

Space travel is a good thing (3)

We don't need space travel (4)

Note how the positions of the authors above relate to the overall argument opposite.

Key terms: Argument

The word 'argument' is used in two ways in critical thinking:
- **Contributing arguments**   Individual reasons are referred to as 'arguments' or 'contributing arguments'.
- **The overall argument**   This is composed of contributing arguments, or reasons. The overall argument presents the author's position. The term 'line of reasoning' is used to refer to a set of reasons, or contributing arguments, structured to support the overall argument.

Overall argument	Contributing arguments
(1) Longer prison sentences should be introduced.	Heavy punishments deter criminals. Current penalties for crime are too lenient and don't deter criminals. Since prison sentences were reduced, crime has increased. Victims need to see that perpetrators of crimes are punished.

Overall argument	Contributing arguments
(2) Increasing prison sentences is not the way to stop crime.	Crime was high even when punishments were more weighty. Prison teaches people how to be more skilled as criminals. Criminals who are imprisoned are more likely to take part in increasingly serious crime when released. Most crime is committed by people who are illiterate and lack work-related skills. Education rather than punishment is needed.

Overall argument	Contributing arguments
(3) We should invest more in space travel.	Many discoveries have come about through space travel. It is important for us to learn more about the universe we live in. The fuel needed for space travel may not be around for much longer so we should use it while we have the chance.

Overall argument	Contributing arguments
(4) We should stop investing in space travel.	Space travel is expensive and the costs far outweigh the benefits. There are much more urgent projects that need investment more than space travel. Better alternatives for fuel for space travel may be available in the future.

Activity: Capturing the author's position

Activity

Read through the following passages and identify the author's position:

- Skim quickly over the passage and note your first impressions, aiming to capture the author's position (the main message of the passage).
- Follow up your rapid read by closer reading to check if you were right. This will give you an idea of how accurately you capture a message when reading at speed.
- Check the answers on page 49.

Passage 3.1

Barristers do not have much direct contact with their clients, but it is possible to find a legal job that suits your preferences for court work. However, if an aspiring barrister wants to spend time in court, they need to select their field carefully, to see if the work patterns associated with it match their preferences. Every field is different. Criminal lawyers may spend most of their time in court. Tax lawyers, on the other hand, may spend only a day a month or less in court. Advocacy work requires less time in court than in the office.

Passage 3.2

The nature and origin of disease was unclear until relatively recently. At the end of the nineteenth century, Koch, a Prussian scientist, introduced a set of procedures now known as *Koch's postulates*. He experimented with bacterial colonies cultivated in the laboratory, made from the blood of dying cattle. When these cultures were injected into healthy live cattle, these also caught the same disease. At the time, these findings were astonishing. Koch had been able to provide proof to support the theory that disease was spread by germs. He contributed one of the most important methodological advances in the history of medicine.

Passage 3.3

The Sahara is a region worthy of serious investigation by travellers. Ancient architectures are no doubt hidden beneath the Sahara sands. Somewhere in the eastern Sahara, there may lie the long-lost oasis of Zerzura. In the west, there lies the fabled city of Timbuktu. Many have tried to find traces of the cultures that once straddled the great area covered by the desert.

Passage 3.4

It was initially believed that young children could not understand other people's points of view or undertake tasks such as counting and measuring until they were at least seven years of age. However, it seems the problem does not lie in children's capacity to do these things so much as in their understanding of what is being asked and why. If there is no obvious purpose, or they do not understand the language used, children find tasks difficult. Even young children can perform tasks formerly considered too advanced for them, as long as these are set up in ways that make sense to them. Problems that involve teddies or drinks, for example, may be meaningful to a very young child, whereas tasks with counters and beakers are not.

Answers: see p. 49. ▶

Further activity

Read the introduction and conclusion of three books or articles in your subject.

How well does the introduction present the author's position: is it clear what the author is trying to persuade you to accept?

How well does the conclusion make it clear what the author's position is?

Argument: Persuasion through reasons

Persuasion and reasons

In everyday language, an 'argument' can suggest poor communication, a difficult relationship, hard feelings and, possibly, aggression. This is not the case with argument as part of critical thinking. An 'argument' merely means presenting reasons to support your position or point of view. If other people accept those reasons, they are more likely to be persuaded to your point of view.

An argument includes:

- a position or point of view;
- an attempt to persuade others to accept that point of view;
- reasons given to support the point of view.

To identify an argument, it is useful to keep in mind such questions as:

- 'What was the point of producing this text or programme?'
- 'What is the main message I am supposed to take from this?'
- 'What does the author/producer want me to believe, accept or do?'
- 'What reasons have they offered to support their position?'

In most circumstances, authors aim to persuade us to a particular point of view because they believe in what they are saying. However, in some cases, they may have an obvious or a hidden vested interest. It may be that they have a long-standing rivalry with academics from a different school of thought. It may be that they work for a company that wants their audience to buy its products or to subscribe to a particular view on health or pollution or genetics.

Authors may also intentionally, or unintentionally, interpret information through the filter of their own political, religious or ideological perspectives. That doesn't necessarily make their argument invalid, but it is often important to know their theoretical position in order to identify the influences on their line of reasoning.

Ambiguous arguments

Sometimes, for everyday purposes, a statement may be clear and uncontroversial. For example:

- 'It's raining' – when clearly it is raining.
- 'Everyone who ate the fish is ill' – when this is an observation of fact.
- 'I ran a mile in 4 minutes' – when this has been timed and observed.

More often, there are complexities in what we hear, see and read. It may not be obvious what point someone is trying to make, or we may suspect that there are half-truths in what they say. We recognise this in speech when we make comments such as 'What's your point?' or 'What are you trying to say? We may wonder how someone has arrived at a particular conclusion: what they say just doesn't seem to 'add up'. When this is obvious, we may be able to point it out and resolve the misunderstanding.

However, when we are reading books or watching television, the author isn't available to answer queries about what is meant. The argument may be very complicated and it can take time to clarify the line of reasoning through careful analysis and close reading or observation. The author may also have presented the information in such a way that the lack of evidence, the illogical arguments or false conclusions are not immediately apparent. Critical thinking skills are then particularly important because we cannot always ask directly for explanations and clarifications.

Identifying the argument (1)

This section looks at ways of isolating key information in a passage in order to identify the argument. You may find it useful to check the glossary of terms on page xii before proceeding. Before you read on, see if you can identify the main argument in the passage below.

Passage 3.5

This area has become well-known, but for unfortunate reasons. The junction of Green Road and Mill Street has been the site of over a dozen major road traffic accidents in the last five years as drivers take the corner too quickly. A local artist has made a rather grim photographic record of all the main accidents that have taken place. Some tourists have been victims. New speed cameras have now been placed at the corner of the road and this will reduce the number of accidents.

You may have noticed that some statements and pieces of information in Passage 3.5 add to our knowledge of the accident site but do not contribute to the overall argument. This general background and detail is highlighted in italics below.

This area has become well-known, but for unfortunate reasons. The junction of Green Road and Mill Street has been the site of over a dozen major road traffic accidents in the last five years as drivers take the corner too quickly. *A local artist has made a rather grim photographic record of all the main accidents that have taken place. Some tourists have been victims.* New speed cameras have now been placed at the corner of the road and this will reduce the number of accidents.

If we remove these, the propositions, or main statements of the argument, become clearer:

> The junction of Green Road and Mill Street has been the site of over a dozen major road traffic accidents in the last five years as drivers take the corner too quickly. New speed cameras have now been placed at the corner of the road and this will reduce the number of accidents.

We can then isolate the main points in our own words:

- *Proposition 1:* Many road traffic accidents occur at the junction of Green Road and Mill Street.
- *Proposition 2:* Drivers take the corner too quickly.
- *Proposition 3:* New speed cameras are in place at the junction.
- *Conclusion:* There should now be fewer accidents.
- *Overall argument:* Speed cameras will reduce the number of accidents at the junction.

The overall argument becomes more obvious when the propositions and the conclusion are identified.

Identifying the argument (2)

Premises   Propositions believed to be true and used as the bases for the argument; the basic building blocks for the argument.

False premise   A proposition that later turns out not to be true or correct.

Predicate   The foundation of the argument; the aims of the argument; an underlying point of view; the assumption that underlies the argument. For example: *the argument was predicated on a Marxist interpretation of wealth; the programme was predicated on the assumption that the prisoner was innocent.*

For Passage 3.5, we can say further that:

- this is an argument because reasons are given to support a conclusion. The reasons supporting the conclusion are:
  - that drivers drive too quickly around the corner;
  - and that accidents happen as a consequence.
- The argument is based, or 'predicated', on the assumption that drivers will take notice of the speed cameras and reduce their speed on that corner. If you disagree with this, you might consider that the conclusion is predicated on a 'false premise'.

Before you read on, see if you can identify the main argument in Passage 3.6a.

As before, general background and detail is highlighted in italics in Passage 3.6b, so that the key points in the argument stand out more clearly. As you read Passage 3.6b, consider whether the conclusion comes at the beginning, the end or elsewhere within the text.

Passage 3.6a

Pit's End should become a site of major archaeological importance. Formerly, it was believed that the three large granite stones found near the village were deposited after the melting of glaciers at the end of the last ice age. Eleven new stones were unearthed during recent excavations. The area had been covered in farmland. Aerial photography suggested that the area was worthy of excavation. The layout of the fourteen stones suggests they were originally part of an unusual oval formation. They are spaced evenly at approximately two metres, which suggests they were laid out by a former settlement, possibly for religious purposes. Geologists confirm they are unlikely to have been laid down by glacial or other natural causes. Tools unearthed there recently are amongst the oldest ever discovered in this country, making them of significant interest. The dig has been funded by the national lottery.

Passage 3.6b

Background information
Pit's End should become a site of major archaeological importance. *Formerly, it was believed that the three large granite stones found near the village were deposited after the melting of glaciers at the end of the last ice age.* Eleven new stones were unearthed *during recent excavations. The area had been covered in farmland. Aerial photography suggested that the area was worthy of excavation.* The layout of the fourteen stones suggests they were originally part of an unusual oval formation. They are spaced evenly at approximately two metres, which suggests they were laid out by a former settlement, possibly for religious purposes. Geologists confirm they are unlikely to have been laid down by glacial or other natural causes. Tools unearthed there recently are amongst the oldest ever discovered in this country, making them of significant interest. *The dig has been funded by the national lottery.*

Identifying the argument (3)

If we remove the general background material from Passage 3.6, the premises and the conclusion become clearer:

Passage 3.6c

Pit's End should become a site of major archaeological importance. Eleven new stones were unearthed. The layout of the fourteen stones suggests they were originally part of an unusual oval formation. They are spaced evenly at approximately two metres, which suggests they were laid out by a former settlement, possibly for religious purposes. Geologists confirm they are unlikely to have been laid down by glacial or other natural causes. Tools unearthed there recently are amongst the oldest ever discovered in this country, making them of significant interest.

We can then isolate the main points, and give them in our own words. Note that the conclusion comes at the beginning of the argument in this instance and the reasons to support the point of view then follow:

- *Conclusion*: Pit's End should become a site of major archaeological importance.
- *Proposition 1*: Eleven new stones have been unearthed that change what was previously known about the area.
- *Proposition 2*: The oval layout of the fourteen stones is unusual
- *Proposition 3*: The even spacing of the stones suggests they were laid down as part of a human settlement.
- *Proposition 4*: The stones are unlikely to have been laid down by natural causes.
- *Proposition 5*: Tools unearthed there recently are amongst the oldest ever discovered in this country.
- *Argument*: The unusual oval stone formation and the very ancient tools found at Pit's End should make it into a site of great archaeological importance.

While we are looking at this passage we can say further that:

- This is an argument because reasons are given to support a conclusion. The reasons given are that the stones form part of an unusual human formation, and that the tools are amongst the oldest in the country. These are likely to create interest.
- The argument is predicated on the assumption that the stone formation dates back to the time of the tools or pre-dates them. However, this may be a false premise as the stones could have been laid down later. That may influence whether the site is interesting archaeologically.

You can see that when presented with a string of information such as in each of the passages above, it isn't always immediately obvious what are propositions, what is the conclusion, and what is simply additional or irrelevant information. If you search out the conclusion first, it is easier to identify the relevant supporting information.

TIP

Search for the conclusions first, and the key messages may become clear quickly.

Activity: Identifying simple arguments

Passage 3.7

I like that picture. The colours create the powerful effect of a sunset, which is pleasant to look at. The figures are interesting and very well drawn. It is a good picture.

Passage 3.8

Biscuits can be bad for your teeth. We often eat mid-morning when the effects of breakfast have worn off. Biscuit companies, like other food manufacturers, require their employees to wear hats to hold back their hair for health and safety reasons.

Passage 3.9

Quantum physics has identified many more dimensions than height, width, depth and time, which most people are familiar with. Such research can take a long time. Discoveries have also been made on other aspects of the time–space continuum.

Passage 3.10

The Pied Piper played a magical pipe and the side of the mountain opened. He encouraged the children from the town to enter into the mountain, which closed behind them so they were lost forever. Their parents never saw them again and he intended this to be the case. The Pied Piper was angry at the townspeople because they refused to pay him for removing rats from the town. His action wasn't accidental; it was one of revenge.

Passage 3.11

The train is late. There must have been a signal failure.

Passage 3.12

The eclipse was expected over Scotland at 9 am yesterday. Lots of people turned up. The sky was still visible when they arrived but it became cloudy. When you watch an eclipse, you have to protect your eyes and you mustn't look directly at the sun.

Passage 3.13

The windows rattled and the doors banged. The air felt charged. We were all frightened. A strange sound filled the air. It must have been a ghost.

Passage 3.14

Many adults learn to read later in life. Although John and Miranda found it difficult to read as children, as adults they caught up with their peers. They enjoyed attending local literacy classes. Almost a million people have improved their literacy skills through adult classes in recent years.

Passage 3.15

Plants need nitrogen in order to grow. Although there is nitrogen in the air, plants cannot absorb it by taking it in from the air. Instead, they are reliant on bacteria in the soil to absorb nitrogen in a process known as 'nitrogen fixation'. The bacteria turn the nitrogen into nitrates which are easier for plants to absorb through their roots.

Activity: Reasons and conclusions

Passage 3.16

A human skeleton was found near the river late last month by a senior couple walking their dog. They believed it was a murder caused by a troublesome local family. The police interviewed the family but ruled out their involvement. The bones are believed to be several hundred years old. Historians confirm that the river Marle passes close to ancient burial grounds and that there are records of other bodies being carried away by the river in the distant past. This was the first for over 150 years. Recent storms have caused the river to rise by half a metre. It is probable that the skeleton was dislodged from its resting place by the river rather than by the local family.

Passage 3.17

There are only 60 species of monocotyledons, more usually known as sea grasses. Nonetheless, sea grasses make important contributions to the coastal ecosystems of every continent except Antarctica. This wasn't discovered until the end of the twentieth century. In shallow waters such as estuaries and bays, sea grasses are indeed the most dominant form of vegetation, supporting a host of marine life. They act as nurseries for fish, including commercial varieties. Moreover, without sea grasses, the bio-diversity of coastal regions would be severely impoverished. The United Nations has sponsored the *World Atlas of Sea Grasses* (Green and Short, 2004) to raise awareness of their importance.

Passage 3.18

According to Csikszentmihalyi, fundamental unhappiness arises in today's world because we are too ruled by the way the world is, rather than the way it ought to be. Although most of us know we gain from being kind, supportive and considerate, we forget this very quickly. We act to satisfy our wants, even though we know there are people who have nothing. We consider them to be far away or less important than ourselves and so we buy another television or CD rather than give money to strangers. We often ignore basic rules which help to keep the environment in balance. For example, we know carbon-based resources are in short supply and yet we use coal, gas and oil as if they were limitless. When we do this, there are consequences which bring unhappiness. In our everyday lives, we often focus on instant rewards and short-term gains, without thinking of the long-term consequences for human happiness. The challenge facing humans is to find a way of acting more co-operatively with each other and more in harmony with our universe.

Passage 3.19

It is important that pregnant women and those with poor immune systems become aware of the potential risks posed by cats. Many of us keep cats as house pets without realising the dangers they may be harbouring. Cats are hosts to infectious *toxoplasma gondii*, a protozoa that causes disease, toxoplasmosis, in mammals such as humans. The protozoa is crescent-shaped and common in nature, but in its infectious stage relies on cats as host bodies. Adult humans rarely show signs of significant disease if they become infected. However, if pregnant women become infected, the foetus can become infected by parasites and suffer serious congenital damage. In the worst cases, infants may lose their eye-sight and acquire motor deficits. In people with poor immune systems or AIDS, toxoplasmosis can cause seizures and death. The symptoms of the disease are not evident in cats so there is no way of knowing if a particular cat is a risk.

Answers: see p. 50. ▶

Hunting out the conclusion

Commentary

Location of the conclusion

The end of the passage is a good place to start looking for a conclusion, as in Passages 3.5, 3.16 and 3.18. Some authors prefer to state their reasons first. They then sum these up as part of their conclusion before going on to make a deduction about the significance of the reasoning.

However, it is useful to check opening sentences of a passage too, as in Passages 3.6, 3.17 and 3.19. Some authors choose to state the conclusion near the beginning to establish their position. They then provide the reasons to back it up, showing how they arrived at the deductions they have made.

Conclusions as interpretative summaries

In Passage 3.16, the conclusion is also an interpretive summary. The final sentence pulls together the information from the passage, which has built the case for the logical deduction about what has occurred. A conclusion in critical thinking is more than a mere summary. However, a summary

can form part of a conclusion. In this case, the conclusion is more than a summary as:

- it contains a selection of salient points which provide an interpretation of events;
- it also makes a judgement about the likelihood of this interpretation.

The author uses these devices to persuade the reader to accept the interpretation offered.

Challenges and recommendations

The conclusions in Passages 3.18 and 3.19 make challenges or recommendations. These are deductions about actions that need to be taken to achieve a desired effect. Such deductions often signal the conclusion.

Signal words

Authors can use words to 'signal', or indicate, that a conclusion is about to be made, such as 'nonetheless' in Passage 3.17. Such words are not always followed by a conclusion, but they signal that it is worth checking. Look for words such as: 'therefore', 'so', 'as a consequence', 'finally', or other phrases that imply 'therefore'.

Words that indicate deduction

As a conclusion is concerned with making deductions, it is worth looking for other words that indicate that the author is making a deduction. These include phrases such as 'this ought to', 'as a result', 'this will', 'this would have', 'this should', 'this must', 'this means that', 'in effect'. Remember to look for words that express this in the negative too, such as 'this ought never to', 'this should never'.

Summary of features

Not all messages contain an argument. When we are reading or listening to a message critically, we can save time if we check for key features of an argument. Later in the book, we will be looking at implicit arguments, where the argument may be hidden. Here, we are concerned with explicit arguments, where the argument is expressed in a relatively open way. So far, we have identified six items to look for in identifying an argument. These are summarised in the table below.

Is it an argument?		
1	Position	Authors have a position, or point of view that they attempt to persuade their audience to accept.
2	Reasons/ propositions	Reasons are provided to support the conclusion. Reasons are also referred to as 'contributing arguments' and 'propositions'.
3	A line of reasoning	A line of reasoning is a set of reasons, presented in logical order. It is like a path leading the audience through the reasons, in steps, towards the desired conclusion. It should be ordered so that it leads clearly and logically from one reason to the next. In a poor line of reasoning, it is difficult to see how each reason contributes to the conclusion.
4	Conclusion	Arguments lead towards a conclusion. The conclusion would normally be the position that the author wants you to accept. However, it is possible that the conclusion stated does not support the position that the author is advocating.
5	Persuasion	The purpose of an argument is to persuade the audience to a point of view.
6	Signal words and phrases	These help the audience follow the direction of the argument.

Locating the conclusion

There are short-cuts we can take to help us locate the main conclusion within a passage more quickly. These are only indicators of where to look as the author may not have chosen to use any of these methods to signal the conclusion.

Clues to finding the conclusion		
1	Start of passage	Conclusions are often set out or indicated early in the message, such as in the first or second sentence, or in the initial paragraph.
2	The end of a passage	Conclusions are frequently located towards the end of a message, such as in the final or penultimate sentence or paragraph.
3	Interpretive summary	Look for a summary that interprets the line of reasoning and/or makes deductions, often towards the end of a text where all the evidence is brought together. However, note page 55: summaries are not always conclusions.
4	Signal words	Look for words used to indicate that a conclusion is about to follow. See p. 178.
5	Challenges and recommendations	These often form part of the conclusion. They often contain the author's position or point towards it.
6	Words indicating a deduction	Look for words that express a probable or possible outcome or interpretation.

Summary

This chapter has looked at ways of identifying an argument. We have seen that an argument begins with a point of view or a perspective. In an argument, the author is attempting to convince the audience of that point of view.

Just because the author intends to do this, it does not mean that their position is clear. In this chapter, and in Chapter 5, we look at how authors can obscure their position through presenting it badly. Furthermore, Chapters 6 and 7 examine how authors may conceal their real position in order to persuade the audience to accept their argument.

If we can identify argument, we are in a better position to recognise when somebody is trying to persuade us of their own point of view. This can make us more alert to their line of reasoning and put us in a better position to analyse their argument. Knowing the basic components of an argument can help us to identify an argument. In checking whether material is an argument or not, we need to look for reasons that aim to persuade, and the conclusion that the author wants us to accept.

The key components of an argument are summed up in the table on p. 47. These, and the 'Clues to finding the conclusion', can help to focus our reading on the main messages of a passage. Using these can make reading faster and more efficient.

An argument in critical thinking consists of reasons organised into a 'line of reasoning' or 'overall argument', with the intention of persuading a potential audience. It also consists of a conclusion, which makes a deduction based on the reasons. The line of reasoning that leads to the conclusion may be surrounded by other material that is not directly relevant to the conclusion, and which may distract the reader from the argument. Good critical reading strategies, including skill in identifying the main features of an argument, may be needed to distinguish the argument from other material.

Information about the sources

The work of barristers: Boyle, F. (1997) *The Guardian Careers Guide: Law* (London: Fourth Estate).

Children's cognitive development: Donaldson, M. (1987) *Children's Minds* (London: Fontana).

The Sahara: Sattin, A. (2004) *The Gates of Africa: Death, Discovery and the Search for Timbuktu* (London: HarperCollins).

Sea grasses: Green, E. P. and Short, F. T. (2004) *World Atlas of Sea Grasses* (Berkeley, CA: University of California Press).

Answers to activities in Chapter 3

Capturing the author's position (p. 39)

Passage 3.1

The author's position is: *It is possible to find a legal job that suits your preferences for court work.* The passage provides advice for aspiring barristers on selecting their field according to how much time they want to spend in court.

Passage 3.2

The author's position is: *Koch contributed one of the most important methodological advances in the history of medicine.* The passage supports this with information about experiments Koch developed that were able to prove the germ theory of disease.

Passage 3.3

The author's position is: *The Sahara is an area worth investigating by those who are interested in history.* The passage supports this by referring to traces of past cultures hidden beneath the sands.

Passage 3.4

The author's position is: *Even young children can perform tasks considered too advanced for them, as long as these are set up in ways that make sense to them.* The passage supports this by arguing that children perform better if the task is presented in language they can understand.

Identifying simple arguments (p. 44)

Passage 3.7

This is an argument. The conclusion is that this is a good picture. The supporting reasons are: the use of colour and the well drawn and interesting figures.

Passage 3.8

This is not an argument. Even if you rearrange the sentences, none of them could act as a conclusion based on reasons provided by the others.

Passage 3.9

This is not an argument even though all the statements are true. If you rearrange the sentences, none of them could act as a conclusion based on reasons provided by the others. Just because the subject sounds scientific, this doesn't make it any more of an argument.

Passage 3.10

This is an argument. The conclusion comes at the end: *The piper's action was one of revenge.* The supporting reasons for the argument are: he was angry at the townspeople as they hadn't paid for his services; he led their children away deliberately and caused their deaths.

Passage 3.11

Although short, this is still an argument. The conclusion is that there must have been a signal failure. The reason for thinking this is that the train is late.

Passage 3.12

This is just a collection of related information and is not an argument. None of the statements serves as a conclusion to the rest.

Passage 3.13

This is an argument, even if you may not agree with the conclusion. The conclusion comes at the end: *It must have been a ghost.* The supporting reasons are the rattling windows, banging doors, charged air and feelings of fear.

Passage 3.14

This is an argument. The conclusion is at the beginning: *Many adults learn to read later in life.* The supporting reasons for the argument are that: John and Miranda caught up with their peers in reading; almost a million adults have improved their literacy skills.

Passage 3.15

This is not an argument. The author is not attempting to persuade the audience to accept a position or a particular conclusion. This passage describes a process.

Reasons and conclusions (p. 45)

Passage 3.16

Main argument: The swollen river dislodged the skeleton.

Reasons that support the argument:

- *Reason 1*: A skeleton was found near the river.
- *Reason 2*: The police have ruled out that a suspected local family was involved.
- *Reason 3*: The bones are believed to be several hundred years old.
- *Reason 4*: Historians confirm that the river passes close to ancient burial grounds.
- *Reason 5*: Other bodies are known to have been carried away by the river in the past.
- *Reason 6*: Recent storms have caused the river to rise by over half a metre.

Conclusion: It is probable that the skeleton was dislodged from its resting place by the swollen river rather than by the local family.

Passage 3.17

Main argument: Sea grasses are important.

Reasons that support the argument:

- *Reason 1*: In shallow waters, sea grasses are the dominant form of vegetation.
- *Reason 2*: They support a host of marine life.
- *Reason 3*: The grasses act as nurseries for fish, including commercial varieties.
- *Reason 4*: Without sea grasses, the bio-diversity of coastal regions would be severely impoverished.

Conclusion: Sea grasses make important contributions to coastal ecosystems.

Passage 3.18

Main argument: We are unhappy because we focus too much on how the world is and on the gratification of short-term objectives, rather than thinking about how we could live more in harmony with other people and the environment over the longer term.

Reasons that support the argument:

- *Reason 1*: We forget to be kind and supportive.
- *Reason 2*: We satisfy our wants first without thinking of people who have greater needs.
- *Reason 3*: We ignore what we know about the needs of the environment.
- *Reason 4*: We focus on instant gratification and short-term gains rather than considering the longer-term consequences.

Conclusion: The challenge facing humans is to find a way of acting more co-operatively with each other and more in harmony with our universe.

Passage 3.19

Main argument: Pregnant women and those with suppressed immune systems need to be aware of the potential danger of toxoplasmosis passed on by cats.

Reasons that support the argument:

- *Reason 1*: Cats are hosts to toxoplasma gondii, a protozoa that can cause disease in humans.
- *Reason 2*: If pregnant women become infected with the protozoa, their foetus could lose its eyesight or have motor deficits.
- *Reason 3*: In people with poor immune systems or AIDS, toxoplasmosis can cause seizures and death.
- *Reason 4*: Infected cats show no symptoms.

Conclusion: It is important that pregnant women and those with poor immune systems become aware of the potential risks posed by cats.

Chapter 4

Is it an argument?
Argument and non-argument

Learning outcomes

This chapter gives you opportunities to:

- understand the distinction between argument and disagreement
- recognise forms of non-argument such as summaries, explanations and description
- distinguish analytical writing from descriptive writing
- select relevant material from extraneous material

Introduction

We saw in Chapter 3 that an argument consists of particular features. However, other messages may also contain some of those features without being an argument. This chapter looks at messages that are sometimes confused with argument, such as disagreement, description, summary and explanation.

Being aware of what is not an argument helps critical analysis by enabling you to categorise different types of material. This, in turn, helps you to find your way around a text or other material more effectively. The most important material is often contained within the argument, so it helps if you can find it quickly.

Critical thinking involves distinguishing what is really relevant from other forms of information. When considering argument, it is easy to be distracted by surrounding material so that you miss the point. If you can distinguish the argument from other material, you can:

- focus your attention more accurately and make better use of your time;
- ensure that your own response is directed to the most appropriate material;
- save the effort of criticising a point of view unnecessarily simply because you missed the point;
- select relevant information more effectively to cite in your own writing and reports.

Argument and disagreement

Argument is not the same as disagreement. You can disagree with someone else's position without pointing out why you disagree or persuading them to think differently. In critical thinking, there is a distinction between a position, an agreement, a disagreement, and an argument.

Key terms

- **Position**   A point of view.
- **Agreement**   To concur with someone else's point of view.
- **Disagreement**   To hold a different point of view from someone else.
- **Argument**   Using reasons to support a point of view, so that known or unknown audiences may be persuaded to agree. An argument may include disagreement, but is more than simply disagreement if it is based on reasons.

Example

- *Position*: Genetic engineering really worries me. I don't think it should be allowed. [No reasons are given so this is simply a position.]
- *Agreement 1*: I don't know much about genetic engineering but I agree with you.

Or

- *Agreement 2*: I know a lot about this subject and I agree with you. [No reasons are given so these are simply agreements.]
- *Disagreement*: That doesn't convince me. I think genetic engineering is really exciting. [No reasons are given so this is simply a disagreement.]
- *Argument 1*: Genetic engineering should be curtailed because there hasn't been sufficient research into what happens when new varieties are created without natural predators to hold them in check.

Or

- *Argument 2*: The possibilities for improving health and longevity through genetic engineering offer hope to sufferers of many conditions that currently don't have an effective cure. We should be pushing ahead to help these people as quickly as we can.

The arguments above use reasons for the position held, to persuade others to the point of view. Note that these are simple arguments: they don't have extended lines of reasoning and they don't present any evidence to support their case. Without these, the power of the argument would have to depend on other factors such as tone of voice, body language, or insider knowledge about the listener, such as that they had a vested interest in the outcome.

Activity: Argument and disagreement

Identify for each whether the author is presenting:

A   an argument, and if so, say why;

B   a disagreement.

Passage 4.1

Bilingualism and multilingualism confer many benefits. Speakers of more than one language have a better understanding of how languages are structured because they can compare across two different systems. People who speak only one language lack this essential point of reference. In many cases, a second language can help people to have a better understanding and appreciation of their first language.

A   B

Passage 4.2

Complementary therapies are an increasingly popular supplement to other forms of treatment. Those who use these therapies argue that treatments such as reflexology, homeopathy and shiatsu complement the care provided by the medical profession. Indeed, some people claim that these therapies are more effective than traditional medicines. Anecdotal cases of miraculous cures abound and there are those who believe such methods can compete on equal terms with medical approaches. This just isn't convincing.

A   B

Passage 4.3

Several young people die each year training for the construction trades. Legislation is in place to cover health and safety at work, but some employers argue that this is too expensive to implement and onerous to monitor. They say that young people are not responsible enough at work and that there is nothing further they can do to prevent their deaths. That cannot be a good argument.

A   B

Passage 4.4

People are less politically aware now than they have been at any time in the past. For hundreds of years, people took great personal risks to fight for causes that would benefit other people more than themselves. This rarely happens today. As late as the 1980s, there were frequent rallies with people in one country demonstrating to show solidarity with people elsewhere. Now, rallies are more likely to be for personal gain such as better salaries or student grants rather than for political issues of wider application. Even low risk activities such as voting in elections attract low turn-outs.

A   B

Passage 4.5

Sea-levels have risen and fallen for generations, as have temperatures. Research suggests that global warming, if it is indeed occurring, is primarily the result of natural changes in the earth's temperature and the effects of solar winds. It is now claimed that industrialisation and the burning of hydro-carbons have little effect upon climatic change. My contention is that arguments against global warming are dangerous.

A   B

Passage 4.6

I cannot agree with people who say that smacking children does them no harm. Of course it harms them, both physically and emotionally. Hitting another person is assault and it would not be tolerated against an adult. Many adults have no sense of the cruelty of smacking precisely because they were smacked themselves as children and erroneously regard this as normal. They then go on to assault other vulnerable people, perpetuating a vicious cycle.

A   B

Answers: see p. 62. ▶

Non-arguments: Description

Descriptions

Descriptions give an account of *how* something is done, or *what* something is like. They do not give reasoned accounts of how or why something occurred nor do they evaluate outcomes. In reports and academic writing, description should be factual, accurate and free of value judgements. Description is sometimes confused with critical analysis as both can investigate an issue in detail. Descriptive detail is not intended to persuade to a point of view but aims, rather, to give the audience a more thorough impression of the item or issue being described.

Example

The solution was placed in a test-tube and heated to 35° centigrade. Small amounts of yellow vapour were emitted. These were odourless. Forty millilitres of water were added to the solution, which was then heated until it began to boil. This time, grey steam was emitted. Water droplets gathered on the side of the test-tube.

This describes the steps taken in an experiment. Careful description of methodological procedures is an important part of writing up any kind of experimental research. No reasons are given for what happened. That critical analysis of the results would be in a separate part of the report.

Example

The painting depicts several figures gathered around a cottage and in the fields. These figures are dressed in peasant dress. All of them are located in the shadows either of the house or of the trees. It is not possible to make out any individual features on their faces or in their clothing. By contrast, the figures of the noblemen who commissioned the painting are dressed in fine and individualised apparel. These figures are all located in the foreground of the painting, in full sunshine, and their facial features are clearly distinguishable.

This passage describes some salient features of a landscape painting. The details that the author has chosen to select suggest a point of view. However, this is not made explicit. If a conclusion was added, these details might provide useful propositions to support an argument about the way rich and poor people are depicted differently in art at a particular time and place. However, the passage does not contain a conclusion and so is a description rather than an argument.

Example

Usually, when people see an object that is familiar to them, such as an elephant, a tree, a bowl, a computer, they grasp immediately what it is. They recognise the overall pattern that the object makes and don't need to work out from other sensory information such as sounds, smell and colour, what the whole object might be. However, people with a condition known as visual agnosia cannot see a whole pattern in this way: they cannot recognise objects visually. If they traced the outline of the object with their hand, they might recognise an elephant, but they can't see an elephant. They can see, and they know they are seeing something, but they can't see an elephant.

In this instance, the author is describing what the condition of visual agnosia is like. The passage is a report of the facts, as far as they were known at the time of writing. The author is not trying to persuade the audience to a point of view. You can check this by looking through the passage for an argument and reasons to support it. The word 'however', which is often associated with a change in the direction of an argument, is used here to indicate a change in the direction of the description of how vision works.

Non-arguments: Explanations and summaries

Non-arguments can look like arguments, especially if they:

- result in a final conclusion;
- use the same signal words as an argument in order to help the flow of the writing.

Explanations

Explanations can appear to have the structure of an argument. They may include statements and reasons, leading to a final conclusion, and be introduced by signal words similar to those used for arguments. However, explanations do not attempt to persuade the audience to a point of view. They are used to:

- account for why or how something occurs;
- draw out the meaning of a theory, argument or other message.

Example

It was found that many drivers become drowsy when travelling and that long hours at the wheel were a major cause of accidents. As a result, more stopping places were set up along motorways to enable drivers to take a break.

The above example explains why more stopping places were set up along motorways.

Example

The children ate the mushrooms because they looked simil ar to those found in supermarkets and on the dinner table. They hadn't been taught to discriminate between safe and dangerous fungi and hadn't been told not to eat mushrooms found in hedgerows.

The above example explains why children ate dangerous mushrooms. If there were an additional sentence, such as 'therefore we need to educate children about fungi', this would become an argument, and the explanation would become a reason.

Summaries

Summaries are reduced versions of longer messages or texts. Typically, a summary repeats the key points as a reminder of what has been said already, drawing attention to the most important aspects. A conclusion may include a summary of what has been said already. New material is not usually introduced in a summary.

In the example below, the text is a list of instructions for making a cake. It does not constitute an argument. The final sentence is merely a summary of what has already been stated. The word 'therefore', which often indicates the conclusion of an argument, here simply introduces the final summary.

Example

For this cake, you need equal weights of self-raising flour, margarine and sugar. Add one egg for approximately each 50 grams of flour. Place all the ingredients in a bowl and beat furiously for three minutes. Blend the ingredients well. Pour into a greased tin and cook in the oven at 190°C for 20 mins until it is risen, golden brown and coming away from the sides of the tin. Different ovens may require different timings. Leave to cool before adding decoration such as jam and cream. Therefore, to make the cake, simply buy the ingredients, mix well, cook at 190°C, leave to cool and decorate to taste.

The passage below is a summary of Passage 3.18 on p. 45.

Example

Csikszentmihalyi argues that there is unhappiness around because we do not focus enough on how we want the world to be. Because of this, we act selfishly and focus on short-term gains, ignoring the longer-term consequences for other people and the environment. His answer is to live more in harmony with the wider world around us.

Activity: What type of message?

Read the passages below, and identify whether each is an example of an argument, a summary, an explanation or a description. How do you know?

Passage 4.7

The solar system is an inhospitable place not just for humans but also for machines. Despite this, over 8000 satellites and spacecraft were launched into space from more than 30 countries between 1957 and 2004. Over 350 people have hurtled through space, not all returning to earth. Launch sites based near the equator, such as that at Kourou in Guyana, enable rockets to make best use of the earth's rotation.

Passage 4.8

New-born babies may lack the capacity to monitor their own breathing and body-temperature during the first three months of life. Babies who sleep alongside their mothers could benefit from learning to regulate their breathing and sleeping, following the rhythm of the parent. These babies wake more frequently than those who sleep alone. Moreover, mothers who sleep next to their babies are better able to monitor their child for movement during the night. Consequently, it may be safer for new-born babies to sleep with their parents.

Passage 4.9

The article outlined the difference between individual yawns and infectious yawning. It referred particularly to research by Professor Platek which suggests that only humans and great apes yawn sympathetically. The article went on to say that people who yawn more easily in response to other people's yawns are also more likely to be good at inferring other people's states of mind. Finally, the article indicates some social benefits of yawning, suggesting that contagious yawning might have helped groups to synchronise their behaviour.

Passage 4.10

The village was located near the outer reaches of the city. The city was starting to encroach upon it, swallowing it up, road by road. It would not be long before the village disappeared altogether, to become part of the huge conurbation forming on the Eastern seaboard. To the west, hills enclosed the village, trapping it between the city and the mountains beyond. A single road led out from the city, through the village and into the mountains.

Passage 4.11

Both of the toy mice were the same size and shape so the dog was confused. Although one mouse was red and one was blue, Misty was unable to tell which mouse was his toy simply by looking. Like other dogs, he needed to sniff them both, using his sense of smell to tell them apart, because he couldn't discriminate between different colours.

Passage 4.12

Shakespeare's *Romeo and Juliet* is set in Verona in Italy. At the beginning of the play, Romeo is pining for another young woman, but quickly falls for Juliet at a ball. Although their two families are hostile to each other, Romeo and Juliet enlist the services of their friends and a friar to bring about their marriage. Unfortunately, in a tragic turn of events, they each kill themselves, believing the other to be already dead.

Answers: see p. 62. ▶

There were many reasons why the student was an hour late for the seminar. First of all, a pan caught fire, causing a minor disaster in his kitchen. It took twenty minutes to restore order. Then, he couldn't find his housekeys. That wasted another ten minutes of his time. Then, just as he closed the door behind him, the postwoman arrived, saying there was a parcel to be signed for. Her pen didn't work which held them up further. Finally, of course, he had to find his keys, which had once more slipped to the bottom of his bag, in order to re-open the door and place the letter on the table.

It was not until 2003 that the first Ice Age engravings of horses, red deer and bison were discovered at Cresswell Crags in Nottinghamshire, England. However, the oversight occurred partly because it was assumed that such work was not to be found in Britain. Indeed, in the initial survey of the cave, the experts did not notice the art that surrounded them.

The bas relief images of horses, bisons and red deer found in Cresswell Crags, England, bear remarkable similarities to those found in Germany. It is unlikely that two separate cultures would have produced drawing of such similarity if there were not links between them. This suggests that there were greater cultural links between continental Europe and Britain during the Ice Age than was formerly believed.

Recently, Ice Age specialists were excited to find evidence of some cultural links between Ice Age peoples across Europe. On a return visit to Cresswell Crags in England, they found images of horses, bison, and red deer similar to those already found in Germany. There is much controversy about other figures found on cave walls, which some experts believe to be images of dancing women, whereas others remain unconvinced.

Answers on page 62. ▶

Distinguishing argument from other material

Extraneous material

Usually, arguments are not provided separately from other material. They may be surrounded by:

- introductions
- descriptions
- explanations
- background information
- summaries
- other extraneous materials.

Example

Satellite imaging has been used to match water temperature swirls drawn on a map of ocean currents made as long ago as 1539. The map was produced by a Swedish cartographer, Olaus Magnus. It had been thought that the rounded swirls, located between pictures of serpents and sea monsters, were there for purely artistic reasons. However, the size, shape and location of the swirls matches changes in water temperature too closely for this to be a coincidence. The map is likely to be an accurate representation of the ocean eddy current found to the south and east of Iceland. It is believed that the map-maker collected his information from German mariners of the Hanseatic League.

Analysis of the example

The overall argument in the example above is that an old sea map is likely to be an accurate chart of part of the ocean.

Description   The passage opens with a description of the method used to test the map: *Satellite imaging has been used to match water temperature swirls drawn on a map of ocean currents . . .*

Background information   *a map of ocean currents . . . made as long ago as 1539. The map was produced by a Swedish cartographer, Olaus Magnus. It had been thought that the rounded swirls, located between pictures of serpents and sea monsters, were there for purely artistic reasons.*

Reason given to support the conclusion   Note that the reason follows logically from the description of the swirls and is well-placed to refute the idea that the swirls were primarily there for artistic reasons: *the size, shape and location of the swirls matches changes in water temperature too closely for this to be a coincidence.*

Conclusion   The conclusion follows on logically from the reason: *The map is likely to be an accurate representation of the ocean eddy current found to the south and east of Iceland.*

Explanatory detail   The passage finishes with information that helps to explain how the map-maker gained information to make the map: *It is believed that the map-maker collected his information from German mariners of the Hanseatic League.*

Developing the skill

When you can identify different kinds of material, you will find that you can categorise parts of the text quickly as you read. You may be able to scan a text and pick out the argument. If not, it can be useful to keep a pencil or a highlighter near you when you read your own books. Use these to underline or mark the conclusion and the reasons. Extract these and note them down in your own words.

Activity: Selecting out the argument (1)

Read Passage 4.17 and identify:

(1) the conclusion;
(2) reasons given to support this;
(3) the author's consideration of opposing arguments;

and other types of message such as:

(4) the introduction;
(5) description;
(6) explanation;
(7) summary;
(8) background information and other extraneous material.

An analysis of the passage is given on the following page.

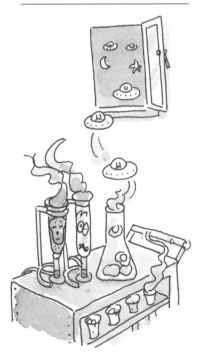

Passage 4.17

Is there anyone out there?

In some countries, the idea that there is life on other planets would make people laugh or sneer. In others, the inhabitants not only believe in life elsewhere in the universe but make efforts to communicate with it. There are certainly doubters and believers on this issue. One traditional argument for the existence of extraterrestrial life, known as the plenitude theory, is that there are so many star systems in the universe that it is unlikely that only earth would bear intelligent life. Indeed, it could be considered the folly of human arrogance to think that we are the only intelligent life in all of space. Not so, argue those who subscribe to contingency theory. Their argument, and it is a compelling one, is that life is a happy accident, a serendipity. They claim that the processes which led to the evolution of life are so complicated that it is extraordinary they occurred even once. They consider it extremely unlikely that the same set of processes could ever occur again. Thus, we have very divergent theories on whether there is life out there or not. It is unlikely that there is extraterrestrial life. For over 100 years, radio waves have been used to track space for signs of life and so far have uncovered nothing. If there was intelligent life out there, it is probable that we would have identified some sign of it by now. The most convincing current argument for extraterrestrial life comes from convergence theory. Convergence theory refers to situations when two different species are faced with a problem and independently arrive at the same solution. For example, both bats and birds evolved wings in order to fly. Similarly, octopus and squid have camera-like eyes. The species evolved separately, arriving at these adaptations independently. This suggests that although there may be infinite possibilities in the universe, nature tends to repeat itself. Morris (2004) has argued that where nature has produced something once, it is likely to produce it again. However, Morris himself recognises that even the basic conditions for life may be rare in the universe. Nature may be willing but the conditions might not be right. It is probable that the exacting conditions required for life are unlikely to be found more than once. It is unlikely that other planets will be exactly the right distance from their sun, with the right gravity, the right combination of chemicals and physics, with water and atmosphere. Although convergence theory indicates that nature tends to reproduce the same outcomes, and plenitude theory argues that the multiplicity of star systems increases the likelihood of extraterrestrial life, the arguments are not convincing. The conditions for life itself are so fragile and complex that it is remarkable that life occurred even once, much less that it could be repeated elsewhere.

5

10

15

20

25

30

35

40

Activity: Selecting out the argument (2)

Analysis of Passage 4.17 *Is there anyone out there?*

The numbers in brackets refer to the tasks set in the activity box on page 59.

(1) **Conclusion**   It is unlikely that there is extraterrestrial life (line 17). The final sentence summarises the argument that supports this conclusion.

(2) **Reason 1**   For over 100 years, radio waves have been used to track space for signs of life and so far have uncovered nothing (lines 18–20).

(2) **Reason 2**   This uses the refuted argument referred to in (3) below, that it is probable that the exacting conditions required for life (chemicals and physics, water and atmosphere) are unlikely to be found again (lines 35–40).

(3) **Author's consideration of opposing theories**   The author considers alternative theories such as convergence and plenitude theories. These are refuted in lines 34–41 and the refutation is harnessed as a reason to support the conclusion.

(4) **Introduction**   Lines 1–5.

(5) **Description**   Lines 11–16 describe contingency theory. They list the key points of the theory. Although the author does describe this argument as 'compelling', no reasons are given to show why it is compelling, so this is description, not argument or explanation. In this case, the description is also likely to be a summary of longer accounts of the theory.

(6) **Explanation**   Lines 23–33 explain convergence theory. Unlike lines 11–16, these lines do more than simply list or describe what the theory says. Instead, they give examples to help clarify what is meant by the theory and draw out general principles from those examples: 'this suggests that . . .' (line 29). They also bring out what is significant about the theory: 'This suggests that although there may be infinite possibilities in the universe, nature tends to repeat itself.'

(7) **Summary** of the material so far: lines 16–17. 'Thus, we have very divergent theories on whether there is life out there or not.'

(8) **Background information**   Lines 5–8 'One traditional argument . . . bear intelligent life', present background information to set the scene. The argument isn't introduced until line 18. Further background information is presented in lines 10 to 16: 'Not so, argue those who subscribe to contingency theory . . . processes could ever occur again.'

Summary

This chapter has looked at ways of distinguishing argument from other types of message that might be confused with arguments, either because of the interpretation of the word 'argument' in everyday language, or because a message bears the appearance of an argument.

Critical thinking is sometimes confused with disagreement. However, in critical thinking, an argument is a way of presenting a set of reasons to support a conclusion and to persuade others to a point of view. This may involve an element of disagreement, but does not necessarily do so. Conversely, in critical thinking, a disagreement that does not involve reasoning is not an argument.

Descriptions give an account of how something is done, or what something is like. They can be detailed, and so are sometimes confused with critical reasoning, which can include detailed analysis. Descriptions do not give reasoned accounts of how or why something occurred nor evaluate outcomes. In reports and academic writing, description should be factual, accurate and free of value judgements. Brief and succinct descriptions can play an important role in introducing a subject, before beginning an evaluation of it.

Explanations and summaries can appear to have the structure of an argument as they may include reasons, conclusions and signal words similar to those used for arguments. However, explanations do not attempt to persuade the audience to a point of view. They are used to account for 'why' or 'how', or to draw out the meaning, rather than to argue 'for' or 'against'. Summaries may be a shorter version of an argument, but their function is to reduce the length of the message.

Being able to identify both what is an argument and what is not, can speed your reading as you can search out the key points in a text more quickly. It can also help comprehension, as you are more likely to identify the salient points for your purpose. These skills will be looked at in more detail in Chapters 9 (reading) and 10 (writing).

Information about the sources

The nature of happiness: Csikszentmihalyi, M. (1992) *Flow: The Psychology of Happiness* (London: Random House).

Social class in eighteenth-century painting: Barrell, J. (1980) *The Dark Side of the Landscape: The Rural Poor in English Painting, 1730–1840* (Cambridge: Cambridge University Press).
Arnheim, R. (1954, 1974) *Art and Visual Perception: The Psychology of the Creative Eye* (Berkeley: University of California Press).

Sudden Infant Death Syndrome: Trevathan, W., McKenna, J. and Smith, E. O. (1999) *Evolutionary Medicine* (Oxford: Oxford University Press).

Contagious yawning: Platek, S. et al. (2003) 'Contagious Yawning: the Role of Self-awareness and Mental State Attribution', *Cognitive Brain Research*, 17(2): 223–7.
Farrar, S. (2004a) 'It is Very Evolved of Us to Ape a Yawn', *Times Higher Educational Supplement*, 12 March 2004, p. 13.

Cresswell Crags cave art: Farrar, S. (2004b) 'It's Brit Art, but Not as We Know It', *Times Higher Educational Supplement*, 16 July 2004.

Research on Olaus Magnus's sea charts: Farrar, S. (2004c) 'Old Sea Chart is So Current', *Times Higher Educational Supplement*, 16 July 2004.

Theories about extra-terrestrial life: Morris, S. (2004) *Life's Solution: Inevitable Humans in a Lonely Universe* (Cambridge: Cambridge University Press).
Mark Pagel (2004) 'No Banana-eating Snakes or Flying Donkeys are to be Found Here', *Times Higher Educational Supplement*, 16 July 2004.

Answers to activities in Chapter 4

Argument or disagreement (p. 53)

Passage 4.1

A   Argument. The overall argument is: *Bilingualism and multilingualism confer many benefits*. The reasons given are: (1) that speakers of more than one language have a better understanding of how languages are structured; (2) a second language can help to understand a first language.

Passage 4.2

B   The final line expresses disagreement with the idea that complementary therapies are the equivalent of medical treatments. No reasons for this are given so this is not an argument.

Passage 4.3

B   The final line expresses disagreement with the idea that employers cannot do more to help save lives in the workplace. No reasons for this are given so this is not an argument.

Passage 4.4

A   This is an argument. The conclusion is in the first line: *People are less politically aware now than they have been at any time in the past*. The reasons given are: (1) people used to fight for causes from which they didn't gain personally; (2) people took more risks for political issues; (3) rallies had a more international perspective; (4) fewer people vote now in elections.

Passage 4.5

B   The final line expresses disagreement with arguments against global warming. No reasons for this are given so this is not an argument.

Passage 4.6

A   Argument. The conclusion is in the second line: *Of course it harms them, both physically and emotionally,* referring back to the issue in the first line about smacking. The reasons given to persuade us are that (1) it is assault; (2) assaults on adults are not accepted; (3) smacking perpetuates a cycle of violence.

What type of message? (p. 56)

Passage 4.7

Description of key aspects of space launches.

Passage 4.8

Argument that babies may benefit from sleeping with their mothers.

Passage 4.9

Summary, by Farrar (2004a) of an article by Platek et al. See Bibliography.

Passage 4.10

Description of the location of a village.

Passage 4.11

Explanation   The text explains why the dog needed to use smell rather than shape or colour to identify his toy mouse.

Passage 4.12

Summary of the plot of a Shakespeare play.

Passage 4.13

Explanation of why the student was late.

Passage 4.14

Explanation of why the cave drawings were identified so recently.

Passage 4.15

Argument that there were greater cultural links between continental Europe and Britain during the Ice Age than was formerly believed.

Passage 4.16

Description of specialists' responses to the cave drawings.

Chapter 5

How well do they say it?
Clarity, consistency and structure

Learning outcomes

This chapter gives you opportunities to:

- check arguments for clarity and internal consistency
- identify logical consistency in an argument
- check for logical order
- understand what is meant by joint and independent reasons
- identify intermediate conclusions and understand their use

Introduction

In Chapter 3, we saw that there are normally six features to check for when searching for an argument, as summarised in the table on page 47:

- author's position;
- propositions and reasons;
- a line of reasoning;
- conclusion;
- persuasion;
- use of indicator and signal words.

However, on their own, these features merely help us to identify whether an author is using an argument. They don't tell us whether the argument is well-structured and consistent. This chapter looks at how authors construct clear, consistent and logical arguments. You will have opportunities to look in more depth at how an argument is structured as a line of reasoning through the use of joint and independent reasons, interim conclusions and logical order.

By understanding how an argument is structured, you can:

- use the structure of the argument to focus reading;
- improve comprehension by understanding how one part of an argument links to another;
- apply this understanding to model your own arguments, such as for essays, reports and dissertations.

How clear is the author's position?

Stating the point

Clarity is important to constructing a good argument. Sometimes an author can present a great deal of interesting information but their point of view, or position, becomes lost in the detail. If the author's position is clear, then it is more likely that their audience will grasp what they are trying to say, and make the effort to follow an argument through to the end.

In a good argument, the author's position will be apparent through a number of means, such as:

- the introductory sentences;
- the final sentences;
- the conclusion;
- the overall line of reasoning;
- an overall summary of the argument;
- careful selection of facts so the argument is not lost.

Activity

Read the following passages. For each, consider:
- Is the author's position clear?
- What makes the author's position clear or unclear?

Passage 5.1

The brain of an elephant is five times larger than that of humans. Some people believe elephants are very intelligent but, even if that were true, are they really five times brighter than humans? But maybe we are looking at this the wrong way. After all, is it fair to compare the brain size of a large animal with that of a small creature? Perhaps it is relative size that matters? Human brains weigh as much as 2.5 per cent of body weight whereas elephants' brains are less than half of a per cent of their total body weight. Proportionally, the brain of a human is ten times greater than that of an elephant. Maybe it is the ratio of brain to body size that matters? If that were the case, then the shrew, with its heavier brain, would be brighter than humans and elephants – and yet shrews do little more than eat.

Passage 5.2

Individuals have free will and so can control their own destiny. On the other hand, groups also have an identity. Research by Campbell (1984), for example, has shown that girls who mix with boys are more likely to have seen a fight and become involved in a fight than girls who mix mostly with girls. This suggests that aggressive behaviour is affected by the social environment and isn't just about character. In everyday life, our sense of self is such that we believe we are making independent decisions. We are aware we have choice and we make decisions for ourselves. Groups can also force decisions upon members, sometimes without them realising.

Passage 5.3

This report researched whether a new sports centre should be constructed in region X. Market research suggests that there is little popular demand for another sports centre in the area. However, very few people in the region use sports facilities to improve their health. The government is trying to encourage more personal responsibility for health and fitness. A sports centre would be useful in promoting this objective. People in the area are not aware of health issues and are not interested in sport. There may be government subsidies available.

Answers can be found on p. 79. ▶

Internal consistency

Clarity and internal consistency

One important aspect of presenting a clear authorial position is creating a consistent argument, so that all parts of the line of reasoning contribute to the conclusion. Nothing then contradicts or undermines the main message. Inconsistencies make an argument hard to follow, leaving the audience uncertain about what the author is trying to persuade them to believe.

Example 1

Apples are good for your teeth. Acid corrodes. Apples consist mainly of acid so they can't be good for teeth.

Here, the message lacks internal consistency. The reader is left wondering whether apples are good for your teeth or not.

Including opposing arguments

A strong line of reasoning will usually give consideration to alternative points of view, including those that appear to contradict the main argument. A good argument manages such apparent contradiction by:

- making it clear throughout the line of reasoning what position it wants the audience to take;
- making it clear when it is introducing an alternative point of view (see signal words on page 175);
- counter arguments to show why the alternative point of view is less convincing;
- resolving any apparent contradictions by showing how the main argument holds true.

Example 2

Apples are better for your teeth than refined sugar snacks. Some people argue that apples are an acid and that acid damages tooth enamel. However, any food, if left on the teeth, is bad for them. Refined sugars are particularly damaging to teeth. Compared with the sugary snacks most people eat, apples provide a more beneficial alternative and have long been recommended by dentists.

Here, the argument is internally consistent: *apples are better for your teeth than refined sugar products.* All the reasons support this. The opposing view (that acids corrode teeth) is included but its importance is minimised.

It is worth noting that the main argument is strong partly because it is worded in a more tentative way so that it is easier to defend. It is easier to argue that something is 'more beneficial than . . .' rather than making an absolute statement such as 'Apples are good . . .', which may not hold true in every circumstance.

Precision

The example above demonstrates that arguments may need to be very precisely worded. Imprecise wording is a common cause of inconsistency, as in the example below.

Example 3

Apples are good for your teeth and have long been recommended by dentists. It may seem strange that this is the case, given that apples consist of acid and acid corrodes enamel. However, the acid is relatively harmless, and certainly apples are more beneficial than alternative snacks made of refined sugar, such as sweets and cakes.

Here, the argument is relatively well structured and is more consistent than Example 1. However, it is still not a consistent argument. The author's opening statement is that 'Apples are good for your teeth.' However, by the end of the passage, the author is arguing that the acid is 'relatively harmless' and that 'apples are more beneficial than alternative snacks'. An argument about the relative benefits is not the same as the absolute statement that 'apples are good', so the message is not internally consistent.

Activity: Internal consistency

Passage 5.4

All drugs which enhance performance should be banned from sport as they confer an unfair advantage on those who take them. Anyone caught taking them should be automatically banned from national and international competition. Sportspeople who take such drugs are not acting in the spirit of fair competition. On the other hand, if someone needs drugs on medical grounds, they should be allowed to compete as they did not intend to cheat.

Passage 5.5

Trainers should discourage sportspeople from taking performance enhancement drugs as these can have serious effects upon their health. Some of these drugs have resulted in distorted body shapes, skin conditions, and increased aggression. The long-term effects of some of these drugs are unknown. On the other hand, some individuals with conditions such as asthma need medication which contains those drugs. For them, taking the drugs may be more beneficial than not taking them. Therefore, it would be wrong to ban performance enhancement drugs altogether.

Passage 5.6

Reality TV is not delivering what the public wants. Too many programmes are cheaply made, turning a camera on the experiences of ordinary people who are duped into wanting their short period of fame. As a result, investment in quality programmes is declining. There is much less variety on television. The promise of choice heralded by digital TV has not materialised. Far from exercising choice, last night almost the whole nation switched on to watch the final episode of the latest reality show. What has happened to television drama, good comedy programmes and well-researched documentaries?

Passage 5.7

The countryside is a lost cause. The green fields and woodlands known as 'green belts' that surround our cities are essential to maintain the beauty of the countryside. Over 8 per cent of the countryside is now built up. Green belts are ever more essential to provide lungs to our growing cities, helping them to 'breathe'. Unfortunately, the countryside is rapidly disappearing as the extensive building of new homes stretches out of the cities. Before long it will be gone and once that happens, it will be difficult, if not impossible, ever to restore the complex ecosystems of lost woodlands and hedgerows.

Passage 5.8

Christopher Columbus was courageous in attempting to sail West to find the East Indies as, before then, everyone believed the world was flat and that he would sail over the edge. Fourth-century Christian writers such as Lactanius and Indicopleustes described the world as rectangular, but their views were not widely known. Leading medieval scholars such as Augustine, Aquinas and Albertus knew the world was round, but their minds were on higher religious issues. In Columbus's time, the scholars of Salamanca had made more accurate calculations than Columbus and, although they knew the shape of the earth, they realised Columbus had under-estimated the distances involved. They opposed his voyage but he persisted. Without his courage, the Americas might never have been discovered.

Answers: see pp. 79–80. ▶

Logical consistency

In clear and consistent arguments, the reasons support the conclusion that the author draws from them. When evaluating an argument, we need to check whether the reasons given by the author do indeed support the conclusion. In other words, we need to check that the argument adds up. When we do this, we are checking for logical consistency.

Sometimes, authors lose track of their own arguments and draw a conclusion that does not follow from the reasons given. Sometimes, there may not be good reasons for the argument and we may feel the author is clutching at straws in the hope we won't notice the lack of logic. For Example 1 below, consider why the reason does not support the conclusion.

Example 1

There was a murder near the station last night. There are always young lads hanging around there. One of them probably did it. The local council should ban young people from hanging around the station.

In the example above, the conclusion is that young people should be banned from hanging around the station. The reason given to support the conclusion is that one set of young people is often found near a station where a murder took place. This reason does not support the conclusion because there is nothing to show that:

- those young people did commit the murder;
- even if they did so, other young people would do the same;
- a general ban on young people would prevent future murders.

This is partly a question of lack of evidence. However, it is also faulty reasoning, as the conclusion does not follow from the reasons presented. An alternative conclusion might have been that if

the young people were in the vicinity when the murder took place, they might have seen or heard something that would help to solve the case. For Example 2, see if you can identify the conclusion and the reasons given to support it before reading on.

Example 2

Behaviour is better in schools in rural areas than in inner city schools. Children brought up in the country have more responsibility for contributing to the family livelihood and care for vulnerable animals. This fosters a more mature attitude and a respect for life in general. Children in inner city schools often have more material possessions but value them less. They show less respect for parents and teachers. Children from the cities should be sent to school in rural schools. This would lead to more children who are respectful and well behaved.

In this case, the conclusion is provided in the last two lines: if children were sent from city to country schools, their attitude and behaviour would improve. The main reason given is that children in rural areas have better behaviour and attitudes.

However, the alleged better behaviour of children in the countryside is attributed to the responsibilities they have at home, not to the schools themselves. As city children would not gain such responsibilities simply by going to rural schools, it does not follow logically that moving school would lead to a change in their behaviour. The reasons provided in the example provide better grounds for an alternative conclusion: that the behaviour of city children might improve if they were given more responsibilities.

Activity: Logical consistency

Activity

Read through the following passages. Decide whether each is logically consistent or not. Give your reasons.

Passage 5.9

The deepest parts of the oceans are known as the abyssal zone. The bathyl zone, which is that part of the abyssal zone found on the continental shelf, is too deep even for light to penetrate. Despite this absolute darkness, animal life still thrives there. Humans form part of the animal kingdom. As animals survive in the bathyl zone, this proves that we do not need light in order to survive.

A consistent   **B inconsistent**

Passage 5.10

Accidents happen on building sites when workers don't take sufficient care of health and safety. Many employees are lax in following health and safety guidance. This means that there will be a rise in accidents on building sites over the next year.

A consistent   **B inconsistent**

Passage 5.11

Although subjects such as sports, media and popular culture involve theoretical understanding of the application of scientific principles, these subjects often have lower status at universities and with the public than subjects such as history and the classics, which are less intellectually demanding. This is partly because the former subjects attract more students from working-class backgrounds. Students who take these subjects go on to earn less than those who take more traditional subjects. This perpetuates working-class people in lower-income jobs. Therefore, working-class students should be encouraged to take traditional subjects, such as history.

A consistent   **B inconsistent**

Passage 5.12

Layers of sediment are laid down over time, and build up to fill the valleys and seas until they form a sequence of rocks. The oldest rocks are always at the bottom, unless the beds of rock have been overturned, such as by folding or faulting. When there is too much molten lava under the earth or in a volcano, molten rock is forced through the layers of sediment. These are known as igneous intrusions and they harden into volcanic dikes that cut through many layers of sedimentary rock. Therefore, where an igneous intrusion cuts through a sequence of sedimentary rock, it is always more recent than the surrounding layers.

A consistent   **B inconsistent**

Passage 5.13

It is impossible to find any place where there is absolute silence. Now, everywhere you go there are mobile phones ringing, people shouting, car horns blaring, music pouring from ghetto-blasters or ringing out in its irritating tinny tones from personal stereos. There is no place where you can go that does not have a sound of some kind breaking the silence. Noise pollution is definitely on the increase.

A consistent   **B inconsistent**

Passage 5.14

Computers can now compete with humans in complex games such as chess and beat them. This was believed impossible until the end of the last century. Since then, computer memories have become ever larger and faster. Now, very large memories can be stored in tiny spaces. Computers do not feel emotions, a faculty which is needed in order to empathise with other people. Nonetheless, computers will one day be able to out-perform humans at everything.

A consistent   **B inconsistent**

Answers: see p. 80. ▶

Independent reasons and joint reasons

If an author gives two or more reasons to support a conclusion, these may be either:

- joint reasons, or
- independent reasons.

Joint reasons

In this case, the reasons are connected in some way and mutually reinforce each other.

Example

It is important that employers in Britain actively encourage older people to remain within the work-force. First of all, as the population ages, there won't be enough young people entering the work-force to meet the needs of the economy. Secondly, the economy benefits from the skills and experience that older people have accrued over their lifetimes. Moreover, older people often have rare skills and useful attitudes that cannot be taught or acquired quickly.

Here, the conclusion is in the first sentence. The reasons given all relate to the skills needs of the economy, and support each other:

- there won't be enough younger people to do the work;
- older people have relevant skills and experience;
- their skills and attitudes are often rare and difficult to acquire.

Independent reasons

The author may use several reasons to support the conclusion, each of which may be valid in its own right but have nothing to do with the other reasons given.

Example

It is important that employers in Britain actively encourage older people to remain within the work-force. Older people often have rare skills and useful attitudes that are wasted when they leave the work-force early. Moreover, staying on longer in full-time or part-time work is believed to be good for the health. Besides, it is unrealistic to expect savings and pensions to be sufficient to meet the needs of people retired for 30 years or more.

Here, all the reasons support the argument but are independent of each other:

- the first is economic (rare skills);
- the second relates to health concerns;
- the third relates to personal finance.

It is useful to identify whether each separate reason is sufficient in its own right to support the argument. Lots of weak reasons do not add up to a good argument, as is demonstrated in the example below.

Example

It is important that employers in Britain actively encourage older people to remain within the work-force. Firstly, older people have a right to a better standard of living. Secondly, many of them will emigrate if they do not remain active here. Thirdly, older people like to meet younger people and rarely get the opportunity outside of the workplace.

The three reasons may all be true in their own right. Having several reasons makes it sound like there must be a good case. However, an employer might consider that these are social issues that do not make a good business case for retaining older employees.

Activity: Independent reasons and joint reasons

Activity

For each of the passages below, identify whether joint or independent reasons are used to support the conclusion. The conclusions are written in italics.

Passage 5.15

Young people over the age of 16 should be allowed to vote. They pay taxes so should have a voice on how their money is spent. They can fight and die for their country so should be entitled to have a voice in the country's political process. If they have political obligations, they should also have political rights.

Passage 5.16

Expeditions leave behind a range of litter, broken equipment and other unwanted items that are gradually ruining the landscape. Few useful discoveries result from the vast numbers of expeditions now taking place. Furthermore, local economies are distorted by the requirements of expedition teams. Expeditions are sometimes unsafe and survival cannot be guaranteed. *Therefore, the number of expeditions to the Arctic should be greatly reduced.*

Passage 5.17

Telling lies is sometimes justifiable. Lies can be hurtful, but the truth can hurt even more. People do not always need to hear the truth – a fantasy can sometimes provide a practical coping mechanism for dealing with difficult circumstances. Moreover, it isn't possible always to tell the truth because it isn't clear what constitutes the 'truth'. For example, exaggeration is a form of lie but it also holds something of the truth. Lies are an important part of social bonding: we lie to maintain friendships and to keep social situations harmonious.

Passage 5.18

The author travelled with the band on tour. She visited their homes, stayed in the same hotels, and attended family parties and funerals. Having had her own band for several years, she knows the life of a rock band from the inside. However, as she was never a member of this band and was not in competition with it, she is able to give an objective account of its highs and lows, its music and the lives of the artists. *As a result, the book gives us a faithful representation of the life of the rock band.*

Passage 5.19

Knowledge management is increasingly important for business. Without it, resources are wasted. For example, companies often make poor use of the training and experience of their staff, failing to cascade it to their other employees. Furthermore, businesses that do not manage knowledge well may appear less up-to-date, and therefore less attractive, to potential customers. With the growth of electronically accessible information, businesses need strategies to help staff cope emotionally with information overload.

Passage 5.20

It took a long time for the world to appreciate the art of Magritte because he gave the public so few clues about how to interpret his work. His art calls heavily upon the unconscious, but he steadfastly refused investigation into aspects of his own life that might have helped others to understand the workings of his own unconscious. He refused to talk even about the basic events of his early life. As he didn't agree with interpretations of art based on personal problems and experiences, he offered little to encourage public interpretations of that nature.

Answers on pp. 80–1. ▶

Intermediate conclusions

In longer and more elaborated lines of reasoning, there may be several sets of reasons to support the overall conclusion. In a well-constructed argument, these will be ordered so that:

- similar reasons are grouped together into sets;
- each set of reasons supports an intermediate conclusion;
- all the intermediate conclusions support the main line of reasoning.

The author may draw an intermediate conclusion on the basis of each set of reasons. This helps the reader to hold in mind the different stages of the argument. Intermediate conclusions help to structure an argument, acting as stepping stones between one stage of an argument and the next.

Example

Smokers should be given more freedom to smoke and more personal responsibility for the choices they make. Many know that cigarettes carry serious health risks, but these are risks that consenting adults are willing to take. Most smokers plan to give up before the risk becomes extreme. Adults should be allowed to make up their own mind about whether they smoke or not, without warnings on cigarette packaging. Smokers pay at least as much tax and insurance as anyone else. They also pay additional taxes through levies on cigarettes and are often required to pay higher insurance. Despite this, some medical practitioners refuse them health care. Smokers should have the same rights to health care as any other tax-payer. They should also have the same access to public spaces. In some countries, it is becoming almost impossible to find a place to smoke. Smokers are forced outside no matter what the weather. They are becoming social pariahs where once smoking was the most social of activities.

In the example above, the conclusion is at the beginning of the passage: *Smokers should be given more personal responsibility for the choices they make.*

In the version of the example reproduced below, the intermediate conclusions are underlined. Note that they can be used either to introduce a new set of reasons or to summarise reasons already introduced.

There are three sets of reasons in this passage, each linked to an intermediate conclusion. The intermediate conclusions are underlined.

Many know that cigarettes carry serious health risks, but these are risks that consenting adults are willing to take. Most smokers plan to give up before the risk becomes extreme. Adults should be allowed to make up their own mind about whether they smoke or not, without warnings on cigarette packaging.

Smokers pay at least as much tax and insurance as anyone else. They also pay additional taxes through levies on cigarettes and are often required to pay higher insurance. Despite this, some medical practitioners refuse them health care. Smokers should have the same rights to health care as any other tax-payer.

They should also have the same access to public spaces. In some countries, it is becoming almost impossible to find a place to smoke. Smokers are forced outside no matter what the weather. They are becoming social pariahs where once smoking was the most social of activities.

Intermediate conclusions used as reasons

Different types of intermediate conclusions

An intermediate conclusion can have two purposes:

- summative;
- to serve as a reason.

Summative

Summing up the argument at intermediate points clarifies the argument by providing it in more manageable bites. It can also reinforce the message, reminding the audience of the overall argument. The example on p. 71 uses this approach. In a good argument, the author will:

- organise reasons into logical groups;
- use a sentence or paragraph to summarise each set of reasons; this summary serves as an intermediate, or interim, conclusion.

To serve as a reason

An intermediate conclusion can also serve as a reason. The author may need to establish a solid case for an intermediate conclusion before it can serve as a reason. In other words, one set of reasons is used to establish an intermediate conclusion, and then that interim conclusion becomes a reason to support the overall conclusion (as in the table below).

Example

Universities want objective methods of marking students' work but objectivity is time-consuming. Lecturers spend a great deal of time checking their interpretations of students' answers. As there is only one correct answer for multiple-choice questions, there are no opportunities for subjective judgements, making the system fairer. These tests can be marked at speed, and objectively, by a computer. Multiple choice offers a quicker and fairer way of marking. With increased numbers of students, universities want to make better use of lecturers' time. Therefore, universities should make more use of multiple-choice tests.

Here, the overall conclusion is that universities should make more use of multiple-choice tests.

The interim conclusion is that *Multiple choice offers a quicker and fairer way of marking.*

The author of the example needed to establish that multiple choice is a quick and objective way of marking in order to argue that universities should use it. The reasons given to support the interim conclusion are that as there is only one correct answer for a multiple-choice question:

- it can be marked objectively;
- it can be marked quickly.

The structure of an argument using intermediate conclusions

Smaller reasons . . .	→	act as supporting detail for intermediate conclusions . . .	→	which form more major reasons . . .	→	to support the main argument or conclusion
reason a reason b reason c		All three reasons support intermediate conclusion 1	→	Intermediate conclusion 1 then becomes Reason 1		These two reasons then support the overall conclusion
reason d reason e		Both reasons support intermediate conclusion 2	→	Intermediate conclusion 2 then becomes Reason 2		

Activity: Intermediate conclusions

Activity

Identify the main argument and the intermediate conclusions for the passage below.

Passage 5.21

Although most smokers say they enjoy smoking, many smokers wish they didn't smoke. 'It feels as if I am setting light to my money,' wrote one correspondent. Cigarettes can account for up to a half of an individual's total spending. As people are borrowing more money in general, and paying interest on it, the overall cost of cigarettes is sometimes hidden. However, as many smokers are all too aware, smoking does not make good financial sense. The effects on long-term health are equally devastating. Just as smokers are often building up debts in the bank, they are also accruing unseen deficits in terms of their health. It is easy to forget the health implications of smoking. Warnings about illness and death can seem a long way away. Unfortunately, once cancer of the bowel, the lung, the throat, or the stomach sets in, it is often too late to take any action. Moreover, these diseases can strike unexpectedly whilst people are still young. Smokers spread strong, unpleasant odours all around them, affecting other people without their consent. Smoking impairs the sense of smell so smokers do not realise how much they are inflicting awful odours on others. Some believe that smoking outdoors washes all those nasty odours away, but this is clearly not the case. Furthermore, studies of the houses of people who always smoke outdoors, have found that the chemicals found in cigarettes are over seven times as prevalent as in the houses of non-smokers. Noxious chemicals linger, affecting the health of other people, sometimes fatally. Whether outdoors or in, smoking doesn't simply kill the smoker, it kills other people and this should not be permitted. The government should take strong action to raise awareness of the risks of smoking and to ban it in public places.

Activity

Identify two intermediate conclusions used as reasons in each of the passages below. In each case, the overall conclusion is in the final sentence.

Passage 5.22

It is a legal offence to assault other people. Hitting and slapping are forms of assault and cause psychological, if not physical, damage. They should always be considered as examples of legal assault. Although this rule is applied to adults, it is often not recognised in the case of children. Slapping is defended as a useful and necessary form of discipline. It is also argued that children are not independent beings. This is not a valid argument. Children may be dependent on adults but they are still people. *Therefore, slapping a child should also count as legal assault.*

Passage 5.23

Many people speak out in discussion too quickly because they are anxious about leaving a silence. When questioned, people often acknowledge that they spoke early in order to ensure there was no gap in the discussion. They are not used to silences in conversation and don't know how to manage them skilfully. They can find silences in discussion to be unnerving and embarrassing. However, silence can be productive. First of all, it allows time for reflection so that speakers can construct a more considered and accurate response, making a more useful contribution to the debate. Secondly, it gives more people the opportunity to speak first. *For more productive discussions, we need to be skilled in managing silences.*

Answers on pp. 81–2. ▶

Summative and logical conclusions

It is important to note the difference between a summative conclusion, and a logical conclusion.

Summative conclusions

Summative conclusions are simply conclusions that draw together previous information into a shorter overall summary. For example, if a text presents two main points of view, a summative conclusion would give a short synopsis of these. Summative conclusions tend to draw a piece of writing or debate to a close, without making a judgement, as in the example below.

Example 1

What causes stomach ulcers?
It used to be assumed that stomach ulcers occurred as a result of stress. People who worked too hard or worried too much were assumed to produce excess stomach acid which would, in turn, cause ulcers. Many still hold this view. On the other hand, research has indicated that 70 per cent of stomach ulcers could be caused by the bacterium *H. Pylori*, which changes the stomach lining so that it is more vulnerable to the effects of stomach acid. This bacterial infection can be treated with antibiotics, rather than forcing the patient to reduce his or her stress levels. Hence, whilst some believe that stomach ulcers are caused by stress, others now believe that they are caused by infection.

In Example 1, the conclusion is in the last sentence and simply summarises what has gone before. In this instance, the author states the two opposing points of view, and does not use the evidence to draw a logical conclusion about which is the most likely explanation for stomach ulcers. As this example does not have a logical conclusion, it is not an example of an argument. This is an example of a summary with a summative conclusion.

Logical conclusions

A logical conclusion is a deduction based on reasons. It is more than simply a summary of the arguments or the evidence. It will include one or more judgements, drawn from an analysis of the reasons given.

Example 2

How can we predict when volcanoes will erupt?
Predicting volcano eruption is not an exact science. Monitoring summit activity often cannot help us predict flank activity such as eruptions down the sides of the volcano. Scientists monitoring Mount Etna in Sicily thought they had established a link whereby such flank activity was preceded by summit activity for a period of a few months. However, in 1995 summit activity began but there was not a flank eruption for a further six years. They decided Etna's eruptive cycle was more complicated than they had first thought in terms of the relationship between summit and flank activity. This may be true of other volcanoes too. Consequently, a period of summit activity cannot necessarily be used as a predictor for flank activity.

In Example 2, the conclusion is signalled by the word 'consequently'. The author deducts a conclusion from the reasons, so this is an example of an argument. The conclusion is that when the summit of a volcano shows a lot of activity, this does not necessarily mean that lava will start pouring down the side of the volcano. This is clearly based on a judgement that the recent research on Etna undermines earlier research which had suggested a closer link between its flank and summit activity.

Activity: Summative and logical conclusions

© Stella Cottrell (2005, 2011) *Critical Thinking Skills*, Palgrave Macmillan

Activity

Identify whether the conclusions in the passages below are summative or logical conclusions. In each case, say whether the passage forms an argument.

Passage 5.24

Are criminals born or made?
In the 1960s, Jacobs suggested a strong genetic component in criminal behaviour. On the other hand, the psychologist Bowlby argued that criminal behaviour is caused by upbringing rather than genetics and noted that a significant number of criminals grew up in families where they experienced abuse or a lack of emotional warmth. More recently, Wilson and Hernstein suggested that a person is more likely to commit a crime if they have genes that predispose them towards criminality as well as facing additional stressors such as childhood abuse or substance misuse in adulthood. Although genes may predispose people towards crime, this is not a cause. As many criminals have experienced abuse and childhood neglect, it is fairer to argue that crime is the result of environment rather than genes, and that criminals are 'made' rather than 'born'.

Passage 5.25

Are 'reality' shows good for television?
In recent years the number of 'reality' shows on television has grown substantially. They are cheap to make and producers argue that viewers want to see 'real people' on their screens. However, critics complain that reality shows are made at the expense of original drama or current affairs programmes and that the overall quality of television is being reduced. Consequently, some people argue that reality shows are good for TV because they are cheap and popular whilst others argue that they result in poor quality television.

Passage 5.26

What is the true cost of cancelling debt?
The Jubilee organization has called for the cancellation of Third World debt. Concerns have been raised that this will mean serious losses that either commercial banks or Western governments will be forced to meet. Rowbotham suggests that debt could actually be cancelled with little cost to anyone. He argues that the dominant form of money in modern economies is bank credit. Although banks have accountancy rules about balancing assets and liabilities, credit does not exist in a physical form. It is not money sitting around in a vault waiting to be used or loaned – it is numerical or 'virtual' money. Consequently, if banks were not obliged to maintain parity between assets and liabilities they could cancel Third World debt without having to move the equivalent amount of money from the reserves to cover this. Therefore, the cancellation relates to 'virtual' money and the banks would experience no real financial loss if Third World debt were to be cancelled.

Passage 5.27

Does organic food taste better?
Supporters of organic produce argue that as well as being healthier than commercially produced food, it tastes better. Fillion and Arazi (2002) carried out blind tastings of organic and non-organic juices and milk with trained panelists. They concluded that although organic juice tasted better, there were no taste distinctions between organic and conventional milk. However, supporters of organic produce maintain that it is 'common sense' that organic food tastes better as it has been produced under healthier conditions. Hence, although scientific support for organic produce tasting better is limited, consumers who choose organic are convinced it does.

Answers: see p. 82. ▶

Logical order

The line of reasoning, or the overall argument, should lead forwards with a clear direction, rather than hopping from one point to another in a random way, or leading the audience round in circles. In the example below, the author moves from one point to another without direction or logical order.

Example 3

Pets add to the quality of life. Any benefits outweigh the costs. However, they can destroy household furniture. Stroking pets is thought to reduce stress. Property values can be affected by the odour animals leave behind them in carpets and curtains. Many people find talking to a pet helps them sort out personal problems. Problems with pets can be sorted out, so they are not insuperable.

The author above could have constructed a more logical argument by:

- grouping similar points together;
- presenting reasons that support their argument first, so as to establish a good case for it;
- considered opposing reasons after they have established their own case, demonstrating why these are not significant or are less convincing.

Note the difference in the example below, which takes a similar position to that above.

Example 4

Pets add to the quality of life. This is evident in several ways. For example, stroking pets can reduce stress. Many people find talking to a pet helps them sort out personal problems. There are some disadvantages to having an animal about the house such as damaged furniture and unpleasant odours. However, these problems can easily be overcome. The benefits of having a pet outweigh the disadvantages.

Dealing with poor logical order

If you are trying to follow a jumbled argument such as the one in Example 1, it can help to order the arguments for yourself:

- as lists of arguments 'for' and 'against', or
- as 'arguments that support the conclusion' and 'arguments that do not support the conclusion'.

Consider how you could do this for Example 3, before reading the box below it.

Example 5

Nuclear power stations are not a viable source of energy for the future. Nuclear reactors are more expensive to build than fossil fuelled power stations. Fossil fuels such as coal, gas and oil are a dwindling resource so nuclear fuel offers a useful alternative for the future. Nuclear reactors are also very expensive to decommission so may not be efficient over the longer term. Coal costs may rise as fossil fuels become harder to find, making nuclear fuel more attractive. No truly safe way of storing nuclear fuel has yet been found. Research into alternative fuels has been underway for some time, with some success. Solar power and use of methane from waste are just two alternatives to fossil fuels.

Arguments for nuclear power stations	Arguments against nuclear power stations
• Fossil fuels will become more expensive as reserves dwindle. • Fossil fuels are likely to run out.	• More expensive to build. • More expensive to decommission. • No truly safe way of storing nuclear waste. • Other alternatives to fossil fuels exist.

Activity: Logical order

Activity

The following passage is not ordered logically. This makes it difficult to follow its line of reasoning. You do not need to be a specialist in the subject to identify how the argument could be better constructed.

Write a short list of the ways the passage is poorly organised – then order the sentences into a more logical sequence yourself. The sentences are numbered to help you write out a preferable order.

Answers
Compare your response with those on pp. 83–4 below.

Passage 5.28

Circadian rhythms

1: In experiments, human volunteers spent several weeks under-ground in constant light. 2: At first, their natural clock and sleep patterns were disrupted. 3: After a few weeks, they reverted back to the natural circadian rhythm with a 24-hour clock more or less in line with the outside world. 4: Our natural clocks are helped to adjust by exposure to sun-light and do respond to patterns of light and dark. 5: Our bodies remain more responsive to biological rhythms than to the demands of clock time or the distractions of the outside world.

6: Since the mapping of human genes as part of the genome project, we have a greater understanding of circadian rhythms and their role in genetic conditions. 7: Some families have genetic conditions which make them less sensitive to circadian rhythms. 8: This may help explain patterns of sleep disturbances found in those families. 9: Our work patterns, leisure patterns, architecture, lighting, food, drugs and medication compete with our natural clocks. 10: These biological rhythms are known as circadian rhythms and we know they are particularly strong in birds.

11: In humans they are particularly controlled by the suprachiasmatic nucleus (SCN) in the anterior hypothalamus at the base of our brains. 12: If this part of the brain is damaged, a person loses all sense of a natural 24-hour clock, where sleep coincides with night-time. 13: In other people, circadian rhythms are much stronger than was expected. 14: Astronauts, who lose this connection to the sun's rhythms for a long time, find it hard to adjust. 15: Many require medication to help them sleep.

16: Night-workers, even after 20 years on shift patterns, do not adjust circadian rhythms to suit the demands of night working. 17: Certain illnesses such as peptic ulcers and heart disease, as well as increased risk of car crashes, are much more common to night-shift workers. 18: As the long-term effects of disrupting circadian rhythms are yet to be discovered, we should take care to ensure the health of shift-workers and those with genetic conditions that make them less sensitive to the biological 24-hour clock. 19: It may be that conditions associated with mental ill-health, such as schizophrenia and bi-polar disorders, are also linked to malfunctions in circadian rhythms.

Summary

This chapter looked at some ways of evaluating how well an argument is presented. A well-presented argument is not necessarily the correct argument, but it can be more convincing. The benefits of understanding how to present an argument well are that you are better able to:

- construct your own arguments in a convincing way;
- identify when you are being convinced by an argument because of the way it is being presented, rather than the quality of the evidence and the inherent merits of the case.

The chapter opened by looking at the author's position. This isn't always evident in an argument. However, if you can identify what the author's underlying position is, it is easier to anticipate the logical conclusion and reasons which support it. This aids comprehension and can help to evaluate the quality of the argument. The author's position is usually reflected in the conclusion. It is much easier to construct your own arguments if you are clear what your position is, and draw up a conclusion that reflects it. If you cannot do this, then your thinking may be muddled and further work is needed to establish what you really think and why.

Many of the other themes covered in this chapter follow on from having a clear authorial position. A clear position helps to sort ideas so that those that support the argument are easily distinguished from those that contradict it. This assists with internal consistency as a strong argument will present apparently contradictory information in such a way that it does not undermine the main argument. Indeed, a well-managed consideration of apparent contradictions can strengthen the main argument.

Once it is clear which information supports the argument, it is easier to order the argument in a logical way, so that similar points are grouped together. This helps the audience to see how the different components of the argument link together. A good argument presents materials in a logical order – that is, one which makes the best sense of the material, so that each point seems to follow on quite naturally from the one that precedes it. There can be more than one way of presenting an argument in a logical order. The important point to bear in mind is that the argument should be presented so that it leads the audience forward in an ordered way through the key points in a way that is clear, structured, and makes sense. This is examined further in Chapter 10.

Information about the sources

Brain size: Greenfield, S. (1997) *The Human Brain: A Guided Tour* (London: Phoenix).

Columbus and the flat or round earth argument: Eco, U. (1998) *Serendipities: Language and Lunacy* (London: Weidenfeld & Nicolson).

Girls fighting: Campbell, A. (1984) *The Girls in the Gang* (Oxford: Basil Blackwell).

Magritte: Hammacher, A. M. (1986) *Magritte* (London: Thames & Hudson).

Circadian rhythms: Foster, R. (2004) *Rhythms of Life* (London: Profile Books).

Telling lies: Stein, C. (1997) *Lying: Achieving Emotional Literacy* (London: Bloomsbury).

Answers to activities in Chapter 5

How clear is the author's position? (p. 64)

Passage 5.1

The author's position is not clear. It could be clarified, for example, by using either the opening sentences to introduce the argument and/or the final sentence to sum it up. The author uses too many questions without providing answers to these. There are many facts, but these do not help clarify the position. The author needs to provide more guidance to the reader about the direction of the argument.

Passage 5.2

The author's position is not clear. The author is aware of different viewpoints, which is good. However, the writing wanders back and forth between different standpoints without being clear which point of view the author wants the audience to accept. The author doesn't fully agree or disagree with either point of view and does not suggest an alternative third point of view. The author needs to sort the issues so that similar points are considered together, and to order them so that they lead towards a conclusion. The passage reads as though the author doesn't know what to believe. In such cases, an author needs to take up a position for the duration of presenting the argument, even if only to say that one point of view has certain advantages over the other.

Passage 5.3

The author's position is not clear. The purpose of the report was to clarify whether a sports centre should be built. The passage looks at points for and against building the sports centre, which is appropriate, but the points are jumbled. It would have been clearer if those for building the centre were given first, and then those against. The relative weighting might have come across better. The author needs to give some indication of whether the sports centre should be built or not, in order for their position to come across.

Internal consistency (p. 66)

Passage 5.4

The answer is **B**: inconsistent. The author argues that performance enhancing drugs should be banned on the grounds that they give an unfair advantage, not on whether someone intended to cheat or not. By the end of the passage, the 'unfair advantage' argument is replaced by arguments about medical need and intention. To be consistent, the author should maintain the position that taking performance enhancing drugs is always wrong, or else argue a more moderate position as in Passage 5.5.

Passage 5.5

The answer is **A**: consistent. In this case, the author argues consistently that drugs should be generally discouraged on health grounds but permitted on an individual basis for health reasons.

Passage 5.6

The answer is **B**: inconsistent. The author argues that reality TV is not giving the public what it wants, but then points out that 'almost the whole nation' is watching it, which suggests it is popular. The author could have made the argument more consistent by, for example:
- offering an explanation for why people watched programmes they did not want;
- giving evidence that there were no other choices;
- presenting evidence of surveys that show people would prefer to watch a good alternative type of programme.

Passage 5.7

The answer is **B**: inconsistent. The author argues that the countryside is disappearing but cites a figure of only around 8 per cent of the countryside as built up so far. To be consistent, the author would need to present further arguments to show why the other 92 per cent is really at risk of disappearing.

Passage 5.8

The answer is **B**: inconsistent. The author argues that before Columbus, 'everyone believed the world was flat'. However, several examples are given of people who didn't believe the world was flat. It is not unusual for people to include this sort of inconsistency in their arguments. People often repeat a commonly held belief, such as that the medieval church believed the world was flat, without noticing that they are citing contradictory evidence. To be consistent, the author could argue that Columbus was courageous on other grounds than that of other people's belief in a flat earth. For example, it could be argued that he was courageous to persist with the voyage when the distances involved, and consequences of these, were not known.

Logical consistency (p. 68)

Passage 5.9

B: This is not logically consistent. It does not follow logically that because some animals can survive without light, all animals can do so.

Passage 5.10

B: This is not logically consistent. The reasons given do not support the conclusion that the number of accidents will rise over the next year.

Passage 5.11

B: This is not logically consistent. A more logical conclusion from the reasons given is that more status should be given to subjects such as sports, media and popular culture. If a subject's low status follows the social class of the students, then if the students change subject, the status of the subject they take might fall, perpetuating the same problems.

Passage 5.12

A: This is logically consistent. The igneous rock could only cut across the layers of sediment if they were already there. They must be older, and the igneous rocks more recent.

Passage 5.13

B: This is not logically consistent. It may be true that it is impossible to find a place of absolute silence but that does not mean noise pollution is increasing. Noise levels may be the same as in previous times but with different causes: we cannot tell from the arguments presented.

Passage 5.14

B: This is not logically consistent. The conclusion is that computers will one day be able to out-perform humans at everything. However, the author has argued that computers lack the qualities needed for empathy. This contradicts the idea of computers being better at 'everything'.

Independent and joint reasons (p. 70)

Passage 5.15

Joint reasons. The reasons are mutually supporting of the rights and responsibilities of young people.

Passage 5.16

Independent reasons. The reasons given concern the environment (litter), value (few discoveries for the number of expeditions taken), economics (effect on local economy), and safety.

Passage 5.17

Independent reasons. Lying is defended on the basis of different arguments: (a) the truth hurts; (b) it provides a useful coping mechanism; (c) it isn't always possible to tell a lie from the truth; (d) the social benefits of lying.

Passage 5.18

Independent reasons. The argument is that the book is a faithful representation of a rock band. The reasons given are based on (1) knowledge: the author's close knowledge of the band; (2) experience: her experience of being in a band herself; (3) objectivity: reasons why the author was able to be objective.

Answers to activities in Chapter 5 (continued)

Passage 5.19

Independent reasons. The reasons given are related to (1) effective use of resources; (2) public image; (3) support for staff.

Passage 5.20

Joint reasons: all support the argument that Magritte gave very few clues to help others to interpret his work.

Intermediate conclusions (p. 73)

Passage 5.21

Overall argument. This is at the end of the passage: *The government should take strong action to raise awareness of the risks of smoking and to ban it in public places.*

The intermediate conclusions are highlighted in bold.

Although most smokers say they enjoy smoking, many smokers wish they didn't smoke. 'It feels as if I am setting light to my money,' wrote one correspondent. Cigarettes can account for up to a half of an individual's total spending. As people are borrowing more money in general, and paying interest on it, the overall cost of cigarettes is sometimes hidden. However, as many smokers are all too aware, **smoking does not make good financial sense**.

The effects on long-term health are equally devastating. Just as smokers are often building up debts in the bank, they are also accruing unseen deficits in terms of their health. It is easy to forget the health implications of smoking. Warnings about illness and death can seem a long way away. Unfortunately, once cancer of the bowel, the lung, the throat, or the stomach sets in, it is often too late to take any action. Moreover, these diseases can strike unexpectedly whilst people are still young.

Smokers spread strong, unpleasant odours all around them, affecting other people without their consent. Smoking impairs the sense of smell so smokers do not realise how much they are inflicting awful odours on others. Some believe that smoking outdoors washes all those nasty odours away, but this is clearly not the case.

Furthermore, studies of the houses of people who always smoke outdoors, have found that the chemicals found in cigarettes are over seven times as prevalent as in the houses of non-smokers. Noxious chemicals linger, affecting the health of other people, sometimes fatally. **Whether outdoors or in, smoking doesn't simply kill the smoker, it kills other people and this should not be permitted**.

Intermediate conclusions used as a reason (p. 73)

The two intermediate conclusions for each passage are highlighted in bold.

Passage 5.22

It is a legal offence to assault other people. Hitting and slapping are forms of assault and cause psychological, if not physical, damage. **They should always be considered as examples of legal assault**. Although this rule is applied to adults, it is often not recognised in the case of children. Slapping is defended as a useful and necessary form of discipline. It is also argued that children are not independent beings. This is not a valid argument. **Children** may be dependent on adults but they **are still people**. Therefore, slapping a child should also count as legal assault.

In this case, in order to argue that slapping a child should count as a legal assault, the author has first to establish that:

(1) slapping should always count as legal assault;

(2) children should count as people.

Passage 5.23

Many people speak out in discussion too quickly because they are anxious about leaving a silence. When questioned, people often acknowledge that they spoke early in order to ensure there was no gap in the discussion. **They are not used to silences in conversation and don't know how to manage them skilfully**. They can find silences in discussion to be unnerving and embarrassing. **However, silence can be productive**. First of all, it allows time for reflection so that speakers can construct a more considered and accurate response, making a more useful contribution to the debate. Secondly, it gives more people the opportunity to speak first. For more productive discussions, we need to be skilled in managing silences.

The author has to establish two interim conclusions that can be used as reasons or arguments in their own right:

- The reason people speak too early is because they don't know how to manage silence.
- Silence can be productive in improving discussion.

(1) The reason people speak too early is because they don't know how to manage silence. If this can be established, then it supports the conclusion that skilful management of silence will improve discussion. The author establishes the interim conclusion by (a) citing people's own acknowledgements that this is accurate; and (b) giving the reason that people are not used to silences in conversation so cannot manage them skilfully.

(2) Silence can improve discussion. The author does this by offering two independent reasons: (a) silences allow thinking time so that responses are better constructed; (b) more people get a chance to speak first.

Summative and logical conclusions (p. 75)

Passage 5.24

Logical conclusion. The author weighs two different sets of arguments and draws, or deducts, a conclusion that the environment is more influential than genes in forming criminal behaviour, so the passage forms an argument.

Passage 5.25

Summative conclusion. The author summarises two positions but does not draw a conclusion about whether reality shows are good for television or not. As there is not a logical conclusion based on the reasons, this is not an argument.

Passage 5.26

Logical conclusion. The author makes a judgement about the level of costs that would be borne by banks if debts in developing countries were cancelled. This conclusion is deduced from the reasons, so this passage constitutes an argument.

Passage 5.27

Summative conclusion. The author merely summarises two points of view without making a judgement about whether organic food tastes better. There isn't a logical conclusion based on reasons so this is not an argument.

Answers to activities in Chapter 5 (continued)

Logical order (p. 77)

Passage 5.28 Circadian rhythms

The passage is badly organised for the following reasons:

- The author hops back and forward between points rather than grouping similar points together into separate sections.
- There is no obvious introduction.
- The conclusion and the author's position are not obvious.
- The passage lacks words to link each new point to highlight the direction of the argument.

Compare the original version with the version below. This contains almost identical material but is ordered differently and phrases are added to indicate the logical links. These are indicated in bold.

5: Our bodies remain more responsive to biological rhythms than to the demands of clock time or the distractions of the outside world. 10: These biological rhythms are known as circadian rhythms and we know they are particularly strong in birds. 11: In humans they are particularly controlled by the suprachiasmatic nucleus (SCN) in the anterior hypothalamus at the base of our brains. 12: **We know this because**, if this part of the brain is damaged, a person loses all sense of a natural 24-hour clock, where sleep coincides with night-time. 13: In other people, circadian rhythms are much stronger than was expected. 1: **For example**, in experiments, human volunteers spent several weeks under-ground in constant light. 2: At first, their natural clock and sleep patterns were disrupted. 3: **However**, after a few weeks, they reverted back to the natural circadian rhythm with a 24-hour clock more or less in line with the outside world.

4: **Nonetheless**, our natural clocks are helped to adjust by exposure to sun-light and do respond to patterns of light and dark. 14: Astronauts, who lose this connection to the sun's rhythms for a long time, find it hard to adjust. 15: Many require medication to help them sleep. 16: Night-workers, even after 20 years on shift patterns, do not adjust circadian rhythms to suit the demands of night working.
17: Certain illnesses such as peptic ulcers and heart disease, as well as increased risk of car crashes, are much more common to night-shift workers.

6: Since the mapping of human genes as part of the genome project, we have a greater understanding of circadian rhythms and their role in genetic conditions. 7: Some families have genetic conditions which make them less sensitive to circadian rhythms. 8: This may help explain patterns of sleep disturbances found in those families. 19: It may be that conditions associated with mental ill-health, such as schizophrenia and bi-polar disorders, are also linked to malfunctions in circadian rhythms.

9: Our work patterns, leisure patterns, architecture, lighting, food, drugs and medication compete with our natural clocks. 18: As the long-term effects of disrupting circadian rhythms are yet to be discovered, we should take care to ensure the health of shift-workers and those with genetic conditions that make them less sensitive to the biological 24-hour clock.

This is not the only possible alternative. Another option would be to order the sentences as:

> 5, 10, 11, 12
> 6, 7, 8, 13
> 9, 1, 2, 3, 4, 14, 15
> 16, 17, 19, 18

This would then read:

Passage 5.28   Circadian rhythms
5: Our bodies remain more responsive to biological rhythms than to the demands of clock time or the distractions of the outside world. 10: These biological rhythms are known as circadian rhythms and we know they are particularly strong in birds. 11: In humans they are particularly

controlled by the suprachiasmatic nucleus (SCN) in the anterior hypothalamus at the base of our brains. 12: If this part of the brain is damaged, a person loses all sense of a natural 24-hour clock, where sleep coincides with night-time.

6: Since the mapping of human genes as part of the genome project, we have a greater understanding of circadian rhythms and their role in genetic conditions. 7: Some families have genetic conditions which make them less sensitive to circadian rhythms. 8: This may help explain patterns of sleep disturbances found in those families. 13: In other people, circadian rhythms are much stronger than was expected.

9: Our work patterns, leisure patterns, architecture, lighting, food, drugs and medication compete with our natural clocks. 1: In experiments, human volunteers spent several weeks underground in constant light. 2: At first, their natural clock and sleep patterns were disrupted. 3: After a few weeks, they reverted back to the natural circadian rhythm with a

24-hour clock more or less in line with the outside world. 4: Nonetheless, our natural clocks are helped to adjust by exposure to sun-light and do respond to patterns of light and dark. 14: Astronauts, who lose this connection to the sun's rhythms for a long time, find it hard to adjust. 15: Many require medication to help them sleep.

16: Night-workers, even after 20 years on shift patterns, do not adjust circadian rhythms to suit the demands of night working. 17: Certain illnesses such as peptic ulcers and heart disease, as well as increased risk of car crashes, are much more common to night-shift workers. 19: It may be that conditions associated with mental ill-health, such as schizophrenia and bi-polar disorders, are also linked to malfunctions in circadian rhythms. 18: As the long-term effects of disrupting circadian rhythms are yet to be discovered, we should take care to ensure the health of shift-workers and those with genetic conditions that make them less sensitive to the biological 24-hour clock.

Chapter 6

Reading between the lines
Recognising underlying assumptions and implicit arguments

Introduction

In earlier chapters, we looked at explicit features of an argument. However, not all aspects of an argument are expressed explicitly. Arguments are often based on unstated assumptions and latent methods of persuasion. This chapter looks at some of the reasons for this, and provides practice in identifying hidden assumptions and implicit arguments.

The premises upon which an argument is based are not always immediately obvious either. These can often contain implicit assumptions or be based on incorrect information. If the premises are not sound, the argument can fall down, no matter how well it is argued. This means that a consideration of the premises of the argument is just as important as a consideration of the reasoning.

This chapter also looks briefly at latent messages used to reinforce an argument. The connotations of a message can add to its ability to persuade. If we can recognise

connoted messages, we are in a better position to see how the argument is structured, and to decide whether we agree with its underlying point of view.

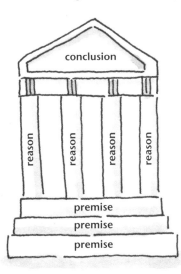

Conclusion: should be well supported

Reasons: the pillars of the argument

Premises: Underlying beliefs, assumptions, foundations, theories

Good conclusions are well-supported by strong reasons based on solid premises.

Assumptions

What is an assumption?

In critical thinking, 'assumptions' refers to anything that is taken for granted in the presentation of an argument. These may be facts, ideas or beliefs that are not stated explicitly but which underlie the argument. Without them, the same conclusion would not be possible.

Proper use of assumptions

Most arguments contain assumptions. In effect, the author invites the audience to accept something as true rather than proving it. Often, this is to save time and to simplify the argument. We don't need to have everything proved to us. When assumptions are made properly, the author has decided that it is reasonable the audience will know what is meant and is likely to agree.

Example

Holidays are a time for relaxation and enjoyment. This year, thousands of people will have their holidays ruined by oil spills along our beaches.

Here, there are a number of assertions which we may not even recognise as assumptions because we agree with the sentiments of the passage. The conclusion is that thousands of people's holidays will be ruined. The underlying assumptions include:

Assumption 1: that holidays are for relaxation and enjoyment. This may seem obvious but the original meaning of holidays was 'holy days', which were intended for religious observation. Some people still use holidays in that way. Others may use them for seeing family or, in the case of students, finding temporary work.

Assumption 2: that thousands of holiday-makers will want to go to the beach.

Assumption 3: that those holiday-makers who go to the beach will not like oil on the beach.

Assumption 4: that oil on the beach in itself can ruin a holiday.

Assumption 5: that the audience will understand words such as *holiday, beach, relaxation, enjoyment, ruined, our,* and *oil spill* and that these do not need to be defined.

All of these are reasonable assumptions. The facts may not be true for every individual: some people may enjoy their holiday even with oil on the local beach. However, the assertions have sufficient general applicability to be fair assumptions. We would not expect the author to provide proof that most people who go to the beach for their holidays want to relax on an oil-free beach. We might be irritated if the author spent time proving such assertions or defining words that we are likely to know.

Taking the context into account

In critical thinking, it is important to identify what are reasonable assumptions and what are not. This can depend on the context, such as the intended audiences: will they share the same assumptions and background knowledge? If the example about oil on the beach was written in a book aimed at people learning English, there might be words such as *oil slick* which the author would need to explain.

Similarly, if the phrase 'our beaches' referred to a small part of local coastland but the article appeared in a national publication, then it would be wrong to assume the audience would be aware that only some local beaches were affected.

Activity: Identify the underlying assumptions

Activity

For each passage below, identify the underlying assumption. Remember that an assumption is not necessarily incorrect or unreasonable.

Passage 6.1

Students of the late twentieth century regularly campaigned against nuclear weapons. Students rarely demonstrate against nuclear weapons any more. Students must be less political than they used to be.

Passage 6.2

House prices rose quickly in the 1980s in many countries. There was a big slump in the 1990s and lots of house-buyers lost money. House prices are now rising very quickly again. House-buyers can expect to lose a lot of money.

Passage 6.3

Children are costing parents more. They demand more of their parents' time, expecting to be taken to activities after school, whereas in the past, parents' own interests took priority. Parents are under more pressure to provide clothes and shoes with expensive designer labels, toys, trips and even more costly brands of breakfast cereal in order for their children to be accepted by their peers. Advertising aimed at children should be banned in order to reduce this excessive peer pressure.

Passage 6.4

According to overture.com, more people search for information about the modern scientist, Emeagwali, on the internet than any other scientist. The number of pages downloaded are the equivalent to a best-selling book. Everybody must have heard about his discoveries by now.

Passage 6.5

Large companies move jobs to other countries where labour is less expensive. When wages rise in one country, the companies look for cheaper options overseas, taking the work to a new set of employees and making the former work-force redundant. Services such as call-handling can be offered from thousands of miles away. Soon, there will be no jobs left in the former high-wage economies.

Passage 6.6

Consumers are keen to eat more healthily. Information on packaging helps people to identify what food contains so they can make more informed judgements about what they eat. However, many people now refuse to eat food if the label refers to any E numbers. This demonstrates that simply putting such information on the label is not necessarily helpful: people need to know what it means.

Answers: see p. 100. ▶

Identifying hidden assumptions

Why identify implicit assumptions?

It is useful to identify the assumptions that underlie an argument as the overall argument can then be better understood and evaluated.

Careless use of implicit assumptions

Implicit or hidden assumptions are often used to support a conclusion. However, these may be made in such a careless way that they do not support the conclusion.

Example 1

Holidays are a time for relaxation and enjoyment. People need this time to recuperate from the stresses of work and family life. This year, thousands of people will have their holidays ruined by oil spills along our beaches. Therefore, people who have already booked their holidays should receive compensation for the stress that these holidays will bring.

The assumption here is that people are entitled to compensation for stress caused by a spoilt holiday. If this assumption was not being made, then there would be no sense in arguing that people in a particular situation should receive such compensation. The passage also carries the assumption that people are entitled not to feel stress at holiday time:

- Holidays are needed to overcome stress.
- If there is stress during a holiday, there should be compensation.

There is also an assumption that if a holiday goes wrong after it was booked, someone somewhere must pay for this. However, this is only likely to be the case in certain circumstances. The passage is not well reasoned as it makes assumptions that are not explained clearly or well-based in fact.

Non-sequiturs

'Non-sequitur' means 'doesn't follow on'. Sometimes, we can guess that there must be a hidden assumption because the conclusion seems to jump out of nowhere, rather than following on from the sequence of reasons.

Example 2

The number of people in prisons continues to rise each year and is much higher than it was over a hundred years ago. Many prisons are now overcrowded. Rehabilitation of criminals would be a much better option.

The conclusion here is that *Rehabilitation of criminals would be a much better option*. This may be the case but it doesn't follow on logically from the reasons that preceded it. The conclusion is a 'non-sequitur'. Overcrowded prisons and a larger prison population may be facts but these do not give information about the relative virtues of rehabilitation versus time in prison. That would require a different set of reasons, such as those given in Example 3 below.

Example 3

Research shows that, far from curing people of crimes, prison teaches criminals about how to succeed at a wider range of crimes – and how not to get caught next time. On the other hand, methods such as further education, increased social responsibilities and coming face to face with their victims have worked in individual cases to change people away from a life of crime. Prison does not have to be the only option.

Here, the conclusion may or may not be correct, but it does follow logically from the sequence of reasons. The author here gives reasons why prison does not work and why rehabilitation can.

Implicit assumptions used as reasons

Authors may use hidden assumptions as reasons to justify their argument. In effect, they 'jump to conclusions'. We can check for this by:

- looking for gaps in the argument
- then working out what the missing link is in the chain of reasons
- then checking to see whether the conclusion would still be supported without those hidden assumptions.

Example

Examinations are a typical way of assessing what students have learnt and we are all familiar with the stress they can bring. How many of us have dreaded hearing those words 'put your pens down', signalling the end of the exam? If students had more time in examinations, they would finish their last questions with less hurry. This would bring them better marks. Students with disabilities can claim additional time so they have an unfair advantage during exams.

The conclusion here is: *Students with disabilities have an unfair advantage during exams.*

Three reasons are given to support this:

Reason 1: If students had more time in examinations, they would finish their last questions with less hurry.

Reason 2: (an interim conclusion used as a reason): If they finished in a less hurried way, they would get better marks.

Reason 3: Students with disabilities can claim additional time.

The implicit assumption, used as a hidden reason to support the conclusion, is that students with disabilities use additional time to complete their final question with less hurry. Without this assumption, there is a gap in the argument.

Furthermore, the effects of coping with a disability, such as sitting through an examination in extreme pain, or dictating an answer to a scribe, or translating back and forth between a signed language for the deaf and the language of the examination, were not considered in the example. It may be just as true that the additional time does not compensate sufficiently for some disabilities, much less confer an advantage. We would need more evidence to know whether any student would benefit unfairly from additional time.

Sometimes there may be several implicit assumptions. This is especially typical of spoken arguments, where we tend to jump more easily from a statement to a conclusion, leaving many assumptions unstated.

Example

Old people are scared of being robbed. They shouldn't keep their money under the bed, then.

The hidden or implicit assumptions in the example are:

- that old people in general fear being robbed, rather than only certain individuals;
- that elderly people keep money under their beds;
- that they are robbed because of this;
- that there is a link between their fear of being robbed and them keeping money under their beds.

There would need to be more evidence to support all of these assumptions. For example, we don't know how common it is for elderly people to worry about being robbed, or what percentage of them conduct their finances through organisations such as banks and building societies. However, it is more likely that senior citizens are scared of being robbed for a range of different reasons, such as the difficulty of recouping stolen money when living on a pension, or the media attention given to the occasional brutal attacks on older people.

Activity: Implicit assumptions used as reasons

Activity

Read the following passages. In each case, identify:

(1) the conclusion;

(2) the implicit assumptions used as reasons to support the conclusion.

Passage 6.7

It has long been the hope of many people that robots would revolutionise mundane chores and hard labour such as construction work and housework. The first humanoid robot was designed by Leonardo da Vinci as long ago as 1495. We have gone for hundreds of years with little progress in gaining humanoid robots to assist around the house and construction site. Labour-saving robots are just a dream. As there has been so little advance on humanoid robots assisting with housework and construction, it will probably never be achieved.

Dinner's ready!

Passage 6.8

The Electoral Commission found that intimidation was used to influence how some voters used their postal vote in the local elections. We should call an end to postal voting. This will ensure a return to fair elections.

Passage 6.9

People used plants as a method of curing illness for centuries before the advent of modern medicines. The same plants are often used by the pharmaceutical industry as the basis for the medicines we use even today. Medicines are now expensive to produce and purchase. It would be better if we returned to traditional methods, using leaves and roots of plants rather than mass-produced pharmaceuticals.

Passage 6.10

We should continue to improve sanitation and diet in order to further increase our life expectancy. People in the past had much shorter life expectancies than today. The life expectancy of pre-industrialised societies tended to be an average of 30 years. Today, people in developed countries can expect to live to over 70 years. Men, in particular, live much longer now.

Passage 6.11

Most new catering businesses collapse within the first year. Entrepreneurs tend to underestimate how long it takes to establish a client base. They run out of operating funds before they have a chance to establish themselves in the market. Many new restaurant owners give clients over-generous portions, often in a misguided attempt to lure them back to the restaurant. Therefore, in order to keep their businesses afloat, new restaurant owners should delay installing new kitchens until the restaurant is established.

Passage 6.12

Many people in the world are under-nourished or do not get enough to eat. More should be done to reduce the world's population so that food supplies can go round.

Answers: see pp. 100–2. ▶

False premises

Predicating an argument on premises

An argument is based on reasons which are used to support the conclusion. However, when an argument is being formulated, it is also based on beliefs, theories or assumptions, known as *premises*. We say that an argument is *predicated* on its premises. *Predicated* means 'based on'. The examples below show how these terms are used.

Example 1

Usually, only 70,000 people attend the summer festival. A recent report has argued that, this year, the organisers need to order sufficient facilities for 500,000 people. People will want to attend the location that day to see the rare solar eclipse.

Here, the argument that the organisers need to order facilities for half a million people is predicated on the premise that many people will be so interested in the solar eclipse that they will come to the festival to see it. In this example, there are underlying assumptions about the popularity of a solar eclipse.

Example 2

The airport authorities have argued that they need additional security because the proportion of football fans using the airport has risen in the last year.

Here, the argument that there is a need for increased security is predicated upon the premise that football fans automatically create more of a security risk at airports.

False premises

As the basis of an argument, the premises act like the foundations of a building. If the premises are not well-founded, the argument can come tumbling down. When the underlying assumptions are incorrect, we say the argument is based, or predicated, on false premises. Usually, we need some knowledge of the circumstances, such as data or the outcome of an event, in order to recognise false premises.

Example 3

A report prior to the festival argued that the organisers needed to provide facilities for 500,000. This was based on the false premise that the public would wish to see the solar eclipse at the same location as the festival. On the day, however, the public stayed home and watched the eclipse on television. Only the usual 70,000 attended.

After the event, it was easy to see that the whole argument was predicated on incorrect assumptions – or false premises.

Example 4

The proportion of football fans using the airport has risen in the last year. The airport used to be used primarily by oil rig workers before work moved further up the coast. In order to maintain the same volume of travellers, the airport is now offering cheap family deals for football fans travelling with children.

Example 2 assumed a particular type of football fan. In Example 4, when we find out more about the fans, we can see there is no obvious reason why families travelling to a football match would create a higher security risk.

Activity: False premises

Passage 6.13

War in the Gulf is likely to have affected how much oil is produced in the next few months. When there is a shortage of oil, petrol prices usually rise. Therefore, the price of petrol is likely to rise this year.

Passage 6.14

Getting wet in the rain gives you a cold. The builders worked for several hours in pouring rain. Therefore, they will get colds.

Passage 6.15

Five per cent of people got married last year, and five per cent the year before. This means that ten per cent of people get married every two years. Therefore, in twenty years time, everybody will be married.

Passage 6.16

Most new restaurants struggle to survive. In order to break even after the first year of opening, we need to earn £2500 pounds a week. To make this, we need to fill every table every night. Other local restaurants fill about half their tables during the week. We have a good menu so we are likely to get a full restaurant every night. This means we will break even.

Passage 6.17

Digital television will increase the number of channels from which viewers can choose. The more choice there is, the better the quality of the programmes that are produced. Therefore, digital television will lead to better television programmes.

Passage 6.18

Bollywood, the Mumbai-based film industry in India, produces around 900 films every year, far more than any rival. These are being distributed to more countries than ever before. Indian films used to appeal mostly to home audiences but now attract large non-Indian audiences. India has diversified into art-films that win international acclaim. Therefore, the Indian film industry is gaining worldwide appeal.

Passage 6.19

National identities are strongly entrenched. When you are on a beach overseas, you can tell which country people come from just by watching their behaviour. French people, for example, play *boules* in the sand, whilst Englishmen are noticeable for walking round without any clothing on their upper bodies. So, there must be something in their genetic make-up that makes the people of a country behave in a similar way.

Passage 6.20

Cities are too polluted by cars' exhaust fumes and chemicals pumped into the air. In the countryside, the air is free of pollution. People ought to stop living in cities as it is healthier to live in the countryside.

Answers: see p. 102. ▶

Implicit arguments

Explicit and implicit arguments

When an argument follows recognisable structures, the argument is explicit. Most of the arguments introduced in the book so far have been explicit.

When it doesn't obviously follow the familiar structure of an argument, the argument is implicit. Implied arguments may lack:

- an obvious line of reasoning;
- a stated conclusion;
- the appearance of attempting to persuade.

Why use implicit arguments?

An argument can be more powerful when it does not appear to be an argument or when there does not appear to be an attempt to persuade an audience. When an argument is explicit, the audience is likely to analyse it in detail, evaluating the strength of the reasoning and the quality of the evidence. This may not suit the purposes of the author.

If a set of statements leads directly to an unstated conclusion, the audience is more likely to draw the desired conclusion for themselves. An argument can be more convincing if the audience thinks they are drawing their own conclusions. It follows that implicit arguments are most likely to be used for purposes such as:

- catching someone unawares or persuading people through an appeal at an unconscious level, for example, in advertising;
- persuading someone to do something they don't really want to do;
- putting an idea into another person's head without appearing to do so;
- threatening others or creating the idea of threatening circumstances;
- maligning other people without actually mentioning their faults;
- suggesting a consequence without stating it, in an attempt to mislead or to make the audience feel they thought of it themselves.

Example

Huge cash prizes of over a million pounds! Your number has been selected out of over 3.4 million entries to win one of our cash prizes! Ring now on this number to find out more.

In this example, the implicit argument is that the recipient of the message has won a large cash prize, probably of over a million pounds. The message doesn't actually say whether all the cash prizes are over a million pounds. It also doesn't state whether the recipient has been selected as a winner of any kind: we only know the number has been selected 'to win'. This may turn out to be a number entered into a draw. Many people are encouraged to respond to such messages, only to find they have paid more in phone bills than the prize is worth.

Ideological assumptions

An implicit argument may be one that is simply not recognised as implicit because it represents what is taken for granted in the author's society or culture – in its body of beliefs or 'ideology'. For example, it was assumed until very recently that men should not express emotion or were incapable of coping with children. This didn't always need to be stated when it underlay an argument, because everyone 'knew' it was true. Implicit arguments can be a society's equivalent of a 'blind spot'.

Subjects such as cultural and media studies today analyse texts to bring out such 'taken for granted', or ideological, aspects so that we are becoming more aware of our hidden assumptions.

Activities: Implicit arguments

Passage 6.21

Employees would do very well to bear in mind that all forms of trade union and association, other than for sports and recreation, are not viewed favourably. Employees are not to discuss their rates of pay with other workers.

Passage 6.22

When our candidate says he fought for his country, he really did fight for his country. When our candidate says that he hasn't stolen from the nation, he really hasn't. And when our candidate makes electoral promises about taxes, he will keep them.

Passage 6.23

There were three hundred copper pipes loaded on lorries in the parking bay at the factory on Saturday afternoon when the manager and other staff left. The pipes had disappeared by Sunday morning. Julian and Ian worked late on Saturday. Both can drive the lorries. Neither has given an alibi for Saturday night.

Passage 6.24

People in our country believe in honesty and decency. We don't believe in stealing or cheating the state. Now, officials are allowing two thousand people to emigrate here from other countries.

Passage 6.25

Most people in this country want the death penalty. This country is a democracy. In a democracy, what most people want should count. This country does not have the death penalty.

Passage 6.26

I don't see why Ernest should be speaking when there are adults present. He is barely twenty and at an age when he should be attending to his seniors. A child should not force himself forward in this way.

Passage 6.27

Anna is eight years old now and it is time she was sent away to work. The farm at Nexby requires a pair of hands to help gather hay and feed the pigs and chickens. They will take her on and pay her room and board. She will only work from 6 a.m. until 6 p.m. every day. They are good people and will see that she does not fall into sin through idleness. Anna will be allowed home most years for Christmas day.

Passage 6.28

Now that Mr Potts has died, we will have to decide on the future of his estate. As he left only three daughters and has no living sons, the estate will have to pass to his dead brother's son, Mr Andrew Potts.

Passage 6.29

It is quite unreasonable to expect women to be employed to read the news. Some of the news is quite upsetting. It isn't all cakes, bazaars and cats stuck up trees. Newscasters often have to report on war, death and political unrest, which require a serious and steady approach.

Answers: see p. 103. ▶

Denoted and connoted meanings (1)

Any message may carry both denoted and connoted meanings. The denoted meaning is the manifest meaning – the one that is most apparent on the surface.

Denoted meanings

The denoted message is the literal or explicit meaning.

Example 1

Denoted meaning
'Today! £100 reductions on all computers!'

The denoted message is: If you buy any computer at the place where the message appears, the price will be reduced by £100.

Example 2

Denoted meaning
You, too, could have a life in the sun.

The denoted message in Example 2 is: You could live where there is sunshine.

However, an argument may also contain latent messages in persuading us to a point of view. These tend to act on our unconscious as we are not necessarily aware that they are being used. Messages that act on the unconscious can be particularly powerful, so it is important to be aware of when an argument sounds convincing because of its connotations rather than its line of reasoning.

The connotations of a message can add to its effectiveness in persuading. If we can recognise connoted messages, we are in a better position to see how the argument is structured, and to decide whether we agree with its underlying point of view.

Connoted meanings

The connoted message carries additional unstated, or latent, meanings and implications. These may be obvious to the reader in some cases, but are often concealed and may need to be teased out.

Example 1a

Connoted meanings
The connotations of Example 1 are:

- These computers are bargains.
- If you don't buy the computer today, you are unlikely to get the £100 reduction so it is best to buy quickly.

Example 2a

Connoted meanings
The connotations of Example 2 are:

- A life in the sun is a desirable state that not everyone can achieve.
- If you do what we suggest, this opportunity will become available to you.

Arguing by association

One common way of creating connotations is by associating the item under discussion with another. This way, the author doesn't have to explicitly argue that an item is a certain way, but implies it through the second item.

Denoted and connoted meanings (2)

3

That's a great car you got for your birthday. I got this CD for mine. This CD is like gold.

The denoted meaning in Example 3 is that the person received a CD as a birthday gift. The connotations of the messages are more complicated. By associating the CD with gold, the CD appears to be rare and therefore more valuable. This confers some importance to the gift and/or to the receiver of the gift. This may be because the CD really is rare. Alternatively, the author may be trying to create the illusion that the gift of a CD is just as good as the more obviously expensive gift of the car.

Products which have no connections with gold often contain the word 'gold' in the name. Alternatively, marketing materials locate a golden image such as a wedding ring prominently where it will catch the eye. The association with gold immediately suggests excellence, wealth, or scarcity. Terms such as 'golden age' suggest a better time. A golden wedding ring suggests a lasting relationship. This may encourage the audience to associate the product with the romance of weddings. The idea of a lasting relationship is useful when encouraging the idea of a long-term relationship between the audience as purchasers and the product being sold.

Latent messages

Latent messages may rely on connotations. In everyday life, we may be familiar with latent messages through the notion of 'reflected glory'. Most of us are familiar with people who don't argue explicitly: 'I am important', but imply it by mentioning all the important people they have met, or significant jobs held by friends and family. Latent messages are used a great deal in advertising and political campaigning. The product being sold, or the candidate for election, or a political argument, are linked with items and ideas that carry positive meanings. Rival political opponents and their campaign messages are associated with negative messages.

Latent messages often depend upon shared social, cultural and ideological values. As we saw above, if the audience is able to make the links for themselves, the intended message can be more powerful. One well-chosen key word or concept can evoke multiple associations, producing an effective latent message.

Latent messages may be conveyed through a number of means such as:

- Playing patriotic music in the background to a political broadcast, to suggest that a particular party is the most patriotic.
- Using an image of a bird flying in an open sky, to suggest freedom and unlimited choice as a consequence of acting in the way that the argument suggests.
- Baking bread when showing viewers around a house that is for sale, to suggest a feeling of home and well-being.

Stereotyping

When an idea or a set of people are continually linked to a small number of associations, such as adjectives, job roles or forms of behaviour, this is known as stereotyping. The more that the group is linked to that set of associations, the harder it is to conceptualise members of that group as individuals.

4

On the left, we have the men's bathrooms, no doubt for the doctors, and over there are the ladies' bathrooms for the nurses.

For decades in Britain, there was a stereotype that doctors were men and nurses were women. Such stereotypes are now challenged. Stereotyping often accompanies the 'in-group' and 'out-group' behaviour described on p. 114.

Activities: Associations and stereotypes

Activity: Word associations

For the table below, identify which set of concepts is associated with each key word.

Key word	Associated concepts
1 mountain	A innocence, caring, love, tenderness, softness
2 child	B danger, bravery, speed, unstoppable
3 fruit extract	C romance, marriage, happiness, being special or chosen
4 wall of fire	D man being independent; a place women aren't meant to go
5 monkey	E healthiness, vitamins, well-being, flowing hair
6 ring	F natural freshness, refreshingly cool, outdoors, hardiness
7 shed or den	G humour, playfulness, tricks

Activity: Associations that sell

Look at several television advertisements. Identify which words or concepts are used the most to sell different types of product. What are the associations of the words used?

Key word or concept used in advert	Associations given to the word or concept

Activity: Stereotypes

Identify which stereotypes are being perpetuated in the following statements.

1   We'll decorate the room pink as they have two girls.
2   There are uniforms here for the pilots, and ladies, your stewards' costumes are over there.
3   We had better make sure there is roast beef on the menu so that the British tourists have something they are able to eat.
4   We should have expected that he couldn't control his temper, seeing he has red hair.
5   We'll play some Reggae for the visitors from the Caribbean and some flamenco music for those from Spain.
6   We should have expected trouble as there were so many football fans in the crowd.
7   There's no point providing washing machines in student halls of residence. It would be better to give them a big laundry bag so they can carry their laundry home to their parents to clean.
8   They won't be interested in fashion or computers: they are both retired now.

The answers are on p. 104. ▶

Activity: Denoted and connoted meanings

Passage 6.30

Although my client has been a bit naughty in the past, her behaviour has now changed. Her children have been through difficult times in the last few months. Her son has been seriously ill and her daughter was very distressed by her grandfather's death. During the period of trial contact with her children, my client has been like a rock to them. They are now reliant on her support.

Passage 6.31

All the other parties change their policies as the wind blows. Only our party has a constant and clear direction. We have our leader to thank for this, as she is the only captain who can steer a clear course through the storms currently facing our country.

Passage 6.32

It shouldn't be difficult to persuade people to take the new scheme on board. We just need to persuade the community leaders to approve our suggestions and the rest of the community will follow like sheep.

Commentary

Passage 6.30

The denoted meaning is that the client's behaviour had been poor but has now improved. She has shown she can provide good support for her children.

The connotations. The word 'naughty' is one associated with children's behaviour and therefore carries the connotation that the woman's behaviour wasn't very serious in adult terms. The mother is associated with the concept of a 'rock' to create the impression of a supportive and dependable mother. 'Rock' carries connotations of firmness, stability, reliability, and providing good support.

Passage 6.31

The denoted meaning is that whereas other parties change their policies, the author's party is constant in its direction irrespective of events.

The connotations. Other political parties are associated with the wind, which is changeable and unreliable. The connotation is that the parties are also unreliable. This creates a greater sense of contrast with the author's party, which is presented as steady even in a storm, rather than in mere wind. The party leader is associated with a captain of a ship. This carries connotations of 'command over the elements', and of steering a steady path towards the shore. This is not an unusual comparison, so, for some people, this association will carry further connotations of previous leaders who were successfully compared to captains of ships in the past.

Passage 6.32

The denoted message is that it will not be difficult to persuade the community to accept the new scheme if the community leaders approve it.

The connotations. The passage associates the people in the community with sheep, an animal that is considered to have little mind of its own. The connotation is that communities have little mind of their own and do whatever community leaders tell them.

Summary

This chapter looked at some aspects of an argument that are not always made explicit, such as assumptions, implicit arguments, underlying premises and the connotations of material used in establishing the argument.

All arguments are dependent on assumptions of some kind. Assumptions may be latent within an argument for good reasons, such as an expectation that the audience will recognise them and know what they mean. This is useful in keeping an argument brief and succinct, avoiding explanations of what everyone is likely to know already.

At times, the author may assume that the audience will share assumptions or have particular knowledge when this is not the case. At other times, authors may choose not to make the underlying assumptions and persuasive techniques obvious, in order to better persuade the audience to their point of view. Assumptions can also act as reasons to support the conclusion. It is important to be able to identify latent persuasion and reasoning in order to be able to evaluate the strength and validity of the argument.

An argument may appear to be well reasoned but if it is based on false premises, it is not a good argument. As the premises are not usually made explicit, it is usually necessary to read between the lines to identify these. To identify whether premises are sound may require some knowledge of the subject, as well as exercising judgement about the likelihood of the premises being well-founded. Often this requires us to call upon our common sense and experience, but we may need to research further to check whether the argument is valid.

Finally, the chapter looked at denoted and connoted meanings. The denoted meaning is the overt or explicit message, which we are more likely to recognise. However, an argument may also contain latent, or connoted, messages to persuade us to a point of view. These tend to act on our unconscious, and we are not necessarily aware that they are being used. Messages that act on the unconscious can be particularly powerful, so it is important to be able to detect latent messages. We can then evaluate whether an argument sounds convincing because of its connotations and hidden messages rather than its line of reasoning.

Information about the sources

For information about the scientist Emeagwali, see www.emeagwali.com

Answers to activities in Chapter 6

Identify the underlying assumptions (p. 87)

Passage 6.1

Underlying assumption: *Campaigning against nuclear weapons is an accurate measure of how politically-minded a group is.* However, it could be that other political issues are just as important to different generations.

Passage 6.2

Underlying assumption: *Whenever house prices rise quickly, there will always be a slump in which people lose money.* It may be, for example, that patterns of investment or interest rates vary during different periods of rapid house-price rises, so that a slump or loss of money might not automatically follow them.

Passage 6.3

Underlying assumption: *Advertising aimed at children is to blame for peer pressure.* This may be true or untrue. The link between advertising and peer pressure isn't established in the passage itself.

Passage 6.4

Underlying assumption: *A high number of searches on the internet means that 'everyone' must know about the subject.* It may be true, but it is probable that many people haven't heard about Emeagwali. A web page which receives many 'hits' is, nonetheless, visited by a relatively small proportion of people. Also, the same people may have visited the web-site many times.

Passage 6.5

Underlying assumption: *All jobs could be moved to lower-wage economies.* This assumption is needed for the conclusion that there would be 'no' jobs left. Some reflection would indicate that this is unlikely to be the case. Many jobs, such as medicine, catering, retailing, teaching and caring services, need to be delivered locally so it is unlikely that 'no jobs' would be left in high-wage economies. The passage also assumes that only 'companies' offer jobs, but other organisations and individuals could also be employers.

Passage 6.6

Underlying assumption: *Some consumers do not understand the information they read about E numbers.* If this was not the assumption, then the conclusion that 'putting information on the label is not necessarily helpful: people need to know what it means' could not be drawn. E numbers mean 'approved for use in every country in Europe' and include chemicals such as vitamins as well as those considered unhealthy. E300 is vitamin C. There is also an assumption that consumers do want to eat more healthily, which may not be the case.

Implicit assumptions used as reasons (p. 90)

Passage 6.7

Conclusion: *As there has been so little advance on humanoid robots assisting with housework and construction, it will probably never be achieved.*

The implicit assumptions used as reasons are:

(1) *Just because a robot was designed a long time ago, there have been continuous efforts since then to design a robot to deal with certain kinds of work.* No evidence is given to show that this is what Leonardo or inventors since him set out to do.

(2) *If something hasn't been done before a certain time, it never can be.* In the case of designing the robot described, the author doesn't prove this.

These assumptions may be true but are not supported in the passage by evidence.

Passage 6.8

The conclusion is: *Ending postal voting will ensure a return to fair elections.*

It may be true or untrue that postal voting is less fair than other forms of voting. However, the implicit assumptions are:

(1) *Elections were fair before postal voting was introduced*. This is not proved in the passage. For example, some people might not consider that elections are fair if those who work away from home on the day of an election through no choice of their own, or those in hospital or serving in the forces overseas, cannot vote.

Other assumptions made are:

(2) *Intimidation is not used in any other kind of voting system*. This is not established in the passage. For example, intimidation could be used to make people surrender their voting papers in other kinds of election.

(3) *Postal voting could not be altered to reduce or remove intimidation*.

Passage 6.9

The conclusion is: *It would be better to return to traditional methods of using leaves and roots of plants rather than mass-produced pharmaceuticals.*

The implicit assumptions are:

(1) *Past methods of using plants were as effective as modern medicines*. This may be true or untrue. The passage does not provide evidence to establish this. Modern medicines often use plants in more concentrated forms and combined with other chemicals that are not locally available. This may make them more, or less, effective.

(2) *Modern medicines are being used to cure the same range and types of illnesses as in the past*.

(3) *The range and amounts of plants would be available and accessible to people in the amounts needed*. When one considers the very large amounts of concentrated chemicals stored on chemists' shelves, it is difficult to imagine that the plant equivalent could be made available so readily.

Passage 6.10

The conclusion is: *We should continue to improve sanitation and diet in order to further increase our life expectancy.*

The implicit assumption being used as a reason is that *life expectancy increased in the past because of sanitation and diet*. This may be the case but it hasn't been established as true in the passage. It might be argued, for example, that many people had good diets but not enough food, and died early as a result of famine. Others died as a result of epidemics and many men died through wars, without these necessarily being affected by poor diet or sanitation.

The passage also contains the implicit assumption that diet, sanitation and life expectancy could be improved further, and that continuing to increase life expectancy is a good thing. Not everyone might agree with this.

Passage 6.11

The conclusion is: *Therefore, in order to keep their businesses afloat, new restaurant owners should delay installing new kitchens until the restaurant is established.*

The implicit assumption which is used as a reason is that *new kitchens are an unnecessary expense when a restaurant is new, contributing to the lack of funds at the end of the year*. This is a reasonable assumption to make but it does not follow from what has been said so far in the passage. This kind of conclusion is also an example of a non-sequitur (see p. 88), as the conclusion seems to jump out of nowhere, rather than following the previous sequence of the reasoning.

Answers to activities in Chapter 6 (continued)

Passage 6.12

The conclusion is: *More should be done to reduce the world's population so that food supplies can go round.*

The implicit assumption used as a reason is that *the size of the world's population is the cause of under-nourishment.* The passage also assumes that there is not enough food to go round. This may or may not be the case: the passage does not present evidence to support this. However, under-nourishment can be caused by eating the wrong foods rather than simply not having food to eat. Some countries consume much more food than their populations actually require so other people might argue that better food distribution is more important than population control.

False premises (p. 92)

Passage 6.13

Sound premises. Petrol prices would be likely to rise for the reasons given.

Passage 6.14

False premises. The argument is based on the false premise that getting wet in the rain gives you a cold. There is no direct link between getting wet and catching a cold. Most of the time, when people get wet, they do not later have a cold.

Passage 6.15

False premises. The false premise is that people would and could continue to marry at the same rate each year, which is unlikely. The passage does not take into consideration that some of the population, such as children, would not be eligible to marry, and that others would not choose to.

Passage 6.16

False premises. It is a false premise that a good menu will lead to a new restaurant being filled every night. Most new restaurants struggle to survive and established restaurants local to the one in the passage do not fill to capacity. Good cooking, low prices or a better location might have been reasons for expecting a full restaurant.

Passage 6.17

False premise. The false premise is that the more choice there is, the better the quality of the programmes. This has not been established – and many people would argue to the contrary.

Passage 6.18

Sound premises. The Indian film industry is growing in its worldwide appeal for the reasons given: it is gaining international acclaim, attracts non-Indian audiences and is shown in more countries than in the past.

Passage 6.19

False premise. Even if it were true that people's nationality could be read from their behaviour, the argument would be based on the false premise that similarities are genetically based. Nations such as the English and the French are not genetically homogeneous but descend from a very wide variety of ancestors. The behaviours described are more likely to be the result of cultural than genetic reasons.

Passage 6.20

False premises. The false premise is that the air in the countryside is free of pollution. There are many pollutants, such as agricultural pesticides, that can affect people living in rural areas.

Answers to activities in Chapter 6 (continued)

Implicit arguments (p. 94)

Passage 6.21

The implicit argument is that if employees do not do as is expected of them, they are likely to lose their jobs or suffer a similar serious penalty such as lack of promotion. This is not stated explicitly but is an implicit threat.

Passage 6.22

The implicit argument is that the opposing candidate lied about fighting for the country and stealing from the nation and won't keep electoral promises about taxes. This is not stated explicitly but is implied.

Passage 6.23

The implicit argument is that Julian and Ian stole the pipes. A series of statements are presented which, if there was a recognisable structure for an argument, would form a series of reasons. The two workers 'worked late', so we are left to assume this means when other people had all gone home; they can drive the lorries so it is implied that they did drive them; they have given no alibi so we are left to assume both that they have no alibi and that this means they must have committed the theft.

Passage 6.24

The implicit argument is that people who emigrate from other countries are more likely to be dishonest. No evidence is presented to support this argument.

Passage 6.25

The implicit argument is that as most people want the death penalty, it should be introduced. This is not stated explicitly.

Ideological assumptions (p. 94)

Passage 6.26

In this passage, people of 20 years old are still considered children. The age at which one becomes an adult has varied at different historical times and according to the society.

Passage 6.27

The passage assumes these are good working conditions. It considers it to be acceptable for children to work rather than attend school, that a twelve-hour working day is reasonable, and that workers don't have extended holidays. In this passage, work is considered a form of morality and not working is regarded as sinful. Novels of the early nineteenth century describe working conditions such as these, which were not unusual at that time.

Passage 6.28

In this case, the ideological assumption is that women cannot inherit estates. This was the case in Britain for several hundred years, and died out mainly in the twentieth century.

Passage 6.29

This passage assumes that women are too emotional to report news about serious issues. For many years, women were not allowed to read the news in Britain, and arguments such as these were commonplace. It was assumed that women would burst into tears at difficult news. It was also argued that if a woman read the news, it would automatically sound trivial because women were associated only with trivial matters.

Associations (p. 97)

1 = F
2 = A
3 = E
4 = B
5 = G
6 = C
7 = D

Stereotypes (p. 97)

1   This reinforces the stereotype that all girls like pink.

2   This reinforces the stereotype that being a pilot is a job for males and being a steward is a job for females.

3   This reinforces the stereotype that British people only eat roast beef and won't eat food from other countries.

4   This reinforces the stereotype that all red-headed people are hot-tempered.

5   This reinforces the stereotypes that people from the Caribbean all like Reggae and only want to listen to that music, and that people from Spain all like flamenco music and only want to listen to that.

6   This reinforces the stereotype that all football fans are trouble-makers.

7   This reinforces the stereotype that students are lazy and can't fend for themselves. It reinforces the idea of students as younger people with parents who live near enough to visit. It doesn't include the concept of students who do not have parents, are older, from overseas, or brought up in care.

8   This reinforces the stereotype that people are not interested in fashion or computers once they reach a certain age.

Chapter 7

Does it add up?
Identifying flaws in the argument

Learning outcomes

This chapter gives you opportunities to:

- consider a range of flaws that may be contained within an argument
- practise identifying flaws in arguments
- recognise the difference between cause and effect, correlation and coincidence
- understand what is meant by necessary and sufficient conditions, and be able to distinguish between the two
- identify a range of ways in which language can be used to distort an argument

Introduction

Chapter 3 demonstrated that an argument has several components: an author's position, a line of reasoning that uses reasons to support a conclusion, and the intention to persuade. In the following chapters, we saw that an argument can collapse even if it appears to have those components. We have already seen how an argument may be weakened by poor structure, logical inconsistency and hidden assumptions. This chapter will look at some other ways of evaluating the strength of an argument. It enables you to consider many common types of flaws that can occur, such as confusing cause and effect; failing to meet necessary conditions; attacking the character of a person rather than evaluating their reasoning; misrepresentation; and using emotive language.

Arguments may be flawed because:

- The authors didn't recognise that their own arguments were flawed. This chapter can help you to recognise flaws in your own arguments so you can improve your reasoning.

- The authors intended to mislead their audiences and deliberately distorted the reasoning, or misused language to create particular responses. This chapter can help you to be more alert to flaws in other people's arguments.

Cats have whiskers.
My grandfather has whiskers.
Therefore, my grandfather must be a cat.

Assuming a causal link

It is flawed reasoning to assume that because two things are found together, or occur at the same time, there must be a link between them. One example of this is assuming a link to be one of cause and effect: that one thing must be the 'cause' of another, or, in effect, jumping to a particular kind of conclusion.

Example 1

Wherever dinosaur imprints are found in rocks, there are geologists around. Therefore, geologists must make the imprints.

The assumption here is that as geologists and dinosaur prints occur in the same place, the geologists create the prints. The underlying assumption is that the dinosaur prints must be fake. If this were not the case, the author couldn't draw the conclusion that geologists must make the prints. The more logical assumption is that the prints attract the geologists as they are a natural subject for geologists to research when they are dating rocks. Other evidence is likely to prove they pre-dated the arrival of the geologists by a great many years.

Example 2

The entire family was ill last night. They all ate fish at the restaurant yesterday. Therefore, the fish must have been contaminated.

Here, the cause of the illness is linked to eating fish. The underlying assumption is that nothing else could have made the family ill. Without this assumption, the author couldn't draw the conclusion that the fish was bad. More evidence than this would be needed to prove that bad fish was the cause of the illness, such as:

- whether anybody else who ate fish from the same batch became ill;
- what the nature of the illness is;
- what else might have caused the illness;
- an examination of the fish remains.

Activity

For each passage, identify the assumed causal link or links.

Passage 7.1

Life expectancy is much higher in Western countries than in the past. Obesity is also much higher. Therefore, obesity must increase our life expectancy.

Passage 7.2

A prisoner who protested his innocence by sitting on the prison roof has been released. This is the second time that a prisoner who has protested in this way has been released. Roof-top protests must be a good way of securing release from the prison.

Passage 7.3

The man's body was found in the kitchen. A bloody knife was found nearby. The lock on the door had been broken. Somebody must have broken in and killed the man.

Answers: see p. 122. ▶

Correlations and false correlations

When trends are related, this is referred to as *correlation* – that is, 'related to each other'. Sometimes, there is a causal link between the correlated trends, and at other times there is not.

Example

As the temperature rises, people drink more water.

Here, the two trends of rising temperature and increased water consumption can be correlated. Drinking water is an effect caused by the increase in temperature.

Example

As the temperature fell, people were more likely to use the indoor swimming pool.

Here, the two trends of falling temperature and increased likelihood of swimming indoors can be correlated. Use of the indoor swimming pool was an effect caused by the fall in temperature. Here, the trends move in opposite directions (one falls as the other increases) so there is an inverse correlation, but the link is still one of cause and effect.

Correlations with 'third causes'

In other cases, there is not a causal link between trends that are correlated. For example, sales of ice cream may rise between May and August each year and so may sales in sandals. The trends move in the same direction and there is a relationship of some kind between the two. This means we can say that increased sales of both ice cream and sandals are correlated. It is reasonable to expect that when sales of sandals rise, there will also be a rise in ice cream sales.

However, increased sales of ice cream don't cause the higher sales of sandals, nor vice versa. If a novel brand of ice cream is launched to coincide with winter festivities, ice cream sales could rise

without there being any effect on sandal sales. A third factor, warmer weather in summer, is responsible for the sales of each.

False correlations

A correlation assumes some kind of mutual relationship. Just because trends move in the same direction, this does not mean there is a correlation between them, as there may be no relationship. If a correlation is assumed where none exists, this is a false correlation.

Example

The number of car crimes has increased. There used to be only a few colours of car from which purchasers could choose. Now there is much more variety. The wider the choice of car colours, the higher the rate of car crime.

It is possible that there is some link between the two trends but it isn't likely. The connection between the two trends is likely to be coincidental rather than correlated.

Checking the relationship

When there appears to be a correlation between trends, it is important to check the ways in which they are linked:

● Are the patterns and trends coincidental rather than there being a direct link between them?
● Are they directly linked as cause and effect?
● Are they linked by a third cause?

Activity: Identify the nature of the link

Passage 7.4

Reason 1: Sugar destroys teeth.
Reason 2: Children eat a lot of sugar.
Reason 3: Children's teeth decay quickly.
Conclusion: Children's teeth decay quickly because of the sugar they eat.

Passage 7.5

Reason 1: More students use the internet for research and for submitting their work than in the past.
Reason 2: The overall number of students has risen but the number of teaching staff has not.
Reason 3: The proportion of students plagiarising the work of other people is likely to have remained the same.
Conclusion: Students are now more at risk of being discovered plagiarising.

Passage 7.6

Marie Curie, Einstein, and Darwin had long hair. They were all great scientists. Therefore, to be a great scientist you need long hair.

Passage 7.7

Reason 1: The price of football tickets has risen.
Reason 2: Football players receive higher wages than ever before.
Conclusion: Spectators are paying more to watch matches in order to pay footballers' high wages.

Passage 7.8

Reason 1: Hedgehogs enjoy eating ice cream.
Reason 2: Hedgehogs eat ice cream if it is stored in containers that they can break open.
Reason 3: Fast food outlets report a lot of ice cream wastage recently.
Conclusion:
Hedgehogs must be breaking in to eat the ice cream at fast food outlets.

Passage 7.9

Reason 1: Dubai's population doubled every ten years between 1940 and 2000 and is continuing to rise.
Reason 2: The port created in 1979 at Jebel Ali provided a prosperous free trade zone that brought in people from all over the world.
Reason 3: Many projects for improving the economic infrastructure, from sporting events and theme parks to world-class technology parks and international finance centres, have encouraged people to settle in Dubai.
Reason 4: Large-scale property development is underway, offering better opportunities for foreign nationals to own property in Dubai.
Conclusion: Dubai's population is increasing because of the opportunities it provides to foreign nationals.

Answers: see p. 122. ▶

Not meeting the necessary conditions

Necessary conditions

In order to prove an argument, certain supporting reasons or evidence will be essential to it. These are called *necessary conditions*. A necessary condition is just as it sounds: it is an essential requirement. If it is not present, there is a gap in the argument, and the outcome could be different. If the outcome could be different, then the argument isn't proved. It is important to bear in mind that there may be many necessary conditions, or requirements, for proving a case.

'Without this, then not that . . .'

You can check whether a reason forms a necessary condition by rephrasing the argument and seeing whether it still holds true. Necessary conditions are expressed in statements such as:

- *If this doesn't happen, then that won't occur.*
- *If this isn't true, then that can't be true either.*
- *If this isn't present, then that won't be present.*
- *If A isn't present, then B can't be true.*
- *If it doesn't have A, then it can't be B.*
- *If it doesn't do A, then B won't result.*

This is easier to grasp through concrete examples.

Example 1

If you don't make advance arrangements for a taxi to come to the house to take you to the station, then a taxi won't arrive in time for you to catch your train.

A necessary condition, or requirement, for the taxi arriving in time, in this case, is that arrangements are made in advance. This is a sound argument.

Example 2

One way of making a lot of money is by winning the lottery. In order to win the lottery, you have to have a lottery ticket for the draw. John has a lottery ticket for the draw so he will make a lot of money.

One necessary condition, or requirement, for making money through the lottery is to have a relevant lottery ticket. John has met this necessary condition by having such a ticket.

Checking for necessary conditions

When you are checking for necessary conditions, it can help to rephrase some or all of the reasons, and see whether the argument still holds.

Example 3

Proposition: Birds have wings. The item has wings. The item is a bird.

To check whether wings are a necessary condition of the item being a bird, apply a statement such as: *If it doesn't have A, then it can't be B*, and check whether this is true or false. In this case:

> *If it doesn't have wings, then it can't be a bird. True or false?*

This is true: if an item did not have wings, it would be hard to argue that it was a bird.

However, it is important to take the context into consideration: if a bird had lost its wings in an accident, or had been born without wings, it would be flawed to argue that this prevented it from being a bird. For example, the underlying DNA that leads birds to have wings would be able to determine that this was a bird.

Not meeting sufficient conditions

'Necessary' is not enough proof

Necessary and sufficient conditions are different. Even if a necessary condition is met, this might not be sufficient to prove a case: there may be other conditions that must be met. You need to consider whether the 'conditions' are sufficient to support the conclusion. If not, then the argument is not yet proved.

For example, simply having a ticket for the lottery draw is not a sufficient condition for making money: the ticket might not win. This illustrates the difference between necessary and sufficient conditions.

'If this, then that . . .'

Sufficient conditions form the totality of all those conditions that must be met in order to secure a particular argument. If sufficient conditions are met, then a particular set of consequences *must* follow. Sufficient conditions are expressed in statements such as:

- *If this is true, then that must always be true.*
- *If A is present, then that proves B.*
- *If this is true, then that must always follow.*
- *If A is present, then B must be true.*

Example 1

The lottery prize money was £10 million. John held the only winning ticket. He met the rules of the competition. Therefore, John made a lot of money.

In Example 1, some necessary conditions for John to make a lot of money are met: the prize was for a large sum, and John was the sole winner. However, if he lost his ticket, didn't claim his prize, or the lottery company went bankrupt, sufficient conditions would not have been met for John to make a lot of money.

Example 2

Bacteria usually have very short life spans. However, in 1989, the skeleton of a well preserved, 11,000-year-old mastedon was found in Ohio. Scientists found an intestinal bacterium in its rib cage that they believe was its last meal. The bacterium was not found in the surrounding peat. Therefore, the bacterium must be over 11,000 years old.

The author is here arguing that bacteria may live much longer than was assumed. A necessary condition is that bacteria found in the skeleton are not also found in the surrounding peat. If they are, then the bacteria might have travelled from the peat to the skeleton only very recently, and might not have been present in the rib cage 11,000 years ago. However, this is not a sufficient condition to prove the age of the bacteria. We don't know, for example, whether the bacteria were blown by the wind into the skeleton at any intervening point during the last 11,000 years, without making contact with the surrounding peat.

Sufficient and/or necessary

When you are checking for sufficient conditions, it can help to rephrase some or all of the reasons, and see whether the argument still holds true. To check whether wings are a sufficient condition to prove that something is a bird, apply a statement such as: If A is present, then that proves B, and check whether this is true or false.

Example 3

Proposition: Birds have wings. The item has wings. Therefore, it is a bird.

If wings are present, then that proves this is a bird. True or false?

The answer is 'false'. Its having wings is not sufficient proof that this is a bird. Other necessary conditions would be that it was, or had been, a living creature, with feathers, and that it had the DNA of a bird. A winged item could simply be an aeroplane.

Activity: Necessary and sufficient conditions

For each proposition below, decide:

- whether the reasons given meet the necessary conditions to support the conclusion. Write *Yes* or *No* in the box headed *Necessary?* Give reasons for your answer.
- whether the reasons given to support the conclusion are sufficient? Write *Yes* or *No* in the box headed *Sufficient?* Give reasons for your answer.
- An example is given in the first box.

The answers are on p. 123. ▶

Ex.	Proposition	Necessary?	Sufficient?
	Example: Birds have wings. The item has wings. Therefore, it is a bird.	*Yes. Wings are a necessary condition for the item being a bird*	*No. The reasons given to support the argument that the item is a bird are not sufficient to satisfy the definition of a bird. This would include: usually flies, is animate, lays eggs, has two legs, has feathers. The information given is not sufficient to rule out an aeroplane or a toy.*
1	The report makes reference to branches. It must be about a tree.		
2	The boxer doesn't eat meat or fish. He does eat dairy products and vegetables. The boxer is a vegetarian.		
3	Amir is under the age of 20. Teenagers are less than 20 years old. Amir must be a teenager.		
4	Claire does not play any musical instrument. Therefore, she is not a musician.		
5	The bishop arrived on a vehicle with two wheels, one in front of the other. The bishop must have been on a bicycle.		
6	A television usually costs more than a radio. This one costs less than a radio, so it must be a bargain.		
7	Li Yeung had the benefit of an exceptionally happy childhood. She must be a very happy adult.		

False analogies

An analogy is a comparison made to draw out similarities between two things.

Creative comparisons

Authors can attempt to persuade their audience through using comparisons. In creative writing such as poetry and fiction, it is legitimate to compare two items that seem at first to be dissimilar in order to produce a literary effect such as surprise, humour or an unexpected perspective. In creative writing, it may be permissible to say 'it was raining wellington boots', or 'the moon is a goddess riding her chariot of clouds'. Literary critics have to decide whether such comparisons work to create the desired effect on the audience.

Valid comparisons

For most types of critical thinking, comparisons must be valid, and add to our understanding of the situation. In scientific terms, for example, it doesn't help to think of the moon as a goddess or clouds as chariots. Comparisons draw attention to those aspects which are similar. As two things are never identical, it takes critical evaluation and judgement to decide whether a comparison is valid for the context. If the comparison helps to give a more accurate understanding, then it is likely to be valid.

Example

The heart works as a pump, moving blood through the body by opening and constricting.

For most purposes, the comparison with a pump helps us to understand the action of the heart, so this is valid.

An analogy is not valid if:

- the two items being compared are not sufficiently similar, or . . .
- the comparison is misleading, or . . .
- the item used for comparison is described inaccurately.

Before reading on, check whether you can identify the weaknesses in the analogy in the example below.

Example

Cloning of human cells should never be allowed: it will create another Frankenstein's monster. We do not want such monsters.

The author's position on cloning is clear: that it is wrong and should be stopped. It may be that the idea of cloning is 'monstrous' to many people and the author is playing on that sentiment. However, the analogy used is not valid as it doesn't compare like with like. A clone is an exact copy of an original. Frankenstein's monster wasn't an exact reproduction or copy of anything, but was, rather, an assembly of pieces. Moreover, by using the term 'another Frankenstein's monster', the author is implying we should have learnt our lesson from the past. However, Frankenstein's monster was only a character in a book. The author wants us to think that a clone will be a 'monster', but if the original used for the clone was not a monster, an exact copy should not be a monster either.

If an author uses a false analogy well, the argument may seem convincing. This is especially true if one half of an analogy seems easy to prove (that Frankenstein's creation was a monster) and the other isn't (the outcomes of cloning). It is easy to assume that because one half of the analogy is true, the other half must be too.

Activity: False analogies

Activity

For each of the passages below, identify:

- What the analogy is: which two things are being compared?
- Whether the comparisons are valid.

Passage 7.10

The earth's atmosphere is like a blanket of gases around the earth. It is only a thin layer but it helps to maintain the temperature of the earth, keeping us warm. It also offers a layer of protection from the intensity of the sun.

Passage 7.11

It may not seem likely that the new political party will be successful in the next elections but we remain optimistic. It is true that the formal membership is small and the party does not have much money with which to campaign. However, what it lacks in these areas, it makes up for in other areas, such as the skill of its politicians and their commitment to success. The party is like a new David, taking on Goliath. It may be small, but it can take on those much bigger than itself.

Passage 7.12

As the basis of an argument, the premises are like the foundations of a building. If the premises are not well-founded, the argument is likely to collapse.

Passage 7.13

There was no way the defendant was able to help himself. He had been under excessive strain for some time and his emotions had been building up like steam under pressure. The witness had been goading the defendant, knowing he was likely to get angry. The defendant was like a pressure cooker, just waiting to explode. Eventually, he just reached boiling point and an explosion became inevitable.

Passage 7.14

Investors in certain businesses lost a great deal of money in recent years as their stocks and shares wavered in the financial markets. Investors may not have a right to compensation for the knocks and bruises they have suffered on the stockmarket but they should be reimbursed for major accidents and serious lapses in the health of the financial markets.

Answers: see pp. 122–3. ▶

Deflection, complicity and exclusion

Language can be used skilfully to construct a powerful argument. However, it can also be used in ways that are unfair and which produce flaws in the line of reasoning. Language can be used to lull the audience into a false sense of security about whether an argument is valid, or can divert the audience from the line of reasoning. Some of these tricks of language are examined below.

Deflective language

An author can use language to suggest there is no need to prove the argument, deflecting the audience from critically evaluating the reasoning.

Suggesting the argument is proved

Use of words such as: *obviously, of course, clearly, naturally* suggests that the argument is so obvious there is no need to evaluate it.

Appeals to modern thinking

Another way of deflecting the audience from the reasoning is by referring to the date, as if that, in itself, added weight to the argument.

Examples

- *We're not in the nineteenth century now!*
- *It's no longer 1940!*
- *It's like being back in the ark!*

As the date is factually accurate, the audience is already drawn into part agreement with the argument. This approach attempts to discredit anyone who disagrees with the argument as being old-fashioned and out-of-date.

Encouraging complicity

Everybody knows

This is a particular form of deflective language where the author acts as if the reader were already part of a group of like-minded thinkers.

This can be a powerful way of enticing the audience into agreement.

Examples

- *As we all know . . . , we all know that . . .*
- *Surely, we all share the view that . . .*
- *Everybody knows that . . . Everyone believes . . .*
- *It is well established that . . .*

If 'everyone' believes something, then the audience would seem unreasonable not to agree.

'People like us': in-groups and out-groups

Another version is to suggest that people with certain attributes, such as 'decent people' or 'anyone with any intelligence', are more likely to agree with the argument. This can be especially convincing if coupled with an appeal to commonly held assumptions and prejudices.

Example

Anyone with any sense knows that women are naturally better at housework than men.

Tajfel (1981) wrote about the way people divide into 'in-groups' and 'out-groups'. The in-group tends to make the out-group appear inferior and undesirable so that others want to avoid being associated with them. Authors can present opponents of their argument as an 'out-group'. The audience is more likely to be persuaded by the arguments of an in-group and less likely to consider the views of the out-group. Appeals to decency, morals, shared values and shared identity can be examples of this:

Examples

- *All decent people would agree that X is immoral.*
- *As British people (or black people/Muslims/ Catholics/deaf people etc.), we all want . . .*

Other types of flawed argument

There are many ways in which an argument may be flawed. As you become more used to critical analysis, you will become more attuned to spotting the weak parts of an argument. You could use a checklist such as that on page 247 to help you identify the main flaws. However, you would need a very long checklist to cover *all* potential weaknesses. It is more useful to develop an increased sensitivity to potential flaws, so that you can recognise them in different kinds of circumstance.

The following sections look at some further potential distortions and weaknesses to look out for. To help develop the sensitivity mentioned above, this section presents texts first and encourages you to find the flaws yourself, if possible, before reading the commentaries that follow.

Activity

Before reading about further types of flawed argument, see if you can identify these for yourself in the passages that follow.

You don't need to worry about whether there are technical names for the flawed arguments: just see if you can recognise when and why the argument isn't watertight. There may be more than one flaw in each passage.

Then read pp. 116–17 to check your answers.

Passage 7.15

Community centre
Closing the community centre will leave our poor little children with nowhere to play after school. Parents are rightly furious. After the death of five children from the area on a school canoeing trip, feelings are running very high. The neighbourhood just cannot take any more. If the community centre closes, parents will worry that their children are being left to suffer all over again.

Passage 7.16

Internet copying
Although it is possible to devise software to catch people who copy on the internet, it is unlikely that everyone who does this could be charged. If you can't enforce a law, then there isn't any point in passing it. If there isn't a law, then there isn't a crime. If there isn't a crime, then nobody has done anything wrong.

Passage 7.17

Tolls
More people should travel by public transport, as this would improve traffic flows in the city. If there were tolls for using roads, people would use public transport. Polls indicate that most people want the traffic flow to be improved. This shows that people would be willing to support the introduction of tolls. Therefore, the council should introduce heavy tolls.

Passage 7.18

Identity cards
Personal identity cards don't present any real dangers to human rights. They add to our security, by making it easier for the police to track and catch criminals. Opponents of identity cards are wishy-washy liberals who live in leafy areas and haven't a clue what it is like to live in run-down areas where crime is rife.

Passage 7.19

The managing director
The rugby team has had a chequered season. It started badly and although it has picked up now, it seems unlikely that it can still win the championship. The managing director says that two new acquisitions will make a great difference to the team's performance for the end of the season. However, the board should give little credence to anything he has to say on the matter. After seeing his seedy affair with the TV quiz hostess broadcast all over the media, despite his constant denials, fans shouldn't give him any further credibility as a manager.

Unwarranted leaps and castle of cards

Unwarranted leaps

Where there are unwarranted leaps, the author appears to add two and two to make five. The argument races ahead, leaving gaps in the reasoning, and relying on unsubstantiated assumptions.

Castle of cards

In *castle of cards* types of argument,

- the author uses a set of interconnected reasons;
- the argument becomes precariously balanced, and depends on the previous reasons being accepted;
- if one reason or assumption is proved incorrect, the argument collapses easily.

Passage 7.17   Tolls (p. 115)

Passage 7.17 contains examples of both unwarranted leaps and *castle of cards* reasoning. The argument relies on a set of interconnected reasons and assumptions and is very delicately balanced. There are unsubstantiated assumptions which could be challenged such as that:

- the traffic problem is caused by the number of cars on the road, rather than, for example, road works or a one-way system;
- if a toll was introduced, people would respond by using public transport.

There is an unwarranted leap to the conclusion that, because a poll shows people want the traffic flow to be improved, they would also support tolls. We are not told whether the poll asked questions about tolls, so we do not know that a toll would be welcomed. The public might have preferred a different solution, such as bus shuttles or car-sharing.

Sleight of hand

A sleight of hand is a 'cunning trick' that can go unnoticed. In Passage 7.17, *Tolls*, the author jumps from a line of reasoning that appears to be discussing tolls, to a conclusion that argues for *heavy* tolls. This slight change of wording is an example of a 'sleight of hand'.

Passage 7.16   Internet copying (p. 115)

The *castle of cards* approach is evident in Passage 7.16. This makes unsubstantiated claims such as that everybody who is caught copying on the internet could not be charged. This is not proved. On the contrary, large-scale fining is possible, and is used for minor traffic offences and for not having a television licence.

The author then argues that if a law can't be enforced, it shouldn't be passed. This is a matter of opinion and the author hasn't proved the law can't be enforced. Using this argument as the next stepping stone, the author argues that without a law there isn't a crime. There is a sleight of hand here, as the author hasn't mentioned whether a law against such copying is already in place at the time of writing.

The author makes a final leap to argue that if there isn't a crime, nobody has done anything wrong. This is not the case. Right and wrong are questions of ethics, not law. Some acts which are wrong might not yet be enshrined in law. For example, when there is a new invention or an advance in medical technology, it can take time for these to result in changes in the law.

Emotive language; Attacking the person

Emotive language

Emotive language uses words, phrases and examples that intend to provoke an emotional response. Some subjects such as children, parents, national pride, religion, crime and security are emotive. Using these unnecessarily as arguments can manipulate the audience's emotions.

People tend to trust their own emotional responses. Strong emotions are usually a signal to the body to act quickly rather than to slow down and use reasoning. If an author can elicit an emotional response, then the audience is likely to be less critical of the reasoning. Where subjects are emotive, it is particularly important to check the underlying reasoning carefully.

Attacking the person

We saw in Chapter 3 that an argument should take counter arguments into consideration. This means making a critical analysis of the line of reasoning, not using personal attacks on those with opposing views. Attacks on the person rather than the argument are often used to undermine the credibility of an opposing point of view – but it is not a valid method of critical reasoning.

The exception is where there is a valid reason for showing that the opponents either have a history of being dishonest or have not revealed their vested interests in the debate.

Passage 7.15   Community centre (p. 115)

In Passage 7.15, *Community centre*, the author appeals to the emotions using words such as 'poor little children' and references to 'feelings running high' and 'suffering'. The passage reminds the audience of a disaster that had happened to other children in the area. The incident was very sad but its relevance to the current argument is not clear. That accident happened away from the area, and when there was already a community centre where children could play. There may be a good case for keeping the community centre open, but the author does not present a reasoned argument to support it.

Passage 7.18   Identity cards (p. 115)

This passage attacks everyone who opposes the introduction of identity cards on personal terms. It also makes unsubstantiated assumptions about the backgrounds and economic circumstances of opponents, in order to undermine their credibility. As the passage relies on these unacceptable methods rather than reasons and evidence, it demonstrates flawed reasoning.

The passage also encourages complicity in the audience (see page 114). By abusing opponents, the author encourages a division between in-groups and out-groups, or 'people like them' and 'people like us'. Furthermore, the passage draws on emotive subjects, referring to crime and security to win over the audience.

Passage 7.19   The managing director (p. 115)

This passage attacks the person of the manager rather than evaluating his judgements about the likely impact of the new players. It attacks the manager on the grounds of his personal life, not his expertise in managing a rugby team. We may not agree with decisions the manager takes in his personal life, but the passage does not show the relevance of this to managing the club. As the manager denies what is in the media, it may not even be true. The use of the term 'seedy' is emotive, suggesting there is an illicit side to the relationship, but this is not substantiated.

More flaws

Just as you did for p. 115, check whether you can identify the flaws in the following passages. There may be more than one flaw in each passage, including flaws covered in previous sections. The answers will be on the following pages.

Nature or nurture
Those who argue that intelligence is not in-born do a disservice to the truly bright individual and hinder attempts to discover excellence. Many of us had intensive training on an instrument such as the piano when we were children, but we obviously did not all turn out to be a Beethoven or Mozart. We are all able to recognise brilliance when we see it. Proponents of the view that intelligence can be nurtured are too ready to blame society or the education system for not turning out more geniuses. They want us to believe that any of our children could be a genius, which is unfair on parents and teachers alike.

Passage 7.21

Curfews
Juvenile crime has risen sharply in cities. Young people are out of control. There are only two options in a situation like this. Either we agree to put up with savage assaults on our persons and property, or we place a curfew on all young people after 10 o'clock.

Passage 7.22

Einstein
Einstein was not very good at maths when he was at school. Many school-children today could solve maths problems that he used to struggle with. The accolade of 'great scientist' shouldn't be ascribed to someone who struggled with basic numerical problems.

Passage 7.23

Health training
The public's knowledge of health is poor and more money is needed for education in this area. Increased sums of money should be spent on courses to make people aware of personal health issues. People don't always know what they can do to take care of their health so further investment is needed in training on health matters.

Passage 7.24

Advantages of maths
More people should be informed of the value of studying maths to a higher level at school or university. A mathematical education can be very advantageous. Therefore, the guidance given to young people should emphasise the benefits of choosing maths.

Passage 7.25

Selling assets
The opposition party is wrong to condemn the leader of the council for selling off public assets at a low price to its own supporters. When the opposition had a majority in the council, they sold off cemeteries and houses below the commercial price, benefiting their own supporters. If they can do it, then the current council can do it too.

Passage 7.26

Stealing at work
Mr Malcolm's employers pay their stylists much lower wages and expect them to work much longer hours than owners of other salons. Mr Malcolm supplemented his income by taking equipment and styling products from the workplace and selling these in his own area. He was justified in stealing from his employer because his employer was exploiting him.

Misrepresentation and trivialisation

One way of distorting an argument is by presenting the options or opposing arguments in an unfair or unbalanced way. Misrepresentation can be engineered in several ways. Three are given below. A consequence of misrepresentation is that important matters can be made to appear trivial.

Ignoring the main opposing reasons

An author can misrepresent an opposing argument by focusing on its minor points and ignoring its chief supporting reasons. If the minor points are not sufficient to support the conclusion, the opposing argument will appear very weak. Sometimes, authors may simply attribute beliefs and arguments to their opponents without any evidence.

Presenting restricted options

Another form of misrepresentation is to present an argument in such a way that it looks as if there are only two possible conclusions or options for action. This approach relies on selecting one conclusion or option that appears very weak and one that seems preferable. The weakness of the alternative conclusion or option makes the author's case appear stronger than it really is.

Misrepresenting a person

A poor form of argument consists of focusing on certain characteristics of a person, especially those irrelevant to the main argument, and ignoring more relevant information about that person.

Passage 7.20   Nature or nurture

Passage 7.20 misrepresents the opponent's arguments. The author's position is clearly one that supports the view that levels of intelligence are innate (i.e. there from birth). The passage attributes arguments to the opponent: 'They want us to believe . . .', 'Proponents . . . are too ready to blame society . . .'. No evidence is given to show that this is what is believed by people who argue that intelligence can be nurtured. Other reasons that people might have for believing that intelligence is not simply a question of birth are not considered. For example, there is no consideration of research evidence.

The argument is trivialised by focusing on relatively rare cases of 'genius' rather than on how intelligence operates for most people. Rather than presenting a well reasoned case, the author uses emotional devices, using an emotive subject such as unfair treatment of teachers and parents. There is an appeal for complicity through assertions aimed at drawing in the audience ('We are all able to recognise brilliance') and by references to potentially common experiences such as childhood piano lessons. These further trivialise the subject.

Passage 7.21   Curfews

The argument in Passage 7.21 is flawed in several ways. The main flaw is that it offers only two options, curfew or assaults. Other options, such as improved policing or changes in lighting, are not considered. 'Out of control' and 'savage' are strong statements using emotive language, but no definitions or explanations are given to substantiate these. It also assumes the crime occurs mostly after 10 o'clock.

Passage 7.22   Einstein

Passage 7.22 misrepresents Einstein by focusing on his early difficulties with maths and ignoring all the discoveries for which he is considered a great scientist. It overlooks that all the people who were better at maths when Einstein was young did not go on to develop such advanced scientific theories.

Tautology; Two wrongs don't make a right

Tautology

A line of reasoning should take an argument forward. Tautological arguments, on the other hand, merely repeat the same points in different words, without advancing the argument. Tautology means using different words to repeat the same concept, as in 'the car was reversing backwards'.

Two wrongs don't make a right

Another form of flawed argument is to argue that an action is acceptable simply because someone else acted in a similar way. Similarly, it is usually considered to be flawed reasoning to argue for consistent treatment when this would mean that an injustice or an illogical outcome was perpetuated by doing so. For example, if one person cheats in an exam, then it is not reasonable to argue that other people should be able to cheat too. If one person lies, it doesn't make it right for others to tell lies.

Passage 7.23   Health training

Passage 7.23 is tautological. Each sentence merely repeats what is said in the other sentences, using different words. 'Spending more money on courses' equates to 'investment in training'; 'make people aware' implies that 'people don't know what they can do'. The argument does not progress, as no further reasons, details or evidence are provided.

Passage 7.24   Advantages of maths

Passage 7.24 is another example of tautology. The empty repetition makes the argument appear to go round in circles. The author doesn't present reasons to substantiate the case for learning higher maths. No details of the potential advantages are given. For example, it could have been argued that a higher qualification in maths can lead to a greater choice of careers or a better income. The author might have included information such as that surveys suggest employees in careers that require higher levels of maths have greater job satisfaction than employees in most other occupations.

Passage 7.25   Selling assets

Passage 7.25 is an example of 'two wrongs not making a right'. It is wrong for any party to sell public assets cheaply in order to secure political advantages for their party. Just because a previous party did so, this does not make it right for other parties to follow suit. It may appear hypocritical to cast blame on another party for behaviour that one's own party has engaged in. However, it would still be in the public interest for an apparently hypocritical politician to expose current wrong-doing. Otherwise, even more public assets would be wasted.

Passage 7.26   Stealing at work

Passage 7.26 is another example of 'two wrongs do not make a right'. The employers may have been in the wrong in the way they treated their employees. However, stealing was not the appropriate response. It isn't either ethical or legal. The argument would not stand up in court.

Summary

This chapter introduces many of the most common types of flawed reasoning. Such flawed reasoning may be a deliberate ploy on the part of an author who intends to deceive the audience. However, flawed reasoning is often the result of insufficiently rigorous critical thinking: many people are not aware of errors in their reasoning.

One group of flaws covered by the chapter relates to the concept of causality. It is a common mistake to assume that if two things appear to be connected in some way, the nature of that connection is one of cause and effect. However, the items may be linked by a third item, a distant relationship, through correlated trends, or simply by coincidence.

A second set of flaws relates to statements or arguments that do not meet the necessary and sufficient conditions to establish proof. If necessary and sufficient conditions are not met, an alternative conclusion could be drawn so the argument is not yet proved.

The third set of flaws is concerned with accuracy and validity in the way language is used to establish an argument. There are many ways that the language used to communicate the argument can distort or conceal. Some examples of this covered within the chapter are: making false analogies, attempting to draw the reader into collusion with the author, using language to conceal gaps in the reasoning, using emotive language with the aim of distorting the audience's response, and misrepresenting opponents' views.

Being able to recognise flaws in an argument is a useful skill. It helps you to identify weak points in other people's arguments and to pinpoint areas for you to investigate more closely so you can make more informed decisions. If you are evaluating an argument within your writing, or as part of a debate, knowing the flaws in the opponent's arguments helps you to formulate better counter arguments. If you are able to recognise such flaws in your own arguments, you are in a better position to put forward more convincing arguments in their place.

Information on the sources

For more about mastedons: Postgate, J. (1994) *The Outer Reaches of Life* (Cambridge: Cambridge University Press).

For more about 'out-groups': Tajfel, H. (1981) *Human Groups and Social Categories* (Cambridge: Cambridge University Press).

Answers to activities in Chapter 7

Assuming a causal link (p. 106)

Passage 7.1

The assumed causal link: obesity leads to longer life expectancy. The link does not follow logically from the reasons given: it hasn't been shown that those who are obese live longer, nor why obesity should lead to longer life.

Passage 7.2

The assumed causal link: that it was the roof-top protest that led to the prisoners' release, rather than, for example, them having been found innocent, the evidence against them being found to be flawed, or them having completed their sentences. Something which has happened only twice does not establish a solid trend.

Passage 7.3

The assumed causal links are that the man was murdered, that somebody broke in to do this, and that the knife was the murder weapon. However, in actuality, no murder may have occurred.

Identify the nature of the link (p. 108)

Passage 7.4

A   The reasons support the conclusion through causal links: children eat sugar; sugar decays teeth; the children's teeth decay.

Passage 7.5

B   The conclusion requires the assumption that students are more likely to be found plagiarising if they work electronically. It assumes that there is something about working electronically which enables this to occur, such as, for example, specialist software, to identify students who copy items found on the internet.

Passage 7.6

C   There may appear to be a link between being a great scientist and having long hair but this would be easy to disprove: all that would be needed would be examples of great scientists with short hair, of which there are many. The argument is illogical as it assumes that long hair is a constant, whereas hair can vary in length over relatively short times. To prove the case, the author would have to establish a link between a decrease in scientific ability when hair was cut, and an increase when it grew back.

Passage 7.7

B   The conclusion requires the assumption that increases in footballers' wages are paid for primarily by match tickets rather than any other means that clubs have for raising money, such as selling players, advertising, prize money and television payments.

Passage 7.8

B   The conclusion requires the assumption that fast food outlets use ice cream containers that hedgehogs can break into. If not, the conclusion would not be supported. It also assumes that nothing or nobody else could have created the wastage except for the hedgehogs, and that there were hedgehogs in the area.

Passage 7.9

A   The reasons support the conclusion through causal links: Dubai provides opportunities for jobs and houses to foreign nationals; foreign nationals have settled; the population is rising.

False analogies (p. 113)

Passage 7.10

This compares the earth's atmosphere to a blanket. In this case, the comparison is valid as both are thin coverings that provide protection and warmth.

Passage 7.11

This passage compares a small political party to the biblical character David, and larger political parties to his opponent, Goliath. David was successful against an apparently greater opponent so the comparison is an effective one in arguing that the new party has a chance of success. The validity of the comparison would be demonstrated at the elections if the smaller party did better than the bigger parties.

Passage 7.12

This compares the premises of an argument to the foundations of a building. This comparison is valid as both provide an underlying structure for what is added later. In both cases, if the basis is not solid, later additions may be unstable.

Passage 7.13

This compares emotions to a pressure cooker. This comparison is made in order to argue that emotions cannot be controlled. However, the comparison isn't valid as it isn't comparing like with like: human emotions are not like steam under pressure. The underlying argument is based on false premises: that emotions cannot be controlled and that pressure cookers inevitably explode at boiling point. However, there are methods for managing emotions. An explosion isn't inevitable, either, when the contents of a pressure cooker reach boiling point, as there are control mechanisms to let out the steam. The comparison does not help us to understand why the defendant couldn't control his emotions.

Passage 7.14

This compares failures in the stock market to health and safety matters for the human body. The passage is based on the assumption that it is reasonable to expect compensation for accidents and ill-health, but, in reality, that varies depending on circumstances such as the country and insurance polices. The author is attempting to make the argument for financial compensation seem more plausible by comparing financial loss to other major events for which compensation seems reasonable. The comparison is not valid because:

- Ill-health and accidents do not automatically bring compensation.
- Even if compensation for major health issues was automatic, the comparison still would not be valid. Health and finance are not comparable in terms of the kinds of choices people have, their control over the risks, and the advance action they can take to avert the consequences.

Answers: Necessary and sufficient conditions (p. 111)

	Proposition	Necessary?	Sufficient?
Ex.	*Example: Birds have wings. The item has wings. Therefore it is a bird.*	*Yes. Wings are a necessary condition for the item being a bird*	*No. The reasons given to support the argument that the item is a bird are not sufficient to satisfy the definition of a bird. This would include 'usually flies', is animate, lays eggs, has two legs, has feathers. The information given is not sufficient to rule out an aeroplane or a toy.*
1	The report makes reference to branches. It must be about a tree.	No. It is not a necessary condition: a report could be about a tree without referring to branches.	No. The reasons given to support the argument that the report is about a tree are not sufficient to prove the case. The report could be referring to branches of an organisation such as a bank.
2	The boxer doesn't eat meat or fish. He does eat dairy products and vegetables. The boxer is a vegetarian.	Yes. It is a necessary condition of being a vegetarian that you don't eat meat or fish but do eat vegetables.	Yes. The reasons given for identifying the boxer as a vegetarian are sufficient to satisfy the definition of a vegetarian.

	Proposition	Necessary?	Sufficient?
3	Amir is under the age of 20. Teenagers are less than 20 years old. Amir must be a teenager.	Yes. Being less than 20 is a necessary condition of being a teenager.	No. The reasons given to support the argument that Amir is a teenager are not sufficient to meet the definition of a teenager. Amir must also be over the age of 12 to qualify as a teenager.
4	Claire does not play any musical instrument. Therefore, she is not a musician.	No. Playing an instrument is not a necessary condition of being a musician. A composer or conductor might not play an instrument.	No. The reason given to support the argument that Claire is not a musician is not sufficient to prove the case. We would need to know other information such as that Claire was not a composer or a conductor and did not meet any other definition of 'musician'.
5	The bishop arrived on a vehicle with two wheels, one in front of the other. The bishop must have been on a bicycle.	Yes. It is necessary that the vehicle had two wheels, one in front of the other, in order for the bishop to have arrived on a bicycle.	No. The details given about the vehicle are not sufficient to establish that it was a bicycle. Therefore, the details do not support the conclusion that the bishop arrived on a bicycle. It might have been a scooter or motorbike.
6	A television usually costs more than a radio. This one costs less than a radio, so it must be a bargain.	No. It isn't always a necessary condition for a television to cost less than a radio for it to be a bargain.	No. We do not know whether the radio is priced at its normal rate. If the radio is more expensive than usual, then the TV could also be more expensive and still cost less than the radio. For the television to be a bargain, we would need to know that there was not a reason for the lower price, such as it being damaged in some way.
7	Li Yeung had the benefit of an exceptionally happy childhood. She must be a very happy adult.	No. Having an exceptionally happy childhood is not a necessary condition of being a happy adult. A person could have had a miserable childhood but their circumstances might change in later life.	No. Even an exceptionally happy childhood is not a sufficient condition for being a happy adult: many events may have intervened to make a person's circumstances unhappy.

Chapter 8

Where's the proof?
Finding and evaluating sources of evidence

Learning outcomes

This chapter gives you opportunities to:

- recognise the difference between primary and secondary sources
- understand what is meant by a literature search
- understand concepts such as authenticity, validity, currency, reliability, relevance, probability, and controlling for variables, as applied to research evidence
- identify ways of evaluating samples used in research projects
- recognise potential weaknesses in oral testimony

Introduction

We do not always need to be an expert in a subject to evaluate an argument. In many instances, we will still be able to evaluate whether the reasons support the conclusion and whether the line of reasoning is ordered in a logical way.

However, in order to evaluate many arguments, we have to know whether the evidence used to support the reasoning is true. This means that we need to go to other sources, either people or material resources, to check the facts that underlie the reasons given.

Evidence may be convincing in one context, such as in everyday conversation or a magazine, but not in others, such as in a court of law or for academic or professional writing. In the latter cases, it is expected that greater efforts are made to check that evidence is all that it appears to be.

Wait! Haven't you heard? Research by mouse.com indicates that 90% of cats find goldfish tastier than mice.

Primary and secondary source materials

Most types of evidence can be divided into one of two categories:

- primary sources: the 'raw material' for the subject, such as data and documents;
- secondary sources: materials such as books and articles based on, or written about, primary sources.

Primary source materials

Primary source materials are those that originate from the time and place of the events being investigated. Primary sources can include:

- contemporary letters, documents, prints, painting and photographs;
- newspapers, books and materials published at that time;
- TV, film and video footage from the time;
- recordings of radio broadcasts;
- remaining body parts, sources of DNA, finger prints and footprints;
- artefacts such as tools, pottery, furniture;
- testimonies of witnesses;
- the raw data from experiments;
- autobiographies;
- material on the internet if the internet or materials on it are the focus of the study;
- individual responses to surveys and questionnaires.

Secondary sources

Secondary sources are any materials written or produced about the event, usually some time later. These include:

- books, articles, web pages, documentaries about an event, person or item;
- interviews with people reporting what they heard from witnesses;
- biographies;
- articles in magazines;
- papers and reports using the results of surveys, questionnaires and experiments.

Crossing between categories

Whether something is a primary source depends on how far it was part of the events at the time. Secondary sources in one circumstance may be primary sources in another. For example, a biography is normally a secondary source, but may reproduce copies of original letters that are primary sources. The biography of a prime minister is a secondary source of information about the political leader but could be a primary source about the life of the author. Magazine articles written in the 1950s were secondary sources when published, but are primary sources for present-day research into life in the 1950s.

Activity: primary sources

What are the main primary sources for your subject?

Searching for evidence

Critical thinking generally requires an active approach to seeking out the most relevant evidence to support your own arguments, and to checking the evidence used by other people.

Checking other people's evidence

When you are reading, or watching a programme, or listening to a lecture, you may encounter a line of argument that is so interesting or relevant that you want to discover more. Alternatively, you may consider that the evidence cited does not sound very credible and you may want to check it for yourself. The higher the level of study or research, the more important it is to check the key evidence, especially if there is any doubt about its being reported accurately.

Use the references

When reading articles and books, you will see a short-hand reference in the text such as '(Gilligan, 1977)' and a more detailed list of references at the end of the text. These references provide the details you need in order to find that source for yourself.

Good references enable any reader who wishes to do so, to check whether:

- the source material really does exist;
- the author represented the source material in an accurate way, and the source really says or contains what the author claimed;
- the source contains any additional information that readers can use for their own projects.

When critically evaluating an argument, don't be afraid to go back to some of the sources and check whether these stand up to scrutiny. Often, it is not possible to form a judgement about an argument until you have more information about the subject.

Evidence for your own arguments

When looking for evidence to support your own arguments, the first questions you are likely to ask are:

- Has anything been written about this already?
- Where can I find that information?
- Which are the most relevant and authoritative sources for this subject?

For everyday purposes

If you need information for casual purposes, such as for a personal project or for contributing to a debate, you may need only to do one or two of the following:

- browse an introductory chapter of a book;
- use a search engine such as *Google* for information about the subject;
- read recent newspapers, or read papers on the internet, using a source such as *guardian.unlimited*;
- ask an expert in the area, such as a librarian;
- visit the web-site of relevant bodies, such as campaign groups, charitable bodies, or government sites.

For academic and professional purposes

If you are looking for material as background for a professional report or for academic work, you will need to conduct a 'literature search'. The rest of this chapter focuses on finding and critically evaluating potential sources of evidence.

Literature searches

A literature search gives you an overview of previous research on the subject. Usually, the larger the project, the more extensive the search. For smaller projects, or where there are word restrictions for the report or essay, careful selection is especially important.

Doing a literature search means:

- finding out what has been written on the subject (secondary sources);
- collating a list of the sources that are potentially relevant for your subject;
- paring down the list, selecting sources for initial investigation to check for relevance;
- browsing selected items to help you select the most useful sources;
- selecting the most relevant sources for more detailed investigation.

On-line literature searches

Many reputable sources are now available on line. If you know the names of journals, government papers or other relevant authoritative sources, enter these as part of your search. Otherwise, enter several key words to help pin-point exactly what you want. Your search will be more effective if you use a relevant search engine. If you are at university, your tutors are likely to recommend the most useful web-sites and search engines. Some useful starting places are given in the Appendix on p. 277.

Using abstracts

Browsing the abstracts of journal articles is a particularly useful way of gaining a sense of all the recent research in the field. The abstract summarises the main argument, research methods, findings and conclusions, which helps you decide whether the article is worth reading in depth. Note, especially, the section which summarises the background literature for that report. This can indicate important leads for your own project.

Deciding whether to use a secondary source

Examine secondary sources critically to decide whether, for your purposes, they are likely to be sufficiently:

- well researched
- trustworthy
- recent
- relevant.

This is especially important if you are considering purchasing books or borrowing them from a library, as it helps you to avoid unnecessary costs and time delays.

Basic questioning of the evidence

Critical thinking is a questioning process. When evaluating evidence, ask such questions as:

- How do we know this is true?
- How reliable is this source?
- Are the examples given truly representative of the whole area?
- Does this match what I already know?
- Does this contradict other evidence?
- What motive might this person have for saying this?
- What are we not being told?
- Are any other explanations possible?
- Do the reasons support the conclusion?
- Is the author's line of reasoning well substantiated by the evidence?

Reputable sources

For academic study and for professional life, evidence is roughly divided into 'reputable sources' (or 'authorities') and then everything else. A reputable source is basically one that:

- has credibility: it can be believed with a high degree of certainty;
- is likely to give accurate information;
- is based on research, first-hand knowledge or expertise;
- is recognised in the field or academic discipline as an authority.

Journal articles

Articles in journals are usually regarded as the most reputable sources as, in order to be published, they have to be reviewed and selected by other leading academics. This is known as 'review by peers'. There is a great deal of competition to get published in leading journals, so articles that succeed in passing such a peer review are generally well regarded.

Subject differences

A reputable source for one subject may not be a reputable source in another field of study. Each academic discipline has its own conventions. For some subjects, such as in science, law, medicine, and accountancy, 'hard' data such as facts and figures are generally regarded as superior forms of evidence. On the other hand, in subjects such as art, music and psychotherapy, qualitative evidence can be regarded as more important: 'feeling the subject' may be more valuable than 'number-crunching'. However, this is not a hard and fast rule, and it can depend on the nature of the subject being studied and the evidence that is available.

Questions to consider

When deciding whether a text is worth reading, consider:

- Has it been recommended by a source you trust, such as your tutor or a reputable journal or a review in a quality newspaper?
- Is there a clear line of reasoning, with supporting evidence?
- Does it include a detailed list of references, or a bibliography, indicating thorough research?
- Does it provide clear references to its sources of information, so that other people could check these? If not, this may not be a suitable text for use in academic contexts.
- Does it use source materials that look reputable, such as journals and relevant books, rather than the popular press?

Using recognised 'authorities'

Older sources, especially those regarded as authorities, may have made a significant contribution to the area of study. It is important then to check:

- exactly how the source contributed to knowledge in the field – don't dismiss something just because it sounds old;
- which parts of the original arguments and evidence are still applicable, and which are not;
- how later research used the source as a stepping stone to further findings – and in what ways the original ideas have been refined or superseded;
- more recent authorities, to see whether the source is still exerting an influence on research.

Authenticity and validity

Authentic evidence

Authentic evidence is of undisputed origin. This means that it can be proved that it is what it is claimed to be, or that it really was written or produced by the persons claimed. It isn't always possible to check for authenticity when hearing or reading an argument, but it is possible to maintain an open mind about whether the evidence is likely to be authentic.

Activity: authenticity

Consider whether each of the following references is likely to be authentic or inauthentic.

1   A medieval illuminated manuscript found in the stacks of a cathedral library.

2   A medieval illuminated manuscript that turns up in a local second-hand bookshop.

3   A collection of 1000 autographs of Elvis Presley being sold over the internet.

4   An unpublished diary written by Shakespeare, in the possession of a second year student.

5   Letters written by Napoleon Buonaparte, dated 1809, contained in a large collection of French Revolution memorabilia.

6   A set of 5 previously unknown Van Gogh paintings discovered in a garage on a housing estate.

7   Decaying remnants of a Viking ship found in recently drained marshland.

8   Letters and art-work written by prisoners in the nineteenth century, in the care of a prison governor.

The answers are on p. 146. ▶

Validity

Valid evidence meets the requirements agreed, or the conventions that are usually followed, for the circumstances. What is valid will vary depending on the circumstances. Evidence may not be valid if, for example, it is not authentic, if it is incomplete or if it isn't based on sound reasoning.

Examples

(1)   A defendant confessed to a crime but the confession wasn't considered valid because it became evident that the defendant had been forced to make it. Legal requirements would not regard a confession exacted under duress as valid evidence of committing a crime.

(2)   To gain a particular qualification, students were required to write eight essays as their own work. Although one student handed in eight essays on relevant subjects, the examiners found that three were too similar to essays available on the internet. These were not accepted as valid evidence of the student's own work, so the requirements of the qualification were not met.

(3)   An athlete argued that she was the fastest runner in the world. Although she had reliable evidence of her running times, these were not considered valid evidence that she was the fastest runner, as they were gained in unusually favourable wind conditions.

(4)   A report claimed that people who smoke are more likely to drink alcohol. The evidence wasn't considered valid as all the participants who smoked were selected in places that sold alcoholic drinks, whereas non-smokers were selected in the street. This meant that the selection of participants was already weighted in favour of the smokers being more likely to drink alcohol. This doesn't meet agreed research conventions, which aim to avoid weighting the evidence.

Currency and reliability

Currency

If a source is described as 'having currency', this means it is still relevant *in the present*. This may be because:

- it was published recently;
- it was updated recently;
- it has been produced in a new edition that takes account of the latest research;
- the material covered is relatively stable and unchanging over time, so that it remains relevant for a long time. Examples of this would be anatomy, biographies, or descriptions of how machinery used to work in the past.

It is always worth checking whether a source is still up to date: new research can appear on any topic at any time.

'Currency' is a term that is applied to secondary sources. Primary sources are contemporary to an event, so may be relevant or not relevant to a topic, but questions of currency are not usually appropriate.

Seminal works

Seminal works are those that are so original or far-reaching in their findings that they continue to exert an influence for a long time. A seminal work could be a text, a film, music, art, architecture or commercial design, or any other item that had a strong impact on the thinking and research in a discipline over time. It helps our understanding of our subject discipline if we have first-hand experience of the seminal works that influenced its research base and theoretical perspectives. We are in a better position to recognise the theoretical perspective informing other research, and to recognise the influence of those works in later works.

Reliability

Evidence is reliable if it can be trusted. This may be because the source of the evidence is:

- someone you know to be trustworthy;
- a recognised expert;
- a person with no vested interest in the outcome;
- a reputable source (see p. 129).

Reliability also refers to whether the evidence is stable over time, so that it can be used to make reasonably secure predictions. In other words, if you have evidence that something worked once, is this sufficient to show that it will work next time?

Example

Climatic conditions are relatively stable for large areas and time-periods and can be used to predict general trends in temperature or rainfall. On the basis of evidence of climatic change, we can predict that the Sahara region is likely to remain hot and dry for many years. Weather, on the other hand, changes quickly, and is less reliable for making predictions. It will rain in the Sahara, but it is hard to predict when or how much rain will fall.

Replication

In scientific writing, you may see references to the results being 'replicated' or 'not replicated'. This means that the results of a survey or experiment were re-tested to see whether they held true. If they didn't, the original outcome might simply have been the result of chance.

It is useful to know whether research was repeated and the findings replicated. If the outcomes were similar, this increases the probability that the findings are reliable.

Activity

Which works are considered seminal for your area of research or the subjects you are studying this year?

Selecting the best evidence

A summary of your background reading, or reasoning based on secondary sources, is normally required as an early section in a report and for dissertations and doctoral theses.

Which sources should I refer to?

It is usually the case that there is a great deal to say about the source materials, but there are word restrictions that limit what can be said. This means you need to consider very carefully the sources to which you will refer.

Be selective

- Include sources regarded as the leading authorities on the issue.
- Refer in brief to any other sources. Select evidence that demonstrates the main pathway, or set of stepping stones, leading up to your own project.

Sources contributing to your argument

The main source materials to which you refer should be those that contribute most to supporting your own line of reasoning. There may be one or two seminal works that you refer to in some detail, a small selection of key works that you cover at some length, and several others that you refer to in passing. It is important, when writing academic reports, to show you can discriminate appropriately between the most relevant sources and those of peripheral importance.

Passing references

References to other research add weight to your own reasoning. A passing reference may be a major study in its own right, but contribute only background detail to your own argument. Usually, you would use a passing reference to support a step in your line of reasoning or to substantiate a minor point in your argument. You do this by either:

- writing a sentence summarising the research findings and naming the source and date; or
- writing your point and then adding a reference in brackets.

Examples

Miles (1988) argues that British Sign Language is a language in its own right.

Sign languages are also languages with their own traditions (Lane, 1984; Miles, 1988).

What should I say about sources?

Most writing tasks have word restrictions. You will usually need to allocate most of your word allowance to critical evaluation of the argument and your sources of evidence, and very few words, if any, to describing them. If you are uncertain of the difference between descriptive and analytical writing, see pp. 54–60.

When selecting sources, ask:

- Did this contribute a major theoretical perspective to the discipline?
- Has this changed thinking in the subject, or made a significant contribution to the questions debated in the discipline?
- Does this provide a contribution to the path of research evidence that leads up to my own project? If so, how? Is this a direct or an indirect link? Is it a key contribution that needs to be discussed or a lesser contribution requiring a passing reference?
- Does this source challenge what was said before or provide an alternative way of thinking about the issue?
- Does it use research methods that are novel or that I could use for my project?

Relevant and irrelevant evidence

Relevance and irrelevance

Relevant evidence is that which is necessary to give a good understanding of the issues. An author can provide evidence that:

(1) supports the conclusion;
(2) is relevant to the subject, but which may not be relevant to the conclusion: in this case, the evidence might even contradict the conclusion;
(3) is relevant neither to the conclusion nor to the subject.

People need to improve their understanding of how language works so that they can use it more effectively. Research studies (Bloggs, 2003; Bloggs, 2006) show that the study of a foreign language improves our understanding of the structure of language, providing a way of comparing different language structures. Therefore, people who only speak one language should be encouraged to study a second language.

Here, the research evidence about the benefits of studying a foreign language is relevant to the conclusion that people who speak only one language should be encouraged to study a second language.

Example 2

People need to improve their understanding of how language works so that they can use it more effectively. Research studies (Bloggs, 2003; Bloggs, 2006) show that many people cannot describe the different components of their own language. A surprising number of people have difficulties remembering the rules even of their mother tongue. Therefore, people who only speak one language should be encouraged to study a second language.

Here the evidence that people have difficulties in their own language could be interpreted to suggest that people who have difficulties with one language should not be encouraged to learn a second. The evidence is relevant to the debate, but does not support the argument. Further information would be needed to support the conclusion.

Example 3

People need to improve their understanding of how language works so that they can use it more effectively. Research studies (Bloggs, 2003; Bloggs, 2006) show people can recognise concepts in a foreign language even when there is no word for that concept in their mother tongue. Therefore, people who only speak one language should be encouraged to study a second language.

Here, the evidence about recognising concepts in a foreign language is loosely related to the topic about languages. However, it has a completely different focus. It has no apparent relevance to the debate about using language effectively or the conclusion that people should learn a second language in order to use language more effectively.

Relevance to the conclusion

In considering whether evidence is relevant, your main focus should be on whether the conclusion would be different if that evidence (or reason) was different or not available?

Check

When evaluating an argument, check:
- Is the evidence relevant to the topic?
- Is it needed to substantiate the reasoning?
- Does it make a difference to the conclusion?
- If so, does it support it or contradict it?
- Is the evidence needed to substantiate interim conclusions?

Activity: Relevant and irrelevant evidence

Activity

For each of the following passages, identify whether the evidence and reasons are relevant to the conclusion. Then read the Commentary opposite.

Passage 8.1

Ice Age

Winters are getting colder. Opinion polls show that most people think there is a new Ice Age on the way. Therefore, we need to take measures to ensure that fuel resources are managed so that nobody is left to suffer from extreme cold during forthcoming winters.

Passage 8.2

Mr Charlton was given information, in confidence, that the price of shares in MKP2 Oils would rise suddenly if news of the new promotion reached the press before the share price was adjusted. Mr Charlton bought 50,000 shares in MKP2 Oils and leaked news of the promotion to the press. As a result, he made ten million pounds personal profit. We can conclude that Mr Charlton abused the trust of the company and cheated it financially.

Passage 8.3

Major catastrophes, rather than gradual evolution, may be the main cause of change. Such a view did not seem plausible in the past as it was assumed that the process of geological change took place in a gradual way, just as it appears to today. However, evidence now suggests that change can be rapid and extreme. Geological evidence indicates that an enormous meteor collided with the earth several hundred million years ago, making most life-forms extinct. Geological science now attracts more funding than it did in the past. Archaeological evidence suggests that sudden changes in the environment brought about the rapid collapse of ancient civilisations.

Commentary

For Passage 8.1, the first reason, that winters are getting colder, is relevant to the conclusion about managing fuel resources. However, no evidence is given to substantiate this reason. The evidence from polls shows opinions, not facts, and this does not support the conclusion. An opinion is still only an opinion, even if held by a lot of people. The validity of an argument or of evidence does not normally rest on a majority decision.

For Passage 8.2, all of the evidence given is relevant to the subject and to the conclusion that Mr Charlton abused the trust of the company and cheated it financially. He betrayed a secret to the press so that he could make money at the company's expense.

In Passage 8.3, the conclusion is that major catastrophes, rather than gradual evolution, may be the main cause of change. The relevant pieces of evidence given to support this are:

- Geological evidence about the effects of a meteor collision in making life-forms extinct.
- Archaeological evidence about the effects of sudden environmental change leading to the fall of ancient civilisations.

The section about the plausibility of this view in the past is useful background information, but does not provide evidence to support the conclusion. Information about funding for geological science is not relevant to the conclusion.

My horoscope's predicting a bad day . . .

Representative samples

Most research topics cannot be tested using very large numbers of people or circumstances. This would usually be too expensive, time-consuming, complicated to organise and unnecessary. Instead, surveys and research projects rely on selected samples. A representative sample is one which gives due consideration to the potential variety of relevant groups and circumstances.

Example

Four animal charities wished to know the views of the public on whether pets taken overseas should be held in quarantine before being allowed to re-enter the country. Each one selected the sample in a different way.

Sample 1
Charity 1 chose 1000 dog-owners from across the nation. The survey was balanced to ensure that roughly equal numbers were interviewed in every part of the country.

Sample 2
Charity 2 chose 1000 dog-owners from across the nation. The survey was balanced to ensure that more people were included in the survey in parts of the country which had large populations, and fewer representatives were questioned if the population was low.

Sample 3
Charity 3 chose 1000 pet-owners from across the nation. The sample was chosen to ensure that a broad range of pet-owners were included, including owners of snakes, budgies and tropical spiders.

Sample 4
Charity 4 chose 1000 people, representing a variety of pet-owners and people who do not own pets. The sample was selected from every county, weighted to include more people from heavily populated areas.

Differing principles of sample selection

Each of these samples selected participants according to a different principle. Sample 1 ensures that all geographical areas are represented equally, whereas sample 2 is more concerned that the sample is representative of population size. Sample 3 aims to ensure that different kinds of pet-owners are represented, whereas sample 4 is representative of both pet-owners and non-pet-owners.

Depending on the aim of the research, any of these methods of selection may be appropriate. For example, if it were known that 99 per cent of pets affected by quarantine were dogs, and that people from poorly populated rural areas were particularly affected, then the approach in sample 1 would be the most appropriate choice. Otherwise, a weighting according to population size is preferable.

If a wide variety of pets were subject to quarantine, then the approaches taken in samples 3 and 4 would be more representative of those affected. Samples 1–3 assume that people without pets do not need to be consulted, whereas sample 4 is more representative of the population in general. Sample 4 is more typical of the kinds of sample you will see in research projects and in articles. Usually, samples need to be representative of several different perspectives.

Check

When reading the 'Methods' section of research papers, articles and reports, check whether the most appropriate sampling method was used. If a group was not represented in the sample, then the findings may not be applicable to it.

Activity: Representative samples

Passage 8.4

The experiment aimed to prove that eating carrots improves night vision in people under the age of 45, excluding children below school age. The sample consisted of 1000 people; 789 were women and the rest were men. For each sex, 25 per cent of participants were from the different age groups, 6–15 years, 16–25 years, 26–35 years and 36–45. Participants ate three capsules of carrot extract every day for ten weeks.

Passage 8.5

The survey set out to discover whether consumers preferred soap perfumed with almond essence or soap perfumed with aloe vera. The sample consisted of 1000 people. Of these, 503 were women and 497 were men; 50% of the sample were aged between 25 and 40, and the rest were aged between 41 and 55.

Passage 8.6

The research project tested the hypothesis that people who receive six sessions of counselling following a bereavement are less likely to take time away from work in the following twelve months than people who do not receive counselling. The sample consisted of 226 participants, in two groups that were matched for age, sex and ethnicity. Group 1 consisted of the 37 participants who opted to receive six sessions of counselling. Group 2 consisted of those who opted not to have counselling.

Commentary

The sample in Passage 8.4 is representative of the age group it set out to test, as it has taken care to ensure a good age distribution. It is not representative in terms of gender, as it includes far more women participants than men. It does not appear to be representative of people with different kinds of eye-sight, which would be important for this experiment.

In Passage 8.5, the sample is representative in terms of gender. Although the numbers of men and women are not exactly the same, the difference is small and not likely to be significant. The sample is not representative in terms of age. The survey does not state that the intention is to discover the preferences of people of a particular age range. It is not representative of people aged under 25 years or over 55 years. It is not clear whether the sample represented people from different economic, social, racial or geographical backgrounds.

In Passage 8.6, the two groups were 'matched' for age, sex and ethnicity. This means the sample was chosen so that a similar proportion of each of the two groups were men and women, from similar age groups and backgrounds. That is useful for ensuring the findings are not the result of differences in the composition of the groups. However, we do not know whether the samples were representative in terms of age, sex or ethnicity. For example, each group might consist entirely of white women aged 25–30. No details are given about whether the sample is representative in any other way, such as by type of job, geographical area or relationship with the deceased person. Most importantly, as only a small number of people received counselling, this is not a balanced sample.

Certainty and probability

Certainty

Arguments cannot always be proved with 100 per cent certainty. Chapter 7 looked at how necessary and sufficient conditions may need to be met in order to prove a conclusion. In many circumstances, it is difficult to prove that sufficient conditions have been met, as there are so many exceptions to the rule.

Reducing uncertainty

Uncertainty is not very satisfying and does not help in decision-making. Academics aim to reduce uncertainty in a number of ways, including:

- selecting reputable sources, which are more likely to be credible;
- critically analysing the evidence, looking for the kinds of flaws outlined in previous chapters;
- calculating the level of probability;
- increasing the level of probability as far as they can.

Probability

When evaluating an argument, the audience needs to decide on a general level of probability. This means deciding whether the evidence is likely to be credible and authentic and, if so, whether the conclusions are likely to follow from the line of reasoning and its supporting evidence. Any conclusion may lie on a spectrum from impossible, to possible, to probable, through to certain. As Chapter 10 shows, academic writing is reluctant to express certainty, even when it has taken significant steps to ensure a highly probable finding.

Probability spectrum

Impossible — possible — probable — certain

Calculating the level of probability

The level of probability is related to the likelihood that something occurred because of the reasons given, compared with how far the outcome could have occurred by chance. If you throw a coin a hundred times so that it lands flat, there are only two options for the way it can fall, heads or tails. The probability is that the coin will land on heads about 50 times and tails about 50 times. This outcome is not certain, but it shouldn't surprise us if it occurs.

To win the lottery, the chances are much less probable. If there are 14 million options for the winning set of numbers, and you have only one set of numbers, the chances of your set being selected are one in 14 million.

Statistical formulae or specialist software can be used to calculate how likely it is that a particular outcome occurred by chance or coincidence. This can be expressed as 'The probability of this happening by chance is . . .'

- less than one in 10
- less than one in a 100
- less than one in a 1000.

Expressing levels of probability

You are likely to see probability expressed as:

$p = <0.1$ (less than a 1 in 10 chance that the outcome could have occurred by chance)
$p = <0.01$ (less than a 1 in 100 chance)
$p = <0.001$ (less than a 1 in 1000 chance)
$p = <0.0001$ (less than a 1 in 10,000 chance).

The words 'The probability of this happening by chance' are abbreviated to 'p ='.
The words 'less than' are abbreviated to <.
The numbers are usually expressed as decimals smaller than the number 1.

Sample sizes and statistical significance

Sample size

The larger the sample size, the greater the degree of probability. The smaller the sample size, the more likely it is that the outcome could have occurred by chance. The appropriate size of sample varies.

An appropriate sample size depends on:

- how essential it is to reduce the element of coincidence;
- whether it is a question of health and safety: a very small sample may suffice to prompt action;
- how necessary it is to be representative of many ages, backgrounds and circumstances;
- the funding available;
- how likely it is that a smaller sample will give reliable results.

Example

Clinical trials on a thousand volunteers indicate a success rate of over 95 per cent. Most patients made a complete recovery and, so far, few side effects have been identified. These trials offer hope of pain relief to a significant proportion of current patients.

Here, a thousand may seem like a significant number of people. However, that sample is unlikely to be representative of all those who may take the drug in future and of the circumstances which would ensure the drug was safe for them. If you needed to take the drug, you would be more reassured if you knew it had been tested on people who share similar circumstances to yourself, such as your blood group, age group, ethnic group, and people with similar allergies or medical conditions.

A study of heart attacks reported in *The Times* (31 August 2004) involved 29,000 participants in 52 countries over ten years. Other medical surveys may be much smaller. Opinion polls are usually based on surveys of about 1000 people.

Statistical significance

When there are very small samples, such as surveys which include fewer than 16 people in each category, it is hard to say that the outcome wasn't just a coincidence. When the sample is small, or the differences between groups are small, we say that these are 'not statistically significant'.

Look for

When evaluating evidence, look out for expressions such as: 'the results are significant at $p = <0.0001$ (see p. 137 above). This shows the level of statistical significance: a one in 10,000 chance. The more zeros after the decimal point, the more reliable the finding and the less likely it is that the result occurred as a coincidence.

If, on the other hand, you see an expression such as 'the results were not statistically significant', this means that the results, or the differences between two things, may just be a coincidence.

Small samples

A small sample may be necessary:

- when surveying people who are unusual in some way, such as people who are exceptionally successful or with rare medical or neurological conditions;
- if it is dangerous to gain larger samples, such as when working at depth under the ocean, travelling into space, exposed to chemicals, or living with extreme sleep deprivation;
- in unusual circumstances, such as large numbers of multiple births.

Over-generalisation

Generalisations are useful as they help us to see patterns and to make judgements more quickly when this is needed. However, a generalisation should be well-founded, based on a reasonable sample.

An over-generalisation is one based on too small a sample to justify the generalisation.

Example

My first child slept through the night but the second one was a very poor sleeper. First-born children are better at getting to sleep than their younger brothers and sisters.

Here, the generalisation about first-born children is made on the basis of only two children. This is a database of two, which is a very small sample. If thousands of other first-born and second-born children showed the same sleeping pattern, then the generalisation might be valid. However, when only two children are involved, there is a large element of chance. The family next door might find that both their children sleep well.

Generalising from a single case

Generalising from a single case means forming a general conclusion on the basis of one instance. This is rarely acceptable.

Example

Some people say that calling people names because of the way they look is offensive. My friend is very overweight and people call him names for being fat. He says he doesn't mind as he finds horrible things to call back. This shows there is no harm in calling people names as they can just retaliate if they want to.

Just because one person appears not to mind offensive language, this does not mean that all other people will react in the same way.

An exception can disprove a rule

However, some generalisations can be made on the basis of a single instance, and be accurate. This is true, for example, when a general rule is already in existence, such as that objects, when dropped, will fall towards the ground. A single case that contradicts that rule would show that the generalisation wasn't universally true: for example, a helium balloon would rise. In such cases, the rule then has to be reconsidered and refined to account for the exception. Much of science and law has progressed by refinements to rules so that they are more accurate about the exact circumstances in which they apply.

Example

Clinical trials showed the drug to be very successful. However, this patient had a severe allergic reaction to the new drug. This means that doctors need to be aware that some people may react negatively to the drug.

Here, a single example is sufficient to necessitate a carefully worded generalisation. Over time, as more exceptions emerge, the generalisation will change to become more precise and accurate.

Example

This drug can create a severe allergic reaction in asthma sufferers and people taking the drug BXR2.

These examples illustrate that a small sample, even a single example, can disprove a theory based on a much larger sample. A single example can disprove a theory or rule. When this happens, the rule or theory has to be re-examined and reformulated to take account of the exception. However, it is also important to bear in mind that a generalisation means 'most of the time' and may be useful in helping to understand a situation despite the exceptions.

Controlling for variables

What are 'variables'?

'Variables' are all those circumstances that might affect the outcome in intended or unintended ways. When evaluating evidence, it is useful to consider whether the author has taken steps to identify potential unintended variables and to prevent them affecting the outcome of the research.

Example

During trials in South Africa, the yield of grapes on a new vine was twice the usual level for red grapes. The yield produced twice the volume of wine. Cuttings of the vine were transported to California to an area with similar soil and rainfall. However, the vine didn't produce the same yields in California.

In this case, the producers controlled for some variables such as soil and rainfall, but these were not enough. In order to find out why the vine yielded more in one area than the other, the producers would need to grow it under controlled conditions, changing just one aspect of the conditions each time, until they isolated the special conditions that doubled the yield. Such variables might include:

- the total hours of daylight available;
- minerals and trace elements in the soil that had been overlooked;
- when the rainfall occurs during the growing process;
- the slope of the land;
- other plants growing nearby and their effect on insects and pests.

When you read research reports or journal articles, check what steps were taken to control for variables. In an article, this will be found in the section on methods. If the research doesn't take steps to control for variables, then the results may have been attributed to the wrong cause.

Control groups

One way of checking that the results support the conclusion is by using a control group. The control group is treated differently from the experimental group and provides a point of reference or comparison. If an experiment was testing for sleep deprivation, the experimental group might be denied sleep for 60 hours, whereas the control group might be allowed to sleep as usual.

Example

A company claims that its SuperVeg juice reduces the incidence of colds and flu. 100 people drink a bottle of SuperVeg every day for a year, and a control group, also of 100 people, is given flavoured water in a SuperVeg bottle.

The flavoured water is known as a 'placebo'. Participants should not know which group they are in, as that can influence their response: participants might wish either to help the experiment along or to sabotage it.

Activity: Controlling for variables

Look again at passages 8.4–8.6 on page 136. For each example, identify what kinds of control groups or controlled conditions are needed.

The answers are on p. 146. ▶

Facts and opinions

Opinion

An opinion is a belief that is believed to be true, but which is not based on proof or substantial evidence. An opinion may be a personal point of view or held by a large number of people, even if it runs contrary to the evidence.

Opinions

I think the butler murdered his employer.

I don't.

Facts

Facts are basically items of information that can be checked and proved through experience, direct observation, testing or comparison against evidence. However, as knowledge of an area increases, facts can later be disproved. A fact checked against reputable evidence generally carries more weight than personal opinion, but that doesn't mean it is true.

Example

Facts
The coroner stated that the time of death was between 2 a.m. and 4 a.m. in the morning. The body was found at 6.30 a.m. by the cook. The footman reports that there were six people in the house overnight. The butler reports that four other people have keys and could have entered the house and left again before 6.30 a.m.

The facts in the example above are:

- The time of death, as given by the coroner. That is likely to be reliable.

- The time the body was found by the cook; however, somebody else could have found the body earlier and remained silent.
- The footman reported certain information.
- The butler reported certain information.

The details of the reports by the footman and the butler may not be facts: these could be personal opinions, or they may have been lying.

False appeals to the 'facts'

People's opinions can vary about what is a fact and what is an opinion.

Example

The butler was in the house all night. His employer was murdered during the night. The butler says he was a loyal servant but maybe he wasn't. I think he was lying and that he had some sort of vendetta against his employer. The facts say he is the murderer.

In this case, the facts appear to be:

- The butler was in the house all night.
- His employer was murdered during the night.
- The butler says he was a loyal servant.

These do not prove that the butler was either a loyal servant or a murderer: either or even both could be true. However, note that the author states his opinion, that the butler is the murderer, as if it were a fact.

Expert opinion

'Expert opinion' is based on specialist knowledge, usually acquired over time or based on research or direct experience. It is often used in court to help a judge or jury to understand the issues. Experts are often asked for their own judgements. This, in itself, is not taken as 'proof', as even experts can be wrong.

Eye-witness testimony

Eye-witness testimony may be useful in a number of circumstances, such as:

- people who saw or experienced accidents, crime and disasters first-hand;
- people who lived through historic events including the more distant past;
- clients' accounts of experiences and/or services received;
- patients' accounts of their experiences.

Levels of accuracy

Untruth

Personal testimonies can provide invaluable evidence, but they are not always accurate.

Interviewees may not reveal the true case because they:

- may want to be helpful, so say what they think the interviewer wants to hear;
- may not like the interviewer;
- may be trying to protect somebody;
- may not remember anything, but like the attention of being interviewed;
- may have a vested interest in the outcome, so benefit from concealing the truth;
- may be being bullied or intimidated and be scared of speaking out;
- may have promised to keep a secret.

If using interviews to gather evidence, remember that the interviewee may have complex motivations for presenting the picture that they give.

Lack of expertise and insider knowledge

The witness may lack information such as expert knowledge or details of why something was taking place which would enable them to make sense of what they saw. They may have seen a camera crew filming a fight in the street as they passed by one afternoon. However, they would not necessarily know whether they were watching a real fight at which a camera crew happened to attend, or whether the fight was staged deliberately for a TV drama. It may also be the case that the interviewee misunderstood what was asked of them.

The limits of memory

Loftus, in *Eyewitness Testimony* (1979), demonstrated, for legal use, how unreliable the memory can be. In one experiment, participants were shown a film of an accident and some were then asked how fast a white car was travelling when it passed a barn. A week later, 17 per cent of those who had been asked this question reported that they had seen a barn in the film, even though there had been no barn. This compared with only 3 per cent of the other viewers. Common memory mistakes include the following.

- Errors in perception: making mistakes about what you have seen and heard.
- Errors in interpretation: misinterpreting what you have seen.
- Errors of retention: simply forgetting.
- Errors of recall: remembering the event inaccurately. Our memory may be altered by going over the event in our mind, discussing it, hearing other people's accounts, or hearing about similar events.
- Composite memories: our brain can blend aspects from several events into one, without us being aware this is happening.

Corroborating sources

It is usually necessary to find other sources of information that corroborate a witness testimony. This can include other witnesses but may also be, for example:

- official records from the time;
- other witness testimony;
- TV footage of the events;
- newspaper, police, social work or court records;
- photographs taken at the time;
- information about similar events that happened elsewhere but which might throw light on the event being considered.

Triangulation

What is triangulation?

Triangulation means checking and comparing different sets of evidence against each other, to see whether they support and complement each other, or whether they contradict each other. This is especially important when relying on first-hand accounts.

Triangulation is something that most of us tend to do in everyday contexts to check whether something is true.

Example

John told his mother that his sister Mary hit him. John was crying and called Mary a bully.

John may or may not be telling the truth. Before his mother took action, she is likely to have triangulated the evidence by:

- listening to Mary's side of the story;
- looking for evidence that John was hit;
- considering John and Mary's usual ways of recounting events;
- checking for alternative explanations.

Example

A head teacher says that a school's record of achievement is better than ever, that most pupils succeed, and that this is because of improvements in teaching at the school.

This statement could be triangulated with:

- published government records over several years to check for general improvement over time at all schools;
- comparing the school's achievement rates with the average for all schools;
- comparing the school's achievement rates with those of schools of a similar type. For example, if the school was situated in an area of high economic deprivation, it is likely to be more appropriate to compare it with schools in similar areas.

You might also wish to investigate whether there are any other reasons for changes to the school's rates of achievement. For example, if the school had started to set difficult entry tests, this might have attracted a very different type of pupil to the school and excluded those less likely to achieve. The improved achievement rates might be because the pupils were different and not because of improvements in teaching.

Comparing like with like

When triangulating information, it is important to check that the different sources used are also referring to the same subject and interpreting words in the same way. If not, you may not be comparing like with like. For example, the head teacher in the example may be talking about sports achievement, not academic, so this would require triangulation with a different set of sources, such as sports records not government records.

Activity: Triangulation

What kinds of evidence would be needed to triangulate the following sources:

(1) A person at the bus stop mentioning that cheap tickets will be available at the door, on the night, to see a band that you really like?

(2) A report by a car manufacturer that new brakes fitted in their latest model of car were safer than other brakes available?

(3) A chapter in a book that argued that, in the past, there were very severe legal penalties for begging?

Answers on p. 144. ▶

Evaluating a body of evidence

When you are researching a subject, or producing an academic assignment, you are likely to refer to many sources of evidence. However, you are not likely to evaluate all of these in the same way.

You can evaluate some sources

by browsing, to evaluate whether they are sufficiently relevant to your research topic and sufficiently reputable for the level of research;

by focusing on the most relevant items, evaluating how these support specific aspects of your line of reasoning;

by selecting and carefully evaluating a relatively small number of key sources, weighing the arguments, and looking for flaws and gaps in the evidence;

by comparing and contrasting different sources, checking for inconsistencies.

The following activity gives you the opportunity to work with a set of short texts to practise discriminating appropriately between them. These texts are also used as the basis for further activities in Chapters 9 and 11.

Activity : identifying reputable sources

Read through the texts on pp. 233–7.

(a) Identify which are the most reputable sources of evidence. Categorise these as:
  • Very reputable
  • Fairly trustworthy
  • Little authority

(b) For which texts might the authors have a vested interest in the outcome?

(c) Which are the most reliable sources for indicating what internet users believe about copying electronic music?

The answers are given on p. 165. ▶

Answers: Triangulation (p. 143)

(1) You would probably want to contact the venue to find out if there really were cheap tickets available on the night.

(2) This could be triangulated with reports from other manufacturers about how their brakes were tested and the results, as well as reports in trade magazines. There may also be general information in consumer magazines about different braking systems. If you knew anybody who had bought a car with the new brakes, you could ask their opinion. If you can drive, you would want to try out the braking system for yourself.

(3) If the book provides references, you can check the original sources to see if they were reported accurately. You would expect to see references to specific 'poor laws' on begging, and the dates of these. You can also check other books to see if these contradict or support the chapter in the book. However, several books may refer to the same secondary source, which itself might be incorrect. Where possible, it is useful to check the primary sources, or published versions of these, for yourself.

Summary

This chapter has looked at some key concepts in evaluating evidence from the point of view of both conducting your own projects, and examining the evidence used by other people.

If you are conducting your own research, whether for a project, report or essay, you will need to ensure that you collect and select the most appropriate evidence, and subject it to critical scrutiny. This chapter introduced the principles of making a literature search. It looked at ways of whittling down a large number of potential sources of evidence to a manageable number for deeper scrutiny. It also showed how to recognise the difference between primary and secondary sources.

When using secondary sources as evidence to support your own arguments, you need to be able to understand the evidence base used by those sources and have criteria you can use to evaluate it. For example, you need to be alert to whether the evidence is what it is claimed to be, checking that it is authentic, accurate, reliable and up-to-date. You also need to understand its significance in terms of probability and the methods taken to ensure reliable findings. When first starting to analyse materials critically, it can seem as though there are a great many aspects to check. However, many of these, such as selecting reputable sources, become automatic. Others are useful to hold lightly in mind whenever you hear or read an argument. It is often useful, and sometimes necessary, to go back to the original sources or published versions of these, to check for accuracy. If sources are well referenced, this makes the task of checking for details much easier.

The earlier section of the chapter looked at ways of analysing individual sources to check for aspects such as their reliability and validity. Later sections of the chapter looked at using one source to check another. Cross-comparison, or triangulation, is something that many of us do naturally in our everyday lives. However, many people take at face value what they read or hear in one source, without checking how this compares with what other sources say. Comparing materials doesn't necessarily lead to the truth, but it often shows where there are different points of view and therefore room for error and further investigation.

You will find that some of the concepts introduced in this chapter will be more relevant for your subject than others. Each academic subject has well-established research methods that develop specialist skills for analysing source materials. Some will use:

- carbon-dating to check the age of materials;
- knowledge of medieval Latin and allegory in order to read and interpret original documents;
- advanced skills in semiotics in order to interpret the meaning of texts;
- specialist equipment to make precise measurements in your subject or detect micro-organisms;
- statistical approaches and formulae to analyse the kinds of data relevant to your subject.

Such advanced skills are likely to be taught within the subject. However, for most subjects, the basic skills in critical thinking will also apply.

Information on the sources

Lane, H. (1984) *When the Mind Hears: A History of Deaf People and their Language* (Cambridge: Cambridge University Press).

Loftus, E. F. (1979) *Eyewitness Testimony* (Cambridge, MA: Cambridge University Press).

Miles, S. (1988) *British Sign Language: A Beginner's Guide* (London: BBC Books).

Palmer, T. (2004) *Perilous Plant Earth: Catastrophes and Catastrophism through the Ages* (Cambridge: Cambridge University Press).

Answers to activities in Chapter 8

Authenticity (p. 130)

1 Probably authentic, as such documents originated in cathedrals and could have become lost in library stacks over the years. Cathedrals are unlikely to forge a document as this would be exposed and would reflect badly on a religious organisation. However, checks would need to be made to validate the manuscript's age and origins, or *provenance.*

2 Probably not authentic. Such items are rare and usually found in libraries, museums, private collections or religious institutions.

3 A collection of 1000 autographs by Elvis Presley could be authentic but such a collection would be valuable and it is unlikely that it would be bought without a viewing. It is more likely that an authentic collection would be sold at auction.

4 Probably not authentic. It is unlikely, though not impossible, that such an unpublished diary would fall into the possession of a student.

5 Probably authentic: such letters are found in collections in major libraries.

6 Probably not authentic: such valuable pictures are found occasionally in attics of old houses or behind other paintings, but not usually in modern garages and not in such large numbers.

7 Probably authentic: it could be carbon dated to check its age so would be difficult to fake.

8 Probably authentic: such items might well be kept at a prison and the governor could have overall responsibility for their care.

Controlling for variables (p. 140)

Passage 8.4 (p. 136)

The experiment requires a control group to compare changes in night vision between those who ate the capsules of carrot extracts and those who didn't. Some variables that would need to be controlled are: diet, which could affect the results; activities which might tire the eyes; previous levels of vision and visual problems; whether participants already had diets high in carrots, allowing no further room for improvement.

Passage 8.5 (p. 136)

The research should take into account such variables as whether participants liked any kind of perfumed soap at all, and whether the scents were equally strong. If not, then participants might have chosen on the basis of the strength of the perfume rather than its scent.

Passage 8.6 (p. 136)

There are many variables that could affect the research outcomes here. The researchers need to check such details as: how closely related the participants were to the bereaved; the frequency and kind of contact and interaction between the people in the sample and the deceased before the bereavement; whether participants attended the funeral; the kinds of work that participants are involved in; for how much time they were usually absent from work before the bereavement; whether they had any illnesses or other conditions likely to make them miss work. Each group would need to have roughly equal numbers of people from each circumstance. However, it could be that a particular combination of these variables has an effect on time off work and it would be hard to control for that in the first set of research.

Chapter 9

Critical reading and note-making
Critical selection, interpretation and noting of source material

Learning outcomes

This chapter offers you opportunities to:

- develop strategies for reading selectively
- understand the relation of theory to argument
- categorise arguments and theories
- check whether interpretations of texts are accurate
- develop strategies for selective and critical note-making

Introduction

Although critical thinking can be used in any context, it is likely that you will apply it most when using written materials. The material presented in previous chapters is relevant to critical reading. This chapter focuses on applying critical thinking skills when reading for a specific purpose, such as writing a report or assignment. It looks at issues such as:

- identifying theoretical perspectives;
- categorising information to assist with its selective use;
- using a critical approach to note-making when reading.

Critical reading is different from other kinds of reading such as skimming or scanning text. The latter are useful strategies for locating where information is in a text and to develop a general feel for a subject. However, they usually result in a more superficial reading of the material.

Critical reading requires you to focus your attention much more closely on certain parts of a written text, holding other information in mind. As it involves analysis, reflection, evaluation and making judgements, it usually involves slower reading than that used for recreational reading or for gaining general background information. As you develop critical reading skills, these reading skills will become faster and more accurate.

Preparing for critical reading

It is not usually easy to make sense of any information taken out of context. When reading new material, some basic preparation can help you to:

- see how the main argument fits together;
- better remember the overall argument;
- better comprehend specific pieces of information;
- recognise how reasons and evidence contribute to the main argument.

The following sections offer suggestions on actions you can take to orientate yourself to a text, in order to facilitate critical reading.

Books

Preliminary skim

First, skim through the book to get a feel for what it contains. Glancing through as you flick the pages a few times, or scanning each page quickly in turn, can give you an initial impression of what the book is about and where relevant information may be located.

Scan the introduction

Check whether the introduction indicates the author's position or refers to the overall argument. Such information can direct you to the most relevant chapters and help you to make sense of detailed information presented in these.

Scan the final chapter

Look at any conclusions drawn at the end of the book. Check whether the final chapter sums up the argument, reasoning and evidence. If so, this is invaluable for keeping track of the line of reasoning when reading about the more detailed evidence in other chapters.

Scan beginnings and ends of chapters

Scan the introductions and final sections of relevant chapters: these are likely to orientate your thinking to the material in the chapter.

Articles

- Browse the abstract to see if the article looks relevant.
- If it does, read the abstract slowly, to identify the main argument.
- If the article is about a research project, the research hypotheses sum up what the author is trying to prove. The results will tell you what they found. The discussion indicates what the author considers to be significant about the research and its findings.
- Use the abstract to locate the most relevant information for you. Decide whether you need to know more about the methods used, the results, the discussion of the results, or the recommendations, depending on your purpose.

Find the argument

Once you have worked quickly to locate where the information is in general terms, apply the critical thinking methods covered in earlier chapters in order to identify the arguments:

- Identify the author's position: what does the text want you to do, think, accept or believe?
- Look for sets of reasons that are used to support conclusions.

Once you have located the argument, you are likely to need to read more slowly and carefully, applying further critical thinking strategies.

Identifying the theoretical perspective

What is a theory?

A theory is a set of ideas that helps to explain why something happens or happened in a particular way, and to predict likely outcomes in the future. Theories are based on evidence and reasoning, but have not yet been proved conclusively.

Everyday and academic use of 'theory'

We use the term 'theory' in everyday language to suggest we don't know yet, for certain, either the reasons or the outcomes.

We've planted twenty bulbs here, in perfect conditions just as it says on the packet, so we should have twenty lovely tulips in the Spring.

Well, that's the theory, anyway!

Everyday use of the word tends to be an expression of opinion, but it shares the characteristics of academic theory in being:

- an attempt to provide an explanation, or a prediction of likely outcomes;
- an idea, or set of abstract ideas, that haven't been fully proved;
- based on the facts as far as they are known at the time, and acknowledging there is still more to find out.

Knowing the theory helps fill the gaps

Most things that we do are based on some kind of theory, but we are not always aware that our opinions fit a theoretical perspective. In Chapter 6, we saw that what we say or write often contains unstated assumptions – which may be unrecognised theories. If we can identify an author's theoretical perspective, we are in a better position to recognise gaps in the reasoning as well as unstated assumptions.

Theory in research and academic life

In professional research and academic thinking, a theory is usually an elaborated system, or 'school', of ideas, based on critical analyses of previous theories and research. Much research sets out to test or further refine existing theories so that they are more useful in providing explanations, and for creating models for future action.

Finding the theoretical position

In the best research and texts, the theoretical position will be stated by the author in an explicit way to assist the reader. In books, this is usually outlined in an early section, or at the beginning of chapters. In articles, reports, dissertations and theses, the theoretical position will be indicated by the following:

- The research hypothesis: this should be stated near the beginning of the research and provides the key theoretical position that the research sets out to prove.
- The literature that has been selected for the literature search: authors' analysis of this should draw out the theories which have influenced the research.

The relation of theory to argument

Arguments can be based on theories

A theory may be used as the basis of an argument.

Example

Marx's theory of economics argues that wealth will become concentrated into a few hands. This research project is based on an interpretation of Marx's theory, and argues that although the denationalisation of public services in Britain led to more companies being set up in the short term, over a few decades, mergers and buy-outs have resulted in many smaller companies closing. As a result, the wealth of those industries is now in the possession of a small number of 'super-companies'. The research hypothesis is that after three decades, 75 per cent of the wealth of former British nationalised industries will, in each case, be in the hands of three or fewer super-companies.

In the example above, the main argument is that after a few decades, industries that were once nationalised, but were later sold to private companies, will become part of a few 'super' companies. The author is explicit that the argument is based on an interpretation of a particular economic theory. Here, the theory is used to develop the research hypothesis.

The inclusion of numbers and proportions helps to make a general theory more specific and measurable. However, the general argument and theory could be valid, even though the specific timing and amounts were not met, if the trend was clearly in the direction predicted.

Theories as arguments

Theories can also be arguments in their own right if they offer reasons and conclusions and attempt to persuade. However, you may find that when theories are used as the basis of an argument, as in the example above, the author refers only to the conclusions or key aspects of the theory. To examine the line of reasoning behind the theory, it may be necessary to return to the original text rather than using second-hand accounts.

An argument is not necessarily a theory

Note that arguments are not always theories. In the example below, the argument for going into town is supported by two reasons, but does not represent a theory.

Example

I know you are keen to return home quickly, but it would be a good idea to go to the shops first. We need to buy a present for Serina's birthday. We also need to get some food for tonight.

Activity: Identifying theory

Identify which of the texts on pp. 233–7 have an explicit (openly stated) theoretical position.

State what the theoretical position is in each case.

The answers are on p. 166. ▶

Subject-specific schools of thought

There will be specific theories, usually organised into schools of thought based around a few key researchers or approaches, for your own subjects. These might be clustered around broad theoretical approaches such as: nativism, humanism, chaos, catastrophism, functionalism, psychodynamics, systems, constructivism, Marxism, feminism, postmodernism and so on.

Activity: Schools of thought

What are the main schools of thought for your own areas of interest?

Categorising and selecting

Critical choices

Research tasks, including reading for reports and assignments, can require us to cover a great deal of information. We can only make active use of a proportion of what we read, but it may seem that everything is useful and interesting. Critical thinking requires us to make decisions about:

- where to allocate available reading time;
- where to focus our critical thinking;
- what to note for future reference;
- what material to use in our own report or assignment, and what to leave out.

Critical choices involve selection, and selection is made easier if we are skilled at categorising information. Practice in categorising information was provided in Chapter 2.

The importance of categorising information

It is easier to make critical choices when we have organised information not simply in files, but within our thinking. Categorising information is an essential process that helps us to recognise links between different kinds of information. This enables us to:

- compare information more easily;
- contrast information more easily;
- refer to sets of information as a group, so that our account is more succinct.

Categorising theory

We saw, above, that identifying the theoretical position helps us to fill in gaps in a line of reasoning. If we can categorise texts according to their theoretical position, we will be better able to:

- sort the information required for our analysis of the literature;
- track how one piece of research builds on previous research;
- better understand why further research into a subject has been undertaken, as we will understand how it fits into a bigger picture. Often, a piece of research can only examine part of the picture.

- Group information under headings that help to clarify our understanding. This also helps us to remember the information.

Generic types of theory

There are some generic headings that are useful as points of reference when starting to group information. It is worth checking whether theories or arguments are primarily:

- *aesthetic*: related to an appreciation of art
- *cultural*: related to the ideas, customs and artefacts of a particular society
- *economic*: related to an economy
- *ethical*: a question of right and wrong
- *financial*: considerations of money
- *legal*: related to the law; what the law says
- *historical*: resulting from past circumstances
- *humanitarian*: with the interests of mankind at heart
- *philanthropic*: acts of kindness to others
- *philosophical*: related to the study of knowledge
- *political*: related to government or state
- *scientific*: resulting from a systematic and/or experimental approach that can be repeated
- *sociological*: related to the development or organisation of human society
- *sophistical*: arguments that seem clever but are misleading

Activity: Categorising arguments

Read through the texts on pp. 233–7. Each text contains one or more types of argument. Categorise these using the generic themes listed above. More than one may apply to each text, or 'none of these' might apply.

Answers are on p. 166. ▶

Accurate interpretation when reading

Reading style and accuracy

Accurate interpretation is particularly important to critical thinking. Donaldson (1978) found that people often get questions wrong because they do not adhere closely enough to the detail of what is asked or stated.

Incorrect interpretations can arise because reading is either over-focused on small details or it pays insufficient attention to details. Some common mistakes are:

- *Over-focused reading*: the reading is too slow, focusing excessively on individual words and sections of the text. Although close reading is a necessary part of critical reading, it is also important to interpret specific details in the wider context of the argument and the theoretical perspective.
- *Insufficient focus*: the reading is too superficial, taking in the big picture but lacking a sense of how the main theories and arguments are supported by specific details and evidence.
- *Insufficient attention to the exact wording*: missing out essential words such as 'not', or not following the exact sequence closely.
- *Failing to draw out correctly the implications* of what is stated.

It follows that, in order to interpret texts accurately, it helps to vary the focus of attention when reading, alternating between:

- the big picture and the fine detail;
- a consideration of the exact words and unstated implications and assumptions.

Activity

Read the interpretations given in the passages below of specific texts given on pp. 233–5. In each case, decide whether the passage:

A makes an accurate interpretation of the writer's overall argument;

B misinterprets the writer's position.

Give reasons for your response, identifying the overall argument.

Passage 9.1

(about Text 1, p. 233)
The author is a true artist who is offering a service to smaller artists who cannot find distributors.

Passage 9.2

(about Text 2, p. 233)
The author argues that as giving garden cuttings is regarded as acceptable and little concern is shown for royalty issues, then downloading music without paying should also be regarded as acceptable.

Passage 9.3

(about Text 3, p. 233)
Piracy is not usually acceptable and most customers should be prepared to go without an item if they are not willing to pay for it.

Passage 9.4

(about Text 6, p. 234)
When people make free copies of music they put the future of distributors of independent artists at risk.

Passage 9.5

(about Text 7, p. 234)
This argues that Plants Breeders are only likely to take action against large companies, so the important issue for gardeners is that they are safe from prosecution.

Passage 9.6

(about Text 10, p. 235)
Individuals should stand up for what they believe is right and stop obeying the law, as it is undemocratic.

Answers are on p. 166. ▶

Making notes to support critical reading

Why make notes?

Note-making is a good idea. It has several benefits over simply reading without making notes:

- If done properly, it breaks up a continuous reading task into many shorter reading sessions alternated with note-making. This rests the eyes and the parts of the brain involved in reading. This is especially useful given the intense reading activity used for critical reading.

- Writing involves the motor memory, making it easier to remember information.

- Many people find it easier to recall information that is written in their own handwriting.

- Selecting what to write, rather than writing everything, means greater interaction with the material, which helps us to recall it in the future.

- Making notes draws together the information that is relevant on the subject, so you have less to read over than all the material contained in the various source materials.

- You can make notes on a copy of the text if it is your own copy, but this doesn't help draw the key ideas into one place.

How do you make notes to support critical reading?

The notes you make should support your main purpose. Avoid making notes on related topics just because they are interesting or might be useful one day. It is possible to write notes to fulfil several different purposes, such as to support a current project and to contribute towards a future project or assignment. If you do this, either use separate sets of notes for each project, or use clear headings in your notes to help you find what you need easily for each. It is worth making a conscious effort to reflect on what you have read.

- What does this really mean?
- Do the reasons support the argument?
- Is there any supporting evidence?
- Does this match what I know about the subject already?
- Does it fit what other people say about the subject?
- Is this relevant and useful to my current purpose?
- How does this add to previous research on the subject?
- Are there any flaws in this?

TIP

Read without a pen in your hand. This helps to avoid writing lots of unnecessary notes that you haven't thought through.

Reading and noting for a purpose

Making notes for analysing argument

If your main purpose is to keep notes to analyse an argument, use headings or a pro-forma such as that on p. 155, to note the following:

- Details for finding the source again easily.
- The author's position/theoretical stance.
- The main argument, or hypothesis.
- The conclusion(s).
- A list of the reasons used to support the conclusion. Number these. If the author repeats a reason in different words, make sure you include it only once on your list.
- Your evaluations of the strengths and weaknesses of the line of reasoning and supporting evidence.

Notes for assignments and reports

When making notes from a book, there is a danger of losing critical focus by taking down information indiscriminately, rather than selecting the most relevant points.

TIP

If you like to make lots of notes about facts and supporting details, keep these on separate sheets from your notes for critical analysis, or write them on the reverse side. If your critical analysis pages remain empty and your background information pages begin to mount up, this will alert you that you are neglecting to evaluate the information for relevance and to select the most salient points. It may also indicate that you have slipped into copying from the text.

The pro-forma on p. 156 provides a model for critical note-making when reading books. It may not suit all your purposes. However, it is structured so that there is, deliberately, very little space for general background. It is rare that you can use more than very minimal background information on any one source material for either academic or professional purposes.

Note-making when reading journal articles

The main difference in note-making when reading from research articles is that you are more likely to make a close analysis of the particular contribution that the research findings or methodology make towards advancing knowledge within the subject area. Such articles tend to be based on a single piece of research and you may be especially interested in the methodology and the discussion of findings. The pro-forma offered on p. 157 puts the emphasis on your analysis rather than on background information.

Choose quotations carefully

Use few quotations and keep them short

Avoid long quotations as they eat into the word limit without providing any additional marks. Select a few short quotations that:

- in a secondary source, sum up a point well in a few words;
- in a primary source, provide direct evidence for your argument;
- are relevant and the best. Use sparingly.

Make quotations stand out in your notes

Develop the habit of using a particular coloured pen, such as red, blue or green, for any copied text such as quotations. This will make it immediately obvious to you, when you read your notes at a later date, what you have copied and what are your own words and ideas.

Note the source of quotations

Note down exactly where the quotation comes from. See pp. 162–3.

Concise critical notes: Analysing argument

Names of author(s)/source			
Title of book/programme			
Web-site address		Date downloaded	
Date and/or time		Edition	
Publisher/channel		Place published	
Volume of journal		Issue	

Author's position/ theoretical position?	
Essential background information	
Overall argument or hypothesis	
Conclusion	
Supporting reasons	1 5 2 6 3 7 4 8
Strengths of the line of reasoning and supporting evidence	
Flaws in the argument and gaps or other weaknesses in the argument and supporting evidence	

Concise critical notes: Books

Names of author(s)			
Full title of book			
Author of chapter			
Chapter title			
Year published		Edition	
Publisher		Place published	

Theoretical position or type of theory?	
Essential background information	
Key arguments	
Reasons and evidence to support the arguments	
Strengths of the arguments	
Weaknesses in the arguments	
Comparison or contrast with other sources	

Concise critical notes: Articles and papers

Names of author(s)	
Full title of article	
Fill title of journal	

Year published		Month	
Volume number		Issue number	

Hypotheses: What is the paper setting out to prove? Are research hypotheses supported?	
What is the theoretical position underlying the research? Type of theory?	
What is the key literature used as background to the article or paper?	
Which research methods are used?	
What kind of sample is used?	
Key results	
Key conclusions or recommendations	
Strengths of the research: ● How does it advance our understanding of the subject or how to research it? ● Are there appropriate hypotheses, methods to test the hypotheses, sample sizes or types, controls for variables, recommendations? ● Consideration of ethics?	
Weaknesses of the research: ● In what ways is it limited? When and where would it not apply? ● What, if any, are the flaws in the research, in the hypotheses, research design and methods, sample size and type, conclusions drawn on the basis of the results?	

Critical selection when note-making

Below, are notes made on Texts 1–11 (pp. 233–5). The purpose of the notes is for use in a report entitled:

'Unfair treatment: The law only seems to apply to business these days.' Discuss.

Look through the sample notes that were made below and underline any sections that are relevant to the report. Give reasons why the notes are relevant, and comment on whether the notes are made in the note-maker's own words.

Then read the commentary and compare your answers.
NB   This activity is focusing on the content of the notes, not their layout.

Sample notes for 'Unfair treatment: The law only seems to apply to business these days.' Discuss.

Evidence that supports the statement

- Legal proceedings are usually only instigated against businesses, not individuals. This is true for copying from the internet, when businesses sell well below market price (Spratt, 2004, Text 4) and for plant breedings (Johl, 2005, Text 7). BUT: this doesn't mean the law only applies to business, just that it is likely to be applied unevenly. This may appear to be unfair to big business. NB Johl (Text 7): the combined effect of plant-sharing is a large financial loss to plant breeders – so business is targeted just because it is easy.

Evidence that contradicts the statement

- Big publishers are only interested in music that has a broad appeal because they hope to make large profits. (Text 1)
- Cuttle (2007): Publishers, including big businesses, can choose the price at which they sell. NB: this can be much higher than it costs to make the item, so in this respect the law supports business. (Text 3)
- The law is scrambled together over time and is often contradictory. There is very little debate on what we want as our concept of justice (Piaskin, 1986, Text 10).
- Isn't it mainly business that can afford to use the law against copying – not small artists?

Commentary on the notes

The notes on Text 1 are about big business but it is not clear why the note-maker considers these relevant to the question. Furthermore, this is not a reputable source for a report.

The notes on Text 10 are about the law in general, but not about business in particular. It is not clear why the note-maker considers these notes relevant to the discussion question.

The notes on Texts 1 and 10 are copied almost word for word from the texts, showing no critical selection. If these were reproduced in a report or assignment, and it was discovered, it would be regarded as plagiarism (unacceptable copying).

The notes on Texts 3, 4 and 7 are better as they are relevant, written in the note-maker's own words, along with reflection that could be used to make a relevant point in the report.

Activity: Critical selection – Notes A

Look at the two sets of notes, A and B, below, which are related to the texts on pp. 233–7. In each case, decide:

- Has the note-maker selected information that is relevant for the purpose given?
- Have they selected the most relevant information?

Notes A. Purpose: 'The internet is corroding moral values.' Discuss.

Points For: internet corrodes moral values

(1) Text 3: Cuttle (2007) argues that people who make illegal copies from the internet try to rationalise this rather than seeing it as wrong, using arguments such as 'everybody else does it'.

(2) Text 1 (Carla, 2006):

Comments made by internet users support Cuttle, as they use rationalisations:

e.g. 'it isn't really stealing to copy off the internet',

and sending and accepting copies without paying for them is:

'performing a useful service' to the arts and individual artists.

(3) Text 1: NB as music can be downloaded off the internet for free, it provides a temptation for people like Carla, and encourages them to look for excuses to justify taking without asking.

(4) Text 9 (KAZ, 2006): Internet user's flawed reasoning to defend non-payment, such as that if you are unlikely to be charged, 'there isn't a crime'.

(5) Texts 4 and 7: The law is mainly used to prosecute other business, and not people who only make a few copies such as for friends.

(6) Text 8: Moral decay isn't just a few people on the internet: even professors now offer flawed reasoning in favour of taking without payment.

e.g. (Lee, 2006) argues in favour of taking material for free from the internet just because people are not caught and punished for copying off the radio ('nobody bothers about this . . .')

Points Against: internet does not corrode values

(1) Text 2: Potter (2005) draws a comparison between downloading from the internet for free and giving away plant cuttings.

(2) If we can compare making cuttings of plants with making copies from the internet, and both are wrong, then the internet is only offering a different way of expressing similar values, not 'corroding' them.

e.g. Text 7 (Johl, 2005) shows plant breeders also suffer from the practice of giving free cuttings. Plant cutting preceded the internet – so these values can't be blamed on the internet.

See commentary on p. 161. ▶

Activity: Critical selection – Notes B

Notes B. Purpose: essay 'Stealing is always wrong.' Discuss this view.

Stealing is wrong

(1) Text 6: Yes, because we don't always know who all the victims are. Kahliney (2006): small music distributors can be severely affected by even a few people losing them royalties, when they copy music to their friends. People's livelihood depends on fair-trading.

(2) And Text 7 (Johl, 2005): Plant breeding is very expensive – so even small royalties which build up over time help producers to invest in new varieties.

(3) Text 3 (Cuttle, 2007): Producers of all media are entitled by law to recoup the costs of their labour or outlay.

Arguments used to support stealing

(1) Text 1: It's other people's fault, such as large publishers that are only interested in music that will give them large profit margins (but see Text 3 above).

(2) Text 1: It can provide a useful service, e.g. sharing music from the internet for free helps bring innovative and radical music to more people, which is better for true artists who want their music to reach as many people as possible. (BUT: Text 6: Small distributors are not necessarily helped.)

(3) Text 2: It's acceptable if you can get away with it – e.g. Ivan Potter (2005): Plants and CDs.

(4) Text 8: also implies that if nobody gets caught or prosecuted, such as for copying from the radio, then stealing doesn't matter. BUT: stealing isn't defined by whether you get caught.

Where stealing might be acceptable?

(1) Text 11 (Soyinka, 2006): No, there can be instances when people don't realise they are stealing, such as students plagiarising – e.g. because the rules are complicated. BUT: ignorance of the 'law' is not accepted as an excuse.

(2) Text 12 (Ebo et al., 2004): Research shows people's behaviour is affected by how easy it is to act in an ethical way. The research hypotheses were that most young people who downloaded music for free pay to download music if this is made easy, and people are less willing to pay for music if they are high earners. The participants were 1206 people aged 15–25, matched for age, sex, and ethnic background across groups and conditions. An advertisement for an alternative web-site where the music could be downloaded for free appeared when the participant was on line. Damblin and Toshima (1986) used a sample of 200 senior citizens and found significant differences in ethical behaviour depending on medical conditions. Several research studies show external conditions can have more impact on behaviour than has ethical understanding (Singh et al., 1991; Colby, 1994; Miah and Brauer, 1997).

Issues of right and wrong are not clear cut

(1) Text 10 (Fred Piaskin, 1986): Right and wrong are 'more properly regarded as dilemmas'. There may be occasions when stealing is wrong in itself, but less wrong than not stealing?

- a person could be stealing and yet not acting in an immoral or unethical way, e.g. to save a life OR
- 'stealing within the law', which would then be an ethical issue, a matter of conscience, not law.

See commentary on p. 161. ▶

Commentary on critical selection activity

Notes A. Collated for 'The internet is corroding moral values.' Discuss.

In this case, most of the notes taken are relevant to the subject.

The notes on Text 3 are relevant as they point out that people look for reasons to justify taking without paying. Searching for reasons to justify an act that may not be right is known as 'rationalisation'.

The note-maker makes a good selection of brief quotations from primary sources, Texts 1 and 9, to illustrate the point. As the quotations are underlined, these stand out properly from the other notes, showing immediately that the words are copied directly from elsewhere. Although personal web-sites such as these are not normally reputable authorities as secondary sources, for this question they are relevant sources of primary evidence, illustrating what some ordinary internet users are saying. It is evident that the note-maker is using Text 8 to provide a contrasting source that also argues for non-payment, which is also relevant.

The notes benefit from being divided into points 'for' and 'against' the argument, but this means that more complex points are not included. For example, when considering values, it would have been useful to consider Text 5 and the issues it raises about the differences between what people say and do. The author argues as if downloading for free is acceptable, although he does pay for the music he downloads himself.

One strong feature of the notes is that they show that the note-maker is thinking whilst reading, and jotting down relevant reflections.

The main weakness of the notes is that they do not select the most relevant material:
- They do not refer to all the relevant sources, such as Texts 10 and 12.
- The note-maker gives no indication why notes on Texts 4 and 7 are relevant to the topic (see note 5, under 'Points For').

Notes B. Collated for 'Stealing is always wrong.' Discuss.

Most of the notes made on the early texts show good critical selection. The note-maker has chosen the most relevant material for the purpose.
The main exception is the set of notes made for Text 12. These are too detailed and are too close to the original text. It is not clear why the note-maker considered that all the details about the research were relevant: these notes do not show evidence of critical selection.

Strong points about these notes are:
- Information is grouped to support different points.
- The notes include evidence of the critical thinking process, which can then be used in reports or essays.

Weak points of these notes are that:
- Quotations and notes copied from the texts do not stand out, and could easily be copied accidentally into a report or essay later without proper acknowledgement. This is especially so for the notes on Texts 1 and 12.
- The words noted down are too close to those used in the original texts, suggesting that the reader has slipped into 'automatic' note-making, or copying, rather than focusing on selecting the most relevant information.

Note your source of information (1)

All of your notes should make it very clear where information comes from.

Long hand and short hand

The first time you use a source, it is useful to write its details in full, preferably in an electronic store, so you can cut and paste it as needed. In your notes, write the details in full the first time you use a source and then use a recognisable abbreviation as a short-hand. Note exact page references or web-site addresses so you can find information again easily when needed.

Details for references

If you are writing an assignment for college or a report for a company, you will be required to make references to the material you use so that your readers know what influenced your thinking and where you found your evidence. Universities and companies usually recommend a particular style of referencing, such as the Harvard or Vancouver system or a house style. These vary in the fine detail, such as whether you write the authors' initials or their full names. Make sure you note the information needed for the referencing system you are required to use. The Harvard system is outlined below. See also pages 187–8.

For books

Note:

- Who wrote it? (Full surnames, followed by the initials, of all writers that appear on the front cover)
- When did they write it? (See pages inside the cover. Give the date it was first published or the date of the current edition, but not the date of the reprint.)
- What exactly is it called, including the subtitle?
- Which edition is it (if not the first edition)?
- The city where it was published (see the pages at the front of the book that give the address of the publisher).
- The name of the publisher.

Example

Details to note about books
Crane, T. (2001) *Elements of Mind: An Introduction to the Philosophy of Mind* (Oxford: Oxford University Press).

Example

Multiple authors
Fisher, D. and Hanstock, T. (1998) *Citing References* (Oxford: Blackwell).

For a chapter from a book

If you are noting information from a book where each of the chapters is written by different authors, note:

- The name of the chapter's author, the date and then the name of the chapter.
- The name of the editor, and the title of the book. Note that the initials of the editor are written before the surname when citing this in references.
- The page numbers, following the title of the book.
- Where it was published and the name of the publisher, in brackets. You may need to note where a chapter was first published.

Example

Chapters from a book
Willis, S. (1994) 'Eruptions of funk: historicizing Toni Morrison'. In L. Gates Jr (ed.), *Black Literature and Literary Theory* (pp. 263–83) (New York: Methuen).

Note your source of information (2)

For articles

Note:

- Who wrote it? (Full surname, followed by the initials of all writers that appear at the top of the article, in the order they appear)
- When did they write it?
- What exactly is it called?
- What is the exact name of the journal the article comes from?
- In which volume and/or issue of the journal did the article appear?
- Page numbers of the entire article.

Example

Articles
Shulman, L. (1986) 'Those who understand: knowledge growth in teaching'. *Educational Researcher*, 15 (2), 4–14.

For electronic sources

Note:

- The authors' names.
- For on-line journals, give the full surnames of the authors, followed by their initials, in the order they appear.
- The date it was written. If no date is given, consider whether this is a good source to use.
- The name of the item (if there is one).
- The name of the journal, and its volume and issue details, for articles.
- If the material is available only on the internet, give exact details of the web-page so somebody else could open that site and page.
- The date it was downloaded from the internet.

Example

Electronic sources
Collins, P. (1998) 'Negotiating selves: Reflections on "unstructured" interviewing'. *Sociological Research Online*, 3 (3). www.socresonline.org.uk/socresonline/3/3/2.html; January 2001.

Newspapers

Note the name of the author, article, the name of the newspaper, the date and the pages.

Example

Farrar, S. (2004) 'Old Sea Chart is so Current', *Times Higher Educational Supplement*, 16 July, p. 5.

If the author's name is not given in the newspaper, give the name of the newspaper first, then the year, then the name of the article, followed by the date and page numbers.

Example

Times Higher Educational Supplement (2004) 'Old Sea Chart is So Current', 16 July, p. 5.

Other sources

There are many other sources of information that you may need to use. Make notes of any details that will help you and others locate that particular source. This might include the name of the library and/or collection, volume numbers and folio numbers. Give exact details of what the source is.

Example

Letter in a collection
Papers in the Bodleian Library. Curzon Collection, vol. 22, ff. 89–90. Letter from Henry Peter Lord Brougham to C. H. Parry, 3 September 1803.

Example

Government and official sources
National Committee of Inquiry into Higher Education (1997) *Higher Education in the Learning Society* (London: HMSO).

Summary

Critical thinking needs to be incorporated at many different stages in the process of producing a critical piece of work. This chapter has focused on applying a critical approach to reading and related note-making.

It is not unusual for people to suspend critical thinking when reading and making notes. For example, they often assume it is acceptable to read and make notes in a non-selective or non-critical way, amass a pile of notes, and then apply critical thinking to the notes that have been made. Whilst this is not an unacceptable strategy, it is not effective in terms of time management. Using such methods, you are more likely to read and take notes on material you will not use, and then repeat your reading of such unnecessary material in order to select what is needed.

Making notes in an uncritical way is also a risky strategy. It is much easier to become confused about which notes have been taken down verbatim from the text and to include these, by accident, in your own work. This would leave you open to charges of cheating and/or plagiarism.

This chapter recommends strategies which, if followed, are more likely to save you time, and to help you develop critical thinking skills as an ongoing process when reading and writing. Guidance on referencing your source materials is included: critical readers will want to ensure that they can find the source of information again in the future if they need it. If the material is to be used within a piece of writing, these details will be needed to refer the reader to the source materials.

Critical reading is assisted by identifying certain key pieces of information that can direct and focus your attention. Earlier chapters identified certain components of an argument, such as identifying the conclusion, as useful ways of finding the argument within a passage. This chapter draws attention to the importance of identifying the underlying theoretical perspective, where possible, in order to better evaluate the significance of the material to the author's point of view.

This chapter also emphasises the importance of developing skills in categorising and selecting information as component skills within critical thinking. Such skills contribute to more effective reasoning abilities, as they require you to find comparisons and exceptions, to look for factors that link and connect information, to develop an understanding of the relative significance of different pieces of information, and to make evaluative judgements.

Information on the sources

Donaldson, M. (1978) *Children's Minds* (London: Fontana).

For background on plant cuttings and PBRs: Hogan, C. (2004) 'Giving Lawyers the Slip'. *The Times*, 24 August, p. 26.

On moral issues: Kohlberg, L. (1981) *Essays on Moral Development*, vol. 1 (New York: Harper & Row).

Peters, R. S. (1974) 'Moral Development: a Plea for Pluralism'. In R. S. Peters (ed.), *Psychology and Ethical Development* (London: Allen & Unwin).

Gilligan, C. (1977) 'In a Different Voice: Women's Conceptions of Self and Morality'. *Harvard Educational Review*, **47**, 418–517.

Answers to activities in Chapter 9

Evaluating a body of evidence (p. 144)

(a) Identifying reputable sources

Very reputable

Text 3: journal article

Text 8: a chapter of an academic book

Text 10: journal article

Text 11: journal article

Text 12: journal article

Fairly trustworthy

Text 2: popular magazines

Text 4: editorial in a smalltown local newspaper

Text 6: trade magazine

Text 7: columnist in a national paper

Little authority

Text 1: internet chat room

Text 5: letter to a national paper

Text 9: personal web-site.

(b) Vested interests

The authors of the following texts may have a vested interest in the outcome of the argument:

Text 1: as the author downloads from the internet

Text 2: as the author may be currying favour with his readers, who are likely to share free cuttings

Text 5 (and possibly Text 9): the argument appears to be a rationalisation for not paying for downloaded copies.

(c) Reliable evidence of internet users' views

The most reliable sources for indicating what internet users believe are those written by internet users themselves, and those indicated by research evidence. In this case, that would be Text 1 and possibly Texts 5 and 9, by internet users. More information would be needed to ensure Texts 5 and 9 were indeed by internet users. Text 12 gives details of the behaviour of internet users, drawn from research, and this behaviour is indicative of their beliefs. However, more investigation would be needed to check on these internet users' motivations for paying.

Answers to activities in Chapter 9

Identifying theory (p. 150)

Only two texts have an explicit theoretical position. These are:

Text 10: that moral and ethical issues should be regarded as 'dilemmas' rather than as simple questions of right and wrong.

Text 12: that behaviour is affected primarily by how easy it is to act in an ethical way.

Categorising arguments (p. 151)

Text 1: sophistical, aesthetic and philanthropic

Text 2: sophistical and philanthropic

Text 3: economic and legal

Text 4: economic

Text 5: philanthropic and sophistical

Text 6: economic

Text 7: legal, economic, ethical

Text 8: sophistical and legal

Text 9: sophistical and legal

Text 10: ethical, legal

Text 11: none of these

Text 12: ethical, economic.

Accurate interpretations when reading (p. 152)

Passage 9.1

B Misinterpretation. The text doesn't state that the author, personally, is offering a service.

Passage 9.2

A Accurate interpretation.

Passage 9.3

B Misinterpretation. The text is very clear that it regards piracy as stealing, and makes no exceptions. Passage 9.3 waters this down, using words such as 'not usually' and 'most customers', suggesting there may be exceptions.

Passage 9.4

A Accurate interpretation.

Passage 9.5

B Misinterpretation. The author's argument is that gardeners who give away cuttings are cheating the people who breed new species of plant. It is true that the text implies that small gardeners will not be prosecuted in practice, but that isn't the argument.

Passage 9.6

B Misinterpretation. The passage does argue that there hasn't been a democratic process to decide that the law should make ultimate decisions of right and wrong. It also argues that positive changes have occurred when people stand up for what they believe. The text does not make recommendations. The argument is more abstract, pointing out that questions of right and wrong are complex and that there are different ways of looking at ethical issues. The implication is that there should be more public discussion of the concept of justice. However, the text doesn't advocate that people stop obeying the law on those grounds.

Chapter 10

Critical, analytical writing
Critical thinking when writing

Learning outcomes

This chapter offers you opportunities to:

- consider the characteristics of critical, analytical writing
- identify the appropriate language structures for indicating, or signposting, the direction of your argument
- compare pieces of writing to identify the characteristics of critical writing
- understand how critical thinking skills are applied to essay-writing

Introduction

Critical writing draws together other aspects of critical thinking in order to present a forceful case to readers. This means that it must continue the process of selection and forming judgements about the evidence. However, the writing must be produced with its eventual readers in mind.

This chapter considers the characteristics of critical, analytical writing from the perspective of writing text, as opposed to considering written arguments from the reader's point of view. As well as looking at general characteristics, it focuses on the language used to present written arguments.

Previous chapters emphasised the importance of developing a clear line of reasoning. When speaking, it is possible to use the tone of voice, pacing and pauses, as well as body language, to help the audience to follow the argument. It is also common to repeat phrases or to raise the voice for emphasis.

These devices are not available to orientate the reader when arguments are written down, especially in formal writings. Therefore, it is all the more important to set the scene well, to summarise key points as you go through and, in particular, to use recognisable words and phrases to signpost the different aspects of the argument.

The process of re-drafting and editing writing is particularly important to critical writing. The writer needs to ensure that the final draft has the characteristics associated with critical writing. The final piece of critical writing should be clearly written and well-structured. It should include devices, such as signal words, that lead readers through the evidence in such a way that they are clear about the conclusion even before they read it.

Finally, the chapter looks at how a range of critical thinking skills are applied to the process of producing essays – a particular kind of writing. Essay-writing is a requirement of most subjects, and the main vehicle used for demonstrating, and assessing, good critical thinking skills.

Characteristics of critical, analytical writing (1)

Content

In critical writing, most of the text is dedicated to presenting a case through providing reasons, using relevant evidence, comparing and evaluating alternative arguments, weighing up conflicting evidence, and forming judgements on the basis of the evidence. Background information of a general nature is used very sparingly, and only essential details are usually included. Description is kept to a minimum.

A sense of audience

Good critical writing always keeps its future audience, or readers, in mind. The aim of an argument is to persuade others. When producing critical writing, it is important to consider how the message might be read by other people, especially people who might disagree with the evidence or the conclusions. A good critical writer knows which aspects of the argument are likely to be the most contentious, and the kind of evidence required in order to counter potential opposition within the reader.

Clarity

Critical writing should aim to be as clear as is possible. The aim is to convince the reader, so it is important that the style of writing makes it easy for the reader to see the point. Long, complicated or poorly punctuated sentences can make it difficult for the reader to follow the argument.

The language used for critical writing is generally sparse. It usually sticks to the facts and avoids emotional content, adjectives and flowery language or jargon. The aim is to present, as far as is possible, the points in a way that an intelligent general reader can understand. Technical language can be used but should not be used simply to sound clever.

Often, an argument can sound clear in our own mind but does not come across clearly in our writing. It is not always easy to see which lines may be interpreted differently when read by someone else, or what might be confusing or ambiguous. Skilful writers check through their writing several times, often by reading aloud, looking for any phrases that may be awkward to read or which could be open to a different interpretation by others.

Analysis

Analytical writing is writing that looks at the evidence in a detailed and critical way. In particular, it weighs up the relative strengths and weaknesses of the evidence, pointing these out to the reader, so that it is clear how the writer has arrived at judgements and conclusions.

Selection

Presenting too much detail can mean the main argument becomes obscured. The reader may lose interest in tracking the line of reasoning and simply conclude that the argument is weak. Usually, writers cannot include detailed critical analyses of every point that supports their arguments. On the other hand, presenting too little detail can make it sound as if there is not enough concrete evidence to support the case.

Skilful writers select the most important points, often the most controversial points, to examine in detail. They may only allude briefly to other points, sometimes several together, in order to indicate that they are aware of these points. Strong critical writing uses a good balance of detailed analysis and sections that summarise arguments and evidence.

Characteristics of critical, analytical writing (2)

Sequence

The more complicated the argument, the more important it is that the information is sequenced in a way that helps the reader. Good critical writing is planned out well so that the most important points stand out clearly. Readers can follow an argument more easily if they can see how each point is connected with the preceding point, and how each point links to the main argument. Good signposting, as described below, helps the reader to understand the sequence used by the writer.

Best order

It is generally more logical to present the points that support your own argument first, so that you establish your case early in the mind of the reader. This helps to align the audience to your position. Audiences are more likely to interpret subsequent reasoning from the perspective of the first argument presented, so it is better to present your own argument first.

However, if your argument aims to show why a well-established argument is wrong, it can make more sense to make a critique of the established argument first, in order to undermine this before presenting an alternative case.

Good critical writing shows an awareness of what are the most important or controversial aspects and dedicates the most space to these. If readers are persuaded on these points, they need less convincing on other points.

Skilful critical writers consider which information their audience needs to read first so as to make best sense of the argument. They ask, repeatedly, questions such as:

- Is this the best order or could it be better?
- Where does this best fit into the argument?
- Is the argument coming across clearly?
- If I moved this information somewhere else, would it be easier to follow the line of reasoning?

Group similar points

Similar points should be located near each other in the writing. For example, the points that support one aspect of the reasoning could be grouped together, followed by the points against. Usually, you should complete your analysis of one piece of evidence before moving on to an analysis of the next. Alternatively, all the aspects of the evidence that support an argument could be grouped together, followed by an analysis of those aspects of the evidence that do not support it. In each case, it is important to consider whether similar points are grouped together in a way that makes the text easy to read. The readers should not feel they are 'hopping' back and forward between points.

Signposting

Good critical writing leads the readers effortlessly through the argument so that they do not need to pause to consider where they are in the argument or whether the writer intends them to agree or disagree with a particular point. A skilful writer will use certain words and phrases as 'signposts' to indicate to the readers where they are in the argument, and how each point links to previous or subsequent points.

In critical writing, it is not usually acceptable to use graphical means to highlight important points. Critical writing avoids methods such as using italics, enboldening text, capital letters, larger font, colour or arrows to make important points stand out. Instead, it relies on good sequencing and use of language to signpost the reader through the line of reasoning.

Activity: Characteristics of critical writing

Read through a recent essay that you have written. Use this to evaluate the following:

- Which of the above characteristics are already strengths in your own writing?
- Which of these characteristics could you improve upon in your writing?

Setting the scene for the reader

When presenting an argument, the author usually has to include more than simply the reasons and conclusions. The circumstances and reasons for producing the argument will usually determine what else is considered to be relevant. When evaluating the likely effectiveness of an argument, it is important to consider:

- what background information the audience needs and expects;
- what they will already know;
- what kind of reasons and evidence are likely to convince that particular sort of audience.

Conventions

For academic subjects, there are conventions which govern the presentation of a line of reasoning. Journal articles, for example, have different conventions from newspaper articles or everyday speech. Usually, the background information in articles is of two types:

1 Key details of previous research relevant to the current article
2 Details of the methods used to gather and analyse the evidence, especially data, for the current article.

Activity

Browse through journal articles and identify the way background information is treated in your subject area. Note how much or how little detail is used in each section of the article. Consider what kind of background information is included, as well as what is not included.

Background and history

In critical writing, general background details are usually kept to a minimum, as in the Feng Shui example on p. 173. The history and general background are only usually included where they form part of the argument.

For example, if the question was: *How did the fish come to take over the estuary?* the history is relevant, and provides a reason that supports the conclusion, as in the example below.

Example

'Background' as a reason
Historically, the fish were subject to many large prey and laid many eggs to increase their chances of survival. When they migrated to the estuary, there were no natural predators to restrain their numbers. They continued to lay as many eggs, and so took over the estuary.

If the question was *Account for changes in banking practices over the last ten years*, the historical background given in the example below would be unnecessary.

Example

Unnecessary detail
Banking is a very old profession. Early examples include the development of the letter of exchange by the Hansa League in the fifteenth century.

Definitions

It is typical in critical thinking to define any terms used in the line of reasoning that might be open to more than one interpretation. This enables the audience to know which interpretation the author is using and reduces misunderstandings.

Example

There has been much debate about whether only humans have consciousness but there is a growing body of research which suggests that animals and even inanimate objects share this capacity. In considering whether animals and objects have consciousness, the first point to consider is what is meant by the term *consciousness*.

Activity: Setting the scene for the reader

Activity

How well do the authors of the following passages set the scene for an essay about a theory of food production?

Passage 10.1

'Is productionism dead?'

Productionism was a theory developed following the recession and famines of the 1930s. Theorists such as Orr, Stapleton and Seebohm Rowntree argued that if farming methods were adapted to include technology, more food could be produced and famines would become a thing of the past. This essay will argue that productionism has been successful to some extent, in that some areas that were formerly subject to famine are no longer prone to famine, and the proportion of starving people worldwide reduced year on year. However, it will also argue that despite the successes of technology in producing more food, other aspects of productionism have undermined its strength as a model for social reform. The essay examines some negative by-products of the productionist approach, such as the threat to bio-diversity, pollution, depopulation of agricultural areas, and the power that lies in the hands of retailers at the expense of small farmers. It will argue that productionism is not dead, but that a new model of food production would now better serve consumers, food producers and the global ecology.

Passage 10.2

'Is productionism dead?'

Productionism is dead. Its main proponents, such as Orr, Staptleton, Orwin and Seebohm Rowntree, were inspired by social altruism. Not for them the traditional farming methods of the past nor the harrowing scenes of famine and collapse presented worldwide in the 1930s. For them, there was a saviour and the saviour was

technology. Today, technology has developed in ways that even a visionary could not have imagined in the 1930s. Nonetheless, it has not been the saviour that was predicted. A new model is needed, and social and ecological forces will ensure that productionism, as a theory, passes into the realms of history.

Passage 10.3

'Is productionism dead?'

The main problem with productionism is that it places too much hope in science when science cannot always deliver. One result of productionism, with its emphasis on producing more and more food, is that people in the developed world think that food supplies can be endless. Child obesity is one result of such an approach. Whilst some people have too much to eat, others do not have enough. A lot of food isn't even a good thing: much of the food we eat is 'junk' and contains little nourishment.

Passage 10.4

'Is productionism dead?'

Food production has always been an important aspect of human activity. Since time began, humans have looked for ways of increasing the amount of food available to them. Without food, we would not be able to survive so this is a critical consideration for any society. Unfortunately, for most of history, the spectre of hunger and often famine have hung over people's heads. One period when this was particularly acute was the 1930s, when even rich economies were affected. It was in the face of such crises that productionism was born.

Answers: see p. 190. ▶

Writing up the literature search

Chapter 8 described methods for conducting a literature search and for identifying reputable sources. You are likely to read many more sources than you can include within your own writing. This requires careful selection of what to include as background information.

For essays

In essays, the focus is on the development of your own argument. It is not typical to include a summary of the literature at the beginning of an essay. Instead, you introduce sources at the relevant point in your argument. In essays, you need to refer to materials used as background reading in order to:

- illustrate a point you are making or add weight to a specific reason you are using to support your argument;
- argue against a point of view, if you wish to challenge what has been previously written;
- provide weight to your own argument by showing that it is supported by the research or arguments of other writers who are well known in the subject area.

For reports, dissertations and projects

It is usual when writing reports, dissertations and projects to start with a relatively brief overview of the background research. This is generally about 10 per cent of the overall piece of writing. You need to identify:

- which two or three pieces, theories, perspectives or previous research articles provide the most significant background information for your own research
- how, if at all, these pieces of research are linked to each other. Usually, this will be by chronological order.

Write most about two to five pieces of research, drawing out the key points. Provide only enough information to ensure the reader understands the significance of the research and its relevance to the rest of your report or dissertation. You may need to allude to most of the other pieces of research in passing, or very briefly.

Accuracy

Always check the original source and/or your notes carefully before writing about the work of other people. Check:

- that you have ascribed the right theory and discoveries to the right people;
- that you give the right dates;
- that you spell their names correctly;
- that you have interpreted their meaning and significance correctly.

Interpretation

Critical reading is an act of interpretation as well as selection. The recommendations made above on pp. 153–4 about how to combine reading with note-making make it more likely that you will produce a personal interpretation for your own assignment or report rather than simply reproducing the work of someone else. For essays, this does not mean that you must find an approach that nobody else has ever considered. Simply through the choices you make and through writing in your own words, you will be making a personal interpretation. The same applies when you are writing up the 'literature search' section for reports, projects and dissertations.

Reminder about referencing

Remember that copying from the internet or a written source is not acceptable, unless it is for a brief quotation and you reference the source correctly. The basics of citing references are given in Chapter 9, pp. 162–3 and pp. 186–7.

Words used to introduce the line of reasoning

Words that signal the direction of an argument

At the end of Chapter 3, there was an introduction to words that indicate conclusions within an argument. Authors may use other words to point out different stages of the argument to the reader. These words signal the direction of the line of reasoning.

It can help to use these words when scanning a text to find the line of reasoning quickly. The table on p. 178 summarises the words and can be used when constructing your own arguments.

Different words have different functions within an argument. Some, for example, are used at the beginning of an argument, others reinforce a point, some signal a change of perspective, others are used for conclusions. These words are sometimes known as *connectives* – as they connect the different parts of the argument.

Introducing the line of reasoning

Certain words are used to signal the opening of the argument. These include words such as *first*; *first of all*; *to begin*; *first and foremost*; *at the outset*; *initially*; *I will start by* . . .

Examples

- I will start by arguing that Feng Shui is important to every aspect of our lives and is not simply a question of decorative art.
- First of all, studying the size of the neo-cortex in the brains of different types of animals such as monkeys or rats can tell us a great deal about their social worlds.
- In considering the role of chemistry in the commercial world, it is important, at the outset, to recognise that chemistry is a commercially viable subject.
- Initially, we will consider whether porous rocks can ever provide solid foundations for new buildings.

Note that the introduction to the argument might not be the first sentence. It may be later in the paragraph. For example, the first example above might follow an introductory sentence or passage, used to set the scene, such as that in the example below.

Example

Feng Shui has formed part of Chinese life for over three thousand years and is increasingly gaining popularity in the West. The reasons for this new popularity are sometimes attributed to a growth in favour of simplicity and minimalism in house decoration. This is a mistake. I will start by arguing that Feng Shui is important to every aspect of our lives and is not simply a question of decorative art.

Words used to reinforce the line of reasoning (2)

Certain words can be used to indicate that new information is being introduced that further reinforces the direction of the line of reasoning. These include words such as *also*; *in addition*; *besides*; *too*; *furthermore*; *moreover*.

Adding similar reasons

When reinforcing a line of reasoning, the author may wish to add reasons similar to those already presented. This can be signalled by words such as: *similarly*; *equally*; *likewise*; *in the same way*.

Examples

- Similarly, the Chinese martial arts are not merely about fighting, but offer tools for understanding mind and motivation.
- In the same way, when we look at the neo-cortex of humans, we learn about the evolution of our own social habits.
- Likewise, applying chemical knowledge to biological problems has opened up new avenues of business and many spin-off industries.

Adding different reasons

At other times, the author may choose to reinforce the overall argument by adding new and different reasons. Authors often indicate that they are adding new reasons by using words such as *in addition*; *besides*; *as well as* . . . ; *not only* . . . *but also* . . .

Examples

- Not only can Feng Shui help to guard your health, it is believed to protect and enhance your wealth and prosperity.
- The amount of time that animals such as chimpanzees spend on grooming each other is not only linked to the composition of the social group, but also to the size of that group.
- In addition to developments within chemistry, developments within information technology have opened up new possibilities for biochemical research at the molecular level.

Strengthening the argument

At other times, authors can use words such as *furthermore*; *moreover*; *indeed*; *what is more*; *such as*; in order to indicate that they believe a reason is particularly good, or that its addition to the line of reasoning makes a more convincing case.

Examples

- Furthermore, Feng Shui is used in business in order to help keep customers and employees happy.
- Moreover, the development of language in humans may be directly related to the size of human communities, which makes grooming impossible as a key form of communication.
- Indeed, the reorganisation of scientific departments to encourage work across disciplines such as physics and material science has led to much excitement about research on the boundaries of each discipline as well as opening up new areas of entrepreneurship.

Signposting alternative points of view

Introducing alternative arguments

A strong argument will usually critically evaluate alternative perspectives or points of view. By doing so, authors show readers that they have considered other possibilities and not simply presented the first argument that entered their heads. This approach usually strengthens an argument as it suggests that the author has researched the subject or has considered all angles.

Words used to signal that an alternative point of view is being considered include: *alternatively*; *others argue that . . .* ; *it might be argued that . . .*

Examples

- It might be argued that Feng Shui has not been proved through rigorous scientific research.
- On the other hand, not everyone believes that animal behaviours have anything to tell us about human behaviours.

- Alternatively, there are those who believe that the prime role of biochemical research should be the advancement of knowledge and that this goal should not be distorted or lost through the demands of the market place.

Rebutting alternative arguments

As we saw above, it is typical, within a line of reasoning, to introduce alternative points of view in order to disprove them or indicate their weaknesses. Normally you would expect the author to show why their own point of view is the more convincing. Words used to rebut alternative arguments are: *however*; *on the other hand*; *nonetheless*; *notwithstanding this*.

Examples

- However, many practitioners of Feng Shui are also scientists.
- Nonetheless, humans are closely related to other primates such as chimpanzees and apes.
- These arguments notwithstanding, there is still much to be gained from a closer alignment between science and business.
- Notwithstanding the argument that chalk is porous and porous rocks provide riskier surfaces for building, under certain circumstances, chalk can provide a solid foundation for building.

Contrasting and contradicting

When other arguments are being considered, authors may move back and forth between their own point of view and opposing arguments. They will normally either weigh up the evidence for one side and then the other for each reason in turn, or they will contrast all the evidence for one point of view against the evidence for their own line of reasoning. Words that indicate this process of contrasting include: *although . . .* ; *conversely*; *by contrast*; *on the one hand . . .* ; *on the other hand . . .* ; *in fact*.

Signposting alternative points of view (continued)

- On the one hand there are those who argue that Feng Shui is based on mysterious principles such as yin and yang that people in the West cannot understand. On the other hand are those who argue that Feng Shui is based on common sense and therefore suitable for everyone.
- Although humans' verbal language can be used in sophisticated ways to express abstract ideas and reasoning, it can also be very restricted in its capacity to communicate our deepest feelings and creative thoughts.

- Some researchers argue that scientists are being forced to patent their work even when they do not want to enter commercial contracts. By contrast, others complain that they do not receive enough support in patenting their discoveries.
- Houses benefit from being built on bedrock. By contrast, houses built on beaches tend to sink over time.

Expressing results and consequences

After several reasons have been considered, the author should draw out how these should be interpreted as a whole. This would normally be found towards the end of the sequence, but the author may do this several times during the line of reasoning, to help the reader keep track of the reasoning and to reinforce the message. This was covered above (on p. 71), early under '*Intermediate conclusions*'.

Words used to express the consequences of the evidence the author has presented include: *as a result*; *as a consequence*; *hence*; *thus*; *consequently*; *because of this*.

Examples

- As a result, we can see that the rules governing Feng Shui at work are similar to those that apply in the home.
- Thus, the introduction of verbal communication allowed us to communicate with more of our species but using less time.
- As a consequence of commercial backing, the infrastructure for scientific research has been improved in a number of institutions.
- Hence, as sand shifts and moves over time, a house built on sand is likely to sink.

Activity

Browse through three or four articles for your subject. What words are used to:

- Introduce the main argument?
- Move an argument along?
- Sum up the argument?

Words used to signpost conclusions

Conclusions

All the reasons and evidence presented should lead towards the conclusion. Even when alternative arguments are put forward, these should be presented in a way that supports the main line of reasoning. Authors usually signal conclusions using words such as *therefore*; *in conclusion*; *thus*; *thus, we can see . . .*

For longer texts, the conclusion may consist of one or more paragraphs rather than just a single sentence. These would normally be placed at the end of the piece of writing. For longer texts, a good piece of writing will usually refer clearly to the overall conclusions as it unfolds, so as to help the reader to make sense of what they read.

In shorter passages, as we have seen, the conclusion may be stated near the beginning rather than the end.

Examples

- In conclusion, Feng Shui is not a decorative art but is, rather, a sophisticated system for arranging our surroundings so that we live in greater balance and harmony with the outer world.
- Thus, we have shown that the human brain evolved as a result of our need for more effective and efficient social communication.
- Therefore, academic research can be greatly advanced by commercial partnership.
- Therefore, it is important to ensure that sufficient tests have been carried out to check the underlying rock structures, and to consider carefully the consequences of building on surfaces other than bedrock.

Activity

Add signal words to signpost the development of the argument in the following passages.

Passage 10.5

Deaf people have their own languages, based on signs, body position and facial expressions. As few hearing people understand these languages, communication between deaf and hearing people is not usually very effective. Deaf people often form strong social and cultural groups, they are often excluded from mainstream culture and their talents are not used effectively within the economy. Hearing people can feel excluded from deaf conversations and uncertain of how to behave around deaf people. It would be in everyone's interests if sign languages were taught in school so that deaf and hearing children grew up able to communicate effectively with each other.

Passage 10.6

Globalisation appears to be inevitable but there is disagreement about whether this is a positive development. There are those who argue that increased contact between countries leads to better understanding and reduces the likelihood of future wars. They see benefits to democracy and human rights from information being widely available electronically, so that different nations can compare conditions in their country with those elsewhere. Some see globalisation as a destructive force. They argue that it leads to less powerful peoples losing their indigenous languages as the languages of more powerful countries are used internationally for business and politics. They argue that globalisation often means big business buying up resources and land in poorer countries, distorting local economies and draining their resources. Although there are some potential benefits to globalisation, some controls are needed to protect poorer economies from exploitation.

Answers: see p. 190. ▶

Words and phrases used to structure the line of reasoning

The signal words introduced above are summarised on the table below.

Function	Words used
Introducing the line of reasoning	
Opening phrases	*Words indicating 'first . . .'* first; first of all; to begin; first and foremost; at the outset; Initially, I will start by . . .
Developing the line of reasoning	
Reinforcing with similar reasons	*Words indicating 'similarly . . .'* similarly; equally; likewise; in the same way; indeed; correspondingly; in the same line; also; too; again; besides
Reinforcing with different reasons or evidence	*Words indicating 'also . . .'* also; in addition; besides; again; as well as; either; too; not only . . . but also . . . ; neither . . . nor . . . ; neither
Stronger reinforcement	*Words indicating 'furthermore'* furthermore; moreover; indeed; what is more
Introducing alternative arguments	*Words indicating 'alternatively . . .'* alternatively; a different perspective on this . . . ; others argue that . . . ; it might be argued that . . . (the words used in 'rebutting alternative arguments' can also be used)
Rebutting alternative arguments	*Words indicating 'however'* however; on the other hand; nonetheless; nevertheless; notwithstanding this; in any case; in spite of this; despite this; at the same time; even though . . .
Contrasting	*Words indicating 'by contrast . . .'* by contrast; although . . . ; conversely; on the one hand . . . on the other hand . . . ; in fact
Concluding	
Expressing results and consequences	*Words indicating 'therefore'* therefore; this suggests that . . . ; this indicates . . . ; as a result; as a consequence; hence; thus; consequently; because of this; from this we can infer that; from this we can deduce that . . .
Conclusions	*Words indicating 'in conclusion'* therefore; in conclusion; thus we can see; thus.

Drawing tentative conclusions

Academic writing, such as that used for research projects, articles and books, tends to avoid words that suggest absolutes and, instead, uses words that express some tentativeness. The kind of alternatives used are indicated below.

Avoids	Uses qualifiers such as:
all, every	most, many, some
always	usually, generally, often, in most cases, so far, haven't yet
never	rarely, in few cases, it is unlikely that
proves	the evidence suggests, indicates, points to, it would appear

Example 1

During the Protestant reformation in Britain in the sixteenth century, the kings' ministers ordered that religious ornaments such as chalices and carved rood screens found in churches be destroyed. These disappeared from churches at that time. However, during the short reign of the Catholic queen, Mary Tudor, these articles reappeared. As chalices and elaborate carved rood screens appeared again so quickly during Mary's reign, this suggests that the items had not been destroyed previously. It would appear that people had simply hidden them away. This further suggests that the reformation had less popular support than had been previously believed, and that many people had been hoping for a return to the old Catholic ways.

Here, the author considers that the sudden reappearance of religious items suggests the items had been hidden rather than destroyed. The author then proposes that this is evidence that the old religious customs were more popular than had been previously believed.

These sound like sensible conclusions. However, the author uses tentative language in drawing these conclusions as there may be other interpretations. For example, it may be that there was a much higher level of skill in reproducing those items than was formerly believed. It is possible the items were destroyed and new items were made quickly.

Alternatively, people would have been aware that there was a possibility that the new religious ways might be overturned in the future and that they might be punished for having destroyed sacred items. They may have preferred the new religion but hidden the forbidden items away in order to protect themselves in the future.

Academic writers are always aware that there may be alternative explanations or unexpected findings that overturn even the most widely held views. In the example above, the writer used phrases such as *this suggests*, *it would appear*, *this further suggests*.

Example 2

A small amount of hydrochloric acid was poured on each rock. The first rock then gave off the smell of hydrogen sulphide, a smell like rotten eggs, suggesting the rock was galena. The second rock fizzed, suggesting that it was giving off carbon dioxide and that the rock may be an oolitic limestone.

Example 2 is science writing. The writer is basing judgements on well-tried tests. The tests used are fairly conclusive, but the writer uses tentative language as, if the rocks did not share other known characteristics of those rocks, such as mineral content or grain size, a different judgement might be needed. It is possible, for example, that the fizzing rock was a different type of calcite rock, such as chalk or marble.

Activity: Writing conclusions

Activity

How well do these passages express their conclusions in a suitably tentative manner?

Passage 10.7

Interpreting new discoveries

We have seen that when explorers found new lands, they tended to interpret what they saw as evidence of what they had intended to find. Travellers to the 'Americas' in the fourteenth and fifteenth centuries sent home reports of finding giants and green men. Earlier, Marco Polo, who had hoped to find unicorns on his travels to China, believed the one-horned creature he found in Java was indeed a unicorn, despite the animal, a rhinoceros, bearing no other resemblance to the fabled beast. However, unlike those who claimed to see giants, or later explorers who really believed they had heard orang utans talking, Marco Polo appears to have described rhinoceroses exactly as he found them. This suggests that not everyone responded to new discoveries by using the same approach. Moreover, it is possible that with the number of discoveries made in recent decades, people are now more likely to take new discoveries in their stride.

Passage 10.8

RNA does the hard work

Although we hear more in the press about DNA, especially after work on mapping human genes, we hear much less about the role of RNA in cell reproduction. RNA, or ribonucleic acid, is essential to the functioning of our genes. One type of RNA reads the messages encoded in the DNA. Various types of RNA are involved in making proteins and carrying these to where they are needed in the body's cells, so that the cell can function as it should, including growing and reproducing. Although the DNA holds encoded messages which help define the nature of the next generation, these would not mean much without RNA. Therefore, it is RNA that appears to do the really hard work in reproduction.

Commentary

Passage 10.7 examines the way people, historically, tried to make sense when they discovered things that were new to them and their cultures. It is difficult to write with absolute certainty about approaches, attitudes and beliefs, and even more so when these took place in the distant past. The writer uses the phrases 'this suggests' and 'it is possible' to indicate the tentative nature of the conclusions being drawn. It is possible, for example, that people today think that there is little more to find out, so are even more surprised by discoveries. The writer uses tentative language appropriately.

Passage 10.8 makes a judgement about the relative importance of RNA in reproduction. Scientific judgements can usually be stated with more certainty, as they can be tested, replicated and measured more exactly than matters such as attitudes and responses. However, even science mainly sets out to support hypotheses and test what appear to be laws. Science recognises that further research can overturn scientific laws, at least under specific conditions. Most of this text is written in more certain language than Passage 10.7, as befits a scientific subject, but the overall conclusion is suitably tentative as it is possible that future research will reveal hitherto unknown roles for DNA or RNA.

Critical analysis for essays: essay titles

Essays are exercises in critical thinking. In academic contexts, they are set primarily for you to demonstrate your understanding of an issue, drawing on your critical analysis of, and engagement with, source materials and a range of theoretical perspectives.

As a rule, essays are set for students on issues where there are multiple perspectives. You are expected to:

- become aware of what those different perspectives are, through attendance at taught sessions and especially by reading around the subject;
- understand how and why the major differences in perspective have arisen;
- understand the theoretical underpinnings for each major area of difference in perspective, and how these compare and contrast with each other;
- critically evaluate the evidence base for the different perspectives and theories, and their applicability to different contexts;
- draw together your critical judgements to form a conclusion or set of conclusions that indicate your own considered position, based on the relative quality of the evidence base.

Critical analysis of the essay title

Essays set for students are usually carefully worded so as to encourage a focus on a particular complex or controversial issue. Before launching into an essay, look carefully at the wording of the title so as to do the following:

- Tease out how many parts or subsections there are to the essay and the relative weighting of each. If there is a word limit, consider how many words you can allocate to each section. This will, in turn, give you a sense of how much time to spend on each.
- Identify the main focus of the essay: what is it that

the tutors want you to address? If this isn't clear, it may become so once you have read around the subject.

- Consider which theoretical perspective or schools of thought to call upon to explore the issues – you will be expected to engage in a 'critical dialogue' with these. Again, these may not be evident until you start reading around the subject.

Setting your own essay title

If you are setting your own essay title, you need to ensure that you set one that encourages you to work in the same way as for an essay title set by a tutor:

- decide on the key issue that you want the essay to address;
- ensure that there are multiple perspectives on the issue, each of which presents good arguments and evidence;
- look for a topic that contains an element of controversy or other complexity;
- ensure that there is a good range of quality reading material on these different perspectives;
- beware of creating an essay title where there is good reading material or evidence for only one perspective – as this will not help you to demonstrate your own critical judgements well.

Resource

An explanatory list of terms commonly used for essay titles is provided below (p. 182).

Academic keywords used in titles

These words indicate the approach or style expected for the piece of writing.

Account for   Give reasons for; explain why something happens.

Analyse   Examine in very close detail; identify important points and chief features.

Comment on   Identify and write about the main issues, giving your reactions based upon what you have read or heard in lectures. Avoid purely personal opinion.

Compare   Show how two or more things are similar. Indicate the relevance or consequences of these similarities.

Contrast   Set two or more items or arguments in opposition so as to draw out differences. Indicate whether the differences are significant. If appropriate, give reasons why one item or argument may be preferable (see Chapter 9).

Critically evaluate   Weigh arguments for and against something, assessing the strength of the evidence on both sides. Use criteria to guide your assessment of which opinions, theories, models or items are preferable.

Define   Give the exact meaning of. Where relevant, show that you understand why the definition may be problematic.

Describe   Give the main characteristics or features of something, or outline the main events.

Discuss   Write about the most important aspects of (probably including criticism); give arguments for and against; consider the implications of.

Distinguish   Bring out the differences between two (possibly confusible) items.

Evaluate   Assess the worth, importance or usefulness of something, using evidence. There will probably be cases to be made both *for* and *against*.

Examine   Put the subject 'under the microscope', looking at it in detail. If appropriate, 'Critically evaluate' it as well.

Explain   Make clear why something happens, or why something is the way it is.

Illustrate   Make something clear and explicit, giving examples or evidence.

Interpret   Give the meaning and relevance of data or other material presented.

Justify   Give evidence which supports an argument or idea; show why decisions or conclusions were made, considering objections that others might make.

Narrate   Concentrate on saying *what* happened, telling it as a story.

Outline   Give only the main points, showing the main structure.

Relate   Show similarities and connections between two or more things.

State   Give the main features, in very clear English (almost like a simple list but written in full sentences).

Summarise   Draw out the main points only (see 'Outline'), omitting details or examples.

To what extent   Consider how far something is true, or contributes to a final outcome. Consider also ways in which the proposition is not true. (The answer is usually somewhere between 'completely' and 'not at all'.)

Trace   Follow the order of different stages in an event or process.

Critical analysis for essays: reading

Critical analysis when reading

For a student essay, much of your time is spent reading around the subject and working with the material that you read. You would be expected to apply the critical skills that you have covered in earlier parts of this book, such as:

- making good critical decisions about the relevance of reading material, given the specific essay title and the issues relevant to it;
- making good critical decisions in what you choose to read, based on the quality of the materials and the evidence base that these draw upon (see pp. 128–32);
- the breadth of what you read and variety of perspectives considered.

Demonstrating critical reading skills

You demonstrate your critical abilities to your tutors through the ways that you make use of reading material. They will look at:

- what you choose to refer to – and what you omit;
- how well you query the findings and opinions in what you read, especially in the light of contradictory findings and judgements;
- whether you can recognise the relative merits and flaws of different perspectives.

Reading for balanced analysis

There is a fine balance in writing essays between ensuring that your position is clear, and not appearing to be dogmatic about it. If you have strong personal opinions or beliefs, then it can be especially difficult to maintain a balanced approach. The following guidelines can help.

Balanced reading

- *Use quality resources*   Justify the position that you believe in on reasons and arguments drawn from good quality sources; if you cannot find these, it will be difficult to present a strong academic case that gains good marks. Cite the sources that you have read that support your position (pp. 187–8 below).

- *Balance your choice of reading*   Read good quality resources for all sides of the argument and select the best evidence for all viewpoints – not just for your own position. If you do this, you demonstrate that you are making a reasonable effort to make objective judgements.

- *Be even-handed*   Bring a similar level of criticality when reading sources that support your own position and those that support positions you reject.

- *Acknowledge good counter arguments*   Even if you are not convinced by alternative viewpoints, be fair in presenting their strengths. If your reading suggests that there are good arguments against your position, then acknowledge the strengths of these. Cite sources for these just as you would for your own position.

What if the evidence is against you?

If the evidence appears stronger for positions that you do not believe in, your reader would then want to know why you are holding to your position against the available evidence. In such a case, it is possible to state that the evidence base, or academic argument, is currently strongest for a particular point of view without this meaning that you accept this personally or have to change your beliefs. Alternatively, you can indicate where you feel evidence may become available in the future that would support your position.

Critical analytical essays: introductions

Parts and components of an essay

An essay consists of three parts, known as:

- The introduction
- The body of the essay
- The conclusion.

Into these, a critical analytical essay integrates the following five components:

1 clarification of the issues;
2 a statement of your own position;
3 analysis of compelling arguments in support of your position;
4 analysis and rebuttal of counter arguments;
5 potential synthesis.

The weighting and sequence of these will vary depending on the issues and the material to be covered, but some guidelines follow below.

The introduction to the essay

An essay isn't like a mystery novel where the plot gradually unfolds and the unexpected suddenly occurs. Rather, in a good essay, the scene is set for the reader through a formal introduction. This should be succinct, precise and brief; it can be as short as a single paragraph and shouldn't be longer than a tenth of your essay.

As part of your introduction, without at this point going into detail, you should make the following clear to your potential reader.

The core issues

Refer to the main issues that will be addressed in the essay and, if this can be done succinctly, include an indication of why these are of significance.

Key perspectives

Indicate the major differences of opinion, perspectives or schools of thought on the issues embedded within the essay title. Avoid straying into the more detailed analysis which would come later in the essay.

Define the terms

Define what you mean by words or phrases that are potentially open to different interpretations, or which are contentious, or that could be used in different ways to produce alternative conclusions. Avoid defining obvious terms, covering every word in a title, or giving dictionary definitions.

Your position

Ensure that your position comes across clearly and that this is consistent with what you write in your conclusion. If possible, indicate the critical perspective that you are taking, such as the school of thought that you lean towards. Your own position should either be stated explicitly or else should be easily inferred from the rest of your introduction.

The direction of your argument

If there are twists and caveats intrinsic to your argument, then mention these succinctly, indicating how they support or modify your overall line of reasoning.

Get to the point

- Avoid giving unnecessary background information that an interested reader can find out for themselves.
- Be specific about 'significance'. Give reasons for why an issue is important now – because of new or high-profile research findings, or recent political or social events, or the anticipated future impact in the sciences, arts, the economy, or in a region, or for a large number of people, or in an area of research where solutions have been hard to find, or where previous research findings have been overturned.
- Avoid the urge to make broad generalisations such as about 'science', 'humanity' or 'the world' as a means of getting started.

Structured argument: the body of the essay

Clarification of the issues

Typically, essays are set on subjects that are multi-faceted and complex – that enable the analysis of different points of view. You are not expected to cover every issue and perspective. The wording of the essay title gives clues to the expected focus for that essay; this narrows down the issues to be addressed. To orientate your reader, clarify the issues either in the introduction or in the opening paragraph of the body of the essay.

Bring out why these issues are significant, controversial or complex. If this seems difficult, it is likely that you have not read sufficiently around the subject. It may help to browse extracts of articles and book reviews for the past few years in key journals for your subject in order to gain a feel for the developing issues.

Your position

Ensure that you provide a clear line of reasoning (pages xii and 47) such that your own position as stated in your introduction comes across clearly and coherently throughout your essay.

Analysis of arguments

The bulk of the essay consists of examining, critically, two or more viewpoints on the issues identified. In doing so, you will identify compelling reasons for espousing some arguments and for dismissing others.

Some arguments may appear persuasive at first but less so when scrutinised further. These could be the dominant views or most interesting recent research. Opinion on these might be different in a few years time. It is worth examining them from that perspective and seeing if you can identify any weak points for yourself.

Other viewpoints may have little following or may be so new that the evidence base is still weak.

Nonetheless, in the future, these might become dominant perspectives in the discipline. It is worth considering what further research might strengthen these viewpoints or give them more credibility.

Make critical judgements

- Make critical judgements on the relative merits of each perspective or school of thought, stating the strengths and weaknesses of each.
- Be prepared to state if there are gaps in the evidence base that make it difficult to make a definitive judgement on a particular aspect.
- Be clear about *exactly* what the evidence does support; it may be very convincing, or weak, in some conditions, but that might not be the case if the conditions were changed in specific ways. Demonstrate that you have given thought to when, where and why an argument might apply in one case but not another, and to where further research is needed to support the case.

Make critical choices

Select only the most compelling arguments for and against. For an undergraduate essay, there is unlikely to be space within the word limit for you to go into detailed analysis of all differences and points of interest.

Your selectivity provides evidence of the strength of your critical thinking skills; your tutors will be looking to see whether you can recognise the most salient arguments and material to include.

Reflection Structured argument in essays

In your own essays:

- How clearly does your own position come across? (Do you tend to 'sit on the fence'?)
- Do you engage in a critical way with different perspectives on the subject – evaluating the arguments of those who have written about the subject?

Essays: Bringing the argument together

Structure your argument

- Use a separate paragraph to analyse each specific point or, if these can be stated briefly, each set of related points.
- Check that paragraphs are sequenced in the best possible order for bringing out your line of reasoning to your reader.
- Use the first or last lines of your paragraphs, and 'sign-posting' vocabulary, to help indicate the flow of your argument to the reader (see pages 173–8).
- Sometimes, it can be difficult to maintain a sense of clear direction when there are complex issues to analyse. If so, give an interim summary of the arguments so far.

Synthesis

It is likely that, in considering different perspectives or theories, you will find some aspects compelling and other aspects less so. You might feel, for example, that some arguments apply well to particular circumstances, but less so in others. You may feel that all arguments contribute something to the debate even if not in equal weight, but that none are entirely satisfactory in all respects.

Your ultimate position in the essay may be a combination, or synthesis, of the most compelling arguments from several different perspectives that you analysed. If so, avoid generalisations such as 'they are all helpful' or 'none are perfect'. Rather, be specific about what you would take from each perspective. Make a judgement about whether your synthesis also has limitations: you should subject your own synthesis to critical scrutiny.

Conclusions in essays

Essay conclusions shouldn't come as a surprise to the reader. Rather, they should appear to be the inevitable end-point of your line of reasoning. The purpose of the conclusion is to stand back from the more detailed reasoning and evidence that you presented in the body of the essay, and clarify the key messages that have emerged. This may include reasons why it is difficult to form firm conclusions, such as gaps you had identified in the evidence.

Your conclusion draws together:

- your position, which may be a synthesis of other viewpoints;
- the most compelling reasons that support that position;
- the strongest counter arguments and a summary rebuttal of these;
- if relevant, it can refer to strengths or weaknesses in the evidence;
- if relevant, what specifically needs to be researched further in order better to clarify the issues or strengthen the arguments.

Give a sense of an ending

Make sure that your conclusion wraps up your essay neatly. It isn't appropriate to introduce new arguments or evidence here, as any new material should be subjected to critical analysis. If you start to analyse these, then you are, in effect, continuing your argument rather than concluding.

Your conclusion does not have to refer back, point by point to all the issues you have already covered, but it should at least allude to these and serve to reinforce your overall argument. Your conclusion should link back, clearly, to the points you raised in your introduction and, especially, to the essay title. If possible, find a way of doing this in your final sentence.

Reflection — Conclusions

In your own essays:

- Do you aim at making a synthesis of the best arguments on the issue?
- Does your final position on the issue come across strongly?

Citing and referencing your sources

It should be evident from previous sections that good written critical analysis will involve drawing on reputable sources of evidence.

It is part of the convention of good critical analysis, whether as a student, writer, artist, inventor or more generally, to acknowledge the sources that you use.

Citations

When you draw on someone's work or ideas in your writing, you should acknowledge this straight away at that point in your writing; this is known as a citation. Typically, after making the point, you write the surname(s) and date of publication: (Bloggs, 2012).

References

References are provided at the end of your work as a list of the full details of all those sources you cited.

Bibliographies

Bibliographies are a list of materials that you used as background, but didn't cite in your text.

'Referencing' in critical writing

For all academic writing, you are required to provide details, or 'references', of all the source materials used to produce your work. For students, as much of your work is based on reading, most references will be to academic books and articles. Depending on your subject, you may use other sources in the public domain such as research papers, newspapers, government reports, parliamentary speeches, websites, television or radio programmes, museum or gallery catalogues and brochures.

What is the purpose of referencing?

For the author of the original source

- It is a courtesy to those whose work you have used or drawn upon to give them proper acknowledgement.

For the reader

- It provides transparency about where your ideas and evidence were drawn from.
- It enables your reader to find the source quickly and easily.
- Readers can go to your source to check the accuracy of your use or interpretation.

The advantages to you

- It strengthens your argument if it is well researched and draws on the authority of reputable sources.
- You will be better able to recall where your ideas came from, either if you wish to use those sources in the future, or if the integrity of your work were to be questioned.
- It is a sign of your integrity to acknowledge your debt to others.
- As a student, there is the added advantage of demonstrating to tutors that you have engaged in background reading, as expected.
- For students, it is a convention that you are required to follow or there are severe penalties.

You don't reference . . .

- Common knowledge (names, dates and well established facts, such as a writer's date of birth or that bees make honey).
- Conversations with friends and students, unless these were formally conducted as part of an agreed research methodology.
- Other students' essays or academic work, as you should not use these for your own work. The exception would be if these had been made available through the university specifically for reference purposes.

What do I include in a reference?

It depends on the source

The detail that you need to provide varies depending on whether the source is a book, chapter in a book, journal article, newspaper article, government paper, manuscript, web-site, radio or TV programme, audio file and so on.

It depends on the style of referencing

The detail that you need to include, and the precise order in which to present this, will vary depending on the referencing style used for your programme of study. Your tutors will advise you which method is used. Typical styles used for academic study are:

- Harvard (widely used)
- Vancouver (especially for science and health subjects)
- Modern Language Association (MLA)
- Modern Humanities Research Association (MHRA)
- OSCOLA (for legal sources).

Typical information to include

- Authors' surnames and initials
- Date of publication
- Full title of the chapter, article or book
- Full title of the book or journal in which a chapter or article is found
- The edition of a book (if not the first)
- Place of publication and the name of the publisher, for books
- Series and volume number, for journal articles
- Location, month and year for conferences
- Digital Object Identifiers (DOI) for internet pages.

Examples

See pages 162–3 on note-taking to support referencing, and examples of references.

How exact do I need to be?

In academic contexts, there are specific conventions for citing sources and referencing. Each type of source, from medieval manuscripts to blogs and tweets, needs to be cited in a very particular way.

Follow referencing rules exactly

You cannot normally pick and choose between referencing systems: whichever system is used on your course should be followed exactly. If in doubt, follow rigidly the examples that are provided by your institution.

'Exactly' for referencing means:

- using the correct referencing style for your programme;
- including a citation within your writing and the full reference at the end, or as a footnote, depending on the style of referencing;
- providing every detail required for the type of source and for the style of referencing;
- providing the information in the exact sequence required;
- using punctuation and abbreviations as stipulated, even down to the use of capitals, brackets, commas, etc.

What if I don't reference my work?

- Weak skills in citing your sources are penalised by poor marks or possibly even a fail. Check your references carefully at least twice.
- If you do not use citations and references correctly, it may appear that you are trying to pass off other people's work or intellectual property (their research or ideas) as your own. This is plagiarism.
- Universities have software and other methods for detecting cheating and plagiarism.
- Plagiarism is treated as an offence and receives severe penalties. You may have to redo part or all of your work for a capped low mark or a zero. You could be removed permanently from your course and college or university.

Summary

Critical writing draws on many of the skills developed earlier in the book, such as developing an argument, analysing, evaluating and selecting evidence, making judgements, and structuring reasons in a logical way towards a conclusion.

However, spoken arguments can draw on devices such as body language and voice modulations to emphasise points, and the dialogue itself can divide the argument into manageable sections. For critical writing, the writer must take care to use language and structure to organise the argument and to signal different stages within it.

In a written argument, care must be taken to set the scene so that readers know from the outset what conclusion the author wants them to draw. Writers normally present their own position, their conclusions and their own supporting reasons first, so that they orientate the reader to their own perspectives early on. It is important to provide just sufficient for the reader to understand the background. Similarly, at the end of the argument, and at points within it, the writer needs to draw out the conclusions clearly.

In other words, throughout a piece of critical writing, the writer must keep the reader in mind constantly. The aim is not to baffle readers with jargon and clever use of language or to bombard them with so much information that they lose sight of the argument. Instead, the writer must select, group, sequence and structure the best reasons, evidence and details, so that the reader can easily make sense of what is written. Once this has been planned into the writing, signal words can be used to signpost the reader to any changes of direction in the argument and to conclusions.

Critical writing usually follows certain conventions, which were outlined at the start of the chapter. For example, the final drafts of critical writing must be fine-tuned so that critical analysis takes precedence over other aspects such as description and background information. Such conventions signal to the reader that this is a piece of critical writing, which prompts a particular approach to reading.

Students are usually asked to demonstrate their understanding of an issue through essays that use critical and analytical skills whilst using particular writing conventions that support the development of an argument. These were outlined in the chapter above.

In the next chapter, you will have the opportunity to look in detail at two critical essays, so that you can see how all these different aspects are combined.

Information on the sources

Marco Polo and unicorns: Eco, U. (1998) *Serendipities: Language and Lunacy* (London: Weidenfeld & Nicolson).

Responses to discoveries of the Americas: Elliott, J. H. (1972) *The Old World and the New, 1492–1650* (Cambridge: Cambridge University Press).

Rocks and minerals: Farndon, J. (1994) *Dictionary of the Earth* (London: Dorling Kindersley).

Productionism: Lang, T. and Heasman, M. A. (2004) *Food Wars: The Global Battle for Mouths, Minds and Markets* (Sterling, VA: Earthscan).

RNA and DNA: Postgate, J. (1994) *The Outer Reaches of Life* (Cambridge: Cambridge University Press).

Answers to activities in Chapter 10

Setting the scene for the reader (p. 171)

'Is productionism dead?'

Passage 10.1 provides a good introduction to the subject that an intelligent reader without an in-depth knowledge of the subject could follow. The author defines what is meant by 'productionism' and summarises why the theory was developed. The introduction informs the reader about positive and negative aspects of productionism covered in the essay. The author's position and conclusions are presented clearly to orientate the reader.

Passage 10.2 is written in a flowery or theatrical style, and makes grand sweeping statements. However, the style makes it difficult for a reader who does not know the subject well to work out what productionism is. The author's general position is clear, but the reader is not told how the argument will be developed.

Passage 10.3 launches too quickly into the subject, giving little introduction to orientate the reader. The author presents examples of the effects of productionism without having explained what it is and how it led to these effects.

Passage 10.4 makes too much use of broad generalisations about human society. Some of these may be true, but would be hard to prove and are not directly relevant to the essay. As a result, the essay starts very slowly, and uses a lot of words to say very little of relevance.

Words used to signpost conclusions (p. 177)

If you used different words to signpost the argument than those used in the passages opposite, check the table on p. 178 to see if you used suitable alternatives. The signal words are indicated in italic.

Passage 10.5

Deaf people have their own languages, based on signs, body position and facial expressions. *However,* as few hearing people understand these languages, communication between deaf and hearing people is not usually very effective. *Although* deaf people often form strong social and cultural groups, they are often excluded from mainstream culture and their talents are not used effectively within the economy. *Similarly,* hearing people can feel excluded from deaf conversations and uncertain of how to behave around deaf people. *Therefore,* it would be in everyone's interests if sign languages were taught in school so that deaf and hearing children grew up able to communicate effectively with each other.

Passage 10.6

Globalisation appears to be inevitable but there is disagreement about whether this is a positive development. *On the one hand,* there are those who argue that increased contact between countries leads to better understanding and has reduced the likelihood of future wars. *Furthermore,* they see benefits to democracy and human rights from information being widely available electronically, so that different nations can compare conditions in their country with those elsewhere. *On the other hand,* there are those who see globalisation as a destructive force. They argue that it leads to less powerful peoples losing their indigenous languages as the languages of more powerful countries are used internationally for business and politics. *Moreover,* they argue that globalisation often means big business buying up resources and land in poorer countries, thus distorting local economies and draining their resources. *Therefore,* although there are some potential benefits to globalisation, some controls are needed to protect poorer economies from exploitation.

Chapter 11

Where's the analysis?
Evaluating critical writing

Learning outcomes

This chapter offers you opportunities to:

- compare two critical essays, to better identify the characteristics of good critical writing
- compare your evaluations of extended pieces of critical writing against a commentary, to check your skills in evaluation
- use a structure for critically evaluating your own writing

Introduction

In this chapter, you have the opportunity to compare two longer pieces of writing on the same subject. These essays are based on the texts found on pp. 233–7, which were also used for the reading and note-making activities in Chapter 9. Assume that the authors of the essays have access to all the texts on pp. 233–7, and, therefore, are making choices about what to include from those materials, and what to leave out.

Below, on p. 192 you will find a checklist to structure your evaluation of Essay 1, followed by the essay and then a commentary. A similar set of materials are provided for Essay 2. The checklists are provided as a tool, and you do not have to use them if you prefer to take a different analytical approach.

As you read each essay, consider how far it meets the requirements for critical thinking that you have covered in the book so far, and what an editor or tutor might provide as feedback if you were to hand this in as your final copy. Note your comments down, either on the checklists or as notes, so that you can compare these with the printed commentaries. The numbers given as superscript in the text (e.g. text[1]) indicate where a note is provided in the commentary.

An adapted checklist has been provided on pp. 204–5 to help you evaluate your own critical writing.

Checklist for evaluating Essay 1

Use this checklist to analyse Essay 1 on the following page. Compare your analysis with the evaluation and commentary on pp. 196–7.

Aspect	Yes/No	Comments
1 The writer's own position on the issues is clear.		
2 It is clear what the reasons are for the writer's point of view.		
3 The writer's conclusion is clear and based on the evidence.		
4 Reasons are presented in a logical order, as a line of reasoning.		
5 The argument is well structured and easy to follow.		
6 Reasons are clearly linked to one another and to the conclusion.		
7 All the text is relevant to the assignment (in this case, about whether stealing is always wrong).		
8 The main reasons and key points stand out clearly to the reader.		
9 The writer makes good use of other people's research as supporting evidence to strengthen the argument.		
10 Does the writer make a reasoned evaluation of other people's views, especially those that contradict his or her own point of view?		
11 Does the writer provide references in the text when introducing other people's ideas?		
12 Does the writer provide a list of references at the end of the essay?		
13 Has the writer successfully removed any non-essential descriptive writing?		
14 Does the writing contain any inconsistencies?		
15 Are the writer's beliefs or self-interests unfairly distorting the argument?		

Evaluate Essay 1

'Stealing is always wrong.' Discuss with reference to unpaid downloading of music from the internet.

There are many forms of stealing. Although most reasonable people would agree that some forms of theft such as burglary or mugging are always wrong,[1] other areas are less clear cut. In this essay, I shall look at downloading music from the internet as a grey area.

Stealing has probably existed since the beginning of time, and certainly as long ago as the Old Testament, where it was banned by the commandments. All religions regard stealing as wrong, so you would think that there were universally understood principles about what is stealing and what is not. However, this is not the case. This is also true of many other types of ethical issue. Despite this long-standing agreement that stealing is wrong, many people steal. In fact, it is a very common crime, so it is worth considering why this has persisted for so long.[2]

Before the internet became popular, people used to tape music from the radio. Lee (2006) says no one was bothered by this because it was impossible to catch people.[3] Everyone knew that it happened but record sales remained high so it clearly had no real impact on artists and labels.[4] Because of this, although home taping was technically illegal, it was only record companies who were worried about profits who could really call it 'stealing'. Nobody knows how much music was copied and it still continues to this day.

Lee goes on to say that just because it is possible to catch people who download from the internet it doesn't make it any worse than people making copies from the radio.[5] Carla (2006) agrees with Lee and says that downloading music from the internet is a 'useful service to music'. She states that without this service the world of music would be 'extremely bland and middle of the road'. Hibbs (2006)[6] says that more and more people are downloading music without paying, and sharing it with their friends. Because everyone is doing it, it cannot be a bad thing and cannot be considered wrong.[7]

The real reason downloading from the internet gets classed as stealing is because big music companies do not like to see big profits escaping from them. Spratt (2004) states that record companies are not even that bothered about ordinary people downloading from the internet. They are only worried about companies who make and sell pirate copies of their recordings. So why do they continue to prosecute file sharers? This can only be about greed, especially as it is the poorest people who have to download for free as they cannot afford to pay for legal downloads.[8]

Cuttle (2007)[9] says that people should pay for the products that they consume and if they cannot pay then they should go without. He sees downloading music for free as stealing. Kahliney (2006) agrees with this. He says that small companies cannot afford to lose money through people downloading their music for free. Even a few copies have a bad effect on companies who only employ a few staff and they might have to make people redundant.[10] The type of music these companies produce tends to be quite obscure and unpopular so there is little effect on the majority of music listeners.[11]

Carla (2006) says that new bands are often overlooked by the major record companies and are only picked up by small, independent companies.[12] These companies are often only able to distribute music on a limited basis. Many have very small staff and resources and cannot get out on the road to sell the music to shops across the country, never mind worldwide. Bigger producers can employ sales teams to take the product out to the market, either promoting it in shops, or even arranging tours to schools to promote the music to school children. School children buy records in the largest numbers so a band that is promoted well to children is likely to rise up the charts and become better known to the general public. It is unrealistic to expect that every band can tour the schools, as schools limit how many bands can visit in a term as they have other things to fit into the school day, and, furthermore, many bands couldn't afford the costs of going on tour. This is where downloading performs a service to the small artist.[13] When people download music for free, it actually helps to get it heard by a range of people who would not know about it otherwise.[14]

The public, especially people with little money, should not have to lose out because of the interests of big business. Business is only motivated by profits. It's in the interest of big business to prevent people downloading. Their argument is all about money, at the end of the day. They were not so bothered about copying from the radio because the quality of the reproductions was bad. If they really had a moral concern about stealing, they would have objected as much to taping as they do about downloading.[15]

There are some forms of stealing that are clearly always wrong, such as mugging a person or robbing their house. We have seen in this essay that stealing is a long-standing ethical problem, and that even though there have long been strictures against stealing, the moral position has not prevented people from stealing. This essay has looked at some areas which are much less clear cut. There are arguments for and against why downloading from the internet might be considered wrong. These depend on what viewpoint you take – companies worried about profit will always see it as wrong but ordinary music listeners think they are providing a helpful service. We also have to think about the artists, both what they can earn and also whether it is good to have their music heard by a wider audience.[16] Not everyone will agree with the arguments presented by either side. This is an interesting debate and one that will doubtless continue for many years.[17]

Evaluation of Essay 1

Aspect	Yes/No	Comments
1 The writer's own position on the issues is clear.	No	It is not stated clearly, but can be guessed.
2 It is clear what the reasons are for the writer's point of view.	No	These are not clearly stated.
3 The writer's conclusion is clear and based on the evidence.	No	The essay appears to favour evidence that supports unpaid downloading as acceptable, but this is not formulated into a conclusion. The final paragraph only summarises the arguments.
4 Reasons are presented in a logical order, as a line of reasoning.	No	The reasons appear to be given in a random order, as the author has not stated clearly what their position is or what conclusions the reader should draw.
5 The argument is well structured and easy to follow.	No	The writing hops back and forward between points. It isn't clear what each paragraph contributes to the argument. The lack of a clear authorial position and conclusion makes the argument hard to follow.
6 Reasons are clearly linked to one another and to the conclusion.	No	It isn't clear how one reason relates to the rest. Interim summaries of the argument would help the reader, as would phrases or sentences to link reasons, and to signal changes of topic.
7 All the text is relevant to the assignment (in this case, about whether stealing is always wrong).	No	The material is mostly related to the subject in some way, but some of it is rather tangential. Too much irrelevant material is included.
8 The main reasons and key points stand out clearly to the reader.	No	The author's opinions, such as about the greed of big business, stand out clearly, but the reasoning is confused. Most reasons don't stand out clearly.
9 The writer makes good use of other people's research as supporting evidence to strengthen the argument.	No	The writer has made little use of research evidence and does not make use of the texts that look at ethical issues (Texts 7, 10 and 12).
10 Does the writer make a reasoned evaluation of other people's views, especially those that contradict his or her own point of view?	No	The writer introduces some views that appear to contradict his or her own view. However, these are dismissed too quickly, without considering the implications in any detail.
11 Does the writer provide references in the text when introducing other people's ideas?	Yes	The writer provides references in the text.
12 Does the writer provide a list of references at the end of the essay?	No	A list of references is not provided so the reader cannot follow up the references. Without this, the references in the text are not much use.
13 Has the writer successfully removed any non-essential descriptive writing?	No	The second paragraph, and the paragraph about music in schools, contain unnecessary description.
14 Does the writing contain any inconsistencies?	Yes	The writing describes the music of small bands as if it is unimportant and 'unpopular', but later argues as if it is a good thing to make such 'unpopular' music better known.
15 Are the writer's beliefs or self-interests unfairly distorting the argument?	Yes	The writer's beliefs come across more strongly than the reasoning or argument.

Commentary for Essay 1

The numbers of the points given below refer to the numbers provided in the text for Essay 1.

1 'Although most reasonable people . . .' – the author is making an assumption that the reader will agree with his or her point of view by appealing to them as a 'reasonable' person. There may be validity in this point of view but there is no evidence given of a universal agreement on which areas of stealing are considered wrong. See Chapter 7, p. 114, for more about this kind of flawed reasoning.

2 This paragraph consists mainly of over-generalisations and repeats the main idea expressed in the first paragraph. It would be considered as 'waffle' by an editor or tutor. It is a waste of the words available.

3 The author states Lee's position on home taping and asserts that record companies were happy to overlook it. The author does not refer to any counter arguments on this issue, which weakens the point. Record companies did, in fact, make strenuous efforts to deter home tapers (such as the 1980s campaign 'Home Taping is Killing Music'). The author assumes that the only possible concern about home taping could have been profit and does not mention the possibility of ethical arguments such as the use of the artists' intellectual property. The author either has not considered the issues in sufficient depth, or is attempting to misrepresent the argument (see p. 119).

4 This is an assumption: the author does not provide convincing evidence that artists were not affected by such copying. Sales might have been even higher if copying had not taken place. Artists might have received a small proportion of the profits, so any reduction in sales may have affected them disproportionately.

5 The author makes uncritical use of Lee's and Carla's texts in this paragraph. Although the 'Lee' source is relatively credible, the 'Carla' text is sourced from a web-site for supporters of free downloading and therefore respondents have a vested interest in their own arguments, which makes them less credible (see p. 131).

There is an unquestioning acceptance that the music industry would be 'bland' without downloading, without critical consideration of this assumption. For example, it is worth considering how music has developed and changed across the centuries, and develops today within many cultures, without use of the internet.

6 The credibility of the 'Hibbs' source is questionable and yet the author re-states these views as if they were 'facts', without any analysis or discussion of what is being said.

7 It is flawed reasoning to argue that because 'everyone' does something, it is then acceptable. See p. 120.

8 The author's argument becomes very polemical at this point. The main thrust of the author's argument is that 'greedy' record companies are desperate to protect profits. It would have been useful to provide supporting evidence to back up this argument. The author would need to do some research to see if there are links between the decline in record company profits and an increase in internet downloading. Similarly, the author would need to find some supporting evidence to convince the reader that the main reason people download from the internet is that they cannot afford to pay. Alternative points of view are presented in the texts that the author has chosen not to use. The author jumps to conclusions, and appears to select facts to support his or her own interests. The position may be justifiable, but it has not been supported by the evidence presented.

9 There seems to be a sudden shift in the line of reasoning here, as the author lists arguments to support the view that internet downloading is wrongful theft. A linking paragraph is needed here to summarise the author's previous arguments and signal the intent to focus on a new topic. See page 173 on words that signpost the direction of the argument.

Commentary for Essay 1 (continued)

10 A linking word or phrase, such as 'however' or 'on the other hand', is needed here.

11 The arguments by Cuttle and Kahliney presented here against illegal downloading appear quite plausible. However, the author dismisses these opposing arguments too quickly, without analysing the evidence. The line of reasoning is flawed, as the conclusion made at the end of the paragraph focuses on how many listeners are affected, which is irrelevant to whether downloading is stealing or not. Even if it were true that the music was obscure, downloading for free might still be considered as stealing. Without further exploration of the author's thinking it is difficult for the reader to see how this interim conclusion has been reached.

12 The argument has switched back to supporting free downloading as a valid activity. Again, the author does not summarise the previous argument to help the reader follow what has been said so far, and does not signal that the topic is going to change.

13 A disproportionate amount of attention is given to talking about school tours. Most of this paragraph is too wordy and irrelevant, and the main argument becomes lost.

14 This paragraph makes unquestioning use of material from Text 1. It may be a good argument that downloading for free helps music made by lesser known groups to reach a wider audience, but no evidence is provided to support this. Moreover, this argument is not consistent with the view raised by the author earlier, that such music is obscure and unpopular. This point also ignores other complexities raised in the texts about the small record companies needing sales in order to survive, and about the legal rights of artists and businesses.

15 An interesting point, but the argument has hopped back to points already raised earlier.

16 Although, in the final paragraph, the author summarises two positions on unpaid downloading, this paragraph does not state the author's own position or draw a logical conclusion.

17 The essay's final sentence is very weak and contributes nothing to the argument.

Overall, the author has shown an ability to describe and summarise texts, but does not demonstrate good reasoning skills. In this essay, the line of reasoning is not clear and the author's position is not reflected in the conclusion. Much of the material is irrelevant or based on sources that are not very credible. There is little critical analysis of the evidence. The author has said the case is a 'grey area' but has not supported this point of view by identifying what factors make something a 'grey area'.

Checklist for evaluating Essay 2

Use this checklist to analyse Essay 2 on the following page. Compare your analysis with the evaluation and commentary on pp. 201–3.

Aspect	Yes/No	Comments
1 The writer's own position on the issues is clear.		
2 It is clear what the reasons are for the writer's point of view.		
3 The writer's conclusion is clear and based on the evidence.		
4 Reasons are presented in a logical order, as a line of reasoning.		
5 The argument is well structured and easy to follow.		
6 Reasons are clearly linked to one another and to the conclusion.		
7 All the text is relevant to the assignment (in this case, about whether stealing is always wrong).		
8 The main reasons and key points stand out clearly to the reader.		
9 The writer makes good use of other people's research as supporting evidence to strengthen the argument.		
10 Does the writer make a reasoned evaluation of other people's views, especially those that contradict his or her own point of view?		
11 Does the writer provide references in the text when introducing other people's ideas?		
12 Does the writer provide a list of references at the end of the essay?		
13 Has the writer successfully removed any non-essential descriptive writing?		
14 Does the writing contain any inconsistencies?		
15 Are the writer's beliefs or self-interests unfairly distorting the argument?		

Evaluate Essay 2

'Stealing is always wrong.' Discuss with reference to unpaid downloading of music from the internet.

There are many different forms of stealing, from theft of property, muggings and burglaries, to theft of ideas through plagiarism. Although there are legal sanctions against many forms of stealing, the issue of moral and social sanctions has always been more complex. For example, Robin Hood, who stole from the rich to give to the poor, is held up as a great British hero. Piaskin (1986) suggests that ethical issues are not simply questions of right and wrong but should be regarded as 'dilemmas'. In this essay I shall use the example of downloading music from the internet to highlight these complexities but, contrary to the view held by Piaskin, to argue that in this case, stealing is always wrong.[1]

In recent years, there have been a number of high profile cases against people who have shared music files for free on the internet. Prior to the development of the internet, music was similarly shared via home taping. Lee (2006) argues that although home taping is technically illegal, no one pursues this as perpetrators cannot be caught.[2] Because it is possible to catch internet file sharers, Lee argues that they are being unfairly punished. Whilst there may be a practical basis to this argument – it is easier to catch downloaders than home tapers – this does not mean that one behaviour should be considered acceptable and the other should not. This kind of argument is a rationalisation, used to make unacceptable actions appear acceptable.

Indeed, this point is made by Cuttle (2007). Cuttle, a legal expert, states that 'piracy of software, video games and music is stealing' and makes it clear that all such copying is illegal.[3] Given that there is a legal argument against both home taping and internet downloading, it appears reasonable to assume that both should be considered as wrong.[4] However, it is important to explore the moral arguments in order to evaluate whether such behaviours should also be considered 'wrong' from an ethical perspective.[5]

Research by Mixim, Moss and Plummer (1934), as well as later studies inspired by Mixim et al., suggest that most people do maintain an ethical sense of right and wrong even in areas where stealing appears to be more socially acceptable. Their findings suggested that people's ethical sense wanes when payment methods are difficult but they do not forget what is ethically right. Ebo, Markham and Malik (2004) examined the effect on internet downloading of easier payment schemes. During the study there was a dramatic decrease in illegal downloads with the majority of users choosing to make use of the easy payment scheme. This indicates that the majority of people in the study acknowledged that to download music for free, in effect stealing it, was wrong.[6]

A different ethical perspective is suggested by those authors who support unpaid downloading, especially those who use ethical and artistic arguments to counter economic arguments. A number of authors such as 'Carla' (2006), an internet downloader, assert that the main argument against downloading comes from record companies who are primarily concerned with their own profits.[7] Economic arguments are treated by such writers as if they are intrinsically weaker than artistic ones. 'Carla' develops this argument to suggest that true artists are driven by a desire to have their music heard by others and welcome the 'service' provided by file sharers. Hibbs (2006), a member of the public, also argues that file sharing is a kindness between friends. These kinds of arguments can sound convincing as they make downloading appear to be altruistic, and altruism appears to have the ethical advantage over the rush for profits. On the other hand, it could be argued that this is altruism at someone else's expense. The economics of free downloading do not help less well known artists, so not paying for downloads of their work is unethical.[8]

Evaluate Essay 2 (continued)

Furthermore,[9] those who defend downloading often act as if they know best the 'real' wishes and interests of artists. Carla, for example, refers to 'true artists', without defining what a 'true artist' is, or providing evidence to show what such 'true' artists would want. Authors such as 'Carla' and Hibbs do not provide evidence to show that artists regard free downloading as being more in their interests than the actions taken by businesses. As music sales are usually of direct financial benefit to artists, many artists may also disagree with free downloading.[10]

Moreover, Cuttle (2007)[11] asserts that arguments such as Carla's and Hibbs's are invalid in free market terms.[12] Publishers have a right to charge the highest price that they are able to obtain, and consumers can choose whether or not to purchase. In that case, business is not in the wrong to charge whatever price the market will sustain. However, there are other economic, and indeed artistic,[13] arguments against Carla's and Hibbs's positions.[14] Such authors assume that objections to downloading come mainly from large corporations who can be dismissed as 'greedy'. Kahliney (2006) argues that small, independent companies and recording artists are most likely to suffer the effects of downloading as their overall reliance on sales is greater. Given that sales for independent artists tend to be low anyway, falling sales could mean the collapse of small labels. Whilst artists could still have their music heard via free downloads, their position is unlikely to remain financially viable for long. Ironically, this increases the likelihood of a music industry populated by the type of 'bland' or 'middle of the road' acts that Carla complains would exist without internet downloading: they will be the only artists that can guarantee reasonable sales.[15]

In conclusion, I have demonstrated in this essay that there are arguments to support the view that all stealing can be regarded as 'wrong'. This holds true even in relation to complex areas such as internet downloading, where social behaviours may appear to support the view that downloading without paying is acceptable.[16] Indeed, in the case of unpaid downloading, there are legal and ethical, economic and artistic arguments to support the view that stealing from the industry is wrong. There are counter arguments, such as that downloading offers a service to music and small artists, but there is little evidence to support such views or to suggest that they represent the view of the majority. On the contrary, when given accessible, affordable payment options, most people chose not to steal, thereby acknowledging that free downloading is wrong. Although moral positions can easily be influenced by practical circumstances such as how easy it is to pay, research suggests people maintain an ethical sense that stealing is always wrong.

References

Carla (2006) internet chat room, Cla@mu.room.host, 7 September 2006.

Cuttle, P. D. (2007) 'Steal it Away', in *National CRI Law Journal*, vol. 7, 4.

Ebo, T., Markham, T. H. and Malik, Y. (2004) 'The effects of ease of payment on willingness to pay. Ethics or ease?' *Proceedings of the Academy for Ethical Dilemmas*, vol. 3 (4).

Hibbs, A. 'Letter to the editor', in *National Press Daily*, 3 November 2006.

Kahliney, C. (2006) 'Is this the end of the road?' In *Small Music Distributor*, 12 August 2006.

Lee, A. (2006) 'Why Buy?' In R. Coe and B. Stepson, *Examining Media*, pp. 36–57 (London: MUP).

Mixim, A., Moss, B. and Plummer, C. (1934) 'Hidden consensus', in *New Ethical Problems*, 17, 2.

Piaskin, F. (1986) 'Moral Dilemmas in Action', in *Joint Universities Journal of Advanced Ethics*, vol. 8, 2.

Spratt, A. (2004) 'The Editorial', in *The Middletown Argus*, 17 June 2004.

Evaluation of Essay 2

Aspect	Yes/No	Comments
1 The writer's own position on the issues is clear.	Yes	This is clearly stated in the opening paragraph and again in the conclusion, and helps to orientate the reader.
2 It is clear what the reasons are for the writer's point of view.	Yes	The author presents legal, ethical, economic and artistic reasons.
3 The writer's conclusion is clear and based on the evidence.	Yes	The conclusion is based on the reasons given, and especially on research into people's behaviour when given a chance to pay rather than steal.
4 Reasons are presented in a logical order, as a line of reasoning.	Yes	The reasons are clearly grouped, starting with the legal reasons and progressing to ethical and other considerations.
5 The argument is well structured and easy to follow.	Yes	The argument groups similar points and details together. It is clear when the argument is changing to consider a different point.
6 Reasons are clearly linked to one another and to the conclusion.	Yes	Good use is made of interim summaries to sum up arguments so far. Linking sentences and signal words are used to develop the line of reasoning.
7 All the text is relevant to the assignment (in this case, about whether stealing is always wrong).	Yes	The text is comprised almost entirely of reasons, summaries, linking phrases, evaluations and judgements.
8 The main reasons and key points stand out clearly to the reader.	Yes	The reasons are stated very clearly and are not lost amongst unnecessary opinion or description.
9 The writer makes good use of other people's research as supporting evidence to strengthen the argument.	Yes	The writer makes effective use of experts, such as the legal expert, to support their own position.
10 Does the writer make a reasoned evaluation of other people's views, especially those that contradict his or her own point of view?	Yes	The writer includes reference to ideas that contradict the main line of reasoning, indicates where opponents may have a point, and provides reasons to show why their points of view are not acceptable overall.
11 Does the writer provide references in the text when introducing other people's ideas?	Yes	There are references to all sources used.
12 Does the writer provide a list of references at the end of the essay?	Yes	
13 Has the writer successfully removed any non-essential descriptive writing?	Yes	There is very little description, except in the introduction, on Robin Hood, to set the scene.
14 Does the writing contain any inconsistencies?	No	
15 Are the writer's beliefs or self-interests unfairly distorting the argument?	No	The writer may have strong beliefs but the argument is firmly based on reasoning.

Commentary on Essay 2

The numbers of the points given below refer to the numbers provided in the text for Essay 2.

1   The author sets out their position clearly in this opening paragraph. The author acknowledges that there are complexities to the issue, but nonetheless, the text clearly states the author's position. We know from the outset that they will be taking up the position that stealing is always wrong.

2   The author begins to create the argument by taking a piece of evidence that appears to go against their position and analysing its argument. In refuting this evidence, the author is establishing their own argument and building credibility for this by weighing it up against a counter argument.

3   The author starts to tease out the different layers within the argument. The argument is clearly based on a legal approach to the issue. Good use is made of a quotation from a legal expert to support the author's position.

4   In this sentence, the author makes an effective interim summary of the argument so far. Good use is made of tentative language, 'it seems reasonable to assume', in order to indicate an awareness that the argument has not yet been won.

5   The final sentence of the paragraph is helpful in signalling to the reader that the argument will now consider a different perspective on the issue, the moral issue. Good use is also made of the signal word 'however', to indicate a change of topic.

6   The author makes good use of research in the field to suggest that most people's behaviour, when they are given a chance to pay or steal, supports the view that downloading for free is recognised as wrong.

7   The author places Carla's position in the context of her being an internet downloader. The author does not explicitly state that Carla's beliefs are necessarily the result of self-interest, but by placing her comments in context the author helps the reader make sense of why she might hold these views.

8   The author strengthens the overall argument by showing why counter arguments can appear convincing, but undermines these counter arguments effectively by questioning who is paying the cost of altruism.

9   The use of a linking word, 'furthermore', indicates that the argument is being continued in a similar vein, but that a new angle is being introduced to strengthen the point being made.

10 The author points out weaknesses and flaws in the counter arguments, using good critical analysis. The author makes a detailed critical analysis of some aspects of the arguments, such as the use of 'true artist' as emotive vocabulary, and points out gaps in opposing arguments. As the counter argument makes suggestions about what artists would think, the author puts forward reasons why artists might have alternative views.

11 By beginning the paragraph with the word 'moreover', the author signals to the reader that a further point will be made to support the current line of reasoning.

12 The views of an expert are again used to support the argument, along with an allusion to a theoretical position, that of the 'free market economy'.

13 The author states that opposing arguments can be dismissed in absolute terms by considering the suppliers' right to charge whatever price they wish. However, this reason may not be persuasive for some audiences, so the author rightly builds further on this argument by considering other angles.

14 Throughout the writing, the author has helped to clarify the nature of the argument by categorising the reasons. Previously, the author stated he or she would refer to legal and moral reasons, and here the text signals that there are also economic and artistic reasons that support their position.

Commentary on Essay 2 (continued)

15 The author effectively undermines the counter argument that free downloading prevents a 'bland' music world, by showing how it could lead to an increase in 'middle-of-the-road' music.

16 This paragraph draws the conclusion that stealing is always wrong. This conclusion has been well supported by the line of reasoning throughout the essay, so should not come as a surprise to the reader. The author summarises their position in the conclusion, clearly asserting this position and recapitulating the key points of the argument. The reader may not agree with this position but will be clear about what the author believes and why.

Overall, this is a much stronger piece of critical writing than Essay 1. The author's position is clear, and the writing is consistent in providing reasons to support this. Good use is made of expert sources to support the author's position, so that it comes across as more than personal opinion. The author makes a careful consideration of opposing arguments, making it clear why these opposing arguments might be attractive, but drawing attention to gaps and flaws in opponents' arguments.

The argument could have been even stronger if it had been more questioning of some of the underlying theoretical arguments for the author's position. The writing takes the position that the law and the free market economy are right, without providing any challenge to this point of view.

Evaluating your writing for critical thinking

You can copy this self-evaluation tool to use for future reports and assignments.

Self-evaluation	Yes/No	Action
1 I am clear on my position on this subject and the reasons for my point of view		Write your position down as a statement in one or two sentences. If you cannot do so, this suggests that your position isn't yet clear in your own mind. If possible, also check whether your point of view is clear to a friend or colleague who knows little about the subject.
2 My conclusion and/or recommendations are clear, based on the evidence, and written in tentative language where appropriate.		Write your conclusions first. Read these aloud; check that they make sense. Imagine someone tells you that your conclusion is wrong. What reasons would you give to defend it? Have you included all these reasons in your writing? For language: see p. 179.
3 The material included is the most relevant to the subject.		Double-check that your line of reasoning meets the task requirements, such as meeting the project brief or answering the questions set for an essay. Does it match the statement you wrote about your position?
4 All sections of the assignment or report are relevant to the exact specifications of the task.		Read through each section or paragraph in turn, checking how the information contributes to your line of reasoning, leading to your conclusion or recommendations. Check that each meets the project brief, or is necessary to answer the set question.
5 I have analysed the structure of my argument. Reasons are presented in the best order and lead clearly towards the conclusion.		If not, write the reasons out in brief and consider how each is linked to the conclusion. Check whether the argument 'hops' from one point to another. Cluster similar reasons together and indicate how each contributes to the main argument or conclusion.
6 The argument stands out clearly from other information. I have selected the best examples.		Check you have not presented so much detail that the main argument is lost. An analysis of a few examples or details is better than a superficial approach to lots of material. Select carefully to meet the task requirement.
7 My reasons are clearly linked to one another and to the conclusion(s).		Check that each paragraph opens with a clear link to what has gone before or signals a change in the direction of your argument using 'signal words' such as those suggested in Chapter 10.
8 My main reasons and key points stand out clearly to the reader.		Take a marker pen and highlight the sentence that sums up the main point or reason covered in each paragraph. If you find this difficult, it is likely that your reader will find it hard to identify your points. If large sections of a paragraph are highlighted, then it is probable that you haven't summarised its main point sufficiently.
9 My facts are accurate.		Don't rely on opinion or memory. Check that your sources are reputable and up to date. Investigate whether anything published more recently gives different information. Check that you have reported the facts accurately, and without distortion.

Self-evaluation	Yes/No	Action
10 I have included reference to relevant theories.		Find out the schools of thought or theories related to this subject. Make a critical evaluation of these to identify where they support or conflict with your argument.
11 I make use of other people's research as supporting evidence to strengthen my argument.		Check what has been written or produced on this subject by other people. Include references to relevant items that best support your point of view.
12 I have cited the source of information for evidence and theories to which I refer.		Write out the details of the references in brief within the text, and in full at the end of the writing.
13 I include a reasoned evaluation of views that do not support my own argument.		Find out what has been written that contradicts your point of view, and consider any other potential objections that could be raised. Evaluate these as part of your line of reasoning. Make it clear why your reasons are more convincing than opposing points of view. Identify any flaws, gaps or inconsistencies in the counter arguments.
14 My writing is mainly analytical and contains only brief, essential descriptive writing.		Check whether all sections of descriptive writing and background information are essential to understanding your reasoning or are part of the conventions of the type of report you are writing. Keep descriptions very brief, look for ways of summarising them and link them clearly to your main argument. Beware of wordy introductions.
15 I have checked my argument for inconsistencies.		Check whether any of the reasons or evidence you have used could be interpreted as contradicting what you have written elsewhere in the piece of writing.
16 I have given clear indications of levels of probability or uncertainty.		Check that your writing indicates your judgement of how likely it is that the conclusion is accurate and irrefutable. If there is a chance that research findings could be interpreted differently by someone else, use appropriate language to indicate a level of uncertainty or ambiguity. See p. 179.
17 My current beliefs are not unfairly distorting my argument.		If any section of your assignment covers a subject where you have strong beliefs or interests, be especially careful that you have checked the evidence supports your reasoning. It is important that your arguments come across in a calm and reasoned way that will convince your reader. Check several times, and be careful not to include emotive language or poorly substantiated opinions.
18 I have covered all the required aspects of the assignment.		Check the assignment's details carefully. Tick aspects already completed so it is clear what else you must do.

Summary

This chapter provided the opportunity to evaluate two pieces of critical writing on a similar subject and to compare these with pre-written evaluations and commentaries. One aim of this activity was to build upon your skills in critical evaluation by applying them to extended pieces of text. However, the key aim was to help you develop the skills to evaluate your own critical writing.

The commentaries provide you with a critical evaluation of two essays, drawing out their weaknesses and strengths. This is the kind of approach that an editor or tutor will take when you submit your own writing. When you produce critical writing for assessment purposes or for publication, you should make an equally rigorous evaluation of your own work before submitting it.

Evaluation, in this case, means making a critique of your work as a single, completed piece of critical writing, checking how all the different components contribute to the strength of the written argument. Before getting to this stage, you should have evaluated, already, the different component parts such as the quality of your evidence, the validity of your selections (what you have chosen to include and what to leave out), whether your reasons support your conclusion, and the validity of your conclusion.

There isn't one correct way to evaluate your overall piece of work. You may find it easier to make rough notes in the form of critical commentary on your text. Alternatively, you may find it easier to use one or more structured checklists, looking for particular aspects in your writing. You may prefer to combine both methods, moving back and forward between them depending on what works best for the way you write.

The important point is that, having made a good critical analysis of your source materials, you apply an equally critical approach to your own writing to ensure that you have presented your argument in a structured, logical and convincing way.

If you wish to practise further in working with longer texts, more practice material is provided on p. 239. ▶

Chapter 12

Critical reflection

Learning outcomes

This chapter offers you opportunities to:

- understand what is meant by critical reflection and appreciate its challenges and benefits for academic study and professional practice
- understand how to undertake critical reflection and decide on the most appropriate approaches for your purposes
- formulate your own model of critical reflection
- understand the difference between phase 1 and phase 2 reflection
- know how to relate theory to practice
- recognise good and bad critical reflection
- understand how to present critical reflection to others, especially for academic assessment

Introduction

It is easy to become caught up in everyday routine such that we lose sight of the reasons for thinking, feeling, believing and acting as we do. Diverse aspects of our experiences and emotional responses – and our interpretations of these – can become entangled in ways that may not be apparent to us. This can distort our perspective and block understanding, which isn't helpful to us in the longer term.

Critical reflection is used increasingly in professional and academic contexts as a means of focusing our attention back onto our own experience. Reflection in this context refers to specific kinds of mental discipline. It involves clarifying our thinking, deepening understanding and reinforcing learning in ways that, ideally, lead to transformation and change.

Although 'reflection' sounds as though it should be easy, in practice, there is a great deal of challenge in working with the raw material of our experience, and especially in doing so with integrity, in ways that support learning, and doing all this within a framework of academic conventions.

This chapter helps you to understand what is required when undertaking critical reflection for academic and professional purposes. It provides structures that can help you to negotiate the various phases and processes of critical reflection, from initial selection of a topic through to presentation of your reflection for assessment.

What is critical reflection?

More than just 'thinking'

In everyday language, the term 'reflection' is used loosely to refer to:

- being engaged in thought;
- vague musings or day dreaming;
- going back over an event in our minds.

Critical reflection for academic and professional purposes is different from this. It is structured, focused and conscious, with the end purpose of developing our understanding. If you undertake critical reflection as a requirement of your programme or profession, there are likely to be expectations about the form this takes and how to present it.

Critical reflection: characteristics

There isn't a single kind of critical reflection, but typical characteristics include:

1 **Selection**: select an aspect of experience, learning or professional practice for analysis.

2 **Changing perspective**: analyse experience from different angles and different levels of detail.

3 **Returning to experience**: once, periodically, or frequently, as best fits the issue.

4 **Analysis of own role**: look at reasons for, and consequences of, your own actions, rather than those of others.

5 **Drawing on received wisdom**: make use of theory, research, professional knowledge.

6 **Deepening your understanding**: look actively for meaning, recognising what is significant, and learning from this.

7 **Using insights to effect change**: use your new understanding to do things differently in the future – ideally to the benefit of others as well as yourself.

'Actions' in this context refers to all salient behaviours, speech, feelings and thoughts, including such matters as body language, assumptions that influence behaviour, failure to take action.

1 Selection

Effective critical reflection is an intensive activity that takes time, mental energy and often, too, emotional energy. Realistically, you won't be able to bring the same level of critical analysis to all areas of your experience. Select one or two areas where that kind of investment of your resources will bring the best returns for you. See pages 212 and 223.

2 Changing perspective

In our everyday routine, we tend to observe our actions from a given perspective and level of detail, referring mainly to our own opinions. It would be difficult to function on a day-to-day basis if we didn't do so. For critical reflection, we look to develop understanding partly by altering our focus, using different levels of detail from those employed on an everyday basis – as if zooming in and out with a camera lens to see surroundings with fresh eyes.

Analysing in detail

This means putting our experiences under a magnifying lens so as to identify component parts and contributing factors. For example, by clarifying an exact sequence of events, we might identify potential causes and effects overlooked at the time. Alternatively, we might recall things that we said or did that did not seem significant at the time but which take on new meaning when we reconsider the context, our motivations or anxieties. We can use these observations to elicit patterns and themes.

What is critical reflection? (continued)

Considering the bigger picture

This means standing back to look at our experience from broader perspectives, as if through a wide-angle lens:

- actively searching out themes or patterns within our reflections;
- testing our personal experience against published theories, research and professional knowledge;
- considering the influence of broader political, social or ideological contexts.

3 Returning to experience

The appropriate timing and frequency will depend on what you want to gain from your critical reflection. You could select:

A significant, one-off, incident to analyse in detail, to help understand better what happened and your own role and reactions.

A recurrent situation to reflect on after each occurrence, so that you build your observations, your sense of potential cause and effect, and of your own role.

An issue or theme, and return to this at frequent and regular intervals so that you can identify patterns in your actions and emotional responses over time.

A particular project or challenge, and record your observations and reflections over its duration. Draw conclusions about your own role and actions, the reasons for these, their consequences for the project, yourself or others and for future action.

4 Analysis of your own role

Critical reflection requires you to look at your own experience – it is not intended to be an occasion to blame others or focus on their actions. Depending on the context, this means looking at such aspects as:

- the impact or consequences of what you did or didn't do – and why;

- the reasons for your actions, moving beyond superficial and immediate reasons to look at latent fears and motivations, displaced emotions, assumptions you had made and whether these helped or hindered the situation;
- changes in the way you acted or responded over time.

5 Drawing on received wisdom

For critical reflection in academic contexts, you are expected to relate your own experience to theory. Ways of doing this are addressed below, page 214.

6 Deepening your understanding

Critical reflection is more than detailed observation or a narrative of events. It involves active working with the raw material of your experience so as to make sense of situations and events, their dynamics, your own role within them and the influence of the broader context. This means sifting through your reflections, selecting key insights and identifying why these are of significance to your performance in study or work, the way you work with others, or your life generally.

7 Using insights to effect change

A key aim of critical reflection is to transform the way you see the world, or an aspect of it, such that you think and act differently. Change of some kind is an implicit aim: this may be a small change but one that will make a difference to you or others. At its best, reflection can have a transformative quality, with a profound effect upon your being and sense of self, others and the world around you.

Why engage in critical reflection?

Challenges of critical reflection

Although we may be aware that we would benefit from putting time aside for reflection, it is not easy for most of us to do so. It takes commitment and discipline because of the following factors.

- *Distractions*: There are usually more compelling things to distract us.
- *Confusion*: We may confuse everyday, unfocused 'thoughtfulness' with the more purposeful and structured critical reflection required.
- *Feelings*: If we select difficult material, this can bring its own challenges such as uncomfortable feelings, unexpected emotional responses, or unwanted conclusions about our own role – it is natural to want to evade these.
- *Skills*: It takes skill to balance a critique of experience with the requirements of academic writing, especially relating to the personal and the theoretical.

It can help to know that these challenges are not unusual. Managing such challenges forms part of the purpose of undertaking critical reflection – and contributes to the sense of achievement.

The benefits of critical reflection

A helpful mental discipline

Critical reflection develops a mental discipline that brings diverse and often unexpected benefits – potentially the transformative results referred to above. Academic or professional requirements for critical reflection are helpful in that they provide an external incentive, and often a framework, that we may otherwise lack for undertaking such in-depth analysis.

The more we create a routine for critical reflection, the more we gain in terms of self-management, critical observation, emotional maturity, and in actively using experience to the benefit of ourselves and others.

Space and time for development

When we commit ourselves to critical reflection, we need to create appropriate conditions, such as making the right mental and emotional space and focusing on ourselves in ways that we wouldn't do otherwise. It helps us organise our time and enables different types of thinking.

More effective study and learning

You can use your own learning as the focus of critical reflection. Stepping back from study, you can benefit from reflecting on your attitudes to learning, your strategies, the effectiveness of these for different subject matter, and what assists or prevents you from achieving well.

You can better understand your own performance through looking critically at:

- your educational history and its impact on achievement and self-belief;
- how your current attitudes and study strategies evolved, and whether these best fit your current context;
- whether your self-perceptions assist or hinder your performance;
- whether, unconsciously, you sabotage your own performance.

To support professional practice

Critical reflection enriches professional practice. By developing your understanding of what you are doing and why, and the consequences of your actions, you are better placed to manage new and unexpected situations in a professional manner that also supports your own needs. This is explored in more detail below (pp. 225–6).

Decide your approach and purpose

Because of the challenges identified above, it can be difficult to:

- get started on a piece of critical reflection;
- keep going with it once started;
- give shape to your reflective thinking so that it becomes meaningful;
- come back to it over time to see what it is really telling you;
- work with your reflective material productively and creatively so that you can learn from the experience and use it.

Some people generate their best reflective thinking by working in impromptu ways, using the moment, and letting the creative flow direct their thoughts. If this is true of you, then go with what works best for you. In that case, you may not need to use a formal approach until you come to shape your final reflective summary for an external audience.

However, for many people, especially those for whom critical reflection is a relatively new activity or one for which they need encouragement to keep going, it is easier to use a more structured approach. This gives a starting point and direction and helps you to produce stronger, more focused critical reflection.

In general, if you spend time early on elaborating what you wish to gain from your critical reflection and the approach you will take to best achieve that outcome, then you are likely to reap benefits in terms of the quality of your reflection and effective use of your time. The section below outlines key considerations for formulating your approach.

> **Reflection** 📖 **What is your style?**
>
> Do you think you would produce better critical reflection by:
>
> - Working in a freer, creative way?
> - Using a structured approach?

Deciding on an approach

Key considerations are:

1 purpose
2 type of desired outcome
3 focus
4 model of reflection to employ
5 your methodology
6 audience
7 relating experience and theory.

These are examined in detail below.

1 Identify your purpose

Start by deciding what it is that you want to achieve from undertaking this reflection – in terms of knowledge, understanding or performance. For example, for particular aspects of your study, life or work, you might want to understand:

- why something went well, and whether the lessons learnt could apply to other situations;
- why a particular situation arose or unfolded the way it did;
- why things don't seem to work out as you hoped or expected;
- why your contributions to seminars or at work aren't as effective as you would wish;
- why you think or react the way you do in particular circumstances.

Once you are clear about your purpose, it is easier to decide on other aspects of your approach, such as the expected outcomes, an appropriate focus, your methods and the model to use.

Approach: outcome, focus, model, method

2 Decide on type of outcome

Before you start your reflections, consider how you will make use of them. This will help you to decide the form that you want your conclusions to take, such as:

- A list of lessons learnt?
- A critical analytical piece of writing based on your reflections?
- Recommendations for personal action?
- Guidelines for future action?
- Instructions for future action?
- A combination of these?

If you are undertaking reflection as a requirement of your programme of study or professional practice, you may be given guidance about how to write up these outcomes.

> ### Reflection 📖 Outcomes
>
> - What kinds of outcomes are expected for the reflection you are expected to undertake for your programme or profession?

3 Select a focus

Select a meaningful focus for your reflection. Choose a particular incident or type of incident, or a recurring issue, concern, set of relationships, or similar that you consider relevant to achieving your purpose above.

You need to select a focus that is relatively challenging, so that there is sufficient material to enable you to develop your understanding. However, the focus should be sufficiently narrow so that you can examine it from multiple perspectives yet without being too superficial.

4 Choose a model of reflection

There are various models of reflection that you can draw upon to provide a framework for your reflection – though this isn't always required or necessary. Particular frameworks may be preferred within your discipline or professional area. If not, you may find it helpful to draw upon one or more of the models outlined on pages 221–4 below.

> ### Reflection 📖 Using a model for reflection
>
> - Is a particular model of reflection recommended for your course or professional area?
> - Do you feel that using a model to structure your reflections would stimulate helpful reflections, or do you feel using a model would stifle your creativity?

5 Method

There isn't a single method of critical reflection. You need to consider:

- whether there is a required methodology for your discipline;
- if you have a choice, the method that will help you engage most effectively.

The following considerations may help you to select what will work best for you.

How best to record your reflections?

For your purposes, would it be better to record your initial reflections on paper, in a notebook, blog or electronic record? Would you prefer to record them digitally?

Approach: method and audience

With whom?

In relation to your identified purpose, are you likely to develop your deepest insights if you do this entirely on your own, or if you use a colleague, friend or peer group to open up your thinking?

Frequency and regularity?

For the purpose and outcomes you have identified, would it be better to undertake critical reflection on a weekly basis, or more or less frequently? Would you gain most by planning specific times each day, week or month, or making notes as and when there are new developments for you to consider?

First steps/prompts?

Consider how you will get started on your reflection. Would you work best by:

- Jotting down your thoughts as they come, and then going back over these for further consideration?
- Using the same set of questions each time, in order to structure your thinking sessions?
- Using a theory as a starting point?
- Discussing an event with a colleague, and then jotting down your thoughts?
- Applying a model of reflection in a systematic way on each occasion?
- Using a pro-forma to guide your reflection?

Working the material

Your initial reflections will generally provide raw material, or phase 1 reflections, that will require further work. Consider when and how you will work with your initial reflections so as to arrive at deeper understandings. See phase 2 reflection, pages 218 and 220 below).

End-point

Consider how you will draw your thoughts together towards conclusions. What format will this take? For example, you may be required to submit a blog that contains your developing ideas, and a piece of reflective writing that draws together key insights and conclusions.

Reflection 📖 Methodology

- Which aspects of your methodology do you think you need to develop the most?
- How will go about this?

---

6 Audience

If you are undertaking critical reflection for your own purposes, then you can decide on the format it takes. However, if you are required to share it with a tutor, peers, work supervisor, assessors, or others, consider how you will adapt your written account in order to take your future audience into consideration.

This may include:

- using different content and styles of writing for phases 1 and 2 (see pp. 218–20);
- including only information and reflections that you are comfortable for others to read;
- providing a well structured and referenced critical summary;
- ensuring confidentiality and anonymity for anyone referred to in reflections – and permission to use workplace material.

Reflection 📖 Confidentiality

- What kinds of information would you not feel comfortable sharing with your peers, tutors or others?
- What kinds of confidentiality issues are there in general for the kinds of reflection you might be asked to undertake for your course?

Approach: relating experience and theory

7 Relating theory and practice

For critical reflection on experience for academic work, you are expected to relate experience to received wisdom or 'theory'. You can approach this in different ways, some of which are listed below.

Check the research basis first

When selecting an area of experience for critical observation, choose an aspect for which you know there is published research. Ideally, there should be research findings that support different theoretical perspectives. If not, it may create difficulties when you come to write up your reflections for assessment. It is much harder to undertake reflection and then start looking for relevant theory and research.

Update yourself on the issues

Investigate the research findings and accepted professional practice for the area you have selected for reflection. Read reputable journals or recently published books on the subject, and find out what the key issues are that are being addressed in that area. What are the 'hot topics'?

Ensure that you are aware of:

- established and new theories related to 'hot topics' or to other areas that you want to investigate through your critical reflection;
- research that supports these;
- any criticisms of that research;
- the direction of debate on these issues within your subject discipline or profession.

In that respect, your background reading will be similar to that undertaken for other kinds of academic work.

Do your experiences support the theory?

Consider when and how your own experiences match or do not match what you would expect from the key theories you have selected to draw upon. If there isn't a good match, consider the reasons for this, such as differences that there might be in the context or data. What is true of one situation may not be the case in your own.

Do theories support your findings?

It is possible that you will develop insights or draw conclusions on matters that were not covered in the initial research items that you used. If so, investigate whether there are theories or research findings that support or contradict what you have found. It adds weight to your own position if you can relate your conclusions to a broader research base. Research into the broader social, political and cultural issues may also help.

Learn from the experts

Use reputable sources of research and their conclusions in order to throw light onto areas of practice or study that you find difficult. Consider what these sources offer you in identifying ways of doing things differently. For example, theories of how memory works may help you in preparing for exams.

Your analysis and your consideration of salient theories should help you to understand better:

- what has been happening up to now and why;
- why you, personally, act as you do and the impact of your actions;
- how wider issues impact upon the everyday and the individual;
- how you can act differently so as to bring about different outcomes.

Decide your approach: summary

Aspect	Decide . . .
Purpose	What is it that you want to understand or do better as a result of this reflection?
Type of outcome	When you look back over your reflections to draw out conclusions, what form do you want or need these to take? For example: • A list of lessons learnt? • Recommendations for personal action? • Guidelines for action? • Instructions on applying what you have learnt?
Focus	What will provide a meaningful focus for your reflection (a particular incident, recurring issue, concern, set of relationships, etc.) that you consider relevant to achieving your purpose above? What makes it worth the time and emotional effort to focus on this?
Model of reflection	• Are you expected to apply a particular model of reflection? If not, would adopting or adapting an existing model help you to structure your reflection? • Would it help to design your own model?
Method	How will you go about your reflection – if you have a choice? • *Recording*: On paper, in a notebook, blog or electronic record? • *With whom*: Individually? With a colleague or peer? In a group? • *Frequency*: Weekly? Daily? As needed? A one-off reflection? • *When*: As a daily log or blog? At a particular time of day? • *First steps/prompts*: How will you get started on your reflection (see stage 1 reflections below)? Would it help to use free association? Using a series of questions or a pro-forma to provide structure? Using a theory as a starting point? Comparing and contrasting with another example? • *Evolution*: How will you develop your initial reflections (see stage 2 reflection, page 218 below)? • *End-point*: How will you draw your thoughts together towards a conclusion?
Theory	• Which theories or research are you going to draw on to bring insight and more depth to your reflection? • How will you go about relating experience and theory? • Are there broader social, political, cultural, ideological, economic or technological issues that you could research that would provide helpful additional perspectives?
Audience	If your written reflection will be seen by peers, tutors or others, how will you adapt this to achieve the following? • Make the key points stand out? • Ensure confidentiality? • Ensure you are reasonably comfortable with them seeing any personal information or reading about personal feelings?

An outline copy of this is provided below. You can copy this and complete it for your work if you would find this helpful.

Resource: Outline approach to reflection

Use the table on page 215 to guide your own approach to the reflection you need to undertake. Write, below, your decisions about your approach, using the right-hand boxes.

Aspect	Decision
Purpose	*What I want to understand better (and why this is significant):*
Type of outcome wanted?	*Conclusions, recommendations, critical observations, personal guidelines, etc.?*
Focus	*Area of experience to focus on:* *How would this focus be useful in achieving my purpose?*
Model	*I will/won't be drawing on a formal model of reflection because . . .* *The model I will use is:*

Aspect	Decision
Method	*With whom:*
	Frequency:
	When:
	First steps/prompts:
	Evolution:
	End-point:
Theory	*Which theoretical perspectives and approaches I am going to draw upon:*
Audience	*To help the reader, I will organise the writing up of these reflections by . . .*
	Confidentiality issues I need to address and how I will do so:

Reflection phases 1 and 2

The process of reflection can be considered in terms of two distinct phases.

- Phase 1: Generating ideas and raw content
- Phase 2: Analysis and synthesis.

Phase 1: Generating ideas and raw content

First-phase reflection refers to jotting down reflections when the details, thoughts and emotions are still fresh, recording these as a stream of initial thoughts. These might be captured in a notebook, file, blog, digital recording or whatever best suits your way of working.

Characteristics of phase 1

- Immediate: written whilst still fresh in the mind.
- Chronological: written 'as it happens' so it may read as an unfolding story.
- Emotional: it provides a chance to explore your feelings – and more emotion may arise as you identify what was happening for you emotionally and why.
- Detailed: likely to contain information and details that seem relevant at the time but which may become less significant as time goes by.
- Fragmented: different things will appear to be significant at different times.

Phase 2: Analysis and synthesis

It is this aspect of reflection that brings depth to your thinking and learning. It is most likely to be phase 2 reflections that are assessed or gain the most marks. It should be clear how phase 2 reflections relate to your stage 1 reflections. In effect, you consider both the issue, and yourself in relation to the issue.

Characteristics of phase 2

- Holistic: you are looking back over an experience, event or project *as a whole*.
- Distance: you stand back to gain perspective. For example, you look at the feelings that were evoked without becoming caught up in them to the same extent.
- Analytical: you analyse your reflections critically.
- Synthesis: you bring together disparate and scattered thoughts and analyses into more rounded judgements and conclusions.
- Extrapolation: you are engaged in a process of teasing out meaning, insights and significance.

At phase 2, you work with your reflections as a whole, looking for significant trends, patterns and conclusions. You may benefit both from sitting quietly with these for a while to see what further thoughts emerge, and also from working with them actively, asking questions of yourself, and drawing out the implications of what you have learnt.

Understand yourself in relation to the issue

At both phases, but especially for phase 2, you need to consider your own role and actions, the impact of these at the time or later, and the consequences of these for yourself or others. For example:

- How well did you handle a situation? How good were your decision-making and other skills?
- How did your views and your understanding develop through the process of reflection?
- What difference will your new understanding make to how you approach similar issues in future?

Examples of phase 1 reflection

For a project for their degree in medicine, Sophie and Charlotte created a resource to help parents and carers communicate with young children about cancer. They each completed a weekly reflective log. The following examples from their logs illustrate the flavour and range of phase 1 reflection.

Their feelings as they undertook new tasks and stretched existing skills

I am slightly worried about my computer abilities and unsure how to create professional looking graphics which could be used in the resource . . .

Evaluations of their current experience

My experience of dealing with bereavement in children is minimal and it is an area that I feel I will have to research in order to help me develop a greater understanding.

Their feelings about dealing with such a sensitive and difficult issue

Although I was excited about the prospect of filling this apparent need and helping parents, I was also anxious about tackling a major topic such as cancer.

Meetings with the tutor

We arrived at the first session with ideas which we had created individually, with a view to discussing these and narrowing them down to create a specific project brief. I felt apprehensive prior to the meeting as both my partner and I were coming up with individual ideas and had not agreed a direction for the project. After . . . I felt less anxious about the project.

The research they undertook

. . . we found many study and journal articles, mainly from the BMJ, which focused directly on this issue. This encouraged me to proceed . . . as initially I was concerned that there would not be much literature for us to base our research on or to indicate that this would be a worthy project. My experience of dealing with bereavement in children is minimal and it is an area that I will have to research in order to develop a greater understanding.

Their responses to their reading

I was shocked to read that many parents put off telling their children about cancer. As a result, children find out themselves through overhearing conversations and finding leaflets around the house.

Lessons they learnt as they went along

I was taken aback when I realised that producing visually appealing cards was not the main aim of the project. This was slightly disheartening as I was looking forward to [that] . . . I then began to understand that the thought process, rationale and development of ideas were more important than creating storyboard cards. With hindsight, it perhaps would have been more useful if [we] had decided on a specific idea . . . prior to the meeting.

How their ideas developed week by week

This week we also considered how the resource may not only help children but also individuals themselves . . . After looking at the fairytale card game, I realised we had missed many important aspects of the story. We then began to reorganise our ideas more logically . . . [and] discovered new ideas. . . .

Recognising contributions from the team

My partner and I definitely complemented each other in other ways. She had a wider vocabulary . . . I was better at . . .

Broader social and cultural issues

. . . religion, language, ethnic origin and family situation. Upon thinking about and discussing this issue, I have realised that . . . these differences in culture are likely to result in different methods of coping with bad news and different family situations and support networks. All these need to be thought about and addressed in our resource . . .

Examples of phase 2 reflection

Sophie and Charlotte drew together their learning in a reflective summary and project report which drew upon, and developed, selections of material recorded in their weekly logs. Some examples are given below. This phase 2 reflection synthesised their reflections, drawing together:

- how their thinking developed, and the effects of this on their project;
- how they made use of research;
- the broader lessons they learnt;
- changes to the way they viewed their future professional roles as doctors.

How and why their assumptions and goals changed over time

Reflecting back to the beginning of the project, I had fixated in my mind that I wanted to create a resource that looked professional and useable . . . this initial aim actually hindered me from thinking more deeply about the concept behind the cards . . . I slowly realised that . . . the cards did not have to look aesthetically perfect – the more important element was what the card represented.

Research that informed their thinking

Barnes et al. (2000) stated that most of the mothers included in their trial of breast cancer . . . were not offered any advice on how to break the news to their children. Many stated that they would have welcomed this opportunity. . . . This is also supported by Kroll et al. which states that research is needed to aid physicians and parents as to what age-appropriate information to give children and at what stage of the disease.

How they learnt from past experiences

I have also been forced to revisit some issues which I learnt about during my mother's illness. . . . The fact that this project has reminded me of those issues . . . has helped me greatly in thinking through some of the topics which need to be addressed in our resource in order for me to help others.

The deeper lessons extrapolated

I think one of the most important aspects that I take away from this project is the effect of cancer not merely on the individual but on their whole family and people close to them. I began this project with a scientific knowledge of cancer and its effects, but I take away . . . an insight into how cancer changes people's lives.

Before this project, I had never considered . . . that different family set-ups can affect the way in which we cope and rely on people. Your culture definitely has a huge impact upon the way you view and deal with disease and adversity. I think that as a doctor, it is vital to bear this in mind and adapt your advice accordingly.

Personal awareness and change

From completing this work for the resource pack, it has made me very aware of a lot of cultural influences which direct me to choosing a certain type of image. I have never before thought about the fact that a picture I might choose to represent a certain issue could convey a completely different meaning to someone from a different culture than me. I think it is important that I have learnt about this as it will make me think twice about using certain images or words in the future.

Suggested changes for the profession and the reasons for doing so

I also think . . . we have identified an important fact, that clinicians should look into increased involvement with their patient's family . . . it is greatly appreciated by patients and their families. This will have a knock on effect . . . as they may feel more comfortable coming to you with subsequent problems . . . [with] medical benefit as it can allow for the problem to be addressed and treated earlier, both minimising the effect on the patient and reducing cost and time for the NHS.

Whether a patient is at home or in hospital it is a doctor's duty to ensure that they have enough information and resources about their cancer. [Otherwise] people are more likely to put off telling their children about their cancer . . .

Models of reflection

What is a model of reflection?

Models provide frameworks that can assist and structure the process of reflection. From a practical perspective, models of reflection vary in complexity, depending on how many steps, or stages, they use to break down the process of reflecting on experience, and how many prompts or cues they provide as potential memory joggers for each stage.

The underlying concept

Reflective models share three basic assumptions. These are that we can:

1 think back over our experiences;
2 understand them at a deeper level; and
3 use that understanding to do things differently in the future – that is, to effect change through learning.

Staged models

Stages present a nominal order for considering different aspects of an experience. Each stage serves as a useful reference point, prompting a different approach to working with an experience. In practice, you are likely to move fluidly between these stages and to include material not covered explicitly by them.

Three-stage model

There are various three-stage models, such as Borton (1970) and Driscoll (1994), that, in essence, simplify the reflective process to:

1 What?
2 So what?
3 Now what?

These map onto the basic assumptions described above broadly as follows.

1 *What?* Go back over the experience and identify what happened.
2 *So what?* Describing your experience is not enough – you need to work out why this is significant. What do you now understand better?

3 *Now what?* Now that you have a better understanding of your experience, what will you do with the insights gained? How will you be different? Or do things differently?

Multi-stage models

It is a complex process to work usefully with experience so as to learn from it. There are many potential components, from identifying what is relevant, exploring personal feelings and understanding other people's perspectives, through to the insights gained from research findings, or a consideration of sociological, political or other dimensions.

Any of the above components, and others, could be extracted for particular emphasis. This could be framed either as a distinct 'stage' within the model or as a distinct set of prompts. For example, Gibbs (1988) provides a model that includes a separate stage on feelings, whereas other models such as Boud et al. (1985) do not, but build consideration of feelings throughout the reflective process.

Prompt-based models

Johns and Freshwater (1998) have developed a model that is popular for professional practice in nursing. This provides prompt questions that relate, broadly, to five different ways of knowing:

- Empirical: the tested knowledge base, such as scientific research.
- Personal: knowing how feelings and motivations influence your actions.
- Aesthetic: knowing how to make meaningful, creative, unconscious responses in the moment.
- Ethical: knowing what it is right to do.
- Reflexive: knowing how to apply learning gained from experience.

Deciding on your model for reflection

Before launching into your reflection, consider the following.

Are you required to use a model?

Do you have to use a model of reflection for your programme? If so, ensure that you understand its rationale so that you can apply this to your own reflection.

Do you want to use an existing model?

If you have a choice about whether you apply a reflective model, consider whether you would find it helpful to draw on one that already exists, to help give structure to your approach and thinking. If so, research the various alternatives available. The references on page 230 provide a good starting place.

Would you prefer to design your own model?

Alternatively, you can design your own model. The advantages of designing your own model are not only that this should better fit your own purposes and circumstances, but that you also gain practice in planning reflective activity. You could also design your own model through active, critical engagement with existing models. This would deepen your understanding of what critical reflection is about.

Designing your own reflective model

Your own model can be as simple or as complex as you find helpful for motivating you and generating deep and useful reflection. You may wish to adapt your model depending on how well it works for you.

Concept
You would need to take on board the underlying concept outlined on page 221.

Characteristics
You would need to ensure your model addressed the characteristics of reflection outlined on page 208.

Adapting a staged model
You can adapt an existing model to suit you. Consider whether you work better with a few overarching stages or with additional stages that draw your attention to areas that are significant to you or your subject discipline or profession. You could adapt either the three-stage model (page 221) or the Core Model (Cottrell, 2010) outlined below, or investigate other models and adapt one of those.

Prompts
Consider whether you would benefit from a list of questions to serve as prompts for each stage of your model. Listing these can help you to decide what it is that you really want to address through your reflection. If you wish to use the Core Model for reflection (page 223), you can build from the prompts provided there. Alternatively, a fuller list of prompts is available in *Skills for Success* (Cottrell, 2010).

Name the stages and the model
Naming the stages of your model helps to make it your own. On a practical level, it also helps to clarify whether the stages are distinct and likely to work well together. It will be easier for you to recall the stages whenever you undertake your reflection.

Once you have named your stages, the distinctive character of your model should be clearer to you. Give your model a name that reflects this.

The Core Model for critical reflection

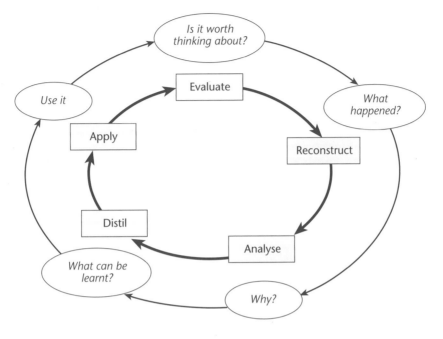

Source: Stella Cottrell (2010).

Core Model: stages and prompts

The Core Model for critical reflection consists of 5 stages, with question-based prompts to support each of these (Cottrell, 2010). You can adapt, select from or delete these stages. You can add further stages if you feel that a particular prompt or set of prompts merits separate attention, either for your own purpose or because these are especially important in your discipline. The five stages are described below.

1 Evaluate

The kind of critical reflection described in this chapter is, as we have seen, intensive, time-consuming and potentially emotionally demanding; you need to select a focus. Given the demands that it makes upon you, it is worth spending time

critically reflecting upon your choice and the direction that you are taking. As this is so important, the first stage of your reflection is a critically evaluative one, examining your purpose and focus and deciding whether these will really yield the best results.

Examples of prompts useful for this stage

- Does this provide enough challenge and material – or have I gone for too easy an option?
- Is this too challenging? Am I too angry or affected by this to address it at this time or as part of an academic assignment?
- Am I ever likely to be in a similar situation again? If not, what will I gain from focusing on it now?

2 Reconstruct

Each time we go over an event in a reflective way, the account is likely to vary. That is why this stage is referred to as 'reconstruction'. This is typical phase 1 reflective activity. We are putting together, again, the events, feelings, details as we now recall them. Going over an event in detail can bring up unexpected reminders or draw attention to items that we may not have noticed previously.

Input from others about the event, or perspectives gained from our reading about the subject, may lead us to reconstruct the event in a slightly different way with different aspects coming to the forefront or gaining a new emphasis or significance. If we write these down and return to them, the differences between one account and another may strike us as significant.

Examples of prompts useful for this stage

- What was I aiming to achieve through my actions, what I said, or what I didn't do or say?
- Did this work out as I expected?
- How did I feel when X happened, and how did I respond?

3 Analyse

Examine your reflective materials, your thoughts or your notes, from different angles; interrogate your material; answer your prompt questions; compare your emerging findings with those expected from your reading or training; question whether you are really confronting your own motivations and taking on board the difficult messages; take a walk; talk to a peer about what you are finding; jot down new thoughts; sleep on them; sit quietly with your reflections; go back over everything again. In other words, work with your material in many ways, so as to encourage fresh insights to emerge.

Examples of prompts useful for this stage

- Which actions or omissions were most significant in the way events unfolded?
- What were the consequences of unexpected or difficult feelings?
- What interpretations or theories help to make sense of what happened?
- Were there deeper roots to this than were apparent at the time?

4 Distil

If your analysis helped to make sense of your experience, then it should be a relatively easy next step to draw out the lessons learnt. Your analysis may have generated many thoughts, of different levels of significance. Draw out the most relevant and synthesise these into a workable set of key ideas or conclusions.

Examples of prompts useful for this stage

- What worked well that I could use again in the future?
- What were the trigger points? How would I manage those differently?
- How does my way of approaching matters or thinking about them help or hinder the desired outcome?

5 Apply

If you have really arrived at new understandings and drawn lessons for yourself, then the logical next step is to consider how you will make use of that learning before you forget it. This may mean that you need to bring others on board so that they understand why you want to do things differently, and are prepared to support you.

Examples of prompts useful for this stage

- To what kinds of situations will I apply these insights?
- What support will I need?
- Who else needs to be on board? How will I persuade them of the benefits?

Applying reflection to professional practice

Why reflect on practice?

Critical reflection has long been used in health-related, caring and teaching professions, and its value is recognised increasingly in other areas such as management and business. There are a number of reasons for this, such as:

- it anchors theory in meaningful, concrete experience, helping to bring it alive;
- it gives recognition to learning gained in non-academic contexts;
- it provides a bridge between practical experience and academic study;
- it helps develop understanding of difficult work situations, improving professional practice.

The workplace as a resource

Work contexts offer rich resources for meaningful study. However, there are ethical considerations that you must take on board. Ensure that you retain confidentiality and anonymity with respect to workplace information. You may be able to use examples if names and details are removed in such a way that the workplace and individuals cannot be identified, or if you gain written permission. You will need permission to use workplace documentation if it is not already in the public arena. It is likely that your programme will ask you to consider the ethical implications of the focus you have selected and the material you will be using.

Reflection on the knowledge base

Your workplace practice is likely to be based, at least in part, on theories, research or established professional wisdom. You can build your own expertise and understanding by drawing on these as part of your critical reflection.

- **Select a relevant theory** or piece of research that relates to your work context.

- **Identify what it would mean in your context.** What, in summary, do the theory or research findings propose? If this theory or research applied to your work context, what would you expect to happen? What would you expect to see, hear, feel, experience, understand better, etc.?

- **Check whether it applies.** In practice, do the theory or research findings apply to your context as expected? How do they throw light on your own experiences? In what ways do they help – or not help – you to make sense of your professional practice?

- **Identify probable cause.** If the theory or research findings do not seem to apply as expected, how do they differ? Why is that likely to be the case? For example, are you working with a different client group than that used for the initial research? Are other conditions different? Do any other theories throw light on your findings?

- **Support for change.** Do your reflections suggest that any change is needed in your workplace – such as a review of procedures or a change in expectations? How do research findings or established theories support your case?

Challenge your own previous practice

Use your critical reflections to challenge your previous thinking, assumptions and actions. Re-examine these in the light of what you have read. If you find that this, in itself, raises difficult issues, reflect on where these difficulties lie, how they have arisen, and how you will address them. Talk to your tutor or your workplace supervisor about any complex issues or concerns.

Reflection and professional judgement

Following procedure

In clinical practice and workplace settings, there are usually set procedures and customary working practices that you are required to follow. These have an important function in ensuring that everyone knows what to do, that teams can work together, and that health, safety, security, quality assurance, statutory obligations and other requirements are met.

When procedure isn't enough

However, from time to time, situations arise that make it difficult or inappropriate to follow procedures exactly. This requires you to make a judgement call – sometimes on the spot. Many poor outcomes in the workplace arise because people don't have sufficient understanding of the relation between theory and practice. This means they are unclear:

- when to deviate from procedure;
- what to do in situations where no procedure yet exists;
- how to read a situation so as to make an appropriate decision for action.

John was a stickler for following protocol to the letter.

Making good judgement calls

If you have a good grasp of the knowledge base and working context that underpin everyday practice, you are better able to make a good call when needed. You are more likely to:

- understand why the normal procedure was established;
- understand the assumptions that inform normal procedure;
- be able to identify whether these apply in the current context;
- judge whether the procedure itself can be adapted or over-ruled;
- evaluate what aspects of the normal procedures still need to be met;
- make a decision that meets the requirements of the current situation.

Reflecting on non-routine action

The following prompts can assist you in reflecting on how you act when routine responses may not be appropriate.

- What is the usual course of action in this kind of instance?
- What is the rationale for that routine procedure (i.e. what are the reasons for doing things that way)?
- What was different in this instance such that it was difficult or inappropriate to follow usual procedures?
- Which aspects of procedure had to be adhered to? Why were these essential?
- Which aspects could be adapted or over-ruled? Why is that the case?
- Did you stick to the routine or adapt it? Why was that?
- Did it work well? What were the immediate effects? What were the consequences?
- What, if anything, would you do if this situation arose again?

Good and bad critical reflection

From what you have read already, you will have started to formulate a sense of what constitutes good reflection. The following table highlights the differences between good and poor critical reflection.

Aspect	Good critical reflection	Poor critical reflection
1 Experience	Draws on personal, group or workplace experience as a means of testing out theory or learning new lessons, looking at experiences with a critical eye.	Assumes 'experience' is an end in itself; that one's own experience is typical of others' without good evidence that this is so; that experience equates to 'insight', without bringing a critical eye to it.
2 Personal responsibility	The best critical reflection demonstrates integrity both in focusing on one's personal role, such as the assumptions brought to a situation or actions taken or omitted, and in taking responsibility for the consequences of these.	Poor critical reflection finds ways of deflecting blame onto other people or the context itself for the way events unfolded. Alternatively, personal responsibility is addressed in a superficial way, so that the relation of action and consequence is not considered in depth. It is also poor practice to assume personal responsibility and guilt for matters that are not simply down to oneself.
3 Focus	Selects a focus such as a particular time-period, set of events, specific kinds of incident or examples of interactions.	Rambles around or covers too many dimensions so it isn't clear what is the focus of the reflection.
4 Scale	The focus is broad enough to offer challenge and meaningful insights but can be reasonably explored in the timescale and word limit.	Is either too narrow to provide the insights needed or too broad to look at things in any depth.
5 Direction	However it may start, good critical reflection begins to take direction as the person starts to identify, and then focus on, selected themes for closer attention.	Rambles or hops about rather than finding a direction.
6 Depth	Delves below the surface: it picks up on initial thoughts and insights, analysing these further with the aim of gaining deeper insights or broader applications.	Is superficial. It doesn't demonstrate any interest in burrowing beneath the surface to understand more.
7 Challenge	Usually tackles a difficult area or enters difficult terrain, such as matters that are personally difficult, or issues that are complex and don't lend themselves to easy answers.	Tends to stay within safe territory or deals with difficult issues in a superficial way or doesn't seem to take the person forward in their understanding.
8 Theory	Draws on relevant theoretical standpoints, research, or established professional practice in ways that demonstrate how these have helped understanding. Where relevant, it relates the particular incident to broader social and political issues.	Draws only on the person's own ideas, experiences and anecdotes, or makes superficial passing references to theory and research.

Aspect	Good critical reflection	Poor critical reflection
9 Criticality	Brings a searching, critical eye to the focus of the reflection, to emerging insights, and to any theories or sources of information. This criticality is used to take the person forward in their understanding of the core emerging issues, such as by challenging their own ideas and actions, or showing how their experience supports or challenges existing knowledge.	Is preoccupied mainly with describing situations, content or events. May include critical analysis but this doesn't seem to be used in a way that really develops an understanding of the core emerging issues.
10 Insight	The reflection takes the person forward in their understanding, such that they can make more sense of their situation, work or study, manage better within it, do things differently, apply understandings to new contexts, etc.	The reflection gives little indication that the person has moved forward in their understanding of the context or issue, or self-knowledge.
11 End-points (Extrapolated conclusions)	The process of reflection may take the person in many different directions. However, by the end, they have stood back, drawn out the key messages of what they have learnt, and summarised these as conclusions or recommendations.	The reflection reads more as description of a process or rambling free association. The lessons learned are not drawn out clearly as conclusions or recommendations.
12 Audience (if reflection is to be shared)	If this is to be used in academic, work or public contexts, the writing up of reflection demonstrates a sound understanding of ethical considerations and stylistic or academic conventions that may apply. Issues of confidentiality have been addressed appropriately.	The reflection is handed in or made public without all due care being taken to ensure that confidentiality and other data protection issues are addressed; no thought is given to how to make the reflection manageable for others to read.

Reflection 📖 The quality of your critical reflection

Using the table above, consider your own critical reflection.

- What do you think are your areas of strength in producing good critical reflection?
- Which aspects do you need to improve?

Presenting your reflection to others

Logs, blog, journals

It is likely that your initial reflections will be written primarily as phase 1 reflection in a journal or blog. If you are asked to submit these as part of an assignment, then read through them following the guidelines in the Audience sections of pages 213 and 228. Amend them accordingly, deleting or blocking out material that you decide not to submit. If your initial reflections are very lengthy, it may be advisable to edit these, or to highlight the salient parts, to help your reader manage the bulk and identify the most relevant sections.

Reflective summary or essay

Typically, you will be asked to produce a critical reflective summary, essay or report. This tends to carry the most weight in an assignment and merits time and attention so as to do justice to what you have learnt. It is important to bear in mind the following.

Academic conventions

Ensure that you apply the usual academic conventions. See pages 167–89.

Referring to theory and research

You may have provided an outline of your background research as part of a project report or made references to different theoretical perspectives within your phase 1 reflection. However, it is essential that you also relate theory to practice within your reflective summary or essay, bringing a critical eye to these, and making clear how they influenced your reflection and practice.

Examples	Making use of theory

Example 1: Business student
When interviewing these participants on their employment history, details of their personal lives emerged. I hadn't expected to become preoccupied by my own anxiety. Smith (1992)

feels that for sensitive topics, there should be an experienced co-leader present 'to adequately monitor the group's comfort level'. I had thought this to be an extreme position for business settings but these interviews made me think again. My difficulty with Smith's suggestion is that having someone present with only that role might be off-putting to the group – and make them feel spied upon. One alternative might be to use two interviewers . . .

Example 2: Education student
A number of authors draw links between feeding and teaching (Coren, 1997; Williams, 1997). Salzberger-Wittenberg (1983) notes that the processes involved in learning and digestion are similar, i.e. taking in, absorbing and producing. . . . Within education, 'spoon-feeding' is often used as a metaphor for poor practice, encouraging shallow learning and 'regurgitation'. My reflections on my teaching are that the process is considerably more complex than I had believed. I shall demonstrate that . . .

Common errors to avoid

When relating theory and practice:

- Avoid putting all references to theory in the opening paragraphs and then forgetting it. If you summarise the research at the outset, make sure that you refer back to it at relevant points throughout the essay.
- Avoid referring to theory without directly linking it to your reflections.
- Avoid reproducing at length the content of theory, such as *Freud said X. He also said Y. He also said Z.* Rather, be specific about how the theory or research is useful or limiting in explaining why something happens.

Summary

This chapter has looked at critical thinking from a different angle, turning the spotlight onto your own actions. Critical reflection of this kind is used increasingly within both academic and professional contexts.

Critical reflection is challenging, requiring you to analyse your own behaviours and assumptions, relating these to broader perspectives from theory and research and, if relevant, professional practice, and doing this with integrity, even when the material itself may be taxing or reveal your actions in a less than perfect light. In addition, initial reflections need to be sifted, the key lessons extracted and related back to theory and practice, and all this presented to others using the conventions of academic writing. Along the way, it is likely that the material will be personally challenging, probably evoking difficult feelings and emotions which you will need to manage well for yourself and others.

The achievement of good critical reflection can feel elusive. Motivation can be an issue, and it can feel difficult to balance the different aspects in a coherent way. This chapter provides ways of addressing these difficulties. It structures the activity into distinct phases and stages, gives examples so that you can see what is expected, and provides step-by-step methods and practical tools that you can use and adapt for your own critical reflection.

It is not surprising that, if you are successful in bringing together all of the above, you are likely to gain enormously. Those who engage deeply in this process generally find that, within a relatively short time, they move from initial, superficial observations to deep, thoughtful conclusions about themselves, their learning, their professional roles, ways of changing things for the better, and even their way of being in the world.

Information about the sources

Borton, T. (1970) *Reach, Touch and Teach* (London: Hutchinson).

Boud, D., Keogh, R. and Walker, D. (eds) (1985) *Reflection: Turning Experience into Learning* (London: Routledge).

Coren, A. (1997) *A Psychodynamic Approach to Education* (London: Sheldon Press).

Cottrell, S. (2010) *Skills for Success: The Personal Development Planning Handbook*, second edition (Basingstoke: Palgrave Macmillan).

Driscoll, J. (1994) 'Reflective Practice for Practice'. *Senior Nurse*, **13** (7), 47–50.

Gibbs, G. (1988) *Learning by Doing: A Guide to Reading and Learning Methods* (Oxford: Further Education Unit, Oxford Polytechnic).

Johns, C. and Freshwater, D. (1998) *Transforming Nursing through Reflective Practice* (Oxford: Blackwell Scientific).

Salzberger-Wittenberg, I., Williams, G. and Osborne, E. (1983) *The Emotional Experience of Learning and Teaching* (London: Karnac Books).

Smith, L. (1992) 'Ethical Issues in Interviewing'. *Journal of Advanced Nursing*, **17**: 98–103.

Williams, G. (1997) *Internal Landscapes and Foreign Bodies: Eating Disorders and Other Pathologies* (London: Tavistock Clinic Series, Duckworth).

Texts for Activities
in Chapters 8, 9 and 11

Texts for activities in Chapters 8, 9 and 11

These texts have been written to support the activities in Chapters 8, 9 and 11. Names, references and data produced in the texts below are fictitious.

Text 1

It isn't really stealing to copy music off the internet. True artists want their music to reach as many people as possible. They are more concerned about the effect of their music on the world than on base concerns such as money. Large publishers are only interested in music that has a broad appeal and which will bring in large profits. They overlook innovative and radical music which is better artistically but which does not sell in such large quantities. Most independent artists cannot find distributors. People who share music with their friends on the internet perform a useful service to music as they make more people aware of small artists and the diversity of music that is available. Without this, the world of music would be extremely bland and middle-of-the-road.

> Carla: in internet chat room, Cla@mu.room. host; 7 Sept. 2006; Carla does not pay for music downloaded from the internet.

Text 2

Neighbours are generous with the cuttings they make from plants. Up and down the country, people are exchanging cuttings from their roses, fuschias and hostas. Many of the plants they share are registered for Plant Breeders' Rights. This entitles the person who bred or discovered the plant to a royalty. Gardeners never bother finding out which plants they must pay a royalty for. A cutting is the gardener's equivalent of burning a CD for music lovers. If gardeners don't bother paying royalties on cuttings, why should other people pay royalties, such as for music downloaded from the internet?

> Ivan Potter, in *Your Gardening Questions*, a popular monthly magazine published by GPX Publishers in London, vol. 6, June 2005.

Text 3

Piracy of software, videos, games and music is stealing, whether this is done by copying films onto video or sharing music files with other people on the internet. Some people argue that it is acceptable to make illegal copies as everybody else does it. Others rationalise this kind of theft on the grounds that publishers set unacceptably high prices. They forget that publishers are entitled to set prices at whatever the market will take. Consumers have a choice. If they want the product enough, they should be prepared to pay for it. If not, they should go without.

> P. D. Cuttle, legal expert, writing in article, 'Steal it Away'. In *National CRI Law Journal*, vol. 7, issue 4, during April 2007.

Text 4

Publishers of modern music are mainly concerned about large-scale copying by what amount to alternative businesses. These businesses make pirate copies and sell them at much lower prices. Publishers are not bothered about ordinary members of the public making a few copies for their friends and family.

> Arnold Spratt, editorial column, in *The Middletown Argus* newspaper, 17 June 2004.

Text 5

More and more people are downloading free music and sharing it with their friends. Such kindness should be applauded. It is likely that everybody will have done this at least once by 2015. If everybody does something, it can't be bad, and if it isn't bad, then where is the crime?

> Alan Hibbs, a member of the public who does pay for music he downloads, in a letter to the editor of the *National Press Daily*, 3 November 2006.

Text 6

Many music distributors are not major business concerns. They employ only a few staff and are reliant on the overall sales of many small artists. This is especially the case for those who distribute independent artists, as sales of these are always low and many don't sell at all. As the market for such artists is low, even a few copies made by each purchaser would have a dramatic effect. Illegal copying is likely to contribute to the shaky financial base of the small distributors upon which independent music depends.

> Callum Kahliney, 'Is this the End of the Road?' In *Small Music Distributor*, 12 August 2006. Article in trade magazine for small distributors.

Text 7

Lawyers argue that gardeners who give away cuttings of plants that are registered for Plant Breeders' Rights (or PBRs) are cheating the people who brought the plant into the market. Breeding a new variety of plant does not come cheaply. It can take many years to develop a new strain so that it is ready for marketing. For a plant to be accepted for PBRs, it must have proved that it is stable and uniform so that those who buy it know what it will look like several years down the line. The plant has to be distinct so that it can't be confused with other plants. For every plant that succeeds, a breeder may have thousands of failures, each of which incurs a cost. Breeding can be costly, requiring investment in research, protected and controlled planting space, and specialised labour. If a breeder is lucky enough to be successful, they then have to pay a large sum to register the plant and there are further costs to renew the registration each year. After all that, the plant will last for only about 20 years, and the royalty runs out after 25 years. This means breeders need to maintain their investment in developing future strains or they will be deprived of an income. The royalty on a plant can be between 20 and 30 pence per cutting, or more. Multiply this by many thousands, and the breeders are really losing out. Whether or not they ever receive this money comes down to the average gardeners' ethical sensitivity and their awareness of PBRs. It is unlikely that the police will descend to recoup the royalties: lawyers focus on the big companies. However, as the lawyers point out, that doesn't mean free cuttings are acceptable: some breeders need every penny if they are to continue to produce new varieties for us to enjoy in the future.

> Anjeli Johl, 'Counting the Cost of Flowers', in the *National Press Daily* newspaper, 10 July 2006. Johl is a regular columnist in the paper's reputable law section.

Text 8

It doesn't make sense to argue that people shouldn't download free copies of music and games over the internet even once, but that it is acceptable to make free copies of music broadcast on the radio ten or twenty times a day if you want. It is illegal to copy from the radio but nobody bothers about this as it is impossible to catch people. Just because it is possible to catch people on the internet shouldn't make it a crime. It is no worse than making copies from the radio.

> Prof. Lee, A. (2006) 'Why Buy?' In R. Coe and B. Stepson, *Examining Media*, pp. 36–57 (London: Many University Press).

Text 9

Although it is possible to devise software to catch people who copy on the internet, it is unlikely that everyone who copies could be charged. If you can't enforce a law, then there isn't any point in passing it. If there isn't a law, then there isn't a crime.

> KAZ, on AskitHere.truth; personal web-site, November 2006.

Text 10

Moral and ethical issues are not simply questions of right and wrong. They should be more properly regarded as dilemmas. The decision that the law, or 'justice', should ultimately decide what is right or wrong has never been made in a democratic way. The law was scrambled together over time, and is often contradictory. There is too little public discussion on whether the whole concept of justice is what we really want as the basis of right and wrong. From time to time, throughout history, brave individuals have stood up to the law, and,

arguably, it is mainly through their defiance that the law has progressed at all. Even today, when an issue really matters to them, individuals will brave prison on the basis of their individual conscience, when the law appears to them to sanction immorality or bad ethics. Peters (1974) and Gilligan (1977) have argued that there are grounds for giving priority to other matters, such as autonomy, courage, and caring about what happens to other people. Even Kohlberg (1981), who took a justice based approach to morality, stated that being able to make judgements about justice was 'a necessary but not a sufficient condition for moral action'.

> Fred Piaskin in an article, 'Moral Dilemmas in Action', in the *Joint Universities Journal of Advanced Ethics*, in 1986. Volume 8, issue 2.

Text 11

It is stealing to copy text from a book, article or the internet without acknowledging the source of the information. It is regarded as theft of the intellectual copyright of another person. This is treated very seriously by universities. However, stealing suggests you know that you are taking something that is not yours to take. Many students are confused. Most know that if they use the exact words in a source, this is a quotation and they must cite the source. However, many believe, erroneously, that it is acceptable to copy whole sections as long as they change a few words here and there.

> Prof. Soyinka, G. (2006) 'Plagiarism Unveiled'. In *Journal of HE Worldwide*, 27 (3), pp. 231–47.

Text 12 (abbreviated version of a research paper)

Ebo, T., Markham, T. H. and Malik, Y. (2004) 'The Effects of Ease of Payment on Willingness to Pay. Ethics or Ease?' *Proceedings of the Academy for Ethical Dilemmas*, vol. 3 (4).

Introduction

This paper sets out to show that behaviour is affected primarily by how easy it is to act in an ethical way. It demonstrates that in the Oldlea area during 1998–2006, there was a decrease in illegal copying of music from the internet following schemes that enabled easy payment online to download the music.

The research builds on the ground-breaking research by Mixim, Moss and Plummer (1934) which showed that some forms of theft were not based on a desire to steal but on inertia when faced with complex or onerous systems of payment. Mixim et al. found that at specific ages, people found it more difficult to queue, and had a tendency to focus on the symptoms associated with queuing rather than the requirement to pay. This resulted in them leaving shops to alleviate their discomfort, forgetting that they were carrying items for which they had not paid.

Damblin and Toshima (1974) acknowledged the theoretical framework of Mixim et al. but criticised the evidence base, which involved only 30 participants over a short time span. Damblin and Toshima (1986), using a sample of 200 senior citizens, found that there were significant differences in ethical behaviour depending on people's medical conditions. Several research studies have shown external conditions can have a greater impact on behaviour than ethical understanding (Singh, McTiern and Brauer, 1991; Colby, 1994; Miah and Brauer, 1997). However, no studies have focused on people under 25 years old nor on the impact of the internet on such behaviours. . . .

The research hypotheses are (1) that most young people who download music for free will pay a fee to download copies of the music if this is made easy, and (2) that the willingness of people to pay for music will depend on income, with high earners being more willing to pay than low earners.

Methodology

Participants were divided into three groups and into two conditions. The three groups were divided into low, middle and high earners. In the first condition, facilities for quick and easy payment for downloaded music were made available. In the second condition, the system for paying was time-consuming and complicated. The participants were 1206 people aged 15–25, matched for age, sex, and ethnic background across groups and conditions. An advertisement for an alternative web-site where the music could be downloaded for free appeared when the participant was on line. This offered free downloads but carried a message that not paying deprived the artist of income.

Results

The results supported the first research hypothesis but not the second. The results for the first hypothesis were significant at . . .

Discussion and conclusions

These research findings suggest, as with older age groups, that when it is easy to pay for a service, most people aged 15–25 act in an ethical way. When given the choice of an easy payment option or an unethical method of free access, 78.6 per cent of purchasers selected the payment route. When payment methods were complicated, only 47 per cent of purchasers paid for their purchase, the others opting instead for the free site. Before making a purchase, almost all participants, 98 per cent, investigated the free site. This shows that they made an ethical choice when they opted to pay, rather than simply choosing the site they were allocated.

However, the second research hypothesis was not supported. This study found that 86 per cent of participants in the low-wage group paid for the music, compared with 64 per cent of those in the middle income group and only 31 per cent in the highest income group. This suggests that ethical responses are stronger in low income groups and weaker amongst high earners.

References

Colby, R. (1994) 'Age, Ethics and Medical Circumstance: A Comparative Study of Behaviours in Senior Populations in West Sussex and Suffolk'. *South West Journal of Age-related Studies*, 19, 2.

Damblin, J. and Toshima, Y. (1974) 'Theft, Personality and Criminality'. *Atalanta Journal of Criminal Theory*, 134, 2.

Damblin, J. and Toshima, Y. (1986) 'Ethics and Aging'. In R. Morecambe, *Is Crime Intentional?* (Cambridge: Pillar Publications).

Miah, M. and Brauer, G. T. (1997) 'The Effect of Previous Trauma on Crime-related Behaviours'. *Atalanta Journal of Criminal Theory*, 214, 4.

Mixim, A., Moss, B. and Plummer, C. (1934) 'Hidden Consensus'. In *New Ethical Problems*, 17, 2.

Singh, K. R., McTiern, S. and Brauer, G. T. (1991) 'Context and Action: Situational Effects upon Non-typical Behaviours in Post-retirement Males'. *West African Journal of Crime Theory*, 63, 3.

Practice activities on longer texts

The following pages provide activities based on longer texts.

The texts for practice activities 1 and 3 provide examples of better critical writing. These give you the opportunity to identify the features of an argument when reading a longer text. They also provide you with a basis for comparison when you go on to analyse the examples of poorer critical writing provided for practice activities 2 and 4.

Texts 2 and 4 provide opportunities to identify examples of poor argument.

Prompts and answers are provided for each practice activity.

Practice 1: Features of an argument

- Read the passage 'Global Warming Requires a Global Solution' and identify the features of the argument, using the numbered prompts below to assist you.
- Label and number each of your answers in the *Comments* margin provided alongside the text. If you use the same numbers as those provided in the prompts table below, this will help you to check your answers.

Prompts		Done (tick when completed)
1	Identify the sentence or sentences that sum up the main argument.	
2	Identify the author's position.	
3	Identify the summative conclusion.	
4	Identify the overall logical conclusion.	
5	Identify the main reasons given to support the logical conclusion.	
6	Identify any intermediate conclusions used as reasons. In the margin, explain the purpose of the interim conclusion (i.e. why the author needed to come to an interim conclusion in order to develop the argument).	
7	Identify evidence given to support reasons.	
8	Identify descriptive text that provides background information for the reader.	
9	Identify words used to signal the development of either the main argument or arguments leading to intermediate conclusions.	
10	Identify any counter arguments put forward by the author.	
11	Identify arguments by the author to address counter arguments.	
12	Identify any use of primary sources.	
13	Identify any use of secondary sources.	

Practice 1: Features of an argument (continued)

Global Warming Requires a Global Solution (Text 1)

The increase in greenhouse gas emissions over the past 50 years is viewed as a major factor in global warming. Research by the leading world authorities on global warming, the Intergovernmental Panel on Climate Change (IPCC), suggests that even if all carbon dioxide emissions ceased today, there would be climate changes for a number of years to come, leading to water shortages for 5 billion people and increased flooding across Northern Europe by 2025. However, scientists have proposed a range of solutions from increasing efficient use of fossil fuels to incentives for using cleaner forms of energy, which they believe, if applied globally, would be sufficient to make a real impact on climate change.

The Kyoto Protocol was proposed in 1997 as a means of working towards a reduction in greenhouse gas emissions and the halting of long-term climate change. It focuses on developed countries, the world's greatest polluters, and seeks to establish an overall reduction in greenhouse gas emissions of 5 per cent on 1990 levels over the period of 2008–2012. Many key developed industrial nations have ratified the Protocol but a number of others have been resistant. Some governments argue that it is not in their countries' interests to form part of a global agreement. However, I shall argue that, although it may need to be applied differentially, a global solution is, ultimately, essential and that developed countries need to take the lead.[2]

Politicians, scientists and businesses in developed countries have given a number of reasons for not signing up to the Protocol. These include doubt about the real link between carbon dioxide emissions and global warming, concerns about the effect on their own economies and a rejection of the need for imposed, rather than voluntary, reductions in emissions. A number of leaders of state have cited the lack of emission reduction targets for developing countries as the key reason behind their rejection of the Protocol. On the surface, this appears a fair argument – global warming is a problem for everyone, not just those in developed countries, and requires every nation to participate. William K. Stevens (1997) makes the point that, if left unchecked, emissions from developing countries will surpass those from developed countries in 20–30 years.

Comments

Practice 1: Features of an argument (continued)

Emissions from developing countries are clearly an important issue. However, for developing countries, the argument that they should be subject to exactly the same restrictions as developed countries does not carry weight. After watching developed countries build their wealth and power on extensive use of fossil fuels this appears to be a case of 'do what I say, not what I do'. Dr Mwandoysa, chair of the developing countries' caucus on climate change, makes the point that many developing countries are struggling just to provide an acceptable standard of living for their citizens but are being asked to support changes which would allow the developed world to maintain its wasteful lifestyle (Stevens, 1997). This is similar to someone dumping their waste in a local field and then complaining that other people are not doing enough to preserve the countryside.

Also, even though developing countries are not required to reduce emissions under the Protocol, Dr Mwandoysa notes that most of them are already working towards this aim, even with limited resources and technology. Developing countries recognise that they have a role to play in halting global warming, but feel that developed countries are better placed to develop the structures and technologies which are needed to support this work further. This is equitable, given developed countries' greater role in the development of global warming.

Greenpeace (2001) suggests that reluctance to offend powerful fossil fuel companies is the key reason behind some developed countries' reluctance to address global warming. Countries which have a heavy reliance on fossil fuels face the possibility that agreeing to reduce emissions will have serious implications for their economy in terms of job losses. However, Stevens (1997) suggests that developed countries, such as the USA and Australia, are actually more fearful of competitive advantages being given to those developing nations such as China and South Korea who stand on the threshold of industrialisation. Whilst such arguments do have validity in terms of developed countries seeking to maintain their current economic power, their validity is short-term.

In the short term, countries who refuse to reduce greenhouse gas emissions are able to continue as economic superpowers. However, ultimately a failure to address greenhouse gas emissions could enforce changes above and beyond those imposed by the Kyoto Protocol. Long-term global warming is anticipated to cause significant climate changes in those developed countries that are reluctant to sign the Protocol. These changes will impact on a range of major industries, for

Comments

example, causing flooding in tourism centres and droughts in key agricultural lands (Penfold, 2001). The extreme economic consequences of such changes undermine the validity of economic preservation as an argument for not ratifying the Kyoto Protocol.

Therefore, although there are economic consequences in taking action to reduce emissions, they are ultimately outweighed by the consequences of unwelcome climate change and long-term economic disaster if we fail to implement global action. Not all countries have played an equal part in the causation of global warming and it is fair that those who have contributed most towards global warming should also contribute most towards finding its solutions. However, given the potential consequences of global warming, it does require a global solution and there is a role and rationale for all countries in reducing greenhouse gas emissions.

Comments

References

1 UNFCCC (undated) *Feeling the Heat*, http://unfccc. int/essential_background; United Nations Framework Convention on Climate Change; downloaded 13/02/05.

2 UNFCCC (undated) *A Summary of the Kyoto Protocol*, http://unfccc.int/essential_background; United Nations Framework Convention on Climate Change; downloaded 13/02/05.

3 Stevens, W. K. (1997) 'Greenhouse Gas Issue Pits Third World Against Richer Nations'. *New York Times*, 30 November 1997. Stevens quotes Dr Mwandoysa.

4 Greenpeace (2001) *A Decade of Dirty Tricks*, www.greenpeace.org.uk; dated July 2001.

5 AFL-CIO Executive Council (1998) *Press Statement on the Kyoto Protocol*, dated 30 January 1998.

6 Penfold, C. (2001) *Global Warming and the Kyoto Protocol*, www.marxist.com/Globalisation/global_ warming.html; dated July 2001.

Answer to Practice 1: Features of an argument

Global Warming Requires a Global Solution (Text 1)

The increase in greenhouse gas emissions over the past 50 years is viewed as a major factor in global warming. Research by the leading world authorities on global warming, the Intergovernmental Panel on Climate Change (IPCC),[13] suggests that even if all carbon dioxide emissions ceased today, there would be climate changes for a number of years to come, leading to water shortages for 5 billion people and increased flooding across Northern Europe by 2025. However, scientists have proposed a range of solutions from increasing efficient use of fossil fuels to incentives for using cleaner forms of energy, which they believe, if applied globally, would be sufficient to make a real impact on climate change.[8]

[8]The Kyoto Protocol was proposed in 1997 as a means of working towards a reduction in greenhouse gas emissions and the halting of long-term climate change. It focuses on developed countries, the world's greatest polluters, and seeks to establish an overall reduction in greenhouse gas emissions of 5 per cent on 1990 levels over the period of 2008–2012. Many key developed industrial nations have ratified the Protocol but a number of others have been resistant. Some governments argue that it is not in their countries' interests to form part of a global agreement. However, I shall argue that, although it may need to be applied differentially, a global solution is, ultimately, essential and that developed countries need to take the lead.[2]

Politicians, scientists and businesses in developed countries have given a number of reasons for not signing up to the Protocol. These include doubt about the real link between carbon dioxide emissions and global warming, concerns about the effect on their own economies and a rejection of the need for imposed, rather than voluntary, reductions in emissions. A number of leaders of state have cited the lack of emission reduction targets for developing countries as the key reason behind their rejection of the Protocol.[10] On the surface, this appears a fair argument – global warming is a problem for everyone, not just those in developed countries, and requires every nation to participate. William K. Stevens (1997)[13] makes the point that, if left unchecked, emissions from developing countries will surpass those from developed countries in 20–30 years.[5, 6, 7]

Comments

Numbers in the text and below refer to the grid on p. 240.

13   The research by the IPCC provides a secondary source for this piece.

8   This descriptive opening paragraph gives essential background information on global climate change.

8   This paragraph gives essential background information about the Kyoto Protocol.

2   This sentence summarises the author's position.

10   The author sets out a number of possible counter arguments against the main argument here.

13   Secondary source

6   Intermediate conclusion: developing countries need to play a role in reducing greenhouse gas emissions.

5   The reason given to support this is: if left unchecked, emissions from developing countries will surpass those from developed countries in 20–30 years.

7   Evidence given for what will happen if emissions are left unchecked.

Answer to Practice 1: Features of an argument

Emissions from developing countries are clearly an important issue. However,[9] for developing countries, the argument that they should be subject to exactly the same restrictions as developed countries does not carry weight.[11] After watching developed countries build their wealth and power on extensive use of fossil fuels this appears to be a case of 'do what I say, not what I do'. Dr Mwandoysa,[12] chair of the developing countries' caucus on climate change, makes the point that many developing countries are struggling just to provide an acceptable standard of living for their citizens but are being asked to support changes which would allow the developed world to maintain its wasteful lifestyle (Stevens, 1997). This is similar to someone dumping their waste in a local field and then complaining that other people are not doing enough to preserve the countryside.[10]

Also,[9] even though developing countries are not required to reduce emissions under the Protocol, Dr Mwandoysa notes that most of them are already working towards this aim, even with limited resources and technology. Developing countries recognise that they have a role to play in halting global warming, but feel that developed countries are better placed to develop the structures and technologies which are needed to support this work further. This is equitable, given developed countries' greater role in the development of global warming.[3, 5, 6.]

Greenpeace (2001)[13] suggests that reluctance to offend powerful fossil fuel companies is the key reason behind some developed countries' reluctance to address global warming. Countries which have a heavy reliance on fossil fuels face the possibility that agreeing to reduce emissions will have serious implications for their economy in terms of job losses. However, Stevens (1997) suggests that developed countries, such as the USA and Australia, are actually more fearful of competitive advantages being given to those developing nations such as China and South Korea who stand on the threshold of industrialisation. Whilst such arguments do have validity in terms of developed countries seeking to maintain their current economic power, their validity is short-term.

Comments

9   'However' is used to signal development of the argument as the author moves to address the counter argument.

11   The author addresses counter arguments here.

12   Dr Mwandoysa is a primary source quoted in a secondary source.

10   The author hints at a counter argument here. It sounds as if it is being suggested that developing countries should be exempt from controls.

9   'Also' is used to signal development of the main argument as the author notes that developing countries are reducing emissions.

3   Summative conclusion of the argument so far: developed countries should make a greater contribution towards reducing emissions.

6   Intermediate conclusion: there are moral reasons for developed countries to be involved in a global solution.

5   The reasons given to support this intermediate conclusion are:
   • developed countries have more resources to invest in new structures and technologies;
   • developed countries played a great role in creating global warming.

13   Greenpeace is a secondary source.

Answer to Practice 1: Features of an argument

In the short term, countries who refuse to reduce greenhouse gas emissions are able to continue as economic superpowers. However,[9] ultimately a failure to address greenhouse gas emissions could enforce changes above and beyond those imposed by the Kyoto Protocol. Long-term global warming is anticipated to cause significant climate changes in those developed countries that are reluctant to sign the Protocol. These changes will impact on a range of major industries, for example, causing flooding in tourism centres and droughts in key agricultural lands (Penfold, 2001).[13, 7] The extreme economic consequences of such changes undermine the validity of economic preservation as an argument for not ratifying the Kyoto Protocol.[6, 5]

Therefore, although there are economic consequences in taking action to reduce emissions, they are ultimately outweighed by the consequences of unwelcome climate change and long-term economic disaster, if we fail to implement global action.[1] Not all countries have played an equal part in the causation of global warming and it is fair that those who have contributed most towards global warming should also contribute most towards finding its solutions. However, given the potential consequences of global warming, it does require a global solution and there is a role and rationale for all countries in reducing greenhouse gas emissions.[4]

References

1 UNFCCC (undated) *Feeling the Heat*, http://unfccc.int/essential_background; United Nations Framework Convention on Climate Change; downloaded 13/02/05.

2 UNFCCC (undated) *A Summary of the Kyoto Protocol*, http://unfccc.int/essential_background; United Nations Framework Convention on Climate Change; downloaded 13/02/05.

3 Stevens, W. K. (1997) 'Greenhouse Gas Issue Pits Third World Against Richer Nations'. *New York Times*, 30 November 1997. Stevens quotes Dr Mwandoysa.

4 Greenpeace (2001) *A Decade of Dirty Tricks*, www.greenpeace.org.uk; dated July 2001.

5 AFL-CIO Executive Council (1998) *Press Statement on the Kyoto Protocol*, dated 30/01/98.

6 Penfold, C. (2001) *Global Warming and the Kyoto Protocol* www.marxist.com/Globalisation/global_warming.html; dated July 2001.

Comments

9 'However' is used to signal a development in the main argument – that the consequences of global warming make it essential for us all to act.

13 and 7 Penfold is a secondary source and is used as evidence to support the author's reasoning.

6 Intermediate conclusion: economic preservation is not a valid argument for not ratifying the Protocol.

5 The reasons given to support the intermediate conclusion are:
   • climate change will cause flooding and drought in those countries;
   • their industries will be affected if no action is taken.

1 These sentences summarise the author's main argument that we all need to address greenhouse gas emissions but that some countries should play a greater role than others.

4 Overall logical conclusion – the consequences of not taking action outweigh those economic consequences of reducing emissions and therefore a global solution is required. This links the conclusion back to the essay title, which strengthens the presentation of the argument.

Practice 2: Finding flaws in the argument

- Read this second passage on global warming, and identify flaws in the argument, using the numbered prompts below as a checklist to assist you.
- *Note*: the practice passage does not contain all the flaws on the list and some flaws occur more than once. You can use the checklist to note whether you believe the passage does or does not contain an example, to make it easier to check your answers.
- Label and number each of your answers in the *Comments* margin provided alongside the text. If you use the same numbers as those provided in the prompts table below, this will help you to check your answers.

Prompts		Example found	There is no example	See page
1	False premises			91
2	Two wrongs don't make a right			120
3	Stereotyping			96
4	Lack of consistency in the argument			65, 67
5	Unnecessary background information			58
6	Lack of precision			65
7	Assumption that is not supported by the evidence			88–9
8	Incorrectly assuming a causal link			106
9	False correlation			107
10	Meeting necessary conditions			109
11	Meeting sufficient conditions			110
12	False analogy			112
13	Deflection			114
14	Complicity			114
15	Exclusion			114
16	Unwarranted leaps (e.g. castle of cards; sleight of hand)			116
17	Emotive language			117
18	Attacking the person			117
19	Misrepresentation			119
20	Trivialisation			119
21	Tautology			120
22	Poor referencing			162

Practice 2: Finding flaws in the argument

Global Warming Requires a Global Solution (Text 2)

The Kyoto Protocol was introduced in 1997 as a means of halting long-term climate change or 'global warming' by forcing countries to sign up to reductions in greenhouse gas emissions. It seeks to establish an overall reduction in greenhouse gas emissions for developed countries of 5% on 1990 levels over the next few years. Although the principles have been accepted by many countries, some developed countries have not ratified the Protocol.

The Intergovernmental Panel on Climate Change (IPCC) suggests that we have probably left it too late to make the changes suggested by the Kyoto Protocol. Even if all carbon dioxide emissions ceased today, there would be ongoing climatic change and global warming leading to effects such as rising sea levels and subsequent contamination of drinking water. At best, the effects will be disruptive and at worst catastrophic. We must act now.

Given the consequences of climate change, it is madness for any nation not to sign up. Those countries refusing to sign have given a number of reasons for this, from calling research on climate change into question and even going so far as to say that carbon dioxide is not a pollutant! This suggests some countries are in denial about the causes and impact of greenhouse gas emissions. However, at the same time, one of the key reasons given by developed countries for non-ratification is that global warming is a global problem. Currently the Protocol hinges on developed nations signing up to specified reduction targets for emissions, whilst there are no similar requirements placed on developing countries. Effectively, the Protocol does not cover 80% of the world's population and many suggest that it is not fair that this burden is borne by developed countries alone.

This argument must really stick in the throat of developing countries. Having watched developed countries growing rich by burning vast amounts of fossil fuel through industry, this behaviour suddenly becomes unacceptable at the point at which they are finally poised to get in on the action. As Dr Mwandoysa, chair of the developing countries' caucus on climate change, points out, many developing countries cannot even afford a basic standard of living for their citizens, let alone put resources into environmental programmes.

Comments

Practice 2: Finding flaws in the argument

As he suggests, why should developing countries modify their behaviour whilst developed countries continue with a wasteful lifestyle? Developing countries will always want to follow in the footsteps of more developed countries. Developed countries are like parents who smoke 60 cigarettes a day but get angry if their little children then threaten to take up the habit themselves.

The sense this gives of a hollow argument is increased when one looks at the real reasons developed countries are jumpy about the Protocol – reluctance to offend major fossil fuel companies. Fossil fuels are big business in many of the developed countries' economies and their power is such that they can influence politicians against ratifying the protocol. Some companies have even made the ludicrous suggestion that global warming is actually good for the planet!

Industry associations in developed countries suggest that agreeing to the Protocol would cost hundreds of thousands of jobs and there would, therefore, be a very real impact on national economies. However, objections go beyond these initial job losses. Not all developing nations are the same and whilst some are too poor to ever be serious competition to the developed countries, others like China or India are just waiting for a chance to take advantage of enforced reductions for developed countries so that they can supersede them as an economic power. Powerful oil companies are clearly anxious about any threat to their market and have a vested interest in making sure the Protocol is not ratified.

Ultimately, countries' failure to address greenhouse gas emissions could mean that they shoot themselves in the foot. Long-term global warming is anticipated to cause significant climate changes and countries will have to contend with floods in their tourist centres and droughts in their wheat belts. However, given that neither of these consequences will have an impact on powerful fossil fuel companies, developed countries can justify adopting this short-term strategy of protecting their interests. The power of fossil fuel companies is such that they can influence developed countries not to sign up to the Protocol. Developed countries are susceptible to the influence of fossil fuel companies so if they are told not to sign up, they are likely to give way to that pressure. Given the impact this has on us all, this is obviously unacceptable. Everybody knows we are facing climatic meltdown. Global warming is a problem for all of us and people can't just opt out because it doesn't suit them.

Comments

Practice 2: Finding flaws in the argument

References

1 United Nations Framework Convention on Climate Change. *A Summary of the Kyoto Protocol* http://unfccc.int/essential_background (downloaded 13/02/05).

2 United Nations Framework Convention on Climate Change – *Feeling the Heat* http://unfccc.int/essential_background (downloaded 13/02/05).

3 Stevens, W. K. (1997) 'Greenhouse Gas Issue Pits Third World Against Richer Nations'. *New York Times*, 30 November 1997.

4 AFL-CIO Executive Council (1998) Press Statement on the Kyoto Protocol, 30 January 1998.

Comments

Answers to Practice 2: Finding flaws in the argument

Prompts		Example found	There is no example	See page
1	False premises	✓		91
2	Two wrongs don't make a right		✓	120
3	Stereotyping	✓		96
4	Lack of consistency in the argument		✓	65, 67
5	Unnecessary background information		✓	58
6	Lack of precision	✓		65
7	Assumption that is not supported by the evidence	✓ (3)		88–9
8	Incorrectly assuming a causal link		✓	106
9	False correlation		✓	107
10	Meeting necessary conditions	✓		109
11	Meeting sufficient conditions		✓	110
12	False analogy	✓		112
13	Deflection	✓		114
14	Complicity	✓ (2)		114
15	Exclusion		✓	114
16	Unwarranted leaps (e.g. castle of cards; sleight of hand)	✓ (2)		116
17	Emotive language	✓ (3)		117
18	Attacking the person	✓		117
19	Misrepresentation	✓		119
20	Trivialisation		✓	119
21	Tautology	✓		120
22	Poor referencing	✓ (2)		162

Answers to Practice 2: Finding flaws in the argument

Global Warming Requires a Global Solution (Text 2)

The Kyoto Protocol was introduced in 1997 as a means of halting long-term climate change or 'global warming' by forcing countries to sign up to reductions in greenhouse gas emissions. It seeks to establish an overall reduction in greenhouse gas emissions for developed countries of 5% on 1990 levels over the next few years.[6] Although the principles have been accepted by many countries, some developed countries have not ratified the Protocol.

The Intergovernmental Panel on Climate Change (IPCC) suggests that we have probably left it too late to make the changes suggested by the Kyoto Protocol. Even if all carbon dioxide emissions ceased today, there would be ongoing climatic change and global warming leading to effects such as rising sea levels and subsequent contamination of drinking water. At best, the effects will be disruptive and at worst catastrophic. We must act now.[10]

Given the consequences of climate change, it is madness for any nation not to sign up.[17] Those countries refusing to sign have given a number of reasons for this, from calling research on climate change into question and even going so far as to say that carbon dioxide is not a pollutant![7] This suggests some countries are in denial about the causes and impact of greenhouse gas emissions.[18, 16] However, at the same time, one of the key reasons given by developed countries for non-ratification is that global warming is a global problem. Currently the Protocol hinges on developed nations signing up to specified reduction targets for emissions, whilst there are no similar requirements placed on developing countries. Effectively, the Protocol does not cover 80% of the world's population and many suggest that it is not fair that this burden is borne by developed countries alone.

This argument must really stick in the throat[17] of developing countries. Having watched developed countries growing rich by burning vast amounts of fossil fuel through industry, this behaviour suddenly becomes unacceptable at the point at which they are finally poised to get in on the action. As Dr Mwandoysa, chair of the developing countries' caucus on climate change, points out,[22] many developing countries cannot even afford a basic standard of living for their citizens, let alone put resources into environmental programmes. As

Comments

Numbers in the text and below refer to the grid on p. 251.

6 **Lack of precision.** The phrase 'next few years' is vague. The Kyoto agreement runs between specific dates, 2008 and 2012. See p. 241.

10 **The necessary conditions** for the argument that 'we must act now' have not been met. If it is too late for us to make changes, as suggested, then why should they be made now? In order to justify the need for immediate changes, the author needs to give evidence that such changes could still have an impact on global warming.

17 Use of **emotive language** with the phrase 'it is madness'.

7 **Assumption.** The author assumes that there is not a valid argument for asserting that carbon dioxide is not a pollutant but gives no evidence that it is a pollutant.

18 **Attacking the person.** Referring to those who disagree as being 'in denial' undermines their argument without properly analysing their reasons.

16 **Unwarranted leap.** This argument makes an unwarranted leap in assuming that because they do not accept some research, opponents must be wrong about global warming. (The style is also rather colloquial.)

17 **Emotive language.**

22 **Poor referencing** of Mwandoysa source. This does not appear in the references and no date is given (compare this with the text for Practice 1).

Answers to Practice 2: Finding flaws in the argument

he suggests, why should developing countries modify their behaviour whilst developed countries continue with a wasteful lifestyle?[19] Developing countries will always want to follow in the footsteps of more developed countries.[3] Developed countries are like parents who smoke 60 cigarettes a day but get angry if their little children then threaten to take up the habit themselves.[12]

The sense this gives of a hollow argument is increased when one looks at the real reasons developed countries are jumpy about the Protocol – reluctance to offend major fossil fuel companies. Fossil fuels are big business in many of the developed countries' economies and their power is such that they can influence politicians against ratifying the Protocol.[7] Some companies have even made the ludicrous suggestion[17] that global warming is actually good for the planet![7, 14]

Industry associations in developed countries suggest that agreeing to the Protocol would cost hundreds of thousands of jobs[22] and there would, therefore, be a very real impact on national economies. However, objections go beyond these initial job losses. Not all developing nations are the same and

Comments

19 **Misrepresentation.** The author misrepresents Dr Mwandoysa's views. Mwandoysa does support developing countries playing their part in reducing emissions but believes that developed countries are better placed to support research and development in this area (see Practice 1).

3 It is **stereotyping** to suggest that all developing countries aspire to be identical to developed countries.

12 **False analogy.** On the surface of it, this looks like a reasonable analogy, suggestive of hypocritical behaviour in both cases. However, it is a poor analogy because parents have a very different relationship with their children from that between developed and developing countries. Parents have a duty of care to protect their children, who are dependants, from the effects of their behaviour, whereas developing countries are independent entities who can make their own decisions. Furthermore, the issue between developed and developing countries described above is one of competition for a limited resource, which is not typically the case when parents wish to prevent children damaging their health.

7 **Assumption.** The author assumes that fossil fuel companies have this power but gives no evidence to support this.

17 **Emotive language** is used in the phrase 'this is a ludicrous suggestion'.

7 **Assumption.** The author assumes that global warming cannot be good for the planet but gives no evidence to support this position.

14 **Complicity.** The writing style here, and the use of an exclamation mark, suggests the author is making the audience feel they must agree, or else they might be considered 'ludicrous' too.

22 **Poor referencing.** The author doesn't state which industry associations are referred to here. A reference for a trade association does appear in the references section, but it is not clearly linked to this statement.

Answers to Practice 2: Finding flaws in the argument

whilst some are too poor to ever be serious competition to the developed countries, others like China or India are just waiting for a chance to take advantage of enforced reductions for developed countries so that they can supersede them as an economic power. Powerful oil companies are clearly anxious about any threat to their market and have a vested interest in making sure the Protocol is not ratified.[16]

Ultimately, countries' failure to address greenhouse gas emissions could mean that they shoot themselves in the foot. Long-term global warming is anticipated to cause significant climate changes and countries will have to contend with floods in their tourist centres and droughts in their wheat belts. However, given that neither of these consequences will have an impact on powerful fossil fuel companies, developed countries can justify adopting this short-term strategy of protecting their interests.[1] The power of fossil fuel companies is such that they can influence developed countries not to sign up to the Protocol. Developed countries are susceptible to the influence of fossil fuel companies so if they are told not to sign up, they are likely to give way to that pressure.[22] Given the impact this has on us all, this is obviously unacceptable.[13] Everybody knows we are facing climatic meltdown.[14] Global warming is a problem for all of us and people can't just opt out because it doesn't suit them.

Comments

16 **Unwarranted leap.** The author uses a sleight of hand here. There is no evidence given to support the suggestion that developing countries intend to seize power or that fossil fuel companies are responding to this.

1 **False premise.** The argument that fossil fuel companies would not be affected by floods or drought caused by climate change is based on a false premise. Both tourists and farmers are likely to be heavy consumers of fossil fuels, which would have a direct impact on fuel companies.

22 **Tautology.** The two sentences here rephrase the same idea in different words. This produced unnecessary repetition without carrying the argument forward.

13 **Deflection.** The author uses the word 'obviously' to imply that the argument has been proved. As we have seen, this is not the case.

14 **Complicity.** The statement 'everybody knows' puts the reader in a position that makes it more difficult to disagree with the argument. The author does this through use of language rather than through reasoning.

References

1 United Nations Framework Convention on Climate Change. *A Summary of the Kyoto Protocol* http://unfccc.int/essential_background (downloaded 13/02/05).

2 United Nations Framework Convention on Climate Change – *Feeling the Heat* http://unfccc.int/essential_background (downloaded 13/02/05).

3 Stevens, W. K. (1997) 'Greenhouse Gas Issue Pits Third World Against Richer Nations'. *New York Times*, 30 November 1997.

4 AFL-CIO Executive Council (1998) Press Statement on the Kyoto Protocol, 30 January 1998.

Practice 3: Features of an argument

- Read the passage 'The Great Chain of Being' and identify the features of the argument, using the numbered prompts below to assist you.
- Label and number each of your answers in the *Comments* margin provided alongside the text. If you use the same numbers as those provided in the prompts table below, this will help you to check your answers.

Prompts		Done (tick when completed)
1	Identify the sentence or sentences that sum up the main argument.	
2	Identify the author's introduction to the argument.	
3	Identify the summative conclusion.	
4	Identify the overall logical conclusion.	
5	Identify the main reasons given to support the logical conclusion.	
6	Identify any intermediate conclusions used as reasons. In the margin, explain the purpose of the interim conclusion (i.e. why the author needed to make an interim conclusion in order to develop the argument).	
7	Identify evidence to support the conclusion.	
8	Identify descriptive text that provides background information for the reader.	
9	Identify words used to signal the development of either the main argument or arguments leading to intermediate conclusions.	
10	Identify any counter arguments put forward by the author.	
11	Identify arguments by the author to address counter arguments.	
12	Identify any use of primary sources.	
13	Identify any use of secondary sources.	

Practice 3: Features of an argument

The Great Chain of Being (Text 1)

'Notions of a "Great Chain of Being" and of a natural order to the universe continued to exert ideological significance during the eighteenth century and beyond.' Discuss.

The idea of the 'Great Chain of Being' was common in medieval Europe. For those who believed in this chain, everything that existed belonged to a pre-assigned place, as if on higher or lower rungs of a ladder. Those lowest items in the universe were at the bottom of the chain whilst humans were nearer the top, below angels but above animals. In considering the influence of the chain of being in the eighteenth century, there are two aspects to consider. Firstly, whether the idea was still familiar in the eighteenth century, and secondly, whether it was used to support political or ideological positions in the important debates of the period.

First of all, it is proposed that the concept of the chain of being was very much alive in the eighteenth century. Such a view is not universally accepted. It has been argued that references to the chain of being had died out by the mid-seventeenth century (Barking, 1957; Madison, 1967). Madison claimed that such notions of the universe were replaced by more enlightened ideas based on scientific observation. It could also be argued that war and trade provided ever increasing opportunities for people to meet with new ideas and ideologies. Colley (2003), for example, refers to how impressed travellers to North African Muslim countries were by its culture and by the tolerance shown by Islam to other faiths. In earlier centuries, Christian rulers burnt people at the stake for expressing such sentiments but this was no longer the case in the eighteenth century.

However, despite such changes in people's outlook, old ideas still continued to hold sway. In the literature of the late eighteenth century, and even the early nineteenth century, it is not unusual to find references to the chain of being. Indeed, in an analysis of pamphlets produced in 1802–3, for example, Pendleton (1976) found that over one in ten pamphlets, a significant proportion, included a reference to the 'Chain of Being'. A much higher proportion of the pamphlets alluded to related concepts, such as the 'natural order' of society. The concept of the 'chain of being', and the idea that there was an inherent order to the universe, was still prevalent in England even in the early nineteenth century.

Practice 3: Features of an argument

As Pendleton's research indicates, there were still many publicists at the end of the eighteenth century who argued that the governing classes in England were a superior type of human being, higher on the great chain of being and closer to God. Many of those in power believed that their own social class was more intelligent, more beautiful, with better morals. They regarded the majority of the population as less intelligent and virtuous, as uglier beings, closer to an animal state, and therefore less deserving of consideration in all respects (Lavater, 1797). People were expected to 'know their place' and to act accordingly at all times. This concept of beings on a higher level of the chain was useful in providing a justification for social superiority.

The hierarchical ordering of nature was also used to provide a powerful defence of political and economic inequalities. In the eighteenth and nineteenth centuries, very few people were allowed to vote in elections, to organise politically or even to speak out against those believed to be their 'betters'. The overwhelming majority of the population still did not have the vote and there were vast differences in wealth, health, and well-being (Thompson, 1963). The notion of a natural chain of being was used to argue that this was as nature or 'Providence' intended.

Furthermore, even after the eighteenth century, the hierarchical ordering of society was still presented as a divine plan, and all people were expected to follow the same religion. This idea of a divinely based order was used to frighten people into submission. A broadside, or poster, pasted around London in 1802 declared that 'It is the ordinance of God, that there should be infinite gradations' and that 'as one star differeth from another star in glory, so shall the plan of subordination be through the whole earthly system.' It was argued that it was natural for some people to have power and riches, and for other people to have none. For example, one pamphleteer (Pratt, 1803) claimed that if the natural order was changed, this would 'unsettle the whole system of the spheres; the planets would rush on each other . . . and the earth be shrivelled, like a scroll, by a spark from the sun'. If everything in the universe formed part of a single continuous chain, then to alter a single part could disrupt the whole chain, causing all society to come to an end and even the universe to collapse. The combining of an ideology of social order with a religious philosophy made the idea of a natural order particularly significant.

Practice 3: Features of an argument

Moreover, in 1802–3, such arguments were of particular importance in fostering patriotic sentiment to support war against France. The political elite encouraged each other to be active in persuading the poor where their interest lay (Ashcroft, 1977). They were worried that large sections of the population would welcome a French invasion that promised social, economic, political and religious freedom, as had been proclaimed in France after the Revolution of 1789. Some expressed fear that if they armed the English people to defend the country, they would turn their weapons against their masters (Cholmeley, 1803). Instead of taking the dangerous risk of arming the country, a propaganda campaign was launched, arguing that the 'natural order' was best and that the English people should accept it rather than join the French if the country were invaded. If the natural order changed, the propaganda argued, the consequences would be famine, disease and death.

Rather than, as Madison suggests, the chain of being becoming an outmoded concept in the eighteenth century, scientists were still active in researching new possible gradations in the hierarchy. They set about measuring bones of people of different skin colours, social classes and geographical origins, in an attempt to set down a hierarchy from best to worst, using their own skin colour as the benchmark for perfection (White, 1779). Lavater, whose writings were translated into English in 1797, referred to this as 'the transition from brutal deformity to ideal beauty' and argued that beauty was a sign of moral superiority. Lavater devised a system for measuring hierarchy, based on bone structure and appearance. His writings were widely published and highly influential in England. Over time, the use of the term 'chain of being' died out, but the belief in the natural or divine hierarchy and its use as a rationale for political and social inequalities continued to hold force.

It is important to note that the concept of a hierarchically ordered universe could be used to justify almost any kind of inequality or oppression. Indeed, Mary Wollstonecraft (1792) argued that the concept of a natural order was being used to justify all kinds of injustice such as cruelty to animals and children, the slave trade, and depriving women of political and economic rights. Literature that used the idea of natural hierarchies also made use of comparisons between all types of people who did not form part of the English ruling oligarchy and growing middle classes. The *Encyclopaedia Britannica*, for example, in its 1797 edition, compared the behaviour of Africans, the English working class, and French revolutionaries,

Comments

Practice 3: Features of an argument

arguing that they shared common characteristics such as 'a lack of moral principles' and an absence of 'natural affections'. Over the next century and a half, these ideas were drawn upon and extended by others to justify policies based on racial and social injustice in many parts of the world.

Ideas based on the chain of being, therefore, far from waning in the eighteenth century, were further developed and extended. The dangers posed by the French Revolution and the proposed invasion of England, added force to the long-established concept of a natural order, especially after these were widely publicised in the anti-invasion and anti-revolutionary propaganda of 1802–4. The scientific methodologies of the eighteenth century resulted in findings that appeared to justify the concept of a natural hierarchy. Although the vocabulary of the chain of being began to die out, the underlying concept was reinforced and used to reinforce negative social, gender and racial stereotypes in the next two centuries. Hence, the concept of the 'great chain of being' did continue to exert ideological significance during the eighteenth century and beyond.

Comments

References

Primary sources

Anon. (1803) *Such is Buonaparte* (London: J. Ginger).

Ashcroft, M. Y. (1977) *To Escape a Monster's Clutches: Notes and Documents Illustrating Preparations in North Yorkshire to Repel the Invasion.* North Yorkshire, CRO Public No. 15.

Cholmeley, C. (1803) Letter of Catherine Cholmeley to Francis Cholmeley, 16 August 1803. In Ashcroft, M. Y. (1977) *To Escape a Monster's Clutches: Notes and Documents Illustrating Preparations in North Yorkshire to Repel the Invasion.* North Yorkshire, CRO Public No. 15.

Encyclopaedia Britannica (1797) 3rd edition, Edinburgh.

Lavater, J. K. (1797) *Essays on Physiognomy*, translated by Rev. C. Moore and illustrated after Lavater by Barlow (London: London publishers).

'Pratt' (1803) *Pratt's Address to His Countrymen or the True Born Englishman's Castle* (London: J. Asperne).

White, C. (1779) *An Account of the Infinite Gradations in Man, and in Different Animals and Vegetables; and from the Former to the Latter.* Read to the Literary and Philosophical Society of Manchester at Different Meetings (Manchester: Literary and Philosophical Society).

Practice 3: Features of an argument

Wollstonecraft, M. (1792) *Vindication of the Rights of Women.* (Republished in 1975 by Penguin, Harmondsworth, Middlesex.)

Secondary sources

Barking, J. K. (1957) *Changes in Conceptions of the Universe* (Cotteridge: Poltergeist Press).*

Colley, L. (2003) *Captives: Britain, Empire and the World 1600–1850* (London: Pimlico).

Madison, S. (1967) 'The End of the Chain of Being: the Impact of Descartian Philosophy on Medieval Conceptions of Being'. *Journal of Medieval and Enlightenment Studies*, 66, 7.*

Pendleton, G. (1976) 'English Conservative Propaganda During the French Revolution, 1780–1802', Ph.D. (unpub.), Emory University.

Thompson, E. P. (1963) *The Making of the English Working Class* (Harmondsworth, Middlesex: Penguin).

*These two sources are hypothetical and provided for the purpose of the practice activity; the other sources are genuine.

Comments

Answers to Practice 3: Features of an argument

The Great Chain of Being (Text 1)

'Notions of a "Great Chain of Being" and of a natural order to the universe continued to exert ideological significance during the eighteenth century and beyond.' Discuss.

The idea of the 'Great Chain of Being' was common in medieval Europe. For those who believed in this chain, everything that existed belonged to a pre-assigned place, as if on higher or lower rungs of a ladder. Those lowest items in the universe were at the bottom of the chain whilst humans were nearer the top, below angels but above animals.[8]

In considering the influence of the chain of being in the eighteenth century, there are two aspects to consider. Firstly, whether the idea was still familiar in the eighteenth century, and secondly, whether it was used to support political or ideological positions in the important debates of the period.[2]

First of all,[9] it is proposed that the concept of the chain of being was very much alive in the eighteenth century.[1] Such a view is not universally accepted. It has been argued that references to the chain of being had died out by the mid-seventeenth century (Barking, 1957; Madison, 1967). Madison claimed that such notions of the universe were replaced by more enlightened ideas based on scientific observation.[10, 13] It could also be argued that war and trade provided ever increasing opportunities for people to meet with new ideas and ideologies. Colley (2003), for example, refers to how impressed travellers to North African Muslim countries were by its culture and by the tolerance shown by Islam to other faiths. In earlier centuries, Christian rulers burnt people at the stake for expressing such sentiments but this was no longer the case in the eighteenth century.[10, 13]

However, despite such changes in people's outlook, old ideas still continued to hold sway.[11] In the literature of the late eighteenth century, and even the early nineteenth century, it is not unusual to find references to the chain of being. Indeed, in an analysis of pamphlets produced in 1802–3, for example, Pendleton (1976) found that over one in ten pamphlets, a significant proportion, included a reference to the 'Chain of Being'.[7, 13] A much higher proportion of the pamphlets alluded to related concepts, such as the 'natural order' of society. The concept of the 'chain of being' and the idea that there was an

Comments

Numbers in the text and below refer to the grid on p. 255.

8   This is descriptive text that tells the reader, briefly, what the 'chain of being' was. This is necessary background information.

2   These two sentences set out how the author intends to approach the argument, breaking it into two sections to help the reader recognise these stages in the argument when they are introduced later.

9   Signal word to introduce the first of the author's reasons.

1   This sentence sums up the main argument.

10   The author considers here counter arguments to the main line of reasoning. In this case, the counter arguments are raised and dealt with early in the line of reasoning as, if it was true that the idea had already died out, there wouldn't be much point continuing with the rest of the argument.

13   Examples of secondary sources (see p. 126 above).

11   This paragraph addresses the counter argument raised by Barking that references to the chain of being had died out. The counter argument raised by Madison is addressed throughout the essay, and in a separate paragraph below.

7   This evidence helps to support the overall conclusion that the idea did continue to have ideological significance.

13   Examples of a secondary sources (see p. 126 above).

Answers to Practice 3: Features of an argument

inherent order to the universe, was still prevalent in England even in the early nineteenth century.[6]

As Pendleton's research indicates, there were still many publicists at the end of the eighteenth century who argued that the governing classes in England were a superior type of human being, higher on the great chain of being and closer to God. Many of those in power believed that their own social class was more intelligent, more beautiful, with better morals. They regarded the majority of the population as less intelligent and virtuous, as uglier beings, closer to an animal state, and therefore less deserving of consideration in all respects (Lavater, 1797).[12] People were expected to 'know their place' and to act accordingly at all times. This concept of beings on a higher level of the chain was useful in providing a justification for social superiority.[5, 6]

The hierarchical ordering of nature was also[9] used to provide a powerful defence of political and economic inequalities.[5, 6] In the eighteenth and nineteenth centuries, very few people were allowed to vote in elections, to organise politically or even to speak out against those believed to be their 'betters'. The overwhelming majority of the population still did not have the vote and there were vast differences in wealth, health, and well-being (Thompson, 1963).[8, 13] The notion of a natural chain of being was used to argue that this was as nature or 'Providence' intended.

Furthermore,[9] even after the eighteenth century, the hierarchical ordering of society was still presented as a divine plan, and all people were expected to follow the same religion. This idea of a divinely based order was used to frighten people into submission.[6] A broadside, or poster, pasted around London in 1802 declared that 'It is the ordinance of God, that there should be infinite gradations' and that 'as one star differeth from another star in glory, so shall the plan of subordination be through the whole earthly system.'[12, 7] It was argued that it was natural for some people

Comments

6 Intermediate conclusion used as a reason: the author establishes first that the notion of a 'great chain of being' was still current. The reasons to support this are:
   • it is not uncommon to find examples;
   • Pendleton's research.

12 Primary source. See p. 126.

5 and 6 Intermediate conclusion used as a reason: the author has established the significance of the concept of the chain of being to maintaining the social structure. This then provides a reason that supports the overall conclusion that the concept is still of significance.

9 Signal word used to indicate to the reader that the author is adding more reasons to support the line of reasoning.

5 and 6 Intermediate conclusion used as a reason: the author has established the significance of the concept of the chain of being to defending the political and economic status quo. This then provides a reason that supports the conclusion.

8 Necessary but brief description of eighteenth-century society, to support the reasoning and to illustrate the significance of the political use of the concept of the chain of being.

13 Secondary source.

9 Signal word to indicate the argument is continuing in a similar direction.

6 Intermediate conclusion: the concept was used to rouse fear and submission.

12 These are examples of primary source materials, see p. 126 above.

7 Source materials used in this paragraph are used as evidence to support the conclusion that the concept had ideological significance.

Answers to Practice 3: Features of an argument

to have power and riches, and for other people to have none. For example, one pamphleteer (Pratt, 1803) claimed that if the natural order was changed, this would 'unsettle the whole system of the spheres; the planets would rush on each other . . . and the earth be shrivelled, like a scroll, by a spark from the sun'.[12] If everything in the universe formed part of a single continuous chain, then to alter a single part could disrupt the whole chain, causing all society to come to an end and even the universe to collapse. The combining of an ideology of social order with a religious philosophy made the idea of a natural order particularly significant.[7]

Moreover,[9] in 1802–3, such arguments were of particular importance in fostering patriotic sentiment to support war against France.[6] The political elite encouraged each other to be active in persuading the poor where their interest lay (Ashcroft, 1977).[12/13] They were worried that large sections of the population would welcome a French invasion that promised social, economic, political and religious freedom, as had been proclaimed in France after the Revolution of 1789.[8] Some expressed fear that if they armed the English people to defend the country, they would turn their weapons against their masters (Cholmeley, 1803).[12] Instead of taking the dangerous risk of arming the country, a propaganda campaign was launched, arguing that the 'natural order' was best and that the English people should accept it rather than join the French if the country were invaded.[5] If the natural order changed, the propaganda argued, the consequences would be famine, disease and death.

Rather than, as Madison suggests, the chain of being becoming an outmoded concept in the eighteenth century, scientists were still active in researching new possible gradations in the hierarchy.[11] They set about measuring bones of people of different skin colours, social classes and geographical origins, in an attempt to set down a hierarchy from best to worst, using their own skin colour as the benchmark for perfection (White, 1779).[12] Lavater, whose writings were translated into English in 1797, referred to this as 'the transition from brutal deformity to ideal beauty' and argued that beauty was a sign of moral superiority. Lavater devised a system for measuring hierarchy, based on bone structure and appearance. His writings were widely published and highly influential in England. Over time, the use of the term 'chain of being' died out, but the belief in the natural or divine hierarchy and its use as a rationale for political and social inequalities continued to hold force.[6, 5]

Comments

12   These are examples of primary source materials, see p. 126 above.

7   Source materials used in this paragraph are used as evidence to support the conclusion that the concept had ideological significance.

9   The word 'moreover' is used to signal that the same line of reasoning is being continued.

6   The intermediate conclusion is that this concept was significant at a particular historical moment.

12/13   This is a collection of primary sources published in 1977. (A modern date does not automatically indicate a secondary source.)

8   Necessary background to illustrate the significance of the concept at a particularly important political moment.

12   Primary source.

5   The reason given to support the intermediate conclusion for this paragraph is:
   • propaganda making use of the chain of being was used as an anti-French device, rather than arming the country.

11   This addresses a counter argument raised in the second paragraph above.

12   Primary sources.

6   Intermediate conclusion used as a reason: the author establishes that the assumptions underlying the chain of being were further developed by scientists and given new life. The reasons to support this interim conclusion are provided by the examples of research and by the acknowledgement that although the term 'chain of being' died out, its assumptions remained in force.

5   The intermediate conclusion is also a main reason used to support the overall conclusion, that the concept retained significance.

Answers to Practice 3: Features of an argument

It is important to note that[9] the concept of a hierarchically ordered universe could be used to justify almost any kind of inequality or oppression.[6, 5] Indeed, Mary Wollstonecraft (1792) argued that the concept of a natural order was being used to justify all kinds of injustice such as cruelty to animals and children, the slave trade, and depriving women of political and economic rights.[12] Literature that used the idea of natural hierarchies also made use of comparisons between all types of people who did not form part of the English ruling oligarchy and growing middle classes. The *Encyclopaedia Britannica*, for example, in its 1797 edition, compared the behaviour of Africans, the English working class, and French revolutionaries, arguing that they shared common characteristics such as 'a lack of moral principles' and an absence of 'natural affections'.[12] Over the next century and a half, these ideas were drawn upon and extended by others to justify policies based on racial and social injustice in many parts of the world.

Ideas based on the chain of being, therefore,[9] far from waning in the eighteenth century, were further developed and extended.[3] The dangers posed by the French Revolution and the proposed invasion of England added force to the long-established concept of a natural order, especially after these were widely publicised in the anti-invasion and anti-revolutionary propaganda of 1802–4. The scientific methodologies of the eighteenth century resulted in findings that appeared to justify the concept of a natural hierarchy. Although the vocabulary of the chain of being began to die out, the underlying concept was reinforced and used to reinforce negative social, gender and racial stereotypes in the next two centuries. Hence, the concept of the 'great chain of being' did continue to exert ideological significance during the eighteenth century and beyond.[4]

Comments

9 This phrase is used to signal a further aspect of the argument, building on previous reasons.

6 The intermediate conclusion is that the concept was used to justify many kinds of oppression. The reasons to support this interim conclusion are evidence drawn from contemporaries such as Mary Wollstonecraft and the *Encyclopaedia Britannica* of 1797, and the uses to which the ideas were put.

5 The intermediate conclusion is another reason to support the overall conclusion that the concept remained significant in the eighteenth century and beyond.

12 These are examples of primary source materials, see p. 126 above.

9 Signal word used to indicate the conclusion.

3 This paragraph is mainly a summative conclusion – summarising key points from the preceding paragraphs.

4 The final sentence provides the logical conclusion here: it makes a deduction drawn from all the reasoning given above.

NB   Linking the final sentence back to the title signals to the reader that the main question posed in the title has been addressed.

References

Primary sources

Anon. (1803) *Such is Buonaparte* (London: J. Ginger).

Ashcroft, M. Y. (1977) *To Escape a Monster's Clutches: Notes and Documents Illustrating Preparations in North Yorkshire to Repel the Invasion.* North Yorkshire, CRO Public No. 15.

Answers to Practice 3: Features of an argument

Cholmeley, C. (1803) Letter of Catherine Cholmeley to Francis Cholmeley, 16 August 1803. In Ashcroft, M. Y. (1977) *To Escape a Monster's Clutches: Notes and Documents Illustrating Preparations in North Yorkshire to Repel the Invasion.* North Yorkshire, CRO Public No. 15.

Encyclopaedia Britannica (1797) 3rd edition, Edinburgh.

Lavater, J. K. (1797) *Essays on Physiognomy*, translated by Rev. C. Moore and illustrated after Lavater by Barlow (London: London publishers).

'Pratt' (1803) *Pratt's Address to His Countrymen or the True Born Englishman's Castle* (London: J. Asperne).

White, C. (1779) *An Account of the Infinite Gradations in Man, and in different Animals and Vegetables; and from the Former to the Latter.* Read to the Literary and Philosophical Society of Manchester at Different Meetings (Manchester: Literary and Philosophical Society).

Wollstonecraft, M. (1792) *Vindication of the Rights of Women* (republished in 1975 by Penguin, Harmondsworth, Middlesex).

Seconday soures

Barking, J. K. (1957) *Changes in Conceptions of the Universe* (Cotteridge: Poltergeist Press).*

Colley, L. (2003) *Captives: Britain, Empire and the World, 1600–1850* (London: Pimlico).

Madison, S. (1967) 'The End of the Chain of Being: the Impact of Descartian Philosophy on Medieval Conceptions of Being'. *Journal of Medieval and Enlightenment Studies*, 66, 7.*

Pendleton, G. (1976) 'English Conservative Propaganda During the French Revolution, 1780–1802', Ph.D. (unpub.), Emory University.

Thompson, E. P. (1963) *The Making of the English Working Class* (Harmondsworth, Middlesex: Penguin).

*These two sources are hypothetical and provided for the purpose of the practice activity; the other sources are genuine.

Comments

Practice 4: Finding flaws in the argument

- Read this second passage on the Great Chain of Being, and identify flaws in the argument, using the numbered prompts below as a checklist to assist you.
- *Note*: the practice passage does not contain all the flaws on the list but there is more than one example of some. You can use the checklist to note whether you believe the passage does or does not contain an example, to make it easier to check your answers.
- Label and number each of your answers in the *Comments* margin provided alongside the text. If you use the same numbers as those provided in the prompts table below, this will help you to check your answers.

Prompts		Example found	There is no example	See page
1	False premises			91
2	Two wrongs don't make a right			120
3	Stereotyping			96
4	Lack of consistency in the argument			65, 67
5	Unnecessary background information			58
6	Lack of precision			65
7	Assumption that is not supported by the evidence			88–9
8	Incorrectly assuming a causal link			106
9	False correlation			107
10	Meeting necessary conditions			109
11	Meeting sufficient conditions			110
12	False analogy			112
13	Deflection			114
14	Complicity			114
15	Exclusion			114
16	Unwarranted leaps (e.g. castle of cards; sleight of hand)			116
17	Emotive language			117
18	Attacking the person			117
19	Misrepresentation			119
20	Trivialisation			119
21	Tautology			120
22	Poor referencing			162

Practice 4: Finding flaws in the argument

The Great Chain of Being (Text 2)

'Notions of a "Great Chain of Being" and of a natural order to the universe continued to exert ideological significance during the eighteenth century and beyond.'
Discuss.

The concept of the 'Great Chain of Being' dominated thinking and writing for many centuries before the eighteenth century. Indeed, Shakespeare and other great writers of the seventeenth century drew on the idea for inspiration. By the eighteenth century, things had started to change radically. This was a period of expansion intellectually and geographically for European states, including Britain. Old ideas were dying out as soldiers travelled the world during the wars against the American colonies and the expanding empire (Colley 2003), and merchants traded more extensively with the east. Barking (1957) and Madison (1967) argue that enlightenment ideas and scientific observation replaced more traditional ideas. A revolution in taste took place as the homes of the rich filled with *chinoiserie*, art from China. Young people came of age through making a 'Grand Tour' of Europe. The concept of the chain of being was being supplanted by other ideas more familiar to our modern world.

In this period of exploration and change, the ongoing wars between England and revolutionary France led to an unusually large production of political propaganda. Pendleton's analysis of this showed that many pamphlets used the concept of the 'chain of being' to encourage the population to support the war. There were many ways that publicists referred to the idea of a natural order to encourage people to refuse the revolutionary ideologies espoused by the French and to encourage them to defend England in the event of an invasion. Those producing pamphlets and other pro-war literature referred to the notion of a natural order to decry French theories of liberty and equality and to argue that English people should take on a patriotic defence of the realm.

The propaganda was very insulting about the French and their new ideas and could easily have caused a diplomatic incident and an earlier outbreak of war. Fortunately, England and France are hundreds of miles apart, and such distances were more significant in the eighteenth century. This means that the French leader, Buonaparte, wouldn't have seen the propaganda and so didn't launch a full-scale invasion.

Practice 4: Finding flaws in the argument

The idea of a natural order was used to bolster the authority of those with social and economic power. Mary Wollstonecraft (1792) argued that the concept of a natural order was used to justify all kinds of injustice.

She argued that people who were cruel to animals and children, were also likely to agree with the slave trade, and the oppression of women, which she opposed. However, she clearly thought it was acceptable to lump humans who lacked money and power into the same bracket as animals. As animals were lower down the chain of being at that time, her comparison of animals with humans who lacked power shows she thought of poor people and slaves as being lower types of being. Her prejudices are typical of ruling class women from that period.

Clearly, rich people in the eighteenth century found the idea of a natural order beneficial. This is particularly outrageous when one considers how vulnerable the poor were at the time, how sad their lives and how dependent on a kind word from their social betters. People were taught to regard those richer than themselves as their 'betters' and to refer to them as their masters. People were meant to accept that they must regard others as superior by virtue of their birth, and to defer to them in all things.

The idea of a natural order was strong even in the beginning of the twentieth century. After the Great War of 1914–18, working men and women gained the vote and social mobility increased. Far fewer people worked as domestic servants after the war. Having a vote on equal terms made people realise that democracy was a good thing and seems to have made them less keen to do jobs as servants. If everyone had the vote, then they were equal before the law, and if they were all equal, then there evidently wasn't a natural order, so the idea of a natural order was bound to die out and the vote would bring about the end of social hierarchies.

Such change would be welcomed. Many judges, priests, politicians and educators, argued that the chain of being was part of God's plan and this effectively frightened people into compliance with the way the country was run. Clerics such as Watson, the Bishop of Llandaff, wrote that it was God who let people get rich and powerful, signs of his favour and proof of their superiority. Other writers said similar things. For example, a poster in 1802 wrote about it being 'the ordinance of God' that the world was graded into different levels of being. Another, a pamphleteer (Pratt, 1803), argued that changing the order established by God would 'unsettle the

Comments

Practice 4: Finding flaws in the argument

whole system of the spheres; the planets would rush on each other . . . and the earth be shrivelled, like a scroll, by a spark from the sun'. However, Pratt was obviously not very bright and had a very poor grasp of science so was not likely to be taken seriously by his contemporaries.

One person who contributed most to perpetuating ideas of a natural order was the Swiss scientist Kaspar Lavater. His work was translated into many languages and used as a manual by the educated classes when they were employing new servants or making judgements about new acquaintances. Lavater invented a new science known as physiognomy which set out to prove that a person's character could be read from their facial features and the shape of the skull. Lavater (1797) argued that certain features were typical of a higher class of people, who were more moral and typical of the European ruling classes. He argued that other features, such as those shared by poorer people, and people with darker skins, were signs of an inferior nature, closer to the animals. Obviously, this was nonsense and no right-minded person would believe that physical features such as your skull would reflect your morals or worth. This would be like assuming that the way people walk tells you how healthy they are. However, many people at that time believed strongly in this method of working out who was superior and who inferior.

In the eighteenth century, people were more likely to believe in progress and change in the surrounding world, rather than a static concept such as the natural order. There were people who used the concept of the chain of being in an instrumental way, to frighten or coerce people into accepting that there was nothing they could do to change their lot. Certain applications of the idea of 'natural order' were adopted by richer people, but this practice was likely to have been a fad or fashion, like doing a quiz in a magazine today. Others used the idea to bolster their own sense of superiority. However, it is not likely that most people took such ideas seriously in the way they led their lives and made choices. In this respect, notions of the great chain of being and the natural order were not significant by the end of the eighteenth century.

Comments

Practice 4: Finding flaws in the argument

References [compare with Practice 3, pp. 259–60]

Comments

Primary sources

Anon (1802) *Such is Buonaparte*, London.

Kaspar Lavater *Essays on Physiognomy*, Translated by Rev. C. Moore and illustrated after Lavater by Barlow, London, 1797.

Pratt, *Pratt's Address to His Countrymen or the True Born Englishman's Castle.* London.

Bishop of Llandaff

Mary Wollstonecraft (1792) *Vindication of the Rights of Women.* Middlesex.

White, C. *An Account of the Infinite Gradations in Man* (Read to the Literary and Philosophical Society of Manchester at Different Meetings) (1779).

Secondary sources

Madison. (1967) 'The end of the Chain of Being: the impact of Descartian. *Journal of Medieval and Enlightenment Studies*, 66; 7.*

Barking, J. K. (1957) *Changes in Conceptions of the Universe.* Cotteridge: Poltergeist Press*

Linda Colley (2003) Captives.

Holmes, Geoffrey. (1977) 'Gregory King and the social structure of pre-industrial England' *Transactions of the Royal History Society*, 27

Pendleton

E. P. Thompson *The Making of the English Working Class* (1963) Middlesex: Penguin

*These two sources are hypothetical and provided for the purpose of the practice activity; the other sources are genuine.

Answers to Practice 4: Finding flaws in the argument

Prompts	Example found	There is no example	See page
1 False premises	✓		91
2 Two wrongs don't make a right		✓	120
3 Stereotyping	✓		96
4 Lack of consistency in the argument	✓ (3)		65, 67
5 Unnecessary background information	✓ (2)		58
6 Lack of precision	✓		65
7 Assumption that is not supported by the evidence	✓ (3)		88–9
8 Incorrectly assuming a causal link	✓		106
9 False correlation	✓		107
10 Meeting necessary conditions	✓		109
11 Meeting sufficient conditions			110
12 False analogy	✓		112
13 Deflection	✓		114
14 Complicity	✓		114
15 Exclusion		✓	114
16 Unwarranted leaps (e.g. castle of cards; sleight of hand)	✓ (2)		116
17 Emotive language	✓		117
18 Attacking the person	✓		117
19 Misrepresentation	✓		119
20 Trivialisation		✓	119
21 Tautology	✓		120
22 Poor referencing	✓		162

Answers to Practice 4: Finding flaws in the argument

The Great Chain of Being (Text 4)

'Notions of a "Great Chain of Being" and of a natural order to the universe continued to exert ideological significance during the eighteenth century and beyond.' Discuss.

The concept of the 'Great Chain of Being' dominated thinking and writing for many centuries before the eighteenth century. Indeed, Shakespeare and other great writers of the seventeenth century drew on the idea for inspiration. By the eighteenth century, things had started to change radically. This was a period of expansion intellectually and geographically for European states, including Britain. Old ideas were dying out as soldiers travelled the world during the wars against the American colonies and the expanding empire (Colley, 2003), and merchants traded more extensively with the east. Barking (1957) and Madison (1967) argue that enlightenment ideas and scientific observation replaced more traditional ideas. A revolution in taste took place as the homes of the rich filled with *chinoiserie*, art from China. Young people came of age through making a 'Grand Tour' of Europe.[5] The concept of the chain of being was being supplanted by other ideas more familiar to our modern world.[4]

In this period of exploration and change, the ongoing wars between England and revolutionary France led to an unusually large production of political propaganda. Pendleton's[22] analysis of this showed that many[6] pamphlets used the concept of the 'chain of being' to encourage the population to support the war.[4] There were many ways that publicists referred to the idea of a natural order to encourage people to refuse the revolutionary ideologies espoused by the French and to encourage them to defend England in the event of an invasion. Those producing pamphlets and other pro-war literature referred to the notion of a natural order to decry French theories of liberty and equality and to argue that English people should take on a patriotic defence of the realm.[21]

[5]The propaganda was very insulting about the French and their new ideas and could easily have caused a diplomatic incident and an earlier outbreak of war. Fortunately, England and France are hundreds of miles apart, and such distances were more significant in the eighteenth century. This means

Comments

5 **Unnecessary background information,** especially as this is not used to look specifically at the idea of the chain of being. On the other hand, important background information, such as explaining what is meant by the 'chain of being', is not provided.

4 **Inconsistency.** This paragraph suggests the concept of the chain of being was waning. The next paragraph suggests it was still widely used (see [4] below). The author doesn't show how these two apparently contradictory ideas could both be true. For example, the idea could have been used in the propaganda for political purposes even if many people no longer believed in it. Apparent contradictions such as this need to be explained and resolved.

22 **Poor reference.** No date is provided here and Pendleton is not fully detailed in the references, so it would be hard for the reader to check this source of information for themselves.

6 **Lack of precision.** 'Many' is a vague term. The reader needs to know how many? What proportion?

21 **Tautology.** This paragraph repeats the same basic idea three times but in different words: i.e. that publicists used the idea of natural order to encourage a pro-war patriotic stance rather than support France and its ideas of liberty and equality. The final sentence, for example, does not take the argument forward or provide any new information for the reader.

5 This paragraph provides **unnecessary background** about the impact of the propaganda on the conduct of the war by the French, which is not what the question asks.

Answers to Practice 4: Finding flaws in the argument

that the French leader, Buonaparte, wouldn't have seen the propaganda and so didn't launch a full-scale invasion.[1, 7, 16]

The idea of a natural order was used to bolster the authority of those with social and economic power. Mary Wollstonecraft (1792) argued that the concept of a natural order was used to justify all kinds of injustice. She argued that people who were cruel to animals and children, were also likely to agree with the slave trade, and the oppression of women, which she opposed. However, she clearly thought it was acceptable to lump humans who lacked money and power into the same bracket as animals. As animals were lower down the chain of being at that time, her comparison of animals with humans who lacked power shows she thought of poor people and slaves as being lower types of being.[19] Her prejudices are typical of ruling class women from that period.[3]

Clearly, rich people in the eighteenth century found the idea of a natural order beneficial.[13] This is particularly outrageous when one considers how vulnerable the poor were at the time, how sad their lives and how dependent on a kind word from their social betters.[17] People were taught to regard those richer than themselves as their 'betters' and to refer to them as their masters. People were meant to accept that they must regard others as superior by virtue of their birth, and to defer to them in all things.

Comments

1. **False premises.** The argument proposed for the lack of an invasion is based on false premises: it is factually inaccurate that England and France are hundreds of miles apart so this would not be a reason for the propaganda not being seen in France. The first paragraph of this piece suggests there was a lot of travel and exchange of ideas, which, if true, would make it more likely that the propaganda would have been seen in France.

7. **Unsupported assumption** about why Buonaparte didn't launch a full-scale invasion.

16. **Unwarranted leaps.** The author jumps from an unsubstantiated point (that the propaganda could have resulted in invasion – we don't know this) to another (that Buonaparte couldn't have seen it), to an unsubstantiated conclusion about why a full-scale invasion didn't happen.

19. **Misrepresentation.** Mary Wollstonecraft draws a comparison between different kinds of oppression, because she saw a common pattern of cruelty, which she opposed. The author misrepresents her intentions by claiming she regarded the poor and slaves as more animal like, simply because the idea of the chain of being was used by others at that time.

3. **Stereotyping.** Although many women of her class may have held such prejudiced opinions, the author stereotypes Mary Wollstonecraft by assuming she held the same ideas, without giving any evidence of this.

13. **Deflection.** The word 'clearly' suggests that the author has established how the rich people used the idea of natural order. This can deflect the reader from noticing that sufficient evidence has not yet been provided to prove the argument.

17. **Emotive language.** Use of words such as 'outrageous' and phrases such as 'sad lives' and 'dependent on a kind word'

Answers to Practice 4: Finding flaws in the argument

The idea of a natural order was strong even in the beginning of the twentieth century. After the Great War of 1914–18, working men and women gained the vote and social mobility increased. Far fewer people worked as domestic servants after the war. Having a vote on equal terms made people realise that democracy was a good thing and seems to have made them less keen to do jobs as servants.[8, 9] If everyone had the vote, then they were equal before the law, and if they were all equal, then there evidently wasn't a natural order, so the idea of a natural order was bound to die out and the vote would bring about the end of social hierarchies.[16, 7]

Comments

appeal to the emotions rather than relying on facts and reasons to advance the argument.

8 **Incorrectly assuming a causal link.** The author assumes a causal link between the extension of voting rights and the reduction in the number of domestic servants. However, there is no obvious reason why having a vote should create a different set of work opportunities for people. The reduction in the number of servants is more likely to be the result of economic changes, such as new kinds of job with better wages becoming available, or families no longer being able to afford to pay competitive wages.

9 This is also an example of a **false correlation:** mistaking the indirect correlation of increased suffrage (more people having the vote) and decreasing numbers of servants as directly connected.

16 and 7 **Unwarranted leaps (castle of cards) and assumptions.** The last sentence is another example of the author jumping from one unsubstantiated claim to another, such as that equality before the law automatically brings about equality of other kinds, such as social equality. However, social hierarchies are usually related to other things such as attitudes to ancestry, occupation, geography and ethnicity rather than depending on whether someone has the vote. Therefore, the author is wrong to draw the conclusion that the vote brought about the end of social hierarchies.

Such change would be welcomed. Many judges, priests, politicians and educators, argued that the chain of being was part of God's plan and this effectively frightened people into compliance with the way the country was run. Clerics such as Watson, the Bishop of Llandaff,[22] wrote that it was God who let people get rich and powerful, signs of his favour and proof of their superiority. Other writers said similar things. For example, a poster in 1802 wrote about it being 'the ordinance of God' that the world was graded into different levels of being. Another, a pamphleteer (Pratt, 1803), argued that

22 **Poor referencing.** No date and no reference given below so the reader can't check this for accuracy.

7 **Unsupported assumption.** The author makes an assumption here that Pratt's contemporaries would not take him seriously but does not provide any evidence to support this. Pratt's views might have been shared by others at that time. (See next page.)

Answers to Practice 4: Finding flaws in the argument

changing the order established by God would 'unsettle the whole system of the spheres; the planets would rush on each other . . . and the earth be shrivelled, like a scroll, by a spark from the sun'. However, Pratt was obviously not very bright and had a very poor grasp of science so was not likely to be taken seriously by his contemporaries.[7, 18, 4]

One person who contributed most to perpetuating ideas of a natural order was the Swiss scientist Kaspar Lavater. His work was translated into many languages and used as a manual by the educated classes when they were employing new servants or making judgements about new acquaintances. Lavater invented a new science known as physiognomy which set out to prove that a person's character could be read from their facial features and the shape of the skull. Lavater (1797) argued that certain features were typical of a higher class of people, who were more moral and typical of the European ruling classes. He argued that other features, such as those shared by poorer people, and people with darker skins, were signs of an inferior nature, closer to the animals. Obviously, this was a nonsense and no right-minded person would believe that your physical features such as your skull would reflect your morals or worth.[14] This would be like assuming that the way people walk tells you how healthy they are.[12] However, many people at that time believed strongly in this method of working out who was superior and who inferior.

In the eighteenth century, people were more likely to believe in progress and change in the surrounding world, rather than a static concept such as the natural order.[7] There were people who used the concept of the chain of being in an instrumental way, to frighten or coerce people into accepting that there was nothing they could do to change their lot. Certain applications of the idea of 'natural order' were adopted by richer people, but this practice was likely to have been a fad or fashion, like doing a quiz in a magazine today.[6, 10] Others used the idea to bolster their own sense of superiority. However, it is not likely that most people took such ideas seriously in the way they led their lives and made choices.[6] In this respect, notions of the great chain of being and the natural order were not significant by the end of the eighteenth century.[11]

Comments

7 See previous page.

18 This amounts to a **personal attack** on Pratt rather than a reasoned analysis of his views.

4 **Inconsistency.** The evidence is presented in a confusing, inconsistent way. The paragraph opens by arguing that references to God were effective. The author seems to cite Pratt as evidence of this effectiveness, but then states that nobody was likely to believe Pratt.

14 The author relies on **complicity** here, writing as if the audience would automatically agree. If the author thinks this is so obvious, then there is no need to state that it is obvious. If the author thinks the audience might not find this approach to be nonsense, then reasons for not accepting it are needed.

12 **False analogy.** The analogy is not useful as the writer argues that Lavater's system is nonsense, whereas the way a person walks can tell you a great deal about some illnesses.

7 This paragraph contains **unsupported assumptions** about what people believed. Not enough evidence has been included to support these assumptions. The assumptions are then used as reasons to support the conclusion proposed in the final sentence.

6 **Lack of precision.** Not enough detail provided.

10 **Meeting necessary conditions.** The necessary conditions for establishing this interim conclusion are not met. To substantiate that the idea of a natural order was used only as a fashionable pursuit, the author would have to do the following:
- provide evidence that the idea was widely used amongst a certain group, and therefore constituted a 'fashion';
- provide evidence that the idea was used in a particular way only for a certain time (as fashions are time-bound); (continued over)

Answers to Practice 4: Finding flaws in the argument

References [compare with pp. 259–60][22]

Primary sources

Anon (1802) *Such is Buonaparte*, London.[c]

Kaspar Lavater[a] *Essays on Physiognomy*, Translated by Rev. C. Moore and illustrated after Lavater by Barlow, London, 1797.

Pratt, *Pratt's Address to His Countrymen or the True Born Englishman's Castle.* London.

Bishop of Llandaff [d, e and f]

Mary Wollstonecraft (1792) *Vindication of the Rights of Women.* Middlesex.[a and f]

White, C. *An Account of the Infinite Gradations in Man* (Read to the Literary and Philosophical Society of Manchester at Different Meetings) 1779.[a, c and e]

Secondary sources

Madison.[d, e and f] (1967) 'The end of the Chain of Being: the impact of Descartian. *Journal of Medieval and Enlightenment Studies*, 66; 7.*

Barking, J. K. (1957) *Changes in Conceptions of the Universe.* Cotteridge: Poltergeist Press*

Linda Colley (2003) Captives.[a, d and e]

Holmes, Geoffrey. (1977) 'Gregory King and the social structure of pre-industrial England' *Transactions of the Royal History Society*, 27 [a and c]

Pendleton [d and e]

E. P. Thompson *The Making of the English Working Class* (1963) Middlesex: Penguin [a and c]

* These two sources are hypothetical and provided for the purpose of the practice activity; the other sources are genuine.

Comments

- provide evidence that those who did use the concept of natural order in one aspect of their life, then acted in a contrary way in other aspects: that is, that the notion was not core to their belief system to such an extent that it ruled their behaviour.

11 The conclusion does not meet **sufficient conditions** as the evidence provided does not adequately support it. (See previous page.)

22 Compare the details of these references with those for Practice 3. Note:

  (a) The order of items within each reference is not consistent from one reference to another, such as the order of the date, and whether initials or names are used.

  (b) Not all the references used in the text are detailed in this list of references.

  (c) Some items in the reference list do not appear in the text so should not appear here. It is possible that the author has used this source but not referenced it properly in the text.

  (d) The information about the author is incomplete for some references so the reader cannot look these up.

  (e) Some titles are not written in full (see list of references from Practice 3).

  (f) Items are not in alphabetical order.

Appendix

Selected search engines and databases for on-line literature searches

Ingenta Connect – www.igentaconnect.com
Finds abstracts for articles for over 30,000 journals and other publications. From university sites, you can also read the full text of these articles, if the university has subscribed to them.

Google Scholar – http://scholar.google.co.uk
A good starting place to look up academic articles.

Questia – www.questia.com
Subscription-based collection of journal articles.

Scitopia – www.scitopia.org
Search engine focused on science and technology. Searches over 3.5 million documents.

Cinahl – www.cinhal.com
Nursing and health care database.

Embase – www.embase.com
Subscription-based biomedical and pharmaceutical database.

Magazines – www.magportal.com
Lets you read magazine articles online.

PubMed – www.ncbi.nlm.nih.gov//pubmed/
Large biomedical and life sciences database.

PsycInfo – www.apa.org.uk/psycinfo
Subscription-based database of psychological articles dating back to the 1800s.

Intute – www.intute.ac.uk
Collection of databases for a range of academic subjects including social sciences, engineering, law and the humanities.

World Wide Art Resources – http://wwar.com
Resources on art news. Art history and contemporary artists.

Bibliography

Arnheim, R. (1954, 1974) *Art and Visual Perception: The Psychology of the Creative Eye* (Berkeley: University of California Press).

Barrell, J. (1980) *The Dark Side of the Landscape: The Rural Poor in English Painting, 1730–1840* (Cambridge: Cambridge University Press).

Bodner, G. M. (1988) 'Consumer Chemistry: Critical Thinking at the Concrete Level'. *Journal of Chemistry Education*, **65** (3), 212–13.

Borton, T. (1970) *Reach, Touch and Teach* (London: Hutchinson).

Boud, D., Keogh, R. and Walker, D. (eds) (1985) *Reflection: Turning Experience into Learning* (London: Routledge).

Bowlby, J. (1980) *Attachment and Loss*, Vol. 3: *Loss, Sadness and Depression* (New York: Basic Books).

Boyle, F. (1997) *The Guardian Careers Guide: Law* (London: Fourth Estate).

Campbell, A. (1984) *The Girls in the Gang* (Oxford: Basil Blackwell).

Carwell, H. (1977) *Blacks in Science: Astrophysicist to Zoologist* (Hicksville, NY: Exposition Press).

Collins, P. (1998) 'Negotiating Selves: Reflections on "Unstructured" Interviewing'. *Sociological Research Online*, **3** (3). www.socresonline.org.uk/3/3/2.html January 2001.

Coren, A. (1997) *A Psychodynamic Approach to Education* (London: Sheldon Press).

Cottrell, S. (2010) *Skills for Success: The Personal Development Planning Handbook*, 2nd edition (Basingstoke: Palgrave Macmillan).

Cowell, B., Keeley, S., Shemberg, M. and Zinnbauer, M. (1995) 'Coping with Student Resistance to Critical Thinking: What the Psychotherapy Literature Can Tell Us'. *College Teaching*, **43** (4).

Crane, T. (2001) *Elements of Mind: An Introduction to the Philosophy of Mind* (Oxford: Oxford University Press).

Csikszentmihalyi, M. (1992) *Flow: The Psychology of Happiness* (London: Random House).

Donaldson, M. (1978) *Children's Minds* (London: Fontana).

Driscoll, J. (1994) 'Reflective Practice for Practice'. *Senior Nurse*, **13** (7), 47–50.

Dunbar, R. (1996) *Grooming, Gossip and the Evolution of Language* (London: Faber & Faber).

Eco, U. (1998) *Serendipities: Language and Lunacy* (London: Weidenfeld & Nicolson).

Elliott, J. H. (1972) *The Old World and the New, 1492–1650* (Cambridge: Cambridge University Press).

Ennis, R. H. (1987) 'A Taxonomy of Critical Thinking Dispositions and Abilities'. In J. Baron and R. Sternberg (eds), *Teaching Thinking Skills: Theory and Practice* (New York: W. H. Freeman).

Farndon, J. (1994) *Dictionary of the Earth* (London: Dorling Kindersley).

Farrar, S. (2004a) 'It's Very Evolved of Us to Ape a Yawn'. *Times Higher Educational Supplement*, 12 March 2004, p. 13.

Farrar, S. (2004b) 'It's Brit Art, but Not as we Know it'. *Times Higher Educational Supplement*, 9 July 2004, p. 8.

Farrar, S. (2004c) 'Old Sea Chart is So Current'. *Times Higher Educational Supplement*, 16 July 2004, p. 5.

Fillion, L. and Arazi, S. (2002) 'Does Organic Food Taste Better? A Claim Substantiation Approach'. *Nutrition & Food Science*, **32** (4), 153–7.

Fisher, A. (1988) *The Logic of Real Arguments* (Cambridge: Cambridge University Press).

Fisher, D. and Hanstock, T. (1998) *Citing References* (Oxford: Blackwell).

Foster, R. (2004) *Rhythms of Life* (London: Profile Books).

Garnham, A. and Oakhill, J. (1994) *Thinking and Reasoning* (Oxford: Blackwell).

Gibbs, G. (1988) *Learning by Doing: A Guide to Reading and Learning Methods* (Oxford: Further Education Unit, Oxford Polytechnic).

Gilligan, C. (1977) 'In a Different Voice: Women's Conceptions of Self and Morality'. *Harvard Educational Review*, **47**, 418–517.

Green, E. P. and Short, F. T. (2004) *World Atlas of Sea Grasses* (Berkeley: University of California Press).

Greenfield, S. (1997) *The Human Brain: A Guided Tour* (London: Phoenix).

Hammacher, A. M. (1986) *Magritte* (London: Thames & Hudson).

Hogan, C. (2004) 'Giving Lawyers the Slip'. *The Times*, 24 August 2004, p. 26.

Jacobs, P. A., Brunton, M., Melville, M. M., Brittain, R. P. and McClermont, W. F. (1965) 'Aggressive Behaviour, Mental Subnormality and the XYY Male'. *Nature*, **208**, 1351–2.

Johns, C. and Freshwater, D. (1998) *Transforming Nursing through Reflective Practice* (Oxford: Blackwell Scientific).

Kohlberg, L. (1981) *Essays on Moral Development*, vol. 1 (New York: Harper & Row).

Lane, H. (1984) *When the Mind Hears: A History of Deaf People and Their Language* (Cambridge: Cambridge University Press).

Lang, T. and Heasman, M. A. (2004) *Food Wars: The Global Battle for Mouths, Minds and Markets* (London; Sterling, VA: Earthscan).

Loftus, E. F. (1979) *Eyewitness Testimony* (Cambridge, MA: Harvard University Press).

McMurray, L. (1981) *George Washington Carver* (New York: Oxford University Press).

McPeck, J. H. (1981) *Critical Thinking and Education* (New York: St Martin's Press).

Miles, S. (1988) *British Sign Language: A Beginner's Guide* (London: BBC Books).

Morris, S. (2004) *Life's Solution: Inevitable Humans in a Lonely Universe* (Cambridge: Cambridge University Press).

National Committee of Inquiry into Higher Education (1997) *Higher Education in the Learning Society* (London: HMSO).

Pagel, M. (2004) 'No Banana-eating Snakes or Flying Donkeys are to be Found Here'. *Times Higher Educational Supplement*, 16 July 2004.

Palmer, T. (2004) *Perilous Plant Earth: Catastrophes and Catastrophism Through the Ages* (Cambridge: Cambridge University Press).

Papers in the Bodleian Library. Curzon Collection, vol. 22, ff. 89–90. Letter from Henry Peter Lord Brougham to C. H. Parry, 3 September 1803.

Pears, R. and Shields, G. (2010) *Cite them Right: The Essential Referencing Guide*, 8th edition (Basingstoke: Palgrave Macmillan).

Peters, R. S. (1974) 'Moral Development: a Plea for Pluralism'. In R. S. Peters (ed.), *Psychology and Ethical Development* (London: Allen & Unwin).

Piliavin, J. A., Dovidio, J. F., Gaertner, S. L. and Clark, R. D. (1981) *Emergency Intervention* (New York: Academic Press).

Platek, S. M., Critton, S. R., Myers, T. E. and Gallup, G. G. Jr (2003) 'Contagious Yawning: the Role of Self-awareness and Mental State Attribution'. *Cognitive Brain Research*, **17** (2), 223–7.

Postgate, J. (1994) *The Outer Reaches of Life* (Cambridge: Cambridge University Press).

Rose, S. (2004) *The New Brain Sciences: Perils and Prospects* (Milton Keynes: Open University Press).

Rowbotham, M. (2000) *Goodbye America! Globalisation, Debt and the Dollar Empire* (New York: John Carpenter).

Sachs, O. (1985) *The Man who Mistook his Wife for a Hat* (London: Picador).

Salzberger-Wittenberg, I., Williams, G. and Osborne, E. (1983) *The Emotional Experience of Learning and Teaching* (London: Karnac Books).

Sattin, A. (2004) *The Gates of Africa: Death, Discovery and the Search for Timbuktu* (London: HarperCollins).

Shulman, L. (1986) 'Those who Understand: Knowledge Growth in Teaching'. *Educational Researcher*, **15** (2), 4–14.

Smith, L. (1992) 'Ethical Issues in Interviewing'. *Journal of Advanced Nursing*, **17**: 98–103.

Stein, C. (1997) *Lying: Achieving Emotional Literacy* (London: Bloomsbury).

Tajfel, H. (1981) *Human Groups and Social Categories* (Cambridge: Cambridge University Press).

Trevathan, W., McKenna, J. and Smith, E. O. (1999) *Evolutionary Medicine* (Oxford: Oxford University Press).

Williams, G. (1997) *Internal Landscapes and Foreign Bodies: Eating Disorders and Other Pathologies* (London: Tavistock Clinic Series, Duckworth).

Willis, S. (1994) 'Eruptions of Funk: Historicizing Toni Morrison'. In L. Gates, Jr (ed.), *Black Literature and Literary Theory* (pp. 263–83) (New York: Methuen).

Wilson, J. Q. and Hernstein, R. J. (1985) *Crime and Human Nature* (New York: Simon).

Worwood, V. A. (1999) *The Fragrant Heavens: The Spiritual Dimension of Fragrance and Aromatherapy* (London: Bantam Books).

www.princeton.edu/~mcbrown/display/carver .html George Washington Carver, Jr: Chemurgist; 6/8/2004.

www.emeagwali.com for the scientist Emeagwali.

Index

abstracts, using, 128
academic writing, 54, 125, 127, 149, 162, 167, 168–9, 172
   see also essays; writing critically
accuracy, 5, 6, 9, 54, 152, 166, 172
   see also precision
agreement, 52
ambiguity, 8, 40
analogies, 112–13, 122, 221, 275
analysis, critical, 1, 4, 8, 51, 54, 58, 60, 117, 155, 168
   use analysis rather than description, 58, 205
   when writing, 167–82, 184–86
   see also argument, identifying; comparison;
      categorising; selection; evidence, evaluating;
      selection
argument, xii, 38, 52
   arguments as reasons, 38
   contributing arguments, 38
   counter arguments, 59–60, 65, 117, 169, 175–6,
      183, 195, 201, 202, 203, 244, 245, 261, 263
   features, 37, 38, 40, 41, 47, 63, 240
   flawed arguments, 105, 106–21, 196
   identifying arguments, 37, 41–3, 47, 51–61
   implicit arguments, 85, 93, 103
   and non-argument 51, 54–61, 62,
   overall argument, xii, 38,
   and theoretical perspective, 149, 150; *see also*
      structuring an argument
   'winning' an argument, 10
assertions, xii
assumptions, 85–90, 99, 252, 253
   ideological, 93, 103
   implicit assumptions, 88–9
   unsupported, 93, 95, 106, 107, 112, 116, 273, 274
   used as reasons, 89–90, 100–1
attention, focusing, 1, 17, 23–6, 29, 34, 51
   to detail, 5, 12, 13–15, 17
audience, ix, 168
authenticity, 130, 146
author, x
author's position, 38–9, 40, 49, 52, 63, 64, 65, 78,
   79–80, 112, 183, 195, 201, 202, 203, 244, 245,

   261, 263
   dealing with evidence against, 183

background information, necessary and unnecessary,
   197, 244, 261, 262, 272
   see also description
barriers to critical thinking, 1, 10–12, 16
benefits of critical thinking skills, 4

castle of cards, 116, 274
categorising, 17, 19, 27–8, 151
   grouping points, 169
   reasons and arguments, 165, 202
   theories, 141, 150, 151, 165
cause and effect, 106–8, 121, 122, 274
citations 187; *see* references
clarity in critical thinking, 64, 65, 168
close reading, 20, 29–31, 147
comparisons, making, 18, 21, 24, 27, 112
complicity, with the reader, 114, 253, 254, 275
conclusions, xii, 41, 46, 47
   as deduction, 46, 74, 195
   evidence-based, 133–4, 195, 197, 201, 204, 261–4
   interim *see* intermediate
   intermediate, xii, 63, 71–2, 201, 202, 244, 245, 246,
      262, 263, 264
   location of, 43, 45–7
   logical conclusions, 74, 246, 264; *see also* deduction
   as reasons *see* conclusions, intermediate
   as summaries, 46, 47, 60, 74, 82, 245, 246, 264
   supported by reasons, 244
   tentative conclusions 179
   writing conclusions, 176–7, 180, 182, 186, 187, 196
connoted meanings, 95–6, 98
consistency
   checking your own writing for, 205
   internal, xii, 65–6, 79–80, 195, 197, 273–275
   logical, xii, 67–8
contributing arguments *see* argument
correlation, 107–8
counter arguments, *see* argument
credible sources, 196

critical reflection, *see* reflection
critical thinking
   in academic contexts, 7–9, 11, 12
   as cognitive activity, 1
critical thinking – *continued*
   as process, 2, 16
   what is critical thinking, viii
criticism
   of peers, 8–9
   what is criticism, 2
currency, 131

deduction, 46, 47, 74
   and unwarranted leaps, 116
deflection, of the reader, 114, 254, 273
denoted meanings, 95–6, 98
description, 54, 60, 61, 195, 244, 262
   identifying background information, 42–3, 51, 58,
      59, 60
difference, identifying, 24
disagreement, 52, 53
distortions to argument, 195, 201, 205

emotion, and critical thinking, 1, 5, 11
emotive language, 117, 196, 252, 253, 273
essays, 3, 172, 181–88, 229
   see also academic writing; writing critically
evidence, 125–46
   evaluating the evidence, 3, 8, 9, 125, 127, 128, 129,
      144, 145, 165
   interpreting evidence, 6
   reputable sources, 129
   selecting evidence, 132–4
   using supporting evidence, 195, 196–7, 201, 202,
      205, 244, 252, 253
   see also primary sources; secondary sources;
      triangulation
exclusion, 114
explanation, 55, 59, 60, 61
extraneous material, 58
eye-witness testimony, 142

facts, 141, 205
false analogies, 112–13, 122, 253, 275
false correlations, 107–8
false premises, 42, 85, 91–2, 102, 254, 273
features of an argument *see* argument
flawed arguments *see* argument
following directions, 19
frames of reference, 23

generalisations, 139, 196

identifying arguments *see* arguments
influences on judgement, 6
in-groups, 114

interim conclusions *see* conclusions, intermediate
intermediate conclusions *see* conclusions
introductions, for critical writing, 170, 184

journal articles as evidence, 129
   notes from, 157
   references from, 163
judgements, making critical, 185, 226

key features of an argument *see* argument, features

latent messages, 96
line of reasoning *see* reasoning
literature searches, 128
   on-line, 128, 245
   writing up, 172
   see also primary source; secondary source
logical conclusions, 74–5, 82
logical order, xii, 63, 76–7, 78, 79, 83, 169, 195, 197,
     201; *see also* sequencing

misrepresentation, 119, 252, 273

necessary conditions, meeting, 109–11, 123–4, 252,
   275
non-sequitors, 88
note-making, 147, 164
   to support reading, 153
   selecting what to note, 158–61
   structuring notes, 155–7
   why make notes, 153
   see also references, quotations

objectivity, 5
opinion, 141
out-groups, 114

personal attacks, 9, 117, 252, 275
personal strategies, 6, 9, 12
personality and critical thinking, 2
persuasion
   and audience, 47, 52, 112, 167, 168
   through flawed argument; *see also* argument, flawed
   through reasons, 40, 47, 52
   through latent methods, 85, 93, 99, 114
   see also presenting an argument
plagiarism, 164, 188; *see also* references
position, *see* author's position
precision, 5, 6, 8, 10, 65, 252, 272
predicate, xii, 42, 91
premises, xiii, 42, 91
   see also false premises
presenting an argument, 2, 3, 4, 9, 14–15, 23, 52, 78
   see also line of reasoning; persuasion; writing critically
primary sources, 125, 126, 142, 245, 262, 263, 264,
     265, 276
priorities for developing critical thinking, 13–17

probability, levels of, 137, 138, 139, 205
professional life, and critical thinking, 4, 8, 17, 125, 210
propositions, xiii, 41, 42, 43, 47

quotations, choosing, 154
    see quotations; references

reading
    and accurate interpretation, 152, 166, 172
        close reading, 29–31, 152, 183
        critically, 2, 4, 147, 183
    efficiently, 37, 51, 63, 147, 148, 152, 153
    selectively, 151, 154
    see also note-making
reasoning, 3
    line of reasoning, xii, 47, 52, 93, 120, 173–4, 178,
        197, 204
    see also logical order
reasons, xiii, 3, 187, 193
    and implicit assumptions, 89
    independent and joint, 69
    intermediate conclusions as reasons, 71–2
    supporting the conclusion, xii, xiii, 42–3, 49–50,
        59–60, 67, 69, 71, 100–2, 109–10, 204
references, 172, 187–8, 204, 205
    using other people's, 127
    to other people's work, 132, 154, 162–3, 172, 195,
        200, 201
    poor referencing, 252, 253, 272, 274, 276
    see also quotations
reflection and critical thinking, xi, 207
    good and bad, 227–8
    characteristics of, 208–9, 218
    experience, 208, 209, 227
    transformative role, 208, 209, 221
    and theory, 209, 214, 215, 227, 229
    and professional practice, 210, 225–6
    approaches to (methodology), 211–17
    audience, 213, 215, 228
    models of, 212, 215, 221–4
    confidentiality, 215
    phases of reflection, 218–20
relevance to the argument, 3, 4, 51, 133, 134, 195,
    201, 204, 262; see also selection
replication, 131
reputable sources see evidence
research skills, 5, 7

salient characteristics, xiii, 27, 54
samples
    representative, 135–6
    significance, 138–40
scepticism, 2, 9
secondary sources, 126, 128, 129, 132, 244, 245, 261,
    262, 276
selection, 8, 132, 151, 158–61, 168
    see also relevance

self-awareness and critical thinking, 3, 4, 5, 6, 8, 10
    see also barriers
self-evaluation, 4, 6, 10, 13–15, 18–22
sequencing, 18, 25–6
    in critical writing, 169
    see also logical order
signal words, 4, 6, 167, 169, 173–8, 201–3, 245, 261,
    262, 263, 264
signposting, 169; see also line of reasoning; signal
    words
similarities, recognising, 21
skills associate with critical thinking, 4, 5, 17
    see also primary sources
sleight of hand, 116, 254
stereotyping, 96–7, 104, 253, 273
structure of an argument, 63, 105, 167
    using intermediate conclusions, 71–2
    when writing, 168–9, 195, 196–7, 201, 204, 261
    see also signal words
substantive points, xiii
sufficient conditions, meeting, 110–11, 123–4, 275
summary, 59–60
    conclusions, 46
    similarity to argument, 55
    summarising the argument, 197, 204, 261
synthesis, 186, 218

tautology, xiii, 120, 254, 272
theoretical perspective, 149
    theory and argument, 150, 203
    types of theory, 151
    using when writing, 205
triangulation, 142, 143–4
two wrongs don't make a right, 120

unwarranted leaps, 116, 252, 254, 273

validity, 130
value judgements, 54
    and own prejudices, 6, 13
variables, 130
    controlling for, 140, 146
vested interest, 40, 52, 131, 196, 202

writing critically, 167, 188
    and audience, 86, 167, 168
    characteristics of, 168–9
    evaluating critical writing, 191–206, 239–76
    evaluating your own writing critically, 204–5, 206
    introducing the line of reasoning, 173
    setting the scene for the reader, 86, 167, 170–1, 189,
        261
    signalling the direction of the argument, 174–8, 261
    tentative style, 179
    see also author's position; consistency; line of
        reasoning; signposting

Loughborough
COLLEGE

the Library